George Valentine Cox

Recollections of Oxford

George Valentine Cox

Recollections of Oxford

ISBN/EAN: 9783742813794

Manufactured in Europe, USA, Canada, Australia, Japa

Cover: Foto ©ninafisch / pixelio.de

Manufactured and distributed by brebook publishing software (www.brebook.com)

George Valentine Cox

Recollections of Oxford

RECOLLECTIONS

OF

OXFORD

BY G. V. COX, M.A.

NEW COLLEGE

LATE ESQUIRE BEDEL AND CORONER IN THE UNIVERSITY OF OXFORD

SECOND EDITION

London:
MACMILLAN AND CO.
1870.

[*All rights reserved*]

OXFORD:
By T. Combe, M.A., E. B. Gardner, E. P. Hall, and H. Latham, M.A.,
PRINTERS TO THE UNIVERSITY.

PREFACE TO THE SECOND EDITION.

THIS Second Edition of 'Recollections of Oxford' has resulted, first, from the frequent hints of friends that the rapid sale of the first edition, and the generally favourable Notices of it, would justify a re-appearance; and, secondly, from a conscientious desire to correct numerous errors and qualify some mis-statements. For the due discharge of this task (I might almost call it a duty) I have been ably assisted by voluntary and even anonymous suggestions, many of them valuable, and most of them thankfully adopted. This help, however, has not prevented the careful exercise of my own labour, both in correcting errata and the insertion of new matter of illustration.

As to the criticisms of periodicals and newspapers, what was favourable I, of course, have read with pleasure: of anything of a contrary character, I can assert that it has no place in my 'Recollections.' I will only say, by way of justification, and in reply to some of my Northern critics, that I never pretended to write as a philosopher, nor even as an historian. To the kind consideration of my future readers I commend this improved edition, adding my special thanks to Messrs. Ellacombe, Rouse, E. Walford, Rigaud, Macray, and though last, not least, Dr. Bloxam, for many valuable hints and corrections.

'OXFORD,
December 9, 1869.

PREFACE TO THE FIRST EDITION.

For many years I have earnestly desired that some well-qualified and loving son of our Alma Mater would arise from among us, to catch her striking but varying features and transmit them to his successors.

Having however looked in vain for such an one, and having again and again been asked why I did not undertake the task myself, I was induced, a few years since, to put together my early and later 'Recollections' of beloved Oxford. From having always lived here, the circumstances of past events have been kept alive by the constant 'admonitio loci'; or rather, having never quite died out, they required but a little fanning of memory's 'mitior aura' to stand out clearly before me.

Having had such frequent occasion in the following pages to use the first person, I will not lengthen this Preface, except to ask indulgence for any apparent discrepancies of dates, caused by the different times of recording my 'Recollections' and the fact that they have been lying on my shelf for seven or eight years.

OXFORD,
July 17, 1868.

CONTENTS.

CHAP.		PAGE
I.	Recollections and Collections from A.D. 1789 to A.D. 1796	1
II.	Recollections of City Preachers, or Lecturers	27
III.	„ from A.D. 1797 to A.D. 1800	33
IV.	„ from A.D. 1801 to A.D. 1817	45
V.	„ from A.D. 1818 to A.D. 1830	91
VI.	„ of Professors	137
VII.	„ of Heads of Houses	160
VIII.	„ of Vice-Chancellors	198
IX.	„ of Proctors	214
X.	„ of University Characters	223
XI.	University Sermons and Preachers	233
XII.	Recollections De Bedellis	244
XIII.	„ from A.D. 1831 to A.D. 1836	257
XIV.	The Hampden Controversy in 1836	280
XV.	The Tractarian Movement	288
XVI.	Recollections from A.D. 1837 to A.D. 1840	295
XVII.	„ from A.D. 1841 to A.D. 1843	317
XVIII.	Proceedings as to Mr. Macmullen	333
	Recollections in 1844	336
	Mr. Ward and his Book, A.D. 1844–5	340
XIX.	Recollections from A.D. 1845 to A.D. 1850	349
XX.	„ from A.D. 1851 to A.D. 1856	377
XXI.	The Statute De Bedellis, and Recollections from A.D. 1857 to A.D. 1858	419
XXII.	Recollections from A.D. 1859 to A.D. 1860	439
	Conclusion	455

CHAPTER I.

Meminisse juvabit.

Recollections and Collections.

A.D. 1789 to A.D. 1796.

IT is obvious that my *early 'Recollections'* may rather be called '*Collections*,' daily impressed by local and traditional sources of information, till my eyes and ears learnt to take a wider range for themselves and received a deeper impression. My young fingers, however, were fully sensible of the severe winter of 1789, which was distinguished by a frost that commenced on the 24th of November and continued, with increasing severity[1], for fifty-one days!

It was in this year that, in order to support the attempt to revive or keep up the languishing Music Room, *Master Crotch*[2], 'The Musical Prodigy,' was regularly engaged to play a concerto on the organ at the weekly concerts. From four years of age, when he was exhibited as a wonder, 'non

---

[1] I have never forgotten some of the circumstances of that time, when I was a young member of a large family. I do not, however, pretend to vie in early recollections with Lord William Lennox, who in his '*Fifty Years' Reminiscences*' records *his own birth* in 1799—'an event of which (he says) I may consider myself the hero!'

[2] My apology for beginning with 'Master Crotch' is, that my first impressions were connected with music and choirs, and especially with wonderful stories of his early musical development.

sine diis animosus infans,' he adhered to Oxford (though not born there), and finally succeeded to the Professorship of Music. The Music Room, which had maintained a fluctuating state of existence ever since its erection (by subscription) in 1742, must at least have been filled at the Commemoration concerts which were given there. How they could *answer* in a room which would scarcely contain with comfort 400 persons, it is difficult to conceive; but public singers, even first-rate ones, did not then ask such extravagant sums for their occasional services[1]. Madam Storace (an Englishwoman who Italianised her husband's name[2]) was for some years the prima donna on these occasions, supported by an Oxford native, Miss Mahon (afterwards Madame Seconde), and 'the four Miss Radcliffes from Worcester.' One of these Miss Radcliffes became a regular weekly-singer at the revived subscription-concerts at the Music Room; she was a very sweet singer of Handel's songs (the only music of that day), a very pleasing, amiable person, and eventually married to a Fellow of a College[3].

[1] The famous Bartleman used to come to Oxford and sing at a concert for ten or fifteen pounds; the tickets at most five shillings. The band was very limited, the leader and some others were paid by an annual benefit-concert; several of the band were amateurs. Dr. Crotch *gave* his services, generally playing a solo on the organ.

[2] As a young chorister, a few years after, I well remember her singing Purcell's 'Mad Bess' with great effect, and the graceful manner in which she transferred a share of the applause to Crotch, for his skilful and brilliant accompaniment, played (as was then not unusual) from a single bass-line amply marked with thorough-bass figures.

[3] Oxford had not been without concerts before the building of the Music Room. Hearne (in the year 1733) speaks with great disgust of 'Concerts given by *one Handel*, with his dirty crew of foreign fidlers, in the Theatre and in Christ-Church hall, at five shilling tickets.' I may be excused for adding, 'Mr. Walter Powel, *Superior Bedel* in Divinity, sang with them *all alone*'—whatever that meant.

This year witnessed great and sincere rejoicings, with feastings and illuminations, on George the Third's recovery from his first mental illness. The University of Oxford of course sent up an address of congratulation, which was presented by *Lord North*, Chancellor of the University, followed by the Vice-Chancellor, Dr. Cooke[1], President of Corpus, and a full Delegacy.

In this year and in several following years an ingenious native of Oxford, Mr. Sadler (afterwards known as 'the Aëronaut'), gave lectures on what he called 'philosophic fire-works;' the taste for *hard words* of Greek formation had not yet set in, or he would probably have called them 'pyrotechnics.' Mr. Sadler was a clever, practical, and experimental manipulator in chemistry, and as such was patronised by the University, or rather by the few scientific men then in the University; what the University, as such, did or even professed to do in scientific matters at that period it were hard to say[2]. The Aldrichian *Professorship* of Chemistry, as we know, was not in full action till 1803; —but the Laboratory under the Museum had not been without a Lecturer. Certainly before Dr. Kidd's time Oxford had the advantage of frequent, or at least occasional Lec-

---

[1] It seems strange (judging from *subsequent* instances of patronage and promotion) that Dr. Cooke never got any ecclesiastical preferment: especially as he received several Royal visits at Corpus, when the Royal Family drove over from Nuneham to lionise Oxford. After one of these visits the President caused a door to be opened from his own premises into the College garden and used to call it 'the King's door,' either (as it was said) from the King (George III) having suggested it, or (as is more probable) from the Doctor having himself perceived the want of it on such an occasion and the convenience at all times.

[2] In a Biographical Dictionary published in 1784 I read, 'Dr. Plot is said to have been appointed by the Vice-Chancellor the first Professor of Chemistry.'

tures, given by Dr. Beddoes 'on Chemistry and also on *Strata and Rocks.*'

It was on June[1] 29, 1789, that the (locally) famous '*Magdalen oak*' fell down, at the entrance of what were then commonly called 'Magdalen *Water-Walks*.' It was twenty-one feet nine inches in girth, and was traditionally said to have been an old tree at the founding of the College; indeed it was supposed to have been six hundred years old at its fall. It fell in the middle of the night, 'accompanied by a violent, rushing noise and a shock felt throughout the College.' A large state-chair made of it was used for many years in the hall of Magdalen[2] College, as a seat for the

---

[1] June, on the authority of the Inscription on the Chair: 'Quercus Magdalenensis corruit Festo S. Petri 1789.' St. Peter's day is the 29th of June. An Oxford artist (and musician) named Malchair published a view of the Oak, both standing and as it lay after its fall.

[2] Having been educated in the School and Choir of Magdalen College, it is but reasonable, as well as natural, that my earliest 'Recollections' should be so often connected with that Society.

> Thou dear old College! by whatever name
> Natives or strangers call our 'Oxford Queen,'
> To me, from days long past, thou'rt aye the same,—
> Maudlin,—or Magdalen,—or Magdalene.

Not Magdalenè—as I have heard it pronounced in church by scrupulous or fantastic persons, who seem not to have learned a lesson from the young man in the Spectator, whose toast 'Elizabetha' was by acclamation cut down to plain 'Bess.' May I add to my earliest 'Recollections' of Magdalen College the strange impression still left on my memory, at seeing the two Bursars, at the first Monday morning-service in Lent, going round the chapel (during the chanting of the Benedicite) and doling out from their caps, to each member, as they passed, a little screw of paper, containing a small sum (from 1s. for the President down to 2d. for a chorister), bequeathed by some pious, thoughtful benefactor 'ad purgandos renes.' 'Physic-money' we called it. I am told it is still kept up!

President on the Gaudy-day, being brought for the occasion from the College Library. I remember it light-coloured and fresh from the carver's hands; it has since turned to a dark colour, and is deposited in President Bulley's hall of entrance.

The number of Determining B.A.'s in the Lent of 1789 was 147.

A.D. 1790.

The neighbourhood of Oxford at this time, and for some time after, had rather a bad reputation for highway robberies of a daring kind; stories were rife of such encounters, some true but many exaggerated[1]. Certainly travelling with pistols, ready-loaded, was a common practice, and banknotes were not unfrequently sewed into the lining of a gentleman's waistcoat or the folds of a lady's dress, for security[2].

The great importance attached to the fact of being possessed of an annual income of £300 (or upwards), at the time of graduating, may be inferred from the fact, that at this period the name of any one who took a degree was not made public, i.e. not mentioned in the newspapers, unless it could be added, 'he went out Grand-Compounder.' This

---

[1] The *real* occurrence was said to have sometimes suggested to idle and reckless minds a somewhat dangerous *imitation*, as a practical joke. Happily no serious mischief is recorded to have attended such rash experiments. Within my own recollection a practical joke of this kind was played upon a New College party going in a post-chaise to a ball at Abingdon. The 'Times' Reviewer of my 'Recollections' wantonly and most incorrectly introduced the venerable name of Howley as an actor in that disreputable scene: Howley was at that time a Fellow of Winchester, and had taken his *M.A.* degree ten years before.

[2] Hence possibly the common phrase of *investing* money.

shows that such persons were considered as 'raræ aves,' and, like other unfrequent visitors, thought worthy of especial notice.

In May, 1790, the University lost one of its most influential and respected residents, by the death of *Thomas Warton*, of Trinity College, the accomplished wit, antiquary and scholar.

It is asserted in the 'Life of Bishop Burgess,' that in 1790 the Heads of Houses refused to grant a D.C.L. degree by Diploma to *Edmund Burke*, though petitioned for that purpose by forty-nine resident Masters of Arts, who thought that his 'Reflections on the French Revolution' highly entitled him to the honour. It is however to be observed that the thing asked was not a mere *Honorary* D.C.L. degree (as in Sheridan's case in 1810), but a Degree *by Diploma*, a Degree which confers immediate and full academical privileges and is a compliment usually confined to persons of high rank or eminent academic services[1]. It is mentioned

---

[1] Oxford Diplomas have never been given lavishly, or without high claims (much less sold)—like those of a foreign University, from which the physician Dr. Pitcairn is said, by way of ridicule, to have asked for a diploma for his footman! This having been granted (on the strength of his recommendation and former connection with the place), he soon after applied for one for his horse!! This however was too much;—he was informed in reply, that search had been made in the records of the University and the nearest approach to anything like a precedent was that of a degree having once been conferred on *an ass*, one Dr. Pitcairn! The Doctor in his turn might have quoted a *precedent* of even a higher title, that of Consul, conferred by an obsequious Senate upon a Roman Emperor's horse! It has been recorded that Pope Clement VI confessed that if Edward III were to ask him to make a bishop of a jackass, he could not say him nay. (Dr. Hook's Archbishops of Canterbury.)

N.B. See in Note [1] (p. 70) in my 'Recollections' for 1810 the rejection of Warburton's proposed Degree of D.D.

in the same work that 'Burgess's English Prize-Essay on the "Study of Antiquities" (gained in 1780) went to a second edition,'—a very rare thing!

Half in joke and half, I believe, in ignorance, I was asked (since the publication of my book) if I remembered the trial of Miss Blandy for poisoning her father. Now, as this trial took place thirty-four years before I was born, there was no need to answer the question. The fact, however, of the trial having been held in the Divinity School will excuse its intrusion here. It so happened that the City or Town Hall was then being built, but not finished; there was then no County Hall, the Assizes being regularly held in the Town Hall. On this occasion the High Sheriff and County Magistrates begged the use of the Divinity School, though ill adapted for such a purpose and for so exciting a trial. I remember when the Town Hall, in which (in those hanging days) two or three poor creatures had been condemned in the morning to be hung for horse or sheep stealing, was hastily and tastefully *got up* for a County ball in the evening!—to be turned into a Court, at both ends, next morning!! I also recollect another strange scene connected with the administration of justice in Oxford, viz. a man raised on a pillory in Corn-Market Street, near Carfax Church. The poor wretch (with head and hands projecting through holes in the fabric) was now and then saluted with a rotten egg or some other worse missile. The pillory was a substantial structure, and high enough to expose the sufferer to the view of the jeering crowd. I do not remember his offence. At that date, about 1794, and long after, one might occasionally see a wretched creature (sometimes even a couple of them) seated in the *stocks* for a long hour, and exposed to the gibes of the rabble. The scene was within the rails in front of the City Police Office.

A.D. 1791.

In April of this year, Dr. George Horne resigned the Headship of Magdalen College on his being made Bishop of Norwich. He had for some years held the Deanery of Canterbury with the Presidency of Magdalen. At Norwich Cathedral he and Dean Lloyd soon collected round them a Choir of Oxford and chiefly Magdalen men as Minor-Canons; some of their names, such as Millard, Walker, and Hansell, are still kept up at Magdalen in the persons of their descendants;—the best evidence of the high character of their progenitors!

In the same month Dr. (or rather Mr.) Routh succeeded Bishop Horne as President. The new President (who then entered upon an office which he held for sixty-seven years), though a man of studious, literary habits, was not the fireside recluse which he afterwards became and long continued to be; he had even discharged the office of Proctor in 1785; for I have heard a story of Dr. Shaw (a rough diamond of the College) saying to him, on hearing him one day calling out in vain 'Siste per fidem[1]' to an Undergraduate *tandem-driver*, 'Ah! Martin, your oratio ad *captandum* don't *take* to-day.'

July 5. The *Honorary* Degree of Doctor in Music was conferred in the Theatre on the celebrated composer *Haydn*—called in the printed Notice of the time 'Joseph Haydn, *Esquire!*' I mention this gladly, because, as a lover of music, I naturally think that the University received as much honour on the occasion as it bestowed, and also because of the rarity of such a degree (I mean an *Honorary*

---

[1] 'Siste per fidem' was the traditional cry of a Proctor to a *fugacious* Undergraduate, sometimes replied to by a good runner with 'Curre per Jovem.'

degree) in Music. Two years before, indeed, it had been conferred (but not in the Theatre, at the Commemoration) on 'F. H. Graaf, Director of Music at Augsburg;'—why or through what influence does not appear,—as a composer he is unknown. Indeed the *Honorary Music Degree* has probably never been granted, except in these two cases[1]; as for Handel, the greatest of all composers, we know that he laughed at the idea of being called 'Dr. Handel! like dat fellow Dr. Grün' (Greene). At this act there were only ninety-three M.A. Regents.

In this year (and in several preceding years) Private Theatricals were got up in great style at Blenheim Palace, where a regular theatre had been constructed, and to which the County families, with the *élite* of Oxford, were invited as spectators. The actors, of course, were gentlemen and ladies; amongst whom was Mr. Nares, Fellow of Merton, afterwards Dr. Nares and Professor of Modern History, but then living in the Palace as Librarian. It happened however that he and one of the Duke's daughters got up a little private drama on their own account, which ended in the lady's eloping and marrying Mr. N.,—a step which the Duchess-mother was said to have never forgiven.

It was in June of this year that the King of France and the Royal Family were *brought back to Paris, under a strong guard*, from the country. In July political riots took place in Birmingham; Oxford however enjoyed its usual state of

---

[1] The *Honorary* Degree in Music might still be conferred, as it still forms an item in the printed forms of the Terminal Account of Fees,— the fees (as in all Honorary Degrees) being paid by the University. Query: Was Graaf presented with others (probably D.C.L.'s) in the train of some German Prince? His *personal* claims as a musician (for who ever heard of him before or since?) could not have gained him this distinction.

repose. Little indeed of any moment occurred there during the rest of the year, except that 'in October Worcester College Chapel was consecrated.' The public *Notice* of it was as follows: 'The characteristic of this Chapel is a simple elegance, which it owes chiefly to the taste of Mr. Wyatt.' Mr. Wyatt is *now*, I believe, generally considered to have inflicted proofs of perverted taste upon several Oxford buildings. All that can be said for the *exterior* of the Chapel is, that it corresponds (Venetian windows and all) with the Hall. The architectural effect of the College front was indeed of no great consequence, so long as it was quite shut out from the public eye; but since it has been thrown open by the construction of Beaumont-street and actually forms the termination of the view, the question of alteration and improvement (for which a subscription was indeed once begun) might well be entertained afresh.

A. D. 1792.

The University was at this period in a state of stagnation; indeed the general interest was absorbed in watching the sad proceedings as to the Royal Family of France, as well as the spread of revolutionary sentiments in the populous towns of our own country. Political discussions (in private at least) ran high at Oxford; and many, who would not willingly disturb their own position (as Englishmen, so much in advance of other nations in point of real liberty), were yet loud in wishing success to the 'National Convention' as opposed to the King's government in France. During the whole of this year Louis XVI and his family were treated with insulting barbarity.

In April died Mr. Eyton, M.A. of Jesus College, and for

forty-seven years Esquire[1] Bedel in Medicine and Arts. He was succeeded by his nephew, Mr. Rhodes, M.A. and Fellow of Worcester, who had acted as Mr. Eyton's deputy during a long illness and absence from Oxford.

In October, 1792, the *Duke of Portland*, who had been elected Chancellor of the University on the death of Lord North (Earl of Guilford), was formally installed at his seat at Bulstrode. Travelling being a serious matter in those days of slow-coachism, the Delegacy, which was sent to Bulstrode Park for the carrying out of that ceremony, slept one night at High Wycombe[2], the neighbouring town!

In November the French Romish clergy, having fled from cruel persecution in their own country, were hospitably received in Protestant England. In aid of a general subscription for their relief, the sum of £1123 was immediately raised in the Colleges of Oxford. Three of these refugees eventually settled in Oxford, and, being men of piety and learning, were highly appreciated in society. Their names were M. Aubry, M. Bertin, and M. Coulon. The first was a man of good family, and at the Restoration he returned to

---

[1] The 'esprit de Corps' must be my excuse for this and similar insertions, with the additional plea that as our office is doomed to expire (by the Statute of 1856), we may one day become subjects of antiquarian curiosity!

[2] An University Address to the Crown, presented by a Delegacy, was formerly a serious and (to the Cista Academica) an expensive business: one whole day was sometimes spent in a leisurely post-chaise journey to London, beginning with a breakfast at Tetsworth or Benson;—a second day was necessarily passed in London;—and a third in an easy return to Oxford,—dinner at Wycombe or Henley, tea or supper at Benson or Tetsworth! Thanks to the railroad, a single day now suffices for the whole ceremony and the journeys to and fro. Within my recollection the Posers (or electors) on their way from New College to Winchester made two days of the journey, dining, supping, and sleeping at Newbury.

France to be made a Bishop. The second, M. Bertin, was a very popular teacher of French. M. Aubry wrote and published a sort of Oxford Guide[1] in very fair Latin verse! He and M. Bertin, on leaving Oxford at the 'Restoration,' were presented to the Honorary Degree of D.C.L. in a special Convocation. M. Coulon, an amiable but less known person, remained in Oxford long after as a teacher of French.

A.D. 1793.

Jan. 6. An effigy of the notorious revolutionary and infidel writer 'Tom Paine' was burnt at night 'on Carfax,' the usual scene of rows and bonfires[2]. It being vacation at Oxford, the act was manifestly a *town* business; the magistrates, in consideration of the *right feeling* thus roughly displayed, wisely connived at the tumultuous and somewhat riotous expression of it. The blazing bonfire and the rush of people with contributions of faggots, nay of hurdles, old doors, empty tubs, tar-barrels, and anything that was combustible, formed a sight not easily forgotten. The open space called Carfax had been *made open* in 1787 by the removal of Otho Nicholson's handsome Conduit, now standing in Nuneham Park[3].

---

[1] Its title was 'Oxonii dux poeticus.' It is a poem consisting of 1880 alternate Hexameters and Pentameters, which in very tolerable Latin, without much of poetry, conducts a supposed stranger all over Oxford in a Matutina and Vespertina Deambulatio.

[2] The same thing took place at this time in many other towns;—the horrible proceedings in France having generally produced a return to better notions, both on religious and political questions, in our own country.

[3] And not, as it ought to do, in some open, roomy part of Oxford, where it might still be *used* as a fountain, without being *abused*, as formerly, by being made to flow with wine or beer at City Elections.

On the 17th of January, 1793, the National Convention at Paris voted 'the *punishment of death*' to be inflicted upon Louis XVI, and on the 24th of the same month the public execution of that sentence followed,—when, after four years of '*detention*,' he was led to the *guillotine*. Whether a public mourning in England was *ordered* or not, I cannot say; but I certainly recollect the general wearing of mourning in Oxford, and the strong feeling of horror impressed on every one, high and low, by that atrocious act. Prints representing the scene were everywhere circulated, and models of the hated guillotine exhibited[1].

As what concerned Winchester School affected New College, and that which affected New College in some measure concerned the University, a few words may be allowed here on a very serious riot in that School. In April of this year there occurred (possibly bred by infection from revolutionary France) a second, and what was called (by comparison) *the great rebellion* at Winchester School. The big boys defied the authorities, and actually shut them out by barricading the College gate[2]; but as they thus shut themselves in and

---

Those persons who occasionally talk of constructing an ornamental Fountain near the south front of St. Giles's Church could not do better than make Otho Nicholson's Conduit their model;—unless indeed they could persuade Mr. Harcourt to *return it* to Oxford.

[1] It seems rather strange that 'the last days of Louis XVI' were not then chosen as the subject for the Latin Verse Prize,—rather than 'Mary Queen of Scots' or 'Marius amidst the Ruins of Carthage.' Even now this national crime (and still more the death of our own king Charles I) would, with its accumulation of historical interest, form a good subject for recitation from either rostrum.

[2] It was said that one of the Fellows, advancing to the closed gate to remonstrate with the rebels, unfortunately had recourse to (what he thought the young scholars would appreciate) a quotation from Virgil, in order to express his grief and astonishment. 'Eloquar an sileam?' he

were rather short of provisions, they capitulated in a day or two. A military detachment was called in from the neighbouring barracks, but, of course, only *in terrorem*. This incident was at least indirectly connected with our Alma Mater; for several of the expelled youths (the whole number of the expelled being very considerable) were admitted into Colleges at Oxford, on showing that they were not among the ringleaders, but unwilling and constrained actors in the scene. Three at least got on the foundation of three several Colleges, and, as exemplary academics, showed that they had had enough of rebellious movements in their early days.

Early in July of this year the Commemoration-week was marked by the '*Public* Installation' of the new Chancellor, the Duke of Portland. Oxford was crowded on the occasion, and beds were let at 'fabulous prices.' Convocations were held for three successive days for reciting prize-compositions and complimentary verses[1] (some of them very edifying, no doubt, to the crowded assemblage, in Greek, Hebrew, &c.!), and for conferring Honorary Degrees to the number of sixty-five. On the first day the crowd in the area and galleries was so great and the heat so oppressive, that the Chancellor, observing the increasing distress and confusion from persons fainting, &c., relieved the almost *dissolved* company by formally *dissolving* the Convocation.

In doing this on the impulse of the moment, he probably

---

commenced;—'*Sileas*,' sounding very like 'silly ass,' was the witty but insolent reply. Of course no further attempt with such weapons was made against such missiles. There is a good account of this *rebellion* in 'The Public Schools,' by Collins.

[1] These complimentary effusions were published (or at least printed for circulation) at the University Press in its best types; an experiment which has not been repeated at subsequent Installations.

forgot the compliment intended for him by the performance of *an Ode*, written for the occasion by the Professor of Poetry, Mr. Holmes of New College[1], and set to music by Dr. Phil. Hayes, the Professor of Music. It might indeed have been done by way of retaliation to Dr. Hayes, who had added to the distressing heat by nailing down all the windows for the sake of musical effect! The effect however was anything but musical to his ears; for the Undergraduates in the galleries most unscrupulously demolished with their caps every pane of glass within their reach. They disregarded, perhaps they were amused by, the piteous remonstrances of the fat Professor, who from the organ-gallery exclaimed (in Recitativo, molto agitato), 'For God's sake, gentlemen, for mercy's sake, for music's sake, for my sake, don't ruin me!'

On the Tuesday of this Commemoration-week the large sum of £268 was collected after the Sermon for the Radcliffe Infirmary.—The only other incident that has been transmitted in connection with this 'Installation-week' is, 'that the pick-pockets,' or 'light-finger'd gentry' from London[2] (some of them, it was said, habited in Masters' Gowns!) made a very successful harvest in the crowded area of the Theatre.

Aug. 10, died Dr. Paget, Fellow of Magdalen and Esquire Bedel in Law. In compliance with the then existing Statute[3] the vacancy was filled up 'intra triduum.' Though it

---

[1] Afterwards Canon of Christ Church, and subsequently Dean of Winchester.

[2] 'May I ask what College you belong to?' said a polite Pro-Proctor to one of these suspicious *Masters of Arts;* 'Oh! I belongs to St. Malen's,' was the satisfactory reply.

[3] This Statute has recently and wisely been altered, as to *holding elections in Vacation time,* the case of M.P.'s only excepted.

was 'in the heart of the Long Vacation,' a hundred and fifty Members of Convocation were found in Oxford and the neighbourhood. In point of fact many more senior men, especially on Foundations, resided in the Long Vacation ('when,' as they used to say, '*the boys* were gone down') than is the case in recent times. On this occasion Robert Hall, a Gentleman-Commoner of Wadham College (then S.C.L., and afterwards B.C.L.), was elected by a considerable majority against Mr. Edward Beckwith, M.A. of New College, afterwards Minor-Canon of St. Paul's.

Oct. 27. A contest took place for the Poetry Professorship between Mr. Kett of Trinity[1], who had preached the Bampton Lectures in 1790, and Mr. Hurdis, of Magdalen, the author of some pleasing but not first-rate poems, and a tragedy entitled ' Sir Thomas More.' Hurdis had 201 votes, Kett 181.

The first edition of Hurdis's poems was printed by himself and his sisters at their private press in the village of Cowley, near Oxford, where they resided. After his death

[1] Mr. Kett was also the author of a trifling novel, called ' Emily,' and of ' Logic made Easy.' This last production was unmercifully cut up by Mr. Copleston, whose Critique was headed with
'Aut haec in nostros fabricata est machina muros,
Aut aliquis latet error; *Equo* ne credite, Teucri.'
The severity and bad taste of this quotation (so remarkable in a person of such gravity as Mr. Copleston) consisted in the allusion to a nickname given to Mr. Kett from his long, *equine* countenance. I have not the Critique by me, but I have been told that 'patet' was substituted for 'latet' in the motto of Mr. Copleston's pamphlet. Not content with being a Bampton Lecturer and also a novelist, Mr. Kett occasionally aspired to be a writer of poetry. These flights were thus quizzed :
'Why Kett is a poet ! at least gossips say so,
And if not an Ovid, we know he's a *Naso*.'
Poor man ! his health and mind gave way, and he is said to have committed suicide, but not in Oxford.

(about 1808) another edition was published, with a very large subscription for copies, in aid of his sisters, who were in rather reduced circumstances.

A.D. 1794.

At this date the military movements of the Democratic French Government began to be so aggressive, that alarm, or at least anxiety, as to so troublesome a neighbour began to be felt in England generally. Under this impression efforts were made and subscriptions raised 'for the Internal Defence of the Country.' Oxford, as usual, answered nobly to the appeal, and (including £200 from the University Chest) the sum of £2,449 was transmitted to Government, as a voluntary aid from the University!

In August, at the Assizes, Mr. Taman[1], a matriculated tonsor, having gradually *extended* his business, was prosecuted by the City of Oxford for encroaching on their privileges, by selling glass and china, without being a Freeman of

---

[1] Mr. Taman's law-suit called forth the following effusion:—

'Never mind poor old Taman, he's only a layman,
  'Our battle he fought, to be sure!'
Thus cried Oxford parsons, thus answered her garçons
  When he knock'd for relief at their door;—

'Why leave your novacula and spread your tentacula
  'To handle the fruits of the pottery?
'You have knock'd your own knuckles, while the City trade chuckles,
  'And gives you no share in their lottery.

'But stay;—Convocation can give compensation,
  '(In their sleeves though the Masters may laugh).
'You must bear the cits' mockery, and sell no more crockery,
  'Be a yeoman and take up your staff.'

the City. [The days of free, unrestricted trade had not yet come.] Mr. Taman chose to dispute the claims of the City, and was *encouraged* (it was said) by the University authorities to fight the battle on the ground of his University matriculation-privilege; certainly he was left to do it single-handed and *proprio Marte!* The Company of Barbers[1], of which he was a member, had formerly been of much consequence. In Roman Catholic times they had the important privilege of superintending the tonsures of the College priests, and in later times of cutting and dressing the junior men's hair and of making and trimming the senior men's wigs. Even then, however, they did not encroach upon other callings, unless it

[1] This 'Company,' which had existed from a remote date, expired in 1859, with the consent of the surviving members, *reduced to the number of three*. They had had great privileges, dined once a year with the Vice-Chancellor, and supped annually with the Proctors.

The barbarous Company, successors to the late Barbers' Company.

'Oxford, 'tis true, no longer harbours
Her ancient Company of Barbers;
But still within her learned Schools
She closely shaves and strictly rules.
There twice a year, for many a day, Sir,
Her tonsors wield their classic razor*;
They ply the trade in magnam partem,
And trim men's heads secundum artem;
They practise well their grave tonsura,
They grope, they bleed cum anxia cura.
Some now and then their bark may save,
Borne on some day's propitious wave;
E'en then, 'tis but a *lucky shave.*
Avoid them idlers, slow, unlucky,
For if they catch, by Jove they'll pluck ye!'

* 'Are you the barber?' said a stranger to Porson in a barber's shop; No, Sir,' (the Greek scholar replied,) 'but I am a *cunning shaver*, at your service.'

were upon that of the medical profession; for as *chirurgeons* (privileged to draw blood, at least in shaving) they had always done a little in the bleeding line in Oxford, as they had elsewhere. 'Very true, Sir,' (the Counsel said at Taman's trial,) 'you and your brother barbers might *hold the basin*, but the gentlemen of the jury will tell you, by their sentence, that you were not privileged to *sell* one.' Accordingly poor Mr. Taman lost his cause, incurred considerable expenses, and had to shut up his shop. He was not however left quite unrecompensed in the end, for he was elected (solatia victo) to the office of a Yeoman Bedel.

A.D. 1795[1].

[Determiners, B.A. 185.]

In the beginning of this year there was again great distress among the Oxford poor from the severity of the weather and the long continuance of the frost. The better-

[1] It was about this time, 1795, that Southey, after a residence of two or three years, left Oxford without a degree. Balliol, of which he was a member, had not then acquired a reputation above other Colleges. Many years afterwards, when he had worked himself into fame (and no man ever worked harder) as a writer in almost every branch of literature, Oxford was proud to see him again and make him an Hon. D.C.L. in the Theatre at Commemoration.

Southey at Balliol was a contemporary with that strange person Walter Savage Landor at Trinity, but avoided an acquaintance with one who, though only seventeen years old, was known as 'the mad young jacobin.' The story of Landor's firing a gun from his room into a window of a room across the quadrangle is given at length from his own pen in his biography (published in 1869), and one cannot but wonder that his punishment was not expulsion rather than rustication for two terms. He never returned to Oxford, though the kind President, Dr. Chapman, in consideration of his youth and unusual abilities, earnestly pressed him to resume his studies there.

provided however, both in the University and City, did not forget their poorer brethren. At that time, and long after, Oxford was dependent on the Canal for the supply of coal; but canals are liable to be frozen, and during a protracted frost there was a daily advance in the price, and at length a total failure in the supply—the wharf being quite cleared out. Such a state of things was now severely felt by all who from want of funds or from want of thought had not laid in a winter's stock; and if many of the middle classes thus suffered, what must have been the misery of the very poor! 'At length on the 4th of March, to the joy and comfort of the inhabitants, Canal-boats arrived with a supply of coal, the navigation having been stopped by ice *for ten weeks*. The price of coals (for some little had been occasionally fetched by land-carriage from Banbury) sunk at once from 4*s*. to 1*s*. 6*d*. the hundred.'

As the Oxford Canal had not existed more than twenty or thirty years before that time, one is led by the above sad account to ask, 'how our predecessors existed through winters of unusual severity and long continuance?' The only[1] answer that presents itself (in the absence of any positive information on the subject) is, that they did what our successors must do (if the world lasts so long) when the existing coal-mines shall be exhausted—that is, *keep moving*

---

[1] An auxiliary answer is suggested by the 'Recollection' that the population (of the town at least) was much less than it has since become, being about 8,000 or 10,000 instead of 30,000, that the neighbourhood of Oxford was not always so bare of woods and forests as it now is, and that the Colleges at least took care to get a supply of fuel from thence. Therefore, unless science shall have discovered some new means of warming houses, planting would again become a matter of necessity, our now naked hills would again wave with foliage, and *Shotover* Hill, or rather *Shotover House*, might again become *Chateau Vert*.

during the short days, and bury themselves under their blankets during the long nights of winter.

March 10. Convocation voted that 2000 copies of the New Testament in Latin (from the University Press) should be placed at the service of the French Refugee Clergy then in England. They had, most of them, made their escape from France in such haste, as to have brought away neither books nor anything else. A Protestant University could not well print for them a supply of Missals and Breviaries; so it did what it could, in conscience as well as charity, by offering them that which is the basis of our common faith.

Even in the summer of 1795 corn was very dear, and there was great distress[1], met however and softened by continued large subscriptions. Toward the end of the year the Vice-Chancellor and the Heads of Houses issued a notice, 'that they had agreed to reduce the consumption of *wheat* in their families by one-third; and they recommended the same measure to their respective Colleges.' We are told that at Blenheim and Nuneham 'a part of the parks was ploughed up, in order to increase the supply of grain[2].'

Nov. 10. An unusual contest (i. e. between *two members of the same College*) took place in Convocation, for the Anglo-Saxon Professorship, then for the first time to be filled up. The candidates were Mr. Mayo and Dr. Finch, both Fellows

---

[1] My 'Recollections' vividly recur to domestic arrangements for meeting this pressure; to loaves of coarser fabric and darker complexion (the quartern loaf of *wheat* being then sold at fifteenpence), to the large introduction of potatoes into puddings and pie-crusts, and to the still larger use of rice to save the potatoes.

[2] At Cambridge (Mr. Gunning informs us), 'this year was marked by very serious *bread-riots;*' perhaps for want of like efforts and precautions.

of St. John's; the former had 101 votes, the latter 67. This *first turn* (as well as every subsequent *fifth turn*[1]) was given by Dr. Rawlinson, the founder of the Professorship, to his own College, St. John's.

A.D. 1796.
[Determiners, B.A. 185.]

The neighbourhood of Oxford had, about this time, been more than once the scene of murder, committed in order to cover violence and robbery. In *very atrocious* cases the convicted murderers were condemned not simply to be hung, but after the execution to be hung in chains on gibbets erected near the bloody spot. My 'Recollections' retain the shocking spectacle of two such gibbets not many miles from Oxford. In other cases of persons executed, the body was given to the Professor of Anatomy[2] for dissection, in illustration of a Lecture given to a class hastily collected. The two skeletons which till lately were hanging in the Anatomy School at Christ Church (said to be the bones of criminals hung at Oxford) are confirmatory of the reminiscence.

There is a tradition that the body of a woman, named Ann Green (who was hung for the murder of her child), was conveyed, according to custom, to Christ Church Anatomy School to be the 'recent subject' for a lecture. It was found however, on unpacking her, that there was still some vital

---

[1] This restriction and other peculiar features of the Professorship were removed by a new statute in 1857; and the office, made tenable for life, was filled by the election of Dr. Bosworth, incorporated from Cambridge.

[2] 'By 2 Car. I. the Anatomy Reader may demand the body or bodies of persons executed within twenty miles of Oxford.' See Gutch's 'Collectanea Curiosa,' vol. ii. p. 45, quoted from Dr. Wallis's 'Abstract of Divers Privileges and Rights of the University of Oxford.'

heat remaining. The care and skill of the Professor and his assistant[1] were accordingly turned to the means of restoring her to life, which (as the story goes) after much perseverance they succeeded[2] in doing. Some attempts at wit were elicited by the double escape of the wretched woman: e. g.[3]

> 'Ann Green was a slippery quean,
> In vain did the jury detect her;—
> She cheated Jack Ketch, and then the vile wretch
> 'Scap'd the knife of the learned dissector.'

April 9. Dr. Wenman, Professor of Civil Law and Fellow of All Souls, was found drowned in the Cherwell; it was supposed that he fell into the river while over-reaching himself in botanising, or in collecting insects for his entomological collection. The pursuit of science or the study of natural history had not at that time many devotees; cer-

[1] I should say *assistants*; for we are told by T. Warton, in his 'Life of President Bathurst,' that he, at that time a Student in Medicine, assisted Drs. Willis and Pelly in this re-animation of Ann Green.

[2] A similar story, though carried much farther, is told of the famous surgeon, Mr. Hunter, under whose hands, ready for dissection, the body of a man, who had just been hung, revived. This was not all, however; for the fellow insisted upon looking upon Hunter *in parentis loco*, as the author of his renewed existence. In this *filial* character he every now and then applied for, and at last demanded, pecuniary aid. To the surgeon's great relief, however, he one morning received a 'recent subject' from Newgate, and who should it be but the identical wretch, *executed a second time*, for a second capital offence! The experiment of resuscitation was not again attempted.

[3] Dr. Bloxam says that Dr. Routh pointed out to him (in some old Map or Plan of Oxford) the gallows-trees *in the Parks*, from which, by a cross-beam, Ann Green was hung. Anthony Wood, on the authority of a special account of the case published in 1651 by a Mr. Watkins, says she was hung in the *Castle Yard* in December, 1650.

There was formerly a gallows near Holywell Church, and, till recently, the stocks were standing in the same neighbourhood, *in terrorem ebriorum*.

tainly Oxford had heard of no other presumed victim. As a Professor of *Law*, he seems to have mistaken his line.

By way of relief to the preceeding melancholy (not to say shocking) topics of this year, something of an amusing character here presents itself. About this date a quarrel took place between two Oxford characters, who ought to have been all harmony and concord, viz. the Professor of Music, Dr. Philip Hayes, and Kit Munro, a violin-player (probably the leader) in the Music Room band :—

'Acres procurrunt, magnum spectaculum uterque.'

Dr. Hayes was 'the fat man' of his day, while his opponent was a very small person. The feud, whatever occasioned it, was '*good-naturedly*' ridiculed by some Oxford wit of the day in the following parody on the well-known scene in Handel's 'Acis and Galatea.' As the *jeu-d'esprit* is of some length, a part only is subjoined from a manuscript copy :—

A NEW MUSICAL INTERLUDE.

KIT TWEEDLEDEE *appears in a pensive posture.*
TWEEDLEDUM *is seen in a rage at a distance.*

CHORUS, *by Members of the Music Room Band.*

> Wretched Kit! thine hour is come;
> Behold the Monster Tweedledum!
> See what shuffling strides he takes;
> See with what wrath his jowl he shakes.
> Wretched Kit! thine hour is come;
> Behold the monster Tweedledum!

Recitative, by TWEEDLEDUM, (*who enters attended by his servant* TOBIAS, *swearing to a martial symphony*).

> Thanks to thee, gentle Toby, for thy swearing,
> It cheers me much.—Toby, 'tis past all bearing
> That Tweedledee, that dabbler in the science,
> Should thus set great Professors at defiance.

Air.

Shall a fiddler, a scraper, a man of brown-paper
  Dare thus to our face to belie us?
Shall the organ submit to the bag-pipe and kit?
  Swear louder, swear louder, Tobias.

(TOBIAS *swears again, accompanied as before.*)

Recitative, by TWEEDLEDEE.

Such insolence provokes my rage,
Weak as I am, I must engage.

Air.

I care not, grim goblin,
  For thy stumping and hobbling;
Wert thou three times as big as thou now art,
  It ne'er should be said
  Tweedledee was afraid,
Or in such a good cause was a coward.

Recitative, by TWEEDLEDUM.

Shall Tweedledum engage so mean a foe?
Hence, caitiff!—or I'll end thee at a blow.

Semi-Chorus.

O Tweedledum, be not so cruel
With Tweedledee to fight a duel;
Since, Tweedledum, the joint of thy thumb
Is as big as the knee of Tweedledee.

This is followed by a *set to* in earnest, in which Tweedledum, mortally wounded, chants, like a dying swan, the following lines, [meant evidently as a quiz on the *then new fitting-up* of the Music School by Dr. P. Hayes].

Dying Strain, by TWEEDLEDUM.

O had I but liv'd to have finish'd my plan,
  I'd been first of all Musical Doctors;
I'd have made such a *cupboard* to hold the Vice-Can.!
  With such neat little *shelves* for the Proctors!

> Then such seats for the ladies! such busts! such devices!
> All o'er so be-carv'd and be-gilded;
> Such sweet pretty pillars, all par'd into slices!
> And my orchestra,—how I'd have fill'd it!
> But now 'tis past! my fame is done away,
> And in St. Peter's Church-yard turn'd to clay[1]!

The above is only half the original *jeu-d'esprit*, but more than enough, perhaps, for those who have no 'Recollections' of the Tweedledum of the 'Interlude.' The name of the author of this absurd but witty production has not been handed down.

[1] It might well have been expected that Dr. P. Hayes, when he *really* died, would be buried in the churchyard of St. Peter's-in-the-East, where there is rather a large tomb over the body of his father, Dr. William Hayes: dying however, as he did, in London, he had the honour of being buried (with a Musical Service) in St. Paul's.

> 'The burial follows where the body falls;
> They rob St. Peter's, but enrich St. Paul's.'

Dr. P. Hayes's arrangements for the Music School (excepting the 'cupboard' and the 'little shelves') have been lately put aside to allow for turning the room into an auxiliary Examination School. The rising gallery and the portraits (curious if not valuable) have disappeared.

CHAPTER II.

'Ye shall call upon him to hear Sermons.'—*Baptismal Service.*

Recollections of City Preachers, or Lecturers.

IN my very early days I had the advantage (?) of *sitting under* the City Lecturers at Carfax or St. Martin's Church. My first reminiscences begin with impressions of wonder at the grandiloquent discourses of my great-uncle, the *Rev. John Cox*, City Lecturer and Rector of St. Martin's. I do not pretend to remember *anything in particular* of his lectures or sermons; and this perhaps from the simple fact, that they were cast in the moral-essay style, and the smooth, well-rounded periods of the day,—characteristics which made them all seem alike, and therefore the less likely to make deep impression individually[1]. In one respect, certainly his preaching differed (quoad me ipsum) from that of other Lecturers, viz. that his avuncular[2] eyes *seemed* to be always upon me.

[1] Just as, at a later period, almost all Low-Church sermons (though quite in a different way and in a very different style) seemed to me all alike,—all, that is, cast in the same mould, and that, probably, the mould prepared for them by Mr. Simeon, the pious, good man of Cambridge. These moulds were called by him '*skeletons,*'—i.e. dry-bones, to be clothed upon ad libitum concionatoris,—but still when thus dressed up, they had all a strong family likeness. ..

[2] N.B. As my relationship to this good old man was on my *father's*

I have used the expression 'lectures or sermons' advisedly, from a conviction that though they are *nominally* the former (being endowed as such), they were generally the latter, and therefore were *preached*, not *read*.

Another Lecturer, of the same date and of the same school, was *Dr. Green*, Vice-Principal, for many years, of Magdalen Hall[1]; his periods, still more rolling, both in structure and intonation, were made more so by a regular rolling about the pulpit, and enforced (as was then the fashion) by a frequent appeal to the dust of the cushion. Dr. Green's brother was at the same time the parish clerk, dressed (as was also then the fashion) in a black gown with tassels down the sleeves; and in those days when congregations were silent and parish clerks sonorous, it was rather striking to hear, throughout the service, the doctorial tones echoed by the truly fraternal responses of the clerk. Dr. Green had the reputation of being a sound scholar, and even in days of academical laxity (as to the exercises for a degree), a stickler for discipline. Indeed he was for a time distinguished from other shades of Green by the title of 'Pluck Green,' having dared to utter the solemn words 'Non stabit pro formâ' in the Schools. Not that he had much occasion to indulge that propensity within his own Hall (the old Magdalen *Hall*,

side, and as *avunculus* is an uncle on the *mother's* side (*patruus* being an uncle on the father's side), I might as well, when coining a word, have *introduced* the adjective *patruel* rather than *avuncular* (neither of them being strictly English), but that the latter has the better sound. Query, is our word 'uncle' borrowed from the latter part of *avunculus*? that latter part being a diminutive termination from *avus*. The Rev. John Cox, here mentioned, was for many years Assessor of the Chancellor's Court.

[1] Dr. Green, in the bidding-prayer before his *rather frequent* University Sermons, used to pray for the good estate of Magdalen Hall *and the college adjoining!*

which then still elbowed Magdalen *College*); for its few members were mostly of a mature age and beyond the restraints of college discipline, being either married gentlemen-commoners or term-trotting[1] schoolmasters or ushers.

I have only a melancholy 'Recollection' of a Lecturer named *Dr. Foster*, the University Registrar, as a dismal-looking preacher with a solemn black wig. But as I can recall nothing more of him or his lectures, 'verbum non amplius addam.'

Next came *Dr. Finch*, Fellow of St. John's, and Bampton Lecturer in 1797, who kept the congregation wide awake by his clever, well-written, but oddly-delivered discourses. As he warmed in his argument, he gradually worked himself up, till at last he actually *foamed at the mouth*, scorning, or at least neglecting, the use of a pocket-handkerchief. On one occasion (which his audience did not soon forget) he finished a sermon 'on lying and slandering' in some such terms as these: 'People, weak and wicked people, are apt to palliate their falsifications by calling them (*when detected*) "white lies[2],

---

[1] 'Term-trotting,' a practice confined to the Halls (and a thing now never heard of), consisted in a man's coming up *now and then*, just to keep a term; so that it required several years at this rate, as well as caused much trouble and anxiety, to get a B.A. degree. The Cambridge 'ten-years men' got a degree much more easily, i.e. by simply keeping their names on the College *books* (or *boards*, as *they* say) and paying dues for ten years; no residence, no examination!

N.B. I may presume that this way of getting a Divinity degree at Cambridge has been discontinued *sub silentio*, as there is no allusion to such practice in the account of Exercises and Degrees in the Cambridge Calendar for 1869.

[2] Dr. F. would have been shocked had he lived to read Mr. Carlyle's attempt to soften down a gross act of falsehood and dishonesty in his hero Frederick William, as 'alas! a kind of lie or fib (white fib or even *gray*)—the pinch of thrift compelling.' But if telling a lie is disgraceful, what epithet is strong enough for the conduct of some, who in those lax

only white lies." Now I beg leave to tell *you*, my brethren (and I hope you will tell *them*), that there is, and can be, no such a thing as a *white* lie; they are all black, intensely black, black as hell' (foam, foam, foam!).

Cotemporaneous with Dr. Finch was *Dr. Collinson*, Fellow and afterwards Provost of Queen's, with a high reputation as a theologian, and subsequently Margaret Professor. His sermons were said to be very good, but from particular circumstances rather unimpressive. As a youngster I certainly could not follow him, though I was obliged[1] to 'sit it out.' In this case, however, my want of comprehension was caused, in a great measure, by the Lecturer's strong Northern dialect (he was, I believe, from Cockermouth in Cumberland), and partly also because a very decided but good-humoured obliquity of vision made me, in my innocence, think that he *was not quite in earnest*.

Mr. Crouch, Vice-Principal of St. Edmund Hall, was a truly pious Christian and earnest preacher. His delivery was not very musical, but was expressive of thorough earnestness, and suggestive of a Paul-like eloquence[2]. His sermons were always at least an hour in length, and, as

---

times may be said to have *lived a* lie? 'How can you hold your fellowship, while you receive so much (contrary to your Statutes) from other sources?' said one to a Senior Fellow. 'Don't you know (was the reply) that you may *hold almost anything*, if you will but *hold your tongue?* And I'll thank you to hold yours.'

[1] An obligation which has attended me through a long official life;—this portion, at least, of my godfathers' duties being in my case very amply fulfilled.

[2] Mr. Crouch was at Oxford the head of the then small party of prayer-loving, Bible-reading, God-seeking Christians, who were called Methodists by the cold majority, but who now (in 1861) would be simply called 'Low-Churchmen,' or would be called *by themselves* 'Evangelicals.'

a consequence, he was not very popular in a one-o'clock dining parish. Mr. C. occasionally assisted his emphasis and strengthened his climax by rising gradually on his toes, and then coming down energetically on his heels at the end of a sentence. He was always, however, listened to with great respect, and even at St. Mary's (though he and his party were quite a minority in the University) his sermons gradually commanded more attention and an increasing audience; so that eventually, when preferment elsewhere took him from Oxford, his loss was for some time felt and acknowledged.

The next City Lecturer I shall mention[1] was Mr. Brown, whose discourses (to use a negative term) were very unimpressive. Mr. B. was well known not only as a City Lecturer and one of the most *frequent* preachers before the University[2], but also as a great pluralist in a small way[3]. It was, I believe, this gentleman (though the story has been told of some other person similarly loaded with small pieces of preferment) to whom the then Bishop of Oxford, at

[1] And the last of whom I have any *early* 'Recollection;' for after 1796 I seldom attended the Carfax service.

[2] Then called *back-preachers*.

[3] A City Lectureship, being remunerated by Canal shares, which were then at a high rate, was worth at least £150 a year, with duty only every fourth Sunday. Mr. Brown, originally of Magdalen Hall but subsequently a Chaplain of Magdalen College, used gratefully to acknowledge (in his University Sermons) William of Wainflete as 'the Founder of Magdalen College *and the Hall adjoining!*' The Hall had not then been *shaken off* by the College as a poor relation and too near a neighbour. Wainflete was not the Founder (properly speaking) of the Hall; it grew, as it were, from accidental, local circumstances, *out of* and *upon* Wainflete's 'Magdalen Grammar School' [like Topsy, it was *raised* not *born*, i.e. not regularly founded]; indeed it was *after Wainflete's death* that it took the name of Magdalen Hall, having previously been called 'Grammar Hall.'

a Visitation, jokingly said: 'Why, Mr. B., you are the greatest pluralist I know.' 'Well, my lord,' he replied, ''tis very true that I hold several pieces of preferment, but I'll swap 'em all with you for your lordship's stall at Windsor.' His lordship smiled 'alienis faucibus,' but he never again alluded to Mr. B.'s *pluralities*.

CHAPTER III.

'In our efforts to track the records of memory ... bright hues come forward, like the colours of the tesselated pavement of antiquity when the renovating water is flung upon them.'—*Lady Morgan's Memoirs.*

Recollections from A.D. 1797 *to* A.D. 1800.

IN the spring of 1797 there was, from a succession of bad crops, the pressure of the war, and other political causes, a *run* upon the Bank of England for payment in gold. Every one, in a sort of panic, was in a hurry to get cash from the Bank for notes[1], thus raising a distrust of Government securities and shaking the public credit. By way of meeting and relieving this state of things, the authorities of the University and City set a good example, or, more accurately, followed the good example set elsewhere, 'by pledging themselves to receive Bank of England notes in all payments.'

It was no uncommon thing at this period for a 'gentleman' (the Oxford tradesman's designation of a member of the University) to ride a *match against time*, from Oxford to London and back again to Oxford (108 miles) in twelve hours or less, with, of course, relays of horses at regular

---

[1] Or, as they were contemptuously called, *paper-money*, or even *rags*. In an address to Convocation (at a much later date) Dr. Tatham says, 'I must do myself the justice of claiming the *Invention* of the Property Tax in the Premiership of Mr. Addington.' He refers for proof to a Letter of his to Mr. Pitt in Dec. 1797.

intervals. In one instance this was done in eight hours and forty-five minutes[1]. What a distinction for a man, not to say a gentleman, to have obtained, at the expense of the poor animals who gained it for him without sharing his triumph! What a pity that, like John Gilpin, his ride and his name have not been handed down in verse, 'caret quia vate sacro.' Betting was, no doubt, the first and chief motive; a foolish vanity the second; the third cause was the absence at that time in the University of a better mode of proving pluck and taming down the animal spirits of non-reading youngsters, such as is *now* found in regular boating, in rifle-practice, in gymnastics, athletics, and even 'rustic sports.' Hunting then, as now, was an expensive amusement, only to be enjoyed by a few, and by them only for a part of the year; racing had not *then* been thought of; bell-ringing, a fashionable academic exercise some twenty years before, was in 1797 voted vulgar. To ride well[2] is

---

[1] It was probably the performer of this piece of cruel sport, a young nobleman, between whom and a friend some such dialogue as the following took place on his return to the paternal mansion, after having thus (not *trotted*, but) galloped away his Term:—

'Nob. In just nine hours I rode on scamp'ring hack
To Town from Oxford, then all the way back!

Friend. Was no one with you when you did the deed?
No one to share it with you but your steed?

Nob. O yes, I had forgot,—my man, Dick Bent,
Follow'd me close for fear of accident.

Friend. Well then, for once give Dick his well-earn'd due,
For he outrode old Time, as well as you.'

[2] 'The Universities are not enemies to exercises of the body, no more than of the mind; and in particular they have a good esteem of *riding the Great Horse*, as contributing to a sure seat and graceful air on horseback.' (Gutch's Collect. Curiosa, vol. ii. p. 23.)

indeed an accomplishment befitting a gentleman, but a gentleman need not learn to ride like a jockey.

At the Act of 1797 the Masters of Arts were 102.

A.D. 1798.

[Determiners, B.A. 165. Regents, M.A. 83.]

A remarkable feature of this period, as a proof of sound English feeling, was exhibited in the voluntary contributions of large sums of money from public bodies and from individuals, '*In aid of the revenue of the country.*' About £4000 were sent to the Government from the University and Colleges of Oxford[1], and the sum of £500, *for three successive years*, was voted by the City Council. What would the City Council of later days say to such a proposal? Perhaps, however, the Council of 1798[2] had the disposal of larger funds than it has at the present time. One of the noblest contributions (to the glory of Manchester and to the amazement of our French enemies) came from 'the house of Peel and Co.,' viz. £45,000! Nor was the patriotic feeling confined to these liberal aids and free gifts; an Association was formed at Oxford to assist the civil power 'at a time (as it was formally announced) when, through the *projected invasion*, Oxford, from its inland situation, might shortly be made the deposit of prisoners of war, and become a place of refuge to the inhabitants of the sea-coast.'

---

[1] Mr. Gunning in his 'Reminiscences' says that the same sum (£4000) was also sent from Cambridge in 1798.

[2] One considerable source of revenue to the City Chest, which then existed, has certainly dried up, viz. the *purchase-money* of the City Freedom, paid by those tradesmen and others who were neither free-born nor the apprentices of freemen. Since the passing of the Reform Bill, mere occupancy of a house for a certain time gives the suffrage and most of the other civic privileges.

All this led very naturally to the enrolment of a Volunteer Corps, or 'Armed Association,' both in the University and City. The City Corps was not very strong in numbers, not more, I believe, than 250 men, commanded by Sir Digby Mackworth, Bart., then resident in Oxford. The University Corps was much stronger, i. e. about 500, commanded by Mr. Coker, of Bicester, formerly Fellow of New College. Such indeed were the zeal and spirit called forth in those stirring times by the threat of invasion, that even clerical members did not hesitate to join the ranks, put on the blue coat for the black one, submit to the discipline of drill, and practise target-shooting. First and foremost of this class was the Rev. Mr. (afterwards Dr.) Barnes, whose active services as *Major* of the Corps were said to have gained him his Canonry[1] at Christ Church. The Rev. Theophilus Leigh Cooke, Fellow of Magdalen, was the acting Adjutant. Some also of the most respectable College servants were enrolled with their masters, and, if actual hostilities had ensued, would have accompanied them, as the Helots did the

---

[1] Local wit was, of course, busy on the occasion, on the difference between a *Major* and a Minor Canon, with the usual play on words; e g.

' 'Twixt Cannons and Canons the diff'rence is small,
   They can both make a noise, can you say which is louder?
 The one fires away from his pulpit and stall,
   Quite as much as the other with shot and with powder.'

Reply.

' I laugh, my good sir, at your late very silly taunt;
 "*Great Guns*" are well plac'd in a Church which is "*militant.*"'

Dr. Barnes however really obtained his Canonry (I have recently been reminded) from having been Chaplain to the House of Commons, an office in those days usually followed by some Crown Preferment, and not, as now, remunerated by a definite income.

Spartans, ready to join them in the battle and to assist them at the camp-fire. The dress or uniform was of a very heavy character, but also very imposing: a blue coat (rather short, but somewhat more than a jacket) faced with white; white duck pantaloons, with a black leathern strap or garter below the knee; and short black cloth gaiters. The head-dress was also heavy; a beaver round-headed hat, surmounted by a formidable roll of bear-skin or fur of some kind!

July 7. A grand ceremony took place in Christ Church Meadow, of the presentation of colours to the University Corps. A sermon, or rather a stirring discourse, was addressed to the Volunteers, *sub dio*, by the Rev. C. Blackstone, of New College. Colonel Coker, who was a fine old man (old, that is, to my young eyes, certainly not a young man), made a speech to his men, drawn up in a square. Indeed, he was rather fond of so addressing them; and, under the influence of patriotic zeal and excited feelings, he generally talked till his tears choked his utterance. Ὡς φάτο δακρυχέων has been said of more than one brave warrior.

A.D. 1799.

[Regent-Masters at the Act, 112.]

This year, as well as the two or three preceding years, brought up a good many Undergraduates to pass the examination[1] for the B.A. degree, under *the old system*. This

---

[1] Lord Eldon's account of his own examination in 1770 (quoted in the Report of the University Commissioners at p. 59) is amusing, but, *me judice*, struck off in a merry mood for a *post prandium* joke. It is this: 'I was examined in Hebrew and in History. "What is the Hebrew for the place of a skull?" I replied, "Golgotha." "Who founded University College?" I stated (though, by the way, the point is some-

examination had dwindled into a formal repetition of threadbare 'Questions and Answers' (in Divinity, Logic, Grammar, 'et in omni scibili') which had been transmitted in manuscript from man to man, and were unblushingly ad-

times doubted) "that King Alfred founded it." "Very well, Sir," said the Examiner, "you are competent for your degree."'

The above is followed (in the Report) by a long extract (in reference to the same period) from Dr. Knox's 77th Essay, in which it is said 'that the greatest dunce usually gets his *testimonium* signed with as much ease and credit as the finest genius. . . . . The poor young man (to be examined in the sciences) often knows no more of them than his bedmaker; and the Masters who examine are sometimes equally unacquainted with such mysteries. But *Schemes* (as they are called) or little books, containing forty or fifty questions in each science, are handed down, from age to age, from one to another. . . . . I have known questions on this occasion to consist of an inquiry into the pedigree of a race-horse!' The author of 'Terrae Filius' (Nicholas Amhurst) gives this account of Examinations, &c., in 1726: 'As the *Public* Lectures are laid aside; as very few Tutors take care to instruct their pupils in anything but a little *bumdrum Logick*; and as very few young fellows are disposed to study more than they are obliged to do, they have found out a new method of performing this *public exercise* with great decency, and very little pains. . . . . As they have ready-made strings of syllogisms for *Disputations*, so for *Examination* they have the *skeletons* of all the arts and sciences, ... containing all the questions in each of them which are usually asked upon this occasion, and the *common answers* that are given to them; which in a week or fortnight they may get at their tongue's end. . . . . Many a school-boy has done more than this for his breaking-up task! . . . . It is well known to be the custom for the candidates either to present their Examiners with a *piece of gold*, or to give them a handsome *entertainment*.' Some further particulars are added which, from the pen of such a writer, were probably *exaggerations*. It is no wonder that Amhurst was expelled from the University. In connection with the subject of Exercises for Degrees, I may be allowed to append an extract from 'The Autobiography of Dr. Alexander Carlyle,' p. 363: 'We arrived at Oxford [i. e. he and Dr. Robertson, John Hóme, and James Adam] before dinner [this was in 1758], and put up at the

mitted, if not adopted, even by 'the Masters of the Schools.' These were Regent-Masters of the year, whose duty it was, by virtue of their Regency, to go through this ceremony, for a mere ceremony it had become. The more scrupulous, joining in the increasing cry for a new Examination-Statute,

Angel..... John Douglas, who knew we were coming, was passing trials [i. e. doing Exercises] for his degree of D.D., and that very day was in the act of one of his *wall*-lectures, as they are called, for there is no audience. At that University, it seems, the trial is strict when one takes a Master's or Bachelor's, but slack when you come to the Doctor's Degree: and *vice versâ* at Cambridge. However that be, we found Douglas sitting in a pulpit, in one of their chapels [i. e. the Divinity School], with not a soul to hear him but three old beggar-women, who came to try if they might get some charity. On seeing us four enter the chapel, he talked to us and wished us away, otherwise he would be obliged to lecture. We would not go away, we answered, as we wished a specimen of Oxford learning; on which he read two or three verses out of the Greek Testament, and began to expound it in Latin. We listened for five minutes, and then, telling where we were to dine, we left him, to walk about.'

As an appendix to this subject, I may add a *personal contribution* to the state of Divinity Exercises in my undergraduate days; I was asked by a B.D. (who often lent, perhaps *sold*, his services as a Respondent, himself furnishing the *arguments*) to supply him with a Latin *Epigram* (sometimes introduced as a finishing-stroke), to fit on to his old '*strings*' on the question, 'An lectio S. Scripturae sit Laicis concedenda.' I gave him the following lines, which more than once had the honour of being recited in the Divinity School:—

> 'Dicis in his Scriptis leges mihi inesse salutis:
> Duc, quaeso, ad fontes,—hinc avido ore bibam.
> "Impie," tu vocitas, "resta! procul esto, profane!
> Pollue ne fontem,—ecce canalis ego!"
> Dum jacui in cunis, animum corpusque tenellus,
> Alterius curâ vivere tunc libuit;
> Nunc *meus esse* licet,—poenas, palmasve merebor;
> Quae monstrent cursum, lumina neu renuas.'

hung back from the farce; but each year was sure to produce a few Masters who did not object even to dine with the *examined*[1] after the fatigues of the morning!

Well might such a state of things expire with the expiring century! The 'New Examination-Statute' was already on the anvil and being worked into shape; Dean Cyril Jackson, Dr. Eveleigh, and Dr. Parsons were labouring hard for the revival of scholarship and the credit of our Alma Mater.

> 'His informatum manibus, jam parte politâ,
> Fulmen erat.'

In short, nothing else (nothing at least of University interest) was thought or talked of but the forthcoming Statute and its probable provisions.

One proof of the stagnation in which the University was at that time involved was the dulness of the Commemo-

---

[1] *Scene*—the room of an Undergraduate just examined. Dinner on the table for two—the Examiner and the Examined.

Examinatus Examinatori:

> 'Now, good Regent-Master, the tables are turn'd,
> Many thanks for your friendly Testamur;
> After such a day's work we our dinner have earn'd,
> And what honest fellow need say more?'

Examinator Examinato (by way of grace):

> 'Say no more, my young friend, we've complied with the "Norma Loquendi, quaerendi and eke respondendi;"
> I'd no reason to sing out "Non stabit pro forma,"
> So now we will stand on no forma edendi.'

'Non stabit pro forma' was the old form of plucking at Oxford. In some *College* Exercises at Cambridge it was 'Descendas,' i.e. from the recitation-desk, the word being sometimes made to sound very like two English words.

ration-week. There was indeed the uninteresting promenade in the Broad Walk on the Sunday evening, and the equally dull 'Radcliffe sermon' on the Tuesday; but there were no pic-nics at Nuneham, no drives to Blenheim; there were no Masonic balls and festivities, no horticultural show, no procession of boats[1]; there were not even any concerts, at least on a large scale; and (greatest proof of all) there was not a single Hon. D.C.L. degree, and only one Hon. M.A. degree, at the Encænia in the Theatre.

Quite at the end of the Act Term, indeed, a move was made, and the academic as well as civic blood was roused by the arrival in Oxford of the Duke of York, with a grand military staff, for the purpose of reviewing the University and City Volunteers. It seems, however, rather strange to us, in our days of combined action and economy of time, that two *separate days* should have been devoted to a purpose so much better effected, *we* should think, in one and the same. But so it was; the University Corps was reviewed one day (of course, with high and well-deserved eulogium on 'their perfect discipline and soldier-like bearing'), and the City Corps on the following day,—compliments again repeated by his Royal Highness, but not quite so exuberant. Port Meadow was the scene (I was going to say of *action*, but, at all events) of inspection. In that wide space the lookers-on might well say, 'Apparent rari .. in gurgite vasto.' How much more effective as a spectacle, and (what is more) how much more expressive of brotherhood in arms, of interest in a common cause, would have been the brigading of the two Corps together! Could it have been a result of the old feud between Gown and Town? And could 'the Horse-Guard Authorities' have thus humoured

---

[1] Indeed there was as yet no *College* boat on the Isis.

the bad feeling? Thank God! there was no such feeling exhibited in 1803, when a great many academics (myself among the number) were enrolled, as officers and privates, in one common but chiefly Civic Volunteer Corps.

The beginning of December brought with it an early and severe frost and the commencement of a trying season for the poor, which, as usual, called forth a large subscription.

A.D. 1800.
[Determiners, B.A. 159.]

The 'trying season' at the close of 1799 was still more sad in its results at the beginning of this year, notwithstanding liberal subscriptions, the distribution of soup, &c. The high price of bread, the frequent badness of its quality, with the other countless trials of poverty, drove the poor inhabitants to acts of violence. Bakers' shops were attacked, and what were called 'bread-riots' regularly commenced. I remember seeing a noisy multitude, men, women, and children, looking very angry as well as hungry, and following a man carrying at the top of a long pole — not indeed the head of a baker or a corn-factor (as the middleman between the grower and the consumer was called), but a loaf of a very mouldy appearance as well as light of weight.

On that occasion (or a similar one) I remember seeing the Vice-Chancellor, Dr. Marlow, going in procession to read, or cause to be read, the Riot Act[1] 'on Carfax.' A portion of the University Corps was quietly assembled within

---

[1] In a similar case *now-a-days* this duty would probably be discharged by the *City* authorities, who were then, no doubt, co-operating. The quartern loaf, weighing 4 lbs. 5 ounces, at one time reached the high price of 1*s.* 10*d.*

the walls of New College, to be ready, if necessity required, to protect the public buildings of the University; and Capt. Haviland, Fellow of New College, gained credit for reconnoitring the movements of the rioters, with a great-coat thrown over his uniform. Happily the special-constables were found sufficient to restore things to order, or the old feud might have been revived with bloodshed!

I believe it was in this year that William Crotch, who had succeeded[1] Dr. Phil. Hayes in the Professorship of Music in 1797, took his Doctor's Degree, having as Professor to *examine and approve his own Musical Exercise* pro gradu. Happily there could be no doubt of its excellence, from the known talents of the composer; but, as if to appeal to the judgment of others, the Exercise, under the title of 'An Ode to Fancy,' was published;—the libretto being formed from Collins's Ode with that title.

At the Commemoration of 1800 (as at that of the preceding year) there was no Honorary D.C.L. Degree. By way of compensation, or to help out the show, there were three Honorary Masters. This, by-the-bye, was adopted in those days as a handsome way of dismissing a dull or idle

[1] Dr. Crotch was as small and short a person as Dr. Hayes was tall and large. This contrast produced the following

JEU-D'ESPRIT.

'*Trying it on.*'

'At length when the big Doctor died
  (Weigh'd down by his fame and his fat),
His light-weighing successor tried
  To succeed to his gown and his hat.

But the three-corner'd hat would not do;
  And the gown (if report you'll believe)
Was too large, even cut into two,—
  So they made him a gown of a *sleeve!*'

Gentleman-Commoner of good family and expectations; especially when the New *Public Examination* Statute was looming in the academical horizon [1].

The 'Presentator' to these Hon. M.A. Degrees was (and is) the Public Orator; but as in most cases of this kind he could have few or no materials for an eulogistic Latin speech, he was generally represented by the College Tutor, who, of course, knew and could say something of the young man or his connections, or his plans for enlarging his mind by foreign travel, &c. 'Hunc igitur, adolescentem ingenuum praesento vobis,' &c.

---

[1] It was well said in the evanescent Oxford and Cambridge Magazine (1856), 'To the end of the last century Oxford has properly no history.' Adam Smith tells us that at the same time 'the greater part of the public Professors had, for many years, given up altogether the practice of teaching.'

CHAPTER IV.

Magnus ab integro saeclorum nascitur ordo.—*Virgil*.

Recollections from A.D. 1801 *to* A.D. 1817.

IN the course of the year 1801 the number of Bachelors of Arts rose to 250; that is, about ninety above the average of the preceding years. This increase was obviously owing to the large number of those who had rushed in to be examined, as their last chance[1], under the old Statute, so soon to be superseded by a new and stringent one.

In the night of April 24, a fire broke out in Oriel College, which for a while threatened great destruction; but by the great exertions of Academics and others it was extinguished, after the complete 'gutting' of two or three sets of rooms and a great amount of injury to books and furniture[2]. The

---

[1] The want of scholarship in many of those who then graduated was notorious; even fellowships did not, at every College, imply classical or any other acquirements, so that *some years after*, as a result of those times, a Head of a College had occasion to say, 'Well! there's our best living gone to *the greatest dunce* in the College!' or rather, in his broad dialect, 'the *gratest doonce*.'

[2] Pitched out of window (as I well remember) from the adjoining rooms into the open quadrangle, not only heedlessly but, in a great degree, unnecessarily. An Irish Gentleman-Commoner was laughed at

Provost's Lodgings were for a time in danger, the fire being in rooms over the passage from one quadrangle into the other. *Of course,* the origin of the fire was not known, at least not acknowledged; though there was no doubt that it arose from a candle left burning by a thoughtless student. How wonderful it is, that so few accidents by fire have occurred amidst such constant risks from heedlessness and other causes! My memory, however, is strongly impressed with a conviction that Oriel College had another escape, and with nearly equal damage, at no great distance of time from that of 1801.

The grand ceremony of the Encænia was held this year in the *Radcliffe Library*[1],—the Sheldonian Theatre being not only under repair, but actually and completely *unroofed*. A notion had got into people's heads, that the roof (at that time one of the largest *unsupported* roofs in the kingdom) was in an unsafe state; and builders and architects advised not merely an examination but even the removal of the roof[2]; the thing, however formidable in idea, was safely done. The allegorical painting which covers the ceiling was carefully *peeled off;* so carefully and successfully, that on its being replaced, no mark of injury was discernible; — as indeed its present perfect condition shows. The striking effect on entering the building when entirely open

for thus *saving from the flames* his and his neighbour's looking-glasses and glazed picture-frames!

[1] A very inadequate substitute, it must be confessed, in point of size and for the classification of the assembly; but as it was intended to be a 'quiet Commemoration,' the comparatively small attendance was well accommodated, and the effect, from the beauty of the building, very striking, as well as singular.

[2] I know not whether the old roof was as scientifically constructed as that which replaced it; but the interior of it in its restored state is well worth inspection, and is easily accessible.

to the sky could be compared to nothing but to that of an ancient amphitheatre; so that, when the work of re-construction began to exclude the blue sky, it excited a feeling of regret for the loss of an effect never again to be enjoyed. On the plea of lightening the roof of the Theatre, the circular windows[1] (richly ornamented and partially gilded), which, to the number of ten or twelve, relieved and all but concealed the old roof, were unscrupulously removed, on the substitution of the new roof. Without pretending to any architectural knowledge, I confess that my eye still regrets the old, ornamental roof, and is hurt by the *entire exposure* of the new one[2]. The old cupola, or lantern, was (in the judgment of many) more elegant, with its streaming gilt flambeau, and more centrally placed, than its larger and more conspicuous successor.

In this year the City of Oxford was stirred up to great excitement by the political *attack* made by *John Ingram Lockhart* (a distinguished barrister, and formerly of University College) on what was considered as a settled, venerable '*institution*,' viz. the 'Marlborough interest' in the representation of the City of Oxford. Recommended by a practised lawyer's cool face and ready tongue, Mr. L.'s addresses were rapturously listened to by the Oxford natives. Never

---

[1] These windows may be seen represented in old Oxford prints and in the title-page of books printed at the University Press; indeed the interior of the roof was used as a deposit for stores of papers and books in sheets, waiting for sale; the University Press being then carried on in the Clarendon, adjoining.

[2] Concealment, or at least partial concealment of the roof, appears to have been a great object with the architects of our old buildings in Oxford; exposure of the roof, and even studied efforts to give it prominence, seem to be intended to catch the eye in all our recent erections.

perhaps, out of Athens or Rome, was greater effect produced by a rough, manly sort of eloquence, than resulted from his subtle and ingenious narration of Æsop's Fable of the Dog and the Wolf, and his running comments on it. Ex. gr. 'Just see how fat and sleek I am,' said the Dog, 'and how thin and rough-coated you are.' 'Very true,' answered the Wolf, 'but, my good friend, what's this deep mark round your neck?' 'Oh! it's only *the collar*[1], by which they tie me up!'—At the ensuing election, Mr. Lockhart supplanted the Blenheim candidate, and long kept his hold upon the citizens.

A.D. 1802.

In this year the new Public Examination Statute[2] (which had already been inaugurated, as a proper accompaniment to the opening of a new century) came into action, rather feebly indeed at first, as might be expected from so great a change and such a sweeping measure. The Statute, with a singular miscalculation as to probable numbers, *limited* the number of those, 'qui se Examinatoribus Publicis *maxime* commendaverint,' to twelve! The only claimants of this honour in 1802 were two; in 1803 there were four; in 1804 three; in 1805 only one; and in 1806 three! Of course a change was necessary; to have fixed a *limit* at all

---

[1] From that moment 'Only the collar' and 'collar'd dogs' became the popular cries in Oxford; for the application to Oxford *Freemen* and the Blenheim patronage was at once felt and acknowledged.

[2] The appointment of Public Examiners, *sworn to do their duty* 'sedulo et fideliter, omni odio et amicitiâ, spe et timore sepositis,' was a striking feature in the new Statute; but the Examiners, though (as was expected of 'Caesar's wife') 'above all suspicion,' have never considered the oath an idle precaution, or kicked at it as an affront.

seems rather absurd, as being, on any reasonable calculation, unnecessary; but that half that number (twelve) should never have been reached, and that zero was so nearly approached, was a proof of something radically wrong in the reckoning or in the nature of the proposed contest for Honours. There was a large staff of Examiners, quite large enough to 'pick the brains' of the annually expected dozen, but the numbers *turned out* by them in the five successive years were 2, 4, 3, 1, 3. There were indeed a few aspirants for the Honours whom they turned back, mistaken individuals, who, residing in the country, had been 'measuring themselves by themselves,' or, as was the case of a country schoolmaster, by their boy-pupils. But, on the other hand, several shy men of first-rate scholarship shrunk from '*challenging* the Honours' (as the phrase was), and so fell back *into the ranks*, as mere 'pass-men,' as they soon began to be called.

The adoption of the *Class System* (the required cure for this sickly state of things) did not take place however till after the experience of five years[1]. Meanwhile there was a falling-off in the number of Degrees, for in 1802 there were only 127 B.A. and 110 M.A. It is also a singular fact (produced, no doubt, by the altered Examination, the difficulty of getting a Testamur, and the shrinking from the chance of being plucked) that in this year *several* of the publicly announced 'Degree-days' passed by without a single B.A. Degree!

---

[1] That desired change and great improvement will be duly noticed in the 'Recollections' of 1807. In this year, 1802, Mr. Copleston was elected Professor of Poetry, the ten years of his Predecessor (Hurdis) having expired. As the Lectures were then given in elaborate Latin few persons offered themselves as candidates. Lowthe's, Copleston's, and Keble's still keep their place in our Libraries.

In this year[1] Oxford, both University and City, shared in the delusive joy of the hollow, short-lived Peace. The Volunteer Corps of each body was disbanded; war was indeed suspended, but only to break out again the more fiercely in the following year. The temple of Janus was shut, but the double-faced god still kept a watchful look-out, ready to throw open the gates even wider than before.

A. D. 1803.

In the Lent Term of this year the number of Determining Bachelors was 140; and, for the first time, while the ordinary Bachelors were *presented* 'ad determinandum' (i. e. to go through the still un-repealed absurdities of the *Quadragesimal* logical disputations), those few who had 'gained

---

[1] In May, 1802, I entered at New College under the patronage of Dr. Gauntlett, and my morning-sleep was there for the first time interrupted by the sound of the 'wakening mallet.' The use of that instrument (still, I believe, retained at New College, and lately adopted at University on Sunday mornings) was a remnant of old times, when the monks were thus called up to their early devotions. In 1802, and for many years after, there was still a curious mode of summoning the members to dinner at New College by the agency of two little choristers, who, at a stated minute, started from the College gateway, shouting in unison and in lengthened syllables, 'Tem-pus-est vo-can-di à-man-ger, O Seig-neurs.' It was their business to make this sentence (itself a remnant of older times) *last out* till they reached with their final note the College kitchen. For the last thirty years (or more) since the choristers' duty 'ministrandi in aula' was discontinued, a *bell from the Tower* has 'called to dinner.' At other Colleges a less ambitious tintinnabulum makes the welcome announcement, with the exception of Queen's, where a trumpet, with no uncertain sound, announces that dinner is about to be served. The '*Guebres*,' in 'The Antiquary,' are said to have used the trumpet as a signal for dinner.

the Honours' (or Maximes) were admitted complete Bachelors '*simpliciter*,' i.e. without going through the subsequent and tedious ceremony of 'determining,'. as it was called.

The Commemoration of 1803 exhibited a slight sign of more life in the University, in the fact that there was one Hon. D.C.L. and one Hon. M.A. degree. But the distinguishing feature of this Commemoration was the excitement (quite a *furore*) produced by *Reginald Heber's* prize poem 'Palestine,' in English verse[1]; *Shuttleworth's* Latin verse too (on Byzantium) was highly estimated; while *the third future bishop, Daniel Wilson* of St. Edmund Hall, carried off the prize for the English Essay on 'Common Sense.' There was as yet no prize for a Latin Essay; the University was indebted for that to Lord Grenville, on his becoming Chancellor in 1810.

In July the war with France broke out afresh, and, of course, with more embittered feelings on both sides; indeed, there had been only an armistice or suspension of hostilities. And so we once more 'cried havoc and let slip the dogs of war;' we literally buckled on our armour before it had had time to become rusty. Now at last, moved by the more serious aspect of affairs, and influenced by exasperated feelings, Englishmen prepared in earnest to meet the threatened[2] invasion. The first thing was to provide 'the sinews of

---

[1] It was thought so superior to the usual run of such productions (and there was also such a peculiar charm in his recitation), that even on the rehearsal-evenings (for in those days there were two public rehearsals) the Theatre was numerously attended.

[2] Moved by a sense of a common interest and a common danger, we at once re-forged our reaping-hooks into swords and bayonets; 'Fall into ranks' was once more the universal cry, 'not loud, but deep,' and nowhere was it better responded to than in Oxford.

war,' and in a very short time the sum of £6,500 [1] was raised in Oxford (the University and City Chests each heading the subscription with £500), to be applied partly in aid of the Government, and partly to the arming, not of two distinct Volunteer Corps (as in the last war), but of one,—and that chiefly composed of citizens, but with a good sprinkling of academics [2]. An efficient Corps of more than 700 men was soon raised and diligently trained. The dress being nearly the same as that of the regular regiments, we were rather flattered to be told we looked like 'common soldiers.' I say 'we,' for during $4\frac{1}{2}$ years I took my place in the Light Company, and shared in the skirmishes on Shotover and the field-days in Port Meadow. In proof of the serious aspect of affairs it may be added (in proof also of the zeal of the University in the cause), that 'a Term' was *granted* to those who might be prevented from *keeping* it by military duties in other parts of the kingdom.

A.D. 1804.

In the course of this year there were 138 B.A.; M.A. only 75. In February *Dr. Holmes*, being made Dean of Winchester, was succeeded in his Ch. Ch. Canonry by *Dr. Howley*, the future Archbishop of Canterbury, whose University sermons, though preached in an unimpressive way, were highly thought of. Both Dr. Holmes and Dr. Howley were originally Fellows of New College; the former had been for some time *preparing for publication* an

---

[1] Mr. Gunning, in his 'Cambridge Reminiscences,' allows that on this occasion Cambridge fell very short of Oxford, raising only £2,000 for military purposes.

[2] Especially in the Flank Companies (as they were then called, i.e. the Grenadier and the Light Companies) and among the officers of those Companies.

elaborate and splendid edition of the Septuagint for the Clarendon (or University) Press[1]. Of the latter (Dr. Howley) but little was previously known, except the fact of his having been tutor in a noble and influential family[2]. But whosoever was his first patron, the University for several years, and the Church for many more, had ample proof of his meek piety, his sound learning, and good judgment. It was said to have been by Cyril Jackson's recommendation that he was afterwards made Bishop of London; his subsequent advancement to the Archbishopric was fairly gained by himself and his own high character.

At the Spring Assizes of this year half Oxford, both Gown and Town, struggled to get admission into the County Court, to witness the trial of the two *Gordons* (one of them a clergyman) for *carrying off* the notorious *Mrs. Leigh*[3]. Luckily for them, her own unblushing evidence soon acquitted them of a *forcible* carrying-off; and so—to the great disappointment of itching ears—the matter ended.

In March, 1804, a long-standing reproach was removed from the University; viz. the *monopoly of half* the Univer-

---

[1] He left, however the work unfinished in the hands of the Rev. James Parsons, by whom it was completed and published.

[2] A mode of getting the foot upon the path which 'leads on to honour,' not uncommon in those days.

[3] This Mrs. Leigh's dangerous character, as a professed unbeliever in Christianity, is well exhibited in one of the early volumes of *De Quincey*, who was thrown into her company in his very early days, and who afterwards (when residing in Oxford at the time of this trial) helped her to escape, in disguise, to a carriage which took her from Oxford. No wonder that one who had no firm standing-ground should come to a fall. De Quincey says that Mrs. Leigh was not allowed to *give her evidence,* the Judge having at once stopped the trial on her confessing (in answer to Counsel) that she did not believe in Christianity nor even the existence of God!

sity sermons by three or four individuals, commonly called
'Hack-Preachers.' The remedy, which had long been called
for, was at length found in the simple plan of appointing
ten 'Select Preachers,'—men, of course, of high character
and qualifications (nominated by the Vice-Chancellor, the
Proctors, the Regius and Margaret Professors of Divinity, and
approved by Convocation),—who should take in succession
the un-accepted preaching turns. By arranging that five of
the ten should go out of office every year, a constant supply
of fresh talent was wisely secured. No scheme ever worked
better from first to last: besides the relief (and oh! how
great a relief!) to those who were officially obliged or conscientiously accustomed to attend at St. Mary's, it gave the
authorities the opportunity of bringing forward promising
preachers, or (what was still better) of bringing back to
Oxford preachers who had left it and had gained a clerical
reputation elsewhere.

A.D. 1805.

My 'Recollections' of this year suggest but little that can
interest others. I do not even find a single note[1] or memo-

---

[1] Valuable helps as I have occasionally found in a few unconnected
notes, I do not go so far as the writer of the following paragraph:—
'A single note (as Gray says) is worth a cart-load of *recollections*.'
What I here add, as a specimen or *spice* of those Oxford days, is an
actual recollection of a real fact. The two adjacent Colleges, All Souls
and New College, though not at that time remarkable as places of
study, engaged in a rivalry of a peculiar kind. In the interchange of
dinners between senior members of the two Societies, a long sitting had
one day been wound up by the introduction of silver jugs of hot negus,
or more properly '*bisbop*.' The appearance of the well-spiced vessels
suggested the idea of a challenge, i.e. a competition of bishop-making
between the Common-room men of the two Colleges. A night was
fixed, when the same party, aided by a few select friends, of acknow-

randum of any academical event or movement. Reginald Heber, a regular '*prize*-fighter,' added another leaf to his academic crown, by gaining the prize for 'The English Essay;' and Tinney of Magdalen (afterwards Fellow of Oriel) alone and single-handed faced (and successfully) the formidable company of six Public Examiners for 'the Honours.'

The lack of serious matter for this year leaves room for something *amusing* (though not so to the parties concerned). The Oxford tradesmen's system of 'giving credit' and their notorious anxiety to get a young man's name 'on their books' had then, as now, their usual effect on thoughtless youths, who were thus entrapped and, for want of funds, could not extricate themselves. Then came the second act of the drama,—the dramatis personæ being, 1st, a young man shut in his room, with door bolted, wanting to go out but afraid even to move; 2ndly, a rather shabby-looking person (the tradesman's collector) at the outside of the door,

---

ledged taste, met at All Souls. Jug after jug was introduced, tasted, and emptied with discriminating *gusto* and assumed gravity. Now New College has it—'so good! so strong!! so heart-warming'!!! And now All Souls calls forth rival ejaculations—'how fine! how genial!! how elegant'!!! But it would not do; votes were called for; each College supported its own production, naturally influenced by previous associations and impressions. The question was referred to the special visiters (i.e. the invited guests, not the *Visitors*), who, after an unsupported proposal to call in the aid of the Queen's College and Brasenose Common-room men, unanimously decided in favour of New College; and Chichele (as was quite proper as to priority in re *bishop*) knocked under to Wykeham! N.B. Andrew Dicks, the successful competitor and compounder of the *mixture*, was soon after successful as a candidate for the office of Yeoman Bedel (*post*, si non *propter*). 'Sir,' said he, 'why do you call it *mixture*? 'Twas no such thing. I got the day by not introducing a drop of water: that was my secret!'

knocking every now and then with an unmistakable, decisive, single stroke; in a word, with a *'dun's-rap.'* An Undergraduate of that day being thus (what he called) *persecuted* (for a well-trained dun would sometimes watch a staircase, like a cat near a mouse-hole, for a whole morning), and not finding his notice, 'Steel-traps and spring-guns set here to catch duns,' successful *in terrorem*, actually charged his door-handle with electricity, and, at the risk of astonishing a friend, frightened away his *persecutor* for a time!

Getting in debt and being *dunned* was, however, no new thing in Oxford, as appears from the following passage in the 'Oxoniana,' quoted from Percy: 'John Grubb, of witty memory in Oxford, in 1688, in celebrating the feats of Guy, Earl of Warwick, thus introduces Oxford duns (who seem to have been what they still are,—having always had the same difficulty to get paid):—

'"Besides, he fought with a dun *cow* (pronounced *coo*),
     As say the poets witty;
 A dreadful dun and horned too,
     Like dun of Oxford city."'

The above is followed by a note: 'A dun is one who is always *dinning*, i.e. knocking at your door.' The word is derived from Dynan (strepere), to din or make a noise.

Oxford studies and amusements[1] went on much as usual; the former were fiercely attacked by the Edinburgh Review,

[1] My own personal *amusement* at this time was chiefly derived from music. I had happily dropped into a College where music (not only in the Choir, but in private practice) was fully enjoyed and scientifically cultivated. One feature (indicative of a transition-state in this as in most other pursuits) may here be mentioned, viz. that pianofortes had not quite *expelled*, though they had *rusticated*, harpsichords from Oxford. We had two harpsichords of the best of Kirkman's manufacture then at

and strenuously defended by Dr. Copleston,—or rather Mr. Copleston, the degree of D.D. being subsequently granted to him, as an extraordinary mark of honour, by *Diploma*, in return for his Defence of Alma Mater and her sons.

The *amusements* (which were more simple in their character and certainly less obtrusive than now in 1860) not having been attacked, required no champion. *Boating*[1] had not yet become a systematic pursuit in Oxford; as for *boat-*

New College, and well played upon. A friend of mine at New College received (about this time) the following invitation from a friend at C. C. C.[*]

> Mecum visne tu cœnare,
> Herbæque fumum inhalare,
> Cum King's in D et Blow's in Are?
> Si non, dic mihi, quæso quare.

[The task of answering in appropriate verse was delegated to me, for my friend and self.]

Answer.

> Tecum lubenter ego cœnabo,
> Et fumum ex et in—halabo;
> Festivum canticum cantabo,
> Sed ventis King et Blow donabo.

Anglicè.

> I'll gladly smoke and sup with you,
>   Ready to feast 'from[†] egg to apple;'
> We'll sing a cheerful catch or two,
>   But leave both Blow and King in chapel.

---

[1] Men went down indeed to Nuneham, for occasional parties, in six-oared boats (eight-oared boats were then unknown): but those boats (such as would now be laughed at as 'tubs') belonged to the boat-people; the crew was a mixed crew, got up for the day, and the dresses were anything but uniform. I belonged to a crew of five, who were,

[*] Mr. Brown, afterwards Bampton Lecturer.
[†] 'Ab ovo usque ad mala.'—Hor.

races, they were no more thought of than were horse-races on Port Meadow. The game of *cricket* was kept up chiefly by the young men from Winchester and Eton, and was confined to the old Bullingdon Club, which was expensive and exclusive[1].

In May died Dr. Hodgson, the fourth and last Head of Hertford College; which indeed may be said to have *died* with him, if it could ever be said to have *lived*. In November Oxford (with all England) mourned for the death of Nelson, at the battle of Trafalgar[2].

A.D. 1806.

[B.A. 134. Honorary Degrees at Commemoration, 7.]

The year 1806 (as may also be said of some of its neighbours) seems to have left very little of academic public interest standing out for recollection or remark. As far as concerns the University generally, scarce anything of novelty or excitement occurred[3]. The system of 'challenging the

I think, the first distinguished by a peculiar (and what would now be thought a ridiculous) dress; viz. a green leather cap, with a jacket and trowsers of nankeen!

[1] The members of it, however, with the exception of a few who kept horses, did not mind walking to and fro: there were no cabs, no char-à-bancs, no 'drags' in those simple days!

[2] I *recollect*, as a boy, running after Nelson (with an admiring crowd) on his only and hasty visit to Oxford, in Long Vacation, near the close of last century. He was then a little, weather-beaten man, but every inch the hero!

[3] The 'Oxford Herald' made its first appearance in 1806, and was conducted with great spirit and judgment. It was for a long time interesting academically from its frequent extracts from old writers in relation to the University; and in a political as well as literary point of view was a formidable rival to the old 'Jackson's Journal,' then the only other Oxford paper.

Honours' not having been found to work so well as had been expected of it, 'put on a spurt' (as our boating-men say) *in its last effort* and produced three distinguished 'maximes;' but, generally speaking, the war and the apprehension of its possible results swallowed up all other interests, and, as a consequence, produced a torpid stagnation and listless apathy in most other matters and on most other questions.

It was in this year that Bonaparte overpowered Prussia; and yet in the summer of this year (vix credetis) an attempt was made to negotiate a peace; Lord Lauderdale being actually sent over to Paris for that purpose! It is hardly necessary to add that it failed, and by its failure made matters worse and the national feelings more embittered.

To myself, personally, it was very far from being an unimportant year; indeed it was a year which settled the complexion of my subsequent life. I ought to apologise for mixing up myself[1] and my humble fortunes with professed 'Recollections' about Oxford and University matters. In March, 1806, I was unanimously elected Esquire Bedel in Law, having been induced at a short notice (for elections then took place 'intra triduum'), by the *immediate advantages* of the appointment, to change my views in life.

[1] My apology is partly *general;* viz. that such has always been and, from the nature of the case, always will be the practice of all Remembrancers; and partly *particular*, inasmuch as I, from my early official position, have been ever mixed up with University interests, personally sharing in its fortunes, in its sunny and its cloudy days. It is in reliance upon the sufficiency of this excuse for any occasional egotism, that I proceed with these Reminiscences.

A.D. 1807.

[B.A. 134. M.A. 71. Hon. Degrees, 6.]

While the University was peacefully carrying out its plans of improvement, bent, as it should be, on raising the standard of academic education and anxious to shake off the sluggish habits of still recent days, the political atmosphere abroad and, in some respects, the social atmosphere at home were in a threatening and disturbed state. Hostilities between France and Russia—or rather between Bonaparte and Alexander—were only for a time averted[1]. At home, that is in different parts of England, there were no political riots indeed, no tumultuous assemblages of pretended patriots or discontented artizans (the pressure from without, i.e. the determined hostility of Napoleon and the consciousness of his growing power had opened men's eyes to the blessings of our Constitution and the advantage of our insular position); but atrocious murders, fatal duels, stage-coach accidents, and pugilistic contests were sadly common.

In June of this year Magdalen Tower was in some danger of injury or even destruction, some part of the interior woodwork having caught fire; but the alarm being soon given, the flames were happily extinguished before any serious damage was sustained. Towards the end of this year the Public Examination for the degree of *Master of Arts* was altogether discontinued[2]; in fact, it had been

[1] And this by means of a singular conference, of two hours' duration, held by the two Emperors on a raft on the river Niemen!

[2] Here again 'self' *crops up*; for I have to confess (what I cannot but 'recollect') that in my anxiety to get all examinations over while yet a *Bachelor* (in both senses), I *unnecessarily* went through this Examination for the M.A. degree; for it was dispensed with before I was of standing to *take* the degree!

found to be very troublesome, and, as being less severe and searching than the previous B.A. Examination, quite redundant. A candidate *took up* what books he pleased, and the work consisted of the Greek Testament with divinity questions at some length, vivâ voce construing in Greek and Latin authors, translation of a 'Spectator' paper into Latin, and questions (not many nor very deep) in connection with a Greek or Latin historian. This *sounds* sufficiently formidable, but in practice it was fast becoming an 'Examination made easy;' for it never, I believe, ended in plucking, and seldom attracted an audience. Michaelmas Term witnessed the *introduction*[1] of *Classes*, and the exciting interest of the *Class List*, into the Examination for the B.A. Degree; an improvement which at once took root, and has ever since, in spite of many experimental alterations, borne good fruit[2].

A. D. 1808.

Those *little* matters, 'quorum pars *magna* fui,' must again fill up the vacant place in the absence of more important 'Recollections.' Those however which I have now to notice have also (it will be seen) something of an University interest. It had been found out, that by virtue of what

---

[1] Then, as now, those who failed of getting a First Class consoled themselves with a new application of Horace's motto for Second Class men:—

'*Tutior* at quanto merx est in *Classe Secundâ!*'
Sat. I. ii. 47.

[2] Daniel Wilson, Vice-Principal of Edmund Hall (subsequently Bishop of Calcutta), printed in 1807 a Remonstrance on the plucking of a member of his Hall. It was a hard case no doubt; but did his pupil thank him a year after for thus proclaiming and perpetuating the memory of his misfortune? 'Save me from my friends!'

is called the Caroline Statute, the University was entitled to have *two* University Coroners, though *one* had been found more than sufficient. The office was forced upon me, not only unsolicited, but rather adversâ Minervâ; Convocation made me a Coroner, nolens volens,—and in this year 1808 I had to hold my first Inquest. The case was a sad, inexplicable one, as to the cause of self-destruction[1]. For some years I was the only University Coroner; the other, after being in abeyance for some years, has been restored. Most of the cases, in which I have been called upon to act, have been from drowning; and of these the number has been greatly exaggerated[2]. Two whole years have often happily passed away without any Inquest at all. There has indeed of late been much more boating, but more men can now swim, and more care is taken by them and for them, notwithstanding the really dangerous structure of the boats.

A.D. 1809.

[B.A. 140. M.A. 112.]

In the Easter Public Examination of this year, Brasenose College *monopolised* the highest honours, the only three First-Class men being all of that College. The introduction of

---

[1] It was that of a Christ Church Chaplain, a quiet and apparently happy and conscientious person, who, nevertheless, shot himself in his College rooms. That being my first Inquest, and having, since my appointment, had but little time to study 'Umfreville on Coroner's Law,' I called in the assistance of the City Coroner. Having thus learnt the routine of such sad inquiries, I have since acted for myself.

[2] Taking thirty years (from 1829 to 1859) there were fifteen cases of academics drowned in boating; and of those, the nine last happened in the last nine years of that period.

Classes evidently worked well at this time[1]; and this, though the Examination was conducted by a smaller staff than before, i. e. four instead of six[2] Examiners.

Public and political interests, however, still threw into the shade all less exciting concerns, University ones among the rest. While Oxford students were quietly plodding for academic honours, Sir John Moore was giving them a new edition, as it were, of the 'Retreat of the Ten Thousand;' displaying, i. e. the most painful but, at the same time, most important of a general's duties, the conducting a retreating army before a force greatly superior in numbers.

In July, 1809, the *Prince of Orange* came to reside in Oxford, and pursued his studies for a long time (in a house in St. Giles's); being a Presbyterian, he was not matriculated, though his studies were assisted by academic private tutors.

At the Commemoration there was no Hon. D.C.L., only three Hon. M.A.

About this time *first appeared* a book, which is now grown into much interest and importance, a book which is, probably, more consulted and referred to, and commands a larger annual sale, than any other publication in Oxford; I mean *The Oxford Calendar*. As becomes all *débutantes*, it was very modest and unpretending at its *entrée;* indeed the authorities of some Colleges looked upon it, at first, with such coldness and suspicion, that the essential information and accurate statements (which *now* constitute so much of the

---

[1] I do not mean *because of that monopoly*, but from the general results in the preceding and subsequent years.

[2] A fanciful alteration was this year introduced, viz. the division of the Second Class by a space and a line;—and this, though so obviously unsatisfactory, was continued till 1825. The work of Examination, having been found (as it might well be) too much for four Examiners, the number was in that year again increased.

value and usefulness of the publication) were in some instances unattainable, in others obtained almost by stealth, and of course imperfectly[1].

The Oxford Herald, August 1, contained the following 'Impromptu:'—

HERTFORD COLLEGE AND NEW INN HALL.

'*Caput, et sine nomine Corpus.*'

'You have heard of acephalous verses
  In this temple of metrical knowledge;
Things stranger my Muse now rehearses,
  For behold an acephalous College[2].
But wonder succeeds yet to wonders,
  (Of greater you scarcely have need,)
Here—a Head lives without any body,
  There—a Body without any head.'

REPLY,

by (or rather *for*) Mr. Hewett, self-created Principal of Hertford College[3].

'Cease, babbler, cease; a greater wonder see,
A Head, a Body, College, all in me.'

In October, Dr. Cyril Jackson having resigned the Deanery of Christ Church, was succeeded by Dr. Hall.

---

[1] It was not till a few years afterwards that the Calendar began to carry with it the weight and authority which it afterwards acquired.

[2] Hertford College had no longer a Head, as no one would take the Headship; and New Inn Hall, though possessed of a Head (Dr. Blackstone), had not a single member on the Books, the Principal not wishing to make the Hall more than a lodging on his very rare visits to Oxford. Indeed, till Dr. Cramer's time, there were no rooms there except the Head's dwelling-place.

[3] Mr. Hewett, a strange sort of person, being one of the Fellows, had *assumed* the government of the wretched place on the death of the last Head.

In November, our Chancellor, the Duke of Portland, died. In the autumn of 1809 an old Norwich clergyman paid Oxford and me a visit; he had driven his daughter in an open carriage all the way from Norfolk, and on approaching Oxford towards 'the Parks,' he turned off in order to enter the city (as he expected) by Wadham; he was *surprised* however, and *annoyed*, at finding the road obstructed by a row of stones; surprised, because he was convinced that in his early Oxford residence (about 1770) the road was *open to the public*,—and annoyed, because when within two hundred yards of his journey's end, he had to retrace his way and drive his weary beast a mile round! Query: Was my friend mistaken in his *recollections*[1]?

Near the end of 1809 the disputed election of a Chancellor took place; the votes were—

For Lord Grenville	406	Majority
Lord Eldon	393	13.
Duke of Beaufort	238	
	1037	

---

[1] This incident is mentioned because the question of a *public road* in that direction has been lately mooted, and because (independently of the public convenience) such a building as the Museum (now also become Radcliffe's Library!) cannot long be left unapproachable by carriages except upon permission and as a matter of favour. If it is true that in Sir Thomas Pope's Statutes for Trinity College (about 1554) 'the Street or Way' running between Trinity Garden and Wadham College is called '*Via regia* juxta Augustinenses,' and if '*Via regia*' means the '*King's high-way*,' how has it come to be claimed as a *private road* by Wadham College? Surely, when 'the Parks' and the adjoining land shall have been made ornamental and attractive (re-inforced too by the approaching claims of the *Keble-ites*), the *privilege* will be graciously given up, or 'Rebecca' may come from her hiding-place in Wales to give lessons in removing obstructions.

A notice had been issued that the voting would go on for two successive days, and as Convocation once commenced must be continued without adjournment (except in elections for an M.P.), the voting was kept up *by a slow fire* (to use a military phrase) throughout the night! the several Committees taking care to send in a few voters now and then. The blunder (for it was a blunder) caused a good deal of annoyance, and some fun. At the conclusion also (late in the second day) there was a mixture of fun and annoyance, when the immense heap of voting-papers was (as the statute then required) 'igne penitus *abolitus*' before the result of the election could be declared by the Proctors [1].

I ought not to conclude my Recollections of 1809 without recording the great struggle about dress between the Proctors and Undergraduates of that period. The former were slow to acknowledge the tendency of the times and the greater liberty and ease in men's lower habiliments, introduced by Wellington in the Peninsular army and generally adopted by civilians at home; the younger Oxonians would no longer conform to the old-fashioned dress' and the *sub-fusc* colours of the Statute [2]. In Mr. Brickenden's proctorship things came to a crisis. In spite of warnings, remonstrances, and impositions, the Undergraduates paraded the High Street, wearing indeed their caps and gowns, but each and all arrayed in white duck trowsers and light-coloured waistcoats.

---

[1] The whole Convocation House was filled with suffocating smoke. That ceremony of burning the voting-papers has since been *abolished*, and the whole process of voting in Convocation greatly shortened and facilitated. One obvious improvement however still remains to be adopted, viz. to do away with the 'quarta pars horæ' proclamations at *uncontested* elections.

[2] 'Vestibus coloris nigri aut subfusci se assuefaciant.' Statute De vestitu et habitu scholastico.

The Proctor fought hard but in vain against increasing numbers, cool perseverance, and open defiance. No wonder that he became most unpopular. It was, I believe, in this year that, in expectation of a riot, forty Masters as extra Pro-proctors, and of course called by the youngsters 'the forty thieves,' were introduced into the Theatre, and even in the gallery, to keep order and note offenders. They did, however, so little good that the experiment was not repeated. The revolution in dress that followed was not to be wondered at; indeed the wonder was that English youths should so long have submitted to such a *régime*. My own Recollections on this subject are confirmed by a friend who had witnessed and gone through these absurdities. 'No Gentleman dared to appear at Dinner or Chapel in undress, nor even take a walk at evening in Christ-Church Meadow except in shorts and silk stockings.'

A.D. 1810.

[B.A. 140. M.A. 122. Hon. Degrees at the Public Installation, 73.]

Jan. 2. Lord Grenville was installed as Chancellor at his house in London.

The disastrous expedition to Walcheren, with the fever called after its name, had occurred in 1809; its unenergetic commander, Lord Chatham, was thus quizzed in Oxford at the beginning of 1810:—

A Dialogue between Lord Chatham and a Friend.

Friend. ' When sent fresh wreaths on Flushing's shores to reap,
    What didst thou do, illustrious Chatham?' (*Chatham.*) 'Sleep.'
Friend. 'To man fatigued with war repose is sweet;
    But when awake, didst thou do nothing?' (*Chatham.*) 'Eat!'

In February of this year I have to lump together several rather incongruous incidents, merely as passing notices. (1) Dr. Barnes was made a Canon of Christ Church. (2) Mr. Duffield, a lay-Fellow of Merton, ran off to Gretna with Miss Elwes, daughter of the *second* old miser of that name. (3) 'Catholic' (i. e. Roman-Catholic) 'petitions' for admission to Parliament now began to make a stir, annually calling forth a counter-petition from our Convocation. (4) The question of Parliamentary Reform also began to be mooted, coldly in Oxford, but with increasing warmth elsewhere. (5) Lancaster, the Quaker, began to give lectures and establish schools on the system of education called, after him, Lancastrian.

April 30. A Diploma D.C.L. Degree was voted to the Prince of Wales; why, I do not *recollect* and cannot think. Certainly Oxford had seen nothing of him, though he did occasionally *change horses* there, on his way to Bibury races, in Gloucestershire[1]. Query: Did not he, about this time, send us some *unrollable Rolls* from Pompeii?

The Oxford Herald of June 2 contained the following amusing extract from Fuller's 'Worthies:'—'When Shotover-woods (bestowed by Charles I on a Person of Honour) were likely to be cut down, the University by letters *laboured* their preservation. In those "letters" occurred this among other *pathetic* expressions: "That Oxford was one of *the eyes* of the land, and Shotover-woods the *hair of the eye-lids*, whereof the loss must needs prejudice the sight with too much moisture flowing therein."' He adds, 'This *retrenched* that

---

[1] On these occasions, the relay of horses was *latterly* ordered to be ready in the outskirts of the city, that he might not be recognised; for he had been annoyed, while changing horses at the ' Star,' by the unpleasant cry 'Where's your Wife?' 'George, where's Caroline?'

design for the present¹.' We may remark here strong evidence that the country about Oxford, now so bare, was once well-wooded. Bagley-wood indeed still, to some extent, remains; but it is carefully inclosed and *preserved*, so that neither botanist nor naturalist can get admission, to pursue his studies there, for fear the game, belonging to the College which owns the wood, should be disturbed²!

A Jubilee was celebrated, in the summer, on the fiftieth anniversary of the King's accession; in Oxford it was kept by giving (by means of a subscription) a dinner, *sub dio*, on a very large scale to the poor. Tables were set out along two sides of the Radcliffe Square; the said tables were covered with a continuous sheet of white paper, of which, it was said, the mills could furnish an unbroken supply of any required length. The appearance was neat, and luckily it did not rain!

At the Commemoration, early in June, *Lord Grenville's* 'Public Reception' or Installation occupied the attention of Oxford and its numerous visitors for four successive days. A *future* Archbishop (Whately) and a *future* Judge (Coleridge) read their Prize-Essays, as B.A.'s, from the rostrum. There were sixty-eight Hon. D.C.L. and five Hon. M.A. Degrees conferred during the successive days, with the other usual ceremonies, complimentary verses and a Musical Ode.

---

[1] That such fantastic language should have produced any effect but that of laughter, seems now a wonder.

[2] The extract here given from Fuller, and an interesting series of 'Historical and Literary Notices,' for some time regularly inserted in the Oxford Herald, were, I believe, communicated by *Philip Bliss*, who had then an interest in the paper, and, from his connection with the Bodleian, and his own antiquarian taste and research, had abundant resources for furnishing such articles.

Sheridan's[1] name, which was inserted in the first printed list of Honorary Degrees, was *withdrawn*[2], owing to a threat of Non-Placets from some scrupulous members of Corpus Common-room. He appeared however in the body of the Theatre, and was at once tumultuously recognised by the whole assembly,—his jolly red face and coarse features being unmistakable. As all other proceedings would evidently be suspended (the Procession had not yet entered, nor Convocation been formally opened), he was *by acclamation* voted to the Doctors' *seat*, and conducted thither by the Curators of the Theatre, though without a *Degree !*

---

[1] I have mentioned the *refusal* of a *Diploma* Doctor's Degree to Burke in 1790; in 1810 Dr. Tatham, in an address to Lord Grenville, tells us (what was hushed up at the time) that the Hebdomadal Board, 'to sleeve-creep the New Chancellor,' proposed the name of Mr. Burke for the *Honorary Degree of M.A.* at this Installation. ' In consequence of a note (says Dr. Tatham) written by me (though totally unacquainted with him) the hon. gentleman saw clearly through the *finesse*, and magnanimously refused the proffered Degree.' Dr. Tatham says he had tried in vain to persuade the Board to offer the *Diploma* Degree formerly refused. ' The work on the French Revolution, formerly a *Prophecy delivered*, had now become a *Prophecy fulfilled*.'

[2] In Watson's Life of Bishop Warburton it is stated that in 1741 (when he was only Rev. W. Warburton, but famous for his 'Divine Legation,' &c.) he was asked by letter from the Vice-Chancellor of Oxford if a Doctor's Degree in Divinity would be acceptable to him. About the same time that of D.C.L. was offered to Pope. By the intrigues of two or three persons, ill affected to Warburton, Warburton's Degree was refused, and Pope would not accept his. 'We will take our Degree together' (Pope said) '*in fame*, whatever we do at Oxford.'

Warburton was subsequently created D.D. in 1754 by the Archbishop of Canterbury. He had been at neither of the Universities, having practised for some time as a Solicitor.

'Recollections' of 1810 ought not to conclude without recording the strong impression made on the whole University by the extraordinary Examination of Mr. (afterwards Sir William) Hamilton of Balliol. He *took up* all the Classics, all Plato and more of Aristotle's works than had ever been heard of in the Examination School before, not to mention the later Platonists, Proclus, Photinus, &c.[1]

A.D. 1811.

[B.A 144. M.A. 133. Hon. Degrees, 3.]

May 9. A cause came on in the University Court which excited great interest in Oxford. A Mr. Williams, an Undergraduate of Jesus College, brought an action against Mr. Brickenden, late Proctor of the University, for illegal imprisonment[2]. Mr. (afterwards Sir Charles) Wetherell was engaged as Counsel for the plaintiff, and used very strong and not very respectful language towards the University authorities[3]. Mr. (afterwards Judge) Taunton was much

---

[1] Nov. 10. One of the leaden Muses was blown down from the top of the old Clarendon. Hearne tells us that these statues were at first refused, and lay at the Wharf for above two years; they cost £600. (Reliquiæ, p. 380.)

[2] That is, for depositing plaintiff *in the Castle* for a night, and for *marching him through the streets next morning* to the Vice-Chancellor's Justice-room, without suffering him to lay aside *the dress of a mail-coach guard*, in which he had been found!

[3] Such appears to have been the traditionary practice on the part of Counsel when *occasionally* employed in our University Court. It was said, that, on a trial, some years before this case of Williams *v.* Brickenden, a learned Counsel (afterwards a Judge) had the audacity to

more mild and sober, but then he was employed for the defendant. It is to be presumed that the plaintiff's case, as to violation of discipline, breach of statutes, disguising dress, &c. was a bad one (academically speaking); and that though Mr. Brickenden, a most unpopular and hot-headed Proctor, had exerted his authority injudiciously and harshly, he had not exceeded it. It was no cause of wonder therefore that the verdict was for the defendant; that it was also 'with costs' did rather astonish even senior men, and, of course, called forth severe remarks out of Oxford,—especially when it was learnt that the Assessor, in summing up, said, 'Authorities are fallible men, and sometimes, as such, may *make a slip;* still authorities, in a place like Oxford, must be supported!'

May 24. In Convocation the sum of £300 was voted for the relief of the '*Détenus*' in France, i. e. the Englishmen (most of them very poor) who had been seized by Bona-

---

assert, that 'such a Court had never sat in judgment since that over which Pontius Pilate presided!' Query: Did he not deserve *to be committed* for *contempt of Court?* It was in the March of 1811 that Shelley, whilst yet a young Undergraduate, was quietly, but necessarily, expelled by the Authorities of University College on his pertinaciously refusing to disclaim the authorship (or any connection with the publication) of a work entitled 'The Necessity of Atheism.' I say *quietly,* for, like most residents in Oxford, I never heard of it till long after; and *necessarily,*— for how could the society, which treated him and his sad case with tender consideration, keep such a rotten sheep in their fold?—At New College, about the year 1803, the University, in the persons of the Proctors, called on Dr. Gauntlett, the Warden, to inform him that they and the Vice-Chancellor had expelled a member of his College for a truly 'grave delictum.' 'Sirs,' said the Warden, 'we have no such member.' 'What!' said the Proctors, 'no Mr. B——, the son of an Irish Bishop?' 'No, indeed, gentlemen; I struck off his name more than six hours ago.'

parte and located, under strict surveillance, at Verdûn; and this out of mere spite and vexation [1].

June 29. The Duke of Gloucester was installed as Chancellor at Cambridge. Among several Oxford graduates I visited our sister University on the occasion, and was admitted M.A. ad eundem [2]. There were fine concerts and liberal entertainments;—especially one grand dinner at Trinity, where the dull Chancellor and the heavy Master (Bishop Mansell) sat and ate in state. In the absence of the young men (with the exception of a few reciters of prize-poems, &c.) Cambridge was not seen to advantage, i.e. in its every-day working-dress.

A.D. 1812.

[B.A. 120. M.A. (?) Hon. Degrees at Commemoration, 7.]

This year offered no striking academical incident to remember or to record, unless it were the carrying off both the Prize Essays by *John Keble*, then of Corpus Christi College. It is worth remarking, that either he had not then developed his talent for poetry (which has been so universally admired in his 'Christian Year[3]'), or he had been

---

[1] Two or three Fellows of Colleges in Oxford were of the number, and for four or five years liberally relieved the wants of their poorer fellow-prisoners and countrymen. At the end of the war, those gentlemen were thankful to return to quiet Oxford, acknowledging that

> 'These fellowships are pretty things;
> We live once more like petty kings,
> And dine untax'd, untroubled under
> The portrait of our pious founder.' (T. Warton.)

[2] My visit, and a very pleasant one, was partly to Dr Clarke Whitfield, and partly to the late amiable Registrary, Mr. Hustler, at Jesus College; where I was lodged.

[3] I had the pleasure of being acquainted with John Keble at that

beaten, as a candidate for the Prize Poems, by such formidable competitors as Rolleston and Coleridge (afterwards Judge Coleridge), his friend and biographer.

This lack of University incidents leaves space for 'Recollections' as to other matters of interest.

While the University of Oxford was doing its work of education, at this period, in a calm, unobtrusive manner, the City of Oxford was (in September) in a state of great excitement. Mr. Lockhart (whose successful and well-applied apologue of 'The collar'd dog' has been mentioned in 1801) at length reaped the fruits of his exertions by being elected Member for the City, and removing the long-standing stigma of its being merely 'a *Blenheim Borough*,' and its freemen 'a pack of *Blenheim spaniels*[1].'

A.D. 1813.

[B.A. 139. M.A. Regents only 72. Hon. Degrees at the Commemoration, 10.]

Early in this year Dr. Landon, Provost of Worcester, ascended one step higher in the scale of preferment, having given up a stall at Norwich (where he was beginning to be highly esteemed) for the Deanery of Exeter.

March 4. The services of the O.L.V. (i.e. the Oxford Loyal Volunteers) were discontinued and the Corps was

---

time; during a walk in the country, while plucking *with some difficulty* a twig of May-blossom, I remarked that 'it was *May* yielding to *must*.' 'Yes,' added my scholar like companion, 'it is the *contingent* yielding to the *positive*.'

[1] Memorandum in an old pocket-book of this date:—

'In 1812 remember
Skated 23rd of November;
And, what's more wonderful than all,
Skated three hours without a fall!'

disbanded, on the ground that Bonaparte[1] was no longer formidable; or, at least, that an invasion was no longer to be apprehended. This disbanding was a rather hasty measure, inasmuch as the snake had only been 'scotch'd, not killed.' The confidence of Englishmen, however, was now justly raised by the glorious consummation of the Peninsular Campaigns, when the French (with Bonaparte's King Joseph at their head) hastily evacuated Spain.

To finish these warlike topics. The papers, throughout the year, were filled with 'Glorious News' in the largest type, especially in the autumn. In October 'Old Blucher' and the allies made great havoc in '*Boney's*' armies, which, notwithstanding the 'Russian Retreat' and subsequent dreadful losses[2], seemed still to rise from the ground, like the offspring of the dragon's teeth. The *prestige* once lost, the tide having once turned, Napoleon found that he had no longer any 'Invincibles;' but as he went down, down, down, others went up, up, up! For instance, the national cry of 'Orange *boven*' was again raised in Holland, and the young Prince of Orange, who had been so quietly residing

---

[1] The great *bug-bear* of so many anxious years, whose very name had been adopted by foolish nurses to frighten naughty children! Indeed, 'Boney is coming' had been a cry not confined to nurseries.

[2] In one of several battles, near Leipsic, 12,000 of his men were killed or taken prisoners; at Dresden, one of his armies, 16,000 strong, surrendered as prisoners of war! Subsequent accounts stated them as 28,000, besides 6,000 sick!

Lord Eldon, writing to a friend in November 1813, says, 'I suppose the promotion of Drs. Parsons and Howley will mortify our gentlemen at Exeter and Brasenose Colleges,—the heads of which (we hear) being unwilling to illuminate for our late glorious successes, have had their lodgings, as far as windows go, most completely demolished.' (Twiss, vol. ii. p. 245.)

N.B. I do not remember any such *demolition*.

at Oxford, took his leave of us, to join his father in his recovered kingdom. On his departure he was made a D.C.L. by diploma, and one of his train an Honorary D.C.L.

August 25. Mr. Bandinel was unanimously elected Bodley's Librarian in Long Vacation, and within a week of Mr. Price's death[1]! The election was, by Statute, to be made 'intra triduum proxime sequuturum;' the only exceptions were, (1) in case the University should be dispersed, 'grassante peste,'—when 'the three days' were to be reckoned from the formal re-assembling of the University; and (2) if the vacancy should occur 'feriis autumnalibus[2].'

I have heard and seen some strange things in Oxford, and even at St. Mary's, but nothing ever so strange as what is related (by Aubrey) of Dr. Kettel[3] of Trinity College, viz.

---

[1] Such was the requirement of the statute; the recent statute fixes the election to be held 'post *viginti dierum* monitionem, et in *pleno termino*.'

[2] This would seem to mean the latter part of the '*Long Vacation*,' since two of its three months (July and August) would rather be called '*feriæ æstivæ*.' Query: If it simply meant the '*Long Vacation*,' ought not Dr. Bandinel's election (*under that second exception*) to have been postponed till Michaelmas Term?

[3] Elected President in 1598. The old picturesque house in Broad Street (facing the Ashmolean Museum) is still called 'Kettel Hall,' from some connection with him and Trinity College. Local tradition says that Dr. Kettel built this Hall to give additional accommodation to the students of his College; and as he was President for forty-five years, he might well have done something for his Society and his particular Hall. In the middle of last century it had become a sort of lodging-house, and in it, as such, Dr. Johnson occupied two rooms (in 1752), busy in collecting materials for his Dictionary and frequenting Trinity Common-room as the friend and guest of Thomas Warton. The old Hall has long since become a private dwelling, and even now its occupants are occasionally requested by strangers to show them his study and bed-room.

that he once concluded a sermon at St. Mary's thus:—'But now, I see it is time for me to shutt up my booke, for I see *the Doctors' men* come in, wiping of their beardes, from the Ale-house.' 'He could, that is from the pulpit, plainly see them, and 'twas their custom in *sermon-time* to goe there, and about the end of sermon to returne to wayte on their masters.' Certainly *most University sermons* would be unprofitable to Doctors' or Proctors' servants; and it is probably from this conviction, that most of the 'Doctors' have lately dispensed with the attendance of their servants, to robe and un-robe them, at St. Mary's, and have brightened up the streets on a Sunday by walking to and from church in their handsome robes.

A.D. 1814.

[B.A. 177. M.A. 133. At the Commemoration, 4 Hon. D.C.L. At the Royal Visit, 14 Hon. D.C.L.]

Jan. 22. There was a tremendous fall of snow; all the roads near Oxford were blocked up, and no letters were received from London for four days! In many places the drifted snow was from ten to twenty feet deep; on the Iffley road, half-a-mile from Oxford, by great labour a passage was cleared, leaving a high wall of snow on either side, for a considerable distance.

At the Lent Assizes, an Oxford drawing-master, Mr. O'Neil, brought an action against the Rev. Mr. Evans, or rather his wife, to recover damages, as a compensation for the breach of a 'promise of marriage,' made by Mrs. Evans when Miss Ireland, daughter of a well-known Oxford apothecary. Verdict for the plaintiff; damages *one farthing!*

About this period *William Cobbett* (the wrong-headed, but strong-headed writer of, at least, good English) routed out some of the statutes and customs of Oxford, and *showed them up* in his *Weekly Register*. Among other things, he brought again into notice (in reference to the excessive power of the Proctors) the case of an old man (aged seventy) named Bayliss, who was carried off to prison, and kept there two nights and a day, because he refused ' to be sent home (as he said) like a dog to his kennel[1].'

April 4. Poor old Mr. Hewett, the last Fellow and quondam Vice-Principal of the extinct Hertford College, gave notice that, on finding that the proper authorities would not appoint a Principal, ' he had nominated, constituted, and admitted himself as Principal[2]!'

May 3. The Duchess of Oldenburgh, sister to the Emperor of Russia, visited Oxford, and was *lionized* by the Vice-Chancellor. She was said to be a busy, influential person among the great people of that day; but at Oxford she excited interest only from the difficulty (almost the impossibility) of getting a view of her fair, round face through the vista of an enormous, elongated ' peak ' or projection of a Leghorn straw-bonnet ! It was like looking at Venus through a telescope.

At the beginning of May a meeting was held in the City Council-chamber for the instituting of an Anti-Mendicity

---

[1] This case of Bayliss *v.* Rev. W. Wood of Ch. Ch., Proctor, is mentioned in the Chapter about Proctors. When the case, which had been commenced in the Common-Law Courts, was claimed by the University for trial in its own Court, Bayliss (as Cobbett said) ' *wisely* dropped the prosecution.'

[2] Of course no notice was taken of this. The *regular* appointment (as mentioned elsewhere) had lapsed.

Society[1]. The plan (like many other good things) was introduced by 'good John Duncan,' of New College, having been successfully tried by him at Bath. The institution has been maintained ever since, wtih more or less efficiency[2]. At first certainly the mistake was made of relieving 'distressed travellers' too liberally, so as to induce regular vagrants to deviate from their road in order to *take in* Oxford. The error was, after a while, found out, acknowledged, and corrected, with good results.

In April of 1814 Louis XVIII was recalled to France to mount the throne of his ancestors. *The great event*, however, of this year for Oxford was the visit of the *Prince Regent* and his royal guests, the *Emperor of Russia* and the *King of Prussia*, with their distinguished suites (June 13). As a thick volume was published by authority, containing a full account of the proceedings, they need not be enlarged upon here. In some respects, indeed, the book tells you rather how everything was *intended* to take place, than how it really happened. For instance, you are told that the Prince was met, in the *middle of Magdalen Bridge*, by the University and City authorities, and that the introductory ceremony took place there; it was certainly so arranged, and,

---

[1] Euphoniously called 'A Society for the Relief of Distressed Travellers.'

[2] Certainly *before that time* beggars hung about the public walks, and some of them seemed even to have established a right to certain frequented places; there was scarcely any City Police, and the University Police acted only *in the night*. Indeed, since the enlargement of that force, the University privilege of 'The Watch and Ward' confines them, in practice at least, to *night work*,—special occasions and public solemnities excepted. [I do not anticipate much good from the much-talked-of plan of amalgamating the University and City Police. The responsibility may be shifted off from one body to the other, and we all know what may be the result of 'sitting between two stools.']

with proper care and forethought, it might easily have been so managed. But it was not[1]. The Prince therefore advanced *beyond* the bridge, pulled up after passing the College gate, and actually *waited* for those who should have been, and really were (but in the wrong place), *waiting for him*. The University authorities, with the Chancellor, Lord Grenville, at their head, were quietly reposing in the hall of Magdalen College; the Mayor and the City authorities in the Common-room;—till at length at the cry of 'The Prince is waiting,' a disorderly, hasty rush took place through the cloisters and out of the College gate. There indeed it was found that the Regent (looking not very well pleased) had actually, according to arrangement, dismounted from his carriage[2]! This first *false start* having been got over, things went smoothly and according to previous arrangement. The progress *on foot* along the middle of the High Street was certainly grand and imposing;—the gownsmen, in full academic dress and arranged according to their Colleges, formed a continuous line on either side the high-way, the pavement, doorways, and windows being crowded with others. Order however could not well be kept after leaving

[1] No trustworthy scouts, for instance, had been stationed to keep a look-out on the Iffley road, no signal appointed to be given, by flag or bell, from Magdalen Tower. 'Is that Magdalen Tower?' said the Prince as he approached Oxford. 'Yes, your Royal Highness,' replied his non-flattering travelling-companion, ' that's the tower against which James II broke his head.'

[2] It was intended that the Chancellor and the Mayor should formally surrender the University staves and the City mace into the Prince's hand; this was done, in a hasty way, as to one of the gold staves; something of the same sort, and in a still more slovenly way, was done as to the City mace. 'Permit me,' said Lord Grenville, ' to surrender the authority of the University into your Royal Highness's hands.' ' It cannot be in better hands,' replied the Regent, with much grace, as he restored the gold staff to his Lordship.

the High Street and entering the narrow approach of the Radcliffe Square; the pressure (notwithstanding a guard of Yeomanry-Cavalry) became great, till the entrance into the Schools-quadrangle (and the Divinity School especially) afforded an acceptable and (by the sudden transition from noise, heat, and tumult, to stillness, coolness, and order) a striking escape from the increasing crowd.

In the Theatre, on the next morning, 'Old Blucher' (as he was familiarly called, but *in form*, 'General Prince Blucher') became after a while (when the Prince Regent, the Emperor Alexander, and the King of Prussia had been duly honoured and gazed upon) the hero of the day[1]. In retiring from the Theatre, he was all but 'pulled in pieces,' —everybody trying to shake hands with him ('sexagenarius iste,' as Dr. Phillimore called him in his presentation speech). In short, the old General was heard to declare that 'it was the hottest struggle he had ever been in[2].' Even at Dr. Barnes's (where he was lodged) he was not safe from this flattering persecution, which he however received with a half-pleased, half-sulky sang-froid. It was soon discovered that he was smoking his pipe in his bed-room (which was also a front-room), and every now and then a cry of 'Blucher, Blucher for ever!' was raised by fresh-comers, till he goodnaturedly came to the window, pipe in mouth, and, after a whiff or two, retired with a rough military salute[3].

---

[1] Indeed a sort of *furore*, excited by his fine head and massy figure, was increased by his manly but simple (I had almost said *English*) bearing.

[2] As he drove to Christ Church (where he was Dr. Barnes's guest) an impudent shoe-maker threw a new pair of boots into his carriage; and thenceforward announced himself as 'boot-maker to General Prince Blucher.'

[3] In the Theatre we were particularly struck with the fine counte-

The Prince Regent (who was grown very stout, but was well got-up for the occasion) went through a great deal of fatigue during this visit, and, now and then, with evident effort; he *groaned audibly* on ascending the Bodleian staircase, and did not seem to enjoy (as the Czar and the King evidently did) the hour's lionizing of Christ Church and the parade in the Broad Walk under a hot sun. At a Levee held in Christ Church Hall, among others the Public Orator, Mr. Crowe, was presented; the Regent gracefully referred to the Orator's Latin Address in the Theatre, and good-naturedly added, 'If, Mr. Orator, I had had to reply in Latin, I might have got as far as "Senex venerabilis," and then I should have broken down[1].'

As to the grand dinner given (strangely enough, but yet most splendidly, and, for effect, most successfully) in the Radcliffe *Library*, and other matter connected with (as it was then called) 'The Visit of the Crowned Heads'—*is it not written* in the elaborate account of the University authorities? I fear that I have dwelt too diffusely on a subject, absorbing *then*, but grown rather cold and uninteresting *now*[2].

---

nance and strong feeling of Sir Charles Stewart (afterwards Lord Londonderry), who (after gaining laurels in the Peninsular War) had accompanied the Allied Armies and written despatches, which had been greedily devoured. Covered as his breast was with all the Orders and Insignia of the Courts of Europe, he was a fine spectacle and a noble-looking Englishman. As he was received, on his presentation, with thundering and persevering applause, *the tears ran down his face!*

[1] The old man, though not fond of kings or princes, retired highly delighted, muttering something like 'Principibus placuisse viris haud ultima laus est.'

[2] It should be mentioned, in connection with the Royal visit, that, at the request of the Prince Regent, a 'Term was granted' in Convocation,—being one of those kindnesses 'quæ commendat rarior usus.'

On the 4th of July a great dinner, set out in the Radcliffe Square, was given (by subscription) to 4000 poor but respectable inhabitants of Oxford, to commemorate 'The General Peace, i.e. *the best* of all Generals,' as was given for their *toast*.

A.D. 1815.

[B.A. 169. M.A. 148. No Hon. Degree at the Commemoration.]

Jan. 29th died Mr. Rhodes, Esquire Bedel in Med. and Arts, and 'intra triduum' (as the Statute *then* required) I was unanimously elected by Convocation into his place, being of considerably more value than the Law staff, which I had held for nine years.

In this year an attempt was said to have been made at Christ Church to get permission for the Students *to wear a silver tassel* to their caps! It was also said to have been[1] met by a reproof from one in high authority, who answered the application at once: 'O yes, certainly; but on condition that you wear on your sleeve a silver badge, marked W.C.B.,' i.e. Westminster Charity Boys.

Another class of events of a most grave and important kind was illustrated on the night of the 28th of February, when 'the scotch'd snake' recovered its venom, if not its former strength. In plain words, Bonaparte slipped away from Elba, and with a handful of men landed in France. In April, so rapid was the march of events, Wellington became Commander-in-Chief of the Allied Armies, and the 18th of June saw *the Battle of Waterloo!* to be followed, on July 6, by the surrender of Paris.

But to return to 'Recollections' properly connected with

---

[1] This is here mentioned only as a prevailing *report*, but the story or something like it, was probably of an older date.

the University and its interests. In this year died *Mr. Lloyd*, B.C.L., of Wadham [1], who had been Curator of the Ashmolean Museum for nineteen years. The Museum itself seldom seemed to occupy the time or thoughts of the Curator; indeed it was a rubbishy, neglected place, where a Deputy Curator sat, apparently for the sole purpose of looking after the sixpences charged per head for admission to the 'Curiosities.'—Having mentioned the death of one Curator, my 'Recollections' of his successors may here find a place. *Mr. Dunbar*, M.A., of Brasenose, who succeeded Mr. Lloyd, was a clever, amusing person, of good family,—whose witticisms (rather studied and elaborate) were occasionally circulated; but being (like his predecessor [2]) rather indolent and unscientific, he made no effort to improve what he found in so neglected a state. Mr. Dunbar held the place, or rather *held to* the place, seven years, and was succeeded by the *Rev. Mr. Philipps*, a Fellow and Mathematical Tutor of Magdalen. Though a man of more solid attainments than his two predecessors, he was a shy, nervous man; and not having the heart to cleanse the Augean institution, nor face enough to keep so unsatisfactory an office, he relinquished it at the end of a year [3]. But the golden age

[1] He was a retired, quiet (not to say idle) gentleman, having no pretensions to science or scholarship; seldom, indeed, coming out of his lodgings in Holywell Street, where he amused himself in what his neighbours called 'strumming' on his harp.

[2] Indeed it looked (in these two last-mentioned appointments, at least) as if the Curatorship (small as the endowment was) had been intended to eke out the income of persons who had done and were doing nothing in the University, but who still clung to the society of Oxford.

[3] Among Mr. Lloyd's predecessors there had been a President of Trinity and a Provost of Worcester, but it does not appear that they did any more for the Ashmolean Museum than the ordinary M.A. or B.C.L. Curators,—except the giving a little more dignity to the post.

of the Institution now commenced, when, under the auspices and through the taste, care, and liberality of the 'par nobile fratrum,'—Mr. *John Duncan* for three years and Mr. *Philip Duncan* for nearly twenty-eight,—the building really became a Museum (though of a limited kind), and not merely a 'curiosity-shop.'

In that improved state of things, *Mr. Phillips*, our Geological Professor, succeeded to the Curatorship in 1854. Query: When the University Museum shall have swallowed up the Ashmolean Collection, and the building shall be turned to other uses, will the name of *Elias Ashmole*[1] quite perish, or be retained unconnected with his 'natural and artificial curiosities?' The building itself was raised by the University, not by Ashmole. By a recent vote of Convocation the building (or a part of it) was converted into Examining Schools. Some ugly projections from the basement (constructed at great expense by Dr. Daubeny, who lived there as Chemical Professor) were also doomed to be removed. Dr. Kidd and his family had previously occupied the rooms of the basement, recently appointed to receive the Arundel Marbles. The old Laboratory under the Museum, where the Chemical Lectures used to be given, has for some time *given up practice* in favour of the grand one

---

[1] Elias Ashmole (according to his Diary) 'had the honour of being made a *Doctor of Phisic* [so spelt] at Oxford, and had a diploma from the University.' Query: Had he any pretension to be a *physician?* Certainly the following extract does not say much for his practice: 'Having the ague, I took early in the morning a good dose of elixir [whatever that might be] and *hung three spiders about my neck*, and *they* (*Deo gratias*) drove my ague away.'!!! His diploma was dated 1669. His epitaph ends thus: 'Sed durante Musæo—nunquam moriturus.' His name has at any rate obliterated the memory of the Tradescants, who originated the collection and afterwards transferred it to Ashmole.

in the New Museum, or rather (in prudent apprehension of a possible explosion) *detached* therefrom.—N.B. I believe that the *upper part* of the Ashmole building (after being prepared, with much expense and the construction of an outside stone staircase) has been found unsuited, from heat or cold or some other cause, for a place of Examination, and is not used for that or any other purpose!

In Michaelmas Term, 1815, Convocation voted £300 in aid of a general subscription 'for the families of the brave men killed at the Battle of Waterloo.' The City of Oxford also voted £100.

A. D. 1816.

[B.A. 143. M.A. Regents, 133. Hon. Degrees at the Commemoration, 8.]

As Savings' Banks were coming in, it was hoped that Lotteries would be going out. It was long, however, before that hope was realized; indeed as their end approached (for their final doom was decided) the mania for this gambling seemed to increase. Oxford was indebted for its Savings' Bank to the philanthropic exertions of the Messrs. Duncan of New College, who left so many marks of their influence for good before they finally retired to Bath; each in his turn, though at a long interval, being at his departure presented to the Honorary Degree of D.C.L. in the Theatre.

In the spring of 1816, it having been generally supposed that the Oxford price of fish (kept up, as it appeared, by a monopoly and the want of competition) might be reduced and regulated by opening a *Fish-shop under the superintendence of a Committee*, the attempt was made in a small tenement[1] close to the Ashmolean Museum. Good, however, as was the idea, either from the choice of an incompetent manager[2] or from the disadvantage of competing with the two established shops in the transactions of the Billingsgate Market, the speculation, after lingering under unforeseen difficulties, soon entirely failed. It was a pity; but, I suppose, political economists would tell us that it could not end otherwise.

At the Commemoration two of the eight Hon. D.C.L. Degrees were conferred on M. Aubrey and M. Bertin, French refugee-priests, who had resided and taught French in Oxford ever since the beginning of the French Revolution. Bertin was cheerful and genial; Aubrey, rather high (being of good family and conscious of it), received his pupils as if he were conferring a favour. The newspapers

---

[1] Since absorbed by the Exeter College improvements.

[2] In connection with what, from its early failure, has become a matter of curiosity, if not of interest, the following Lines are quoted from the Oxford Herald of May 18 :—

'*The Oxford Fish Company.*

'When I heard that our City had named a Committee
    For selling cheap fish, I was glad ;
And my tongue ran so glib, that I said to my rib,
    She should taste the first cargo they had.

'So I went to the mart, at the time set apart,
    But they told me the fish was not come ;
There I waited an hour, brav'd hail-storm and show'r,
    And at last disappointed went home.

'Cries my wife. "Where's the fish to fill the top dish ?"
    "None is come, dear," I said, and caress'd her.
"It won't do," said my Kitty,—" so, to spite the Committee,
    Go and buy some of Carter or Tester."'

said that the University paid the fees for their Degree; but, more correctly, they were charged no fees, because *foreigners* paid none.

In July died in Oxford *Constantine Demetriades*, a dirty old Greek (not at all answering to his sounding name), who had hung about the University for some time, professedly as a teacher of Modern Greek, but really as a butt for the young men's jokes, a sponge for their eatables and drinkables, and a recipient of their loose silver[1]. He was never seen without a thick staff, ' to keep the dogs and scouts from the pockets of his old great coat! '

Oct. 18. The Duke of Clarence (afterwards William IV) visited Oxford and was made D.C.L. by diploma; he was accompanied by his brother-sailor Lord Exmouth, who, fresh from the bombardment of Algiers, was made Hon. D.C.L.

---

[1] Demetriades was, of course, thoroughly hated and sometimes roughly treated by the scouts, as not only devouring breakfasts, but also not scrupling to carry off the fragments, as he said, ἐν ποκέτεσσιν. He was one of the odd set of people who took refuge in the deserted rooms of Hertford College.

His supposed Epitaph.

' Here in his dirt lies poor old Demetriades,
  Your tricks, ye wanton boys, no more can try him;
  Laugh not, ye scouts, weep rather, like the Hyades,
  But see ye wake him not,—his staff lies by him.'

He is here supposed to have requested, as the old philosopher did in jest: 'Ponitote baculum juxta me, quo abigam canes,' &c. N.B.—I have been told that I have ante-dated the death of Demetriades by two or three years. I may be wrong; (if so, may his shade forgive me!) but not so wrong as one of my critics, who confounds him with Mr. Roberson, a solicitor, who lived in the ruins of Hertford College by sufferance.

Lord Exmouth was presented by Dr. Copleston. A Doctor in *Divinity* presenting a candidate for a *Law* Degree was rather an anomalous, certainly an unusual thing. But, first, it was *only* an Honorary Degree; and secondly, Dr. Copleston was, like Lord Exmouth, a *Devonshire* man,—both able and willing to eulogise the naval hero.

A.D. 1817.

[B.A. 143. M.A. 111. Hon. Degrees at Commemoration, 8.]

Jan. 11. The Grand Duke *Nicholas* of Russia (afterwards Emperor) paid a visit to Oxford, and a fine-looking man he was. He was *Doctored* by diploma, and four of his suite had the Honorary Degree of D.C.L. conferred on them.

This year, while there was peace abroad, was marked at home by riotous and seditious meetings, under the auspices of Hunt and Co. A Bill was passed in April for the express purpose of strengthening the hands of the magistrates in putting down such proceedings. Loyal meetings were held in Oxford and loyal addresses voted.

On the 6th of November, the Princess Charlotte (who had been married to Prince Leopold, afterwards King of Belgium), after the birth of a still-born child, disappointed the hopes of the nation by her own premature death:—

> 'When she, the star that shone the brightest here,
> Left earth,—to flourish in a fitter sphere.' (Oxford Spy.)

Never perhaps was a public loss more generally or more strongly felt, never was a 'general mourning' less a mere form[1] or matter of respect. The English nation had calculated upon a successor to the throne in that direct line,— 'ast aliter visum est!'— Her death after child-birth was followed by sad consequences in the person of Dr. Sir R. Croft, her accoucheur, who soon after destroyed himself.

[1] The choirs and organs of our Cathedral and College Chapels were hushed till after her funeral; and an Address of Condolence was voted in Convocation to be sent to the Prince Regent.

CHAPTER V.

'Equidem memini; fama est obscurior annis.'—*Virgil.*

Recollections from A.D. 1818 *to* A.D. 1830.

A.D. 1818.

[B.A. 162. M.A. 137. Hon. D.C.L. at Commemoration, 5.]

A CLEVER satirical poem, called 'The Oxford Spy,' published at this time, was intended 'to throw *a searching light*[1]' on some of the dark or weak points in the discipline, &c. of the University. It came out (anonymously of course) in five successive numbers or cantos, and reached a third edition. It was attributed to the late Rev. I. Shergold Boone of Christ Church, who carried off both the English and Latin Verse Prize in 1817[2], but who, from some strange

---

[1] '*A searching light*' also (in a literal sense) was now about to open on our ill-lighted city. Oxford, like most other cities, having hitherto been content to live (by night at least) in comparative darkness, at length awoke to a consciousness of its inconvenience and a desire for enlightenment. With a view to effect this, the first meeting was held (March 1) for getting an Act of Parliament for the establishment of a *Gas Company.*

[2] The third and fourth rate of the unsuccessful candidates for 'the Newdigate' had a new field opened for their poetic talents about this time,—in the composition of the well-paid copies of verses (almost poems) with which not only the Lotteries and Potteries but even blacking-manufacturers and Jew tailors inundated the papers and covered the walls. 'La! Sir,' said the vulgar wife of a wealthy 'merchant' of that stamp, 'd'ye think we wastes our time in writing them stuffs and puffs? No, indeed; we keeps a poet from Oxford College.'

motive or other (to spite his College, probably, though really spiting himself), did not choose *to go in for a Class*, which he might have commanded. The real cause, I suppose, was to be found in his satire and the spirit which prompted it; ex. gr.

> 'E'en should *the Paper* show his blazon'd name
> In the First Class of Academic fame,
> Still, still the care remains to form his mind,
> No College honours fit him for mankind.'

And again:—
> 'While all that makes "The Graduate highly Class'd"
> Is but mechanic drudgery at last.'

As many things which 'The Spy' satirised have since been amended, he might (had he written in a different mood and less offensive form) have been hailed as a prophet of better things and accepted as a corrector of abuses. But neither individuals nor bodies of men like to be quizzed (much less to be lashed) into amendment. At this distance of time the satire, as a poem, can be read with calmness and found to contain much that is sensible, cast in a manly, poetical form. That the writer, however talented, never rose very high in point of preferment, was perhaps a natural result of being a satirist and (worse) 'a spy[1].'

Having allowed so much space to the last topic, I must crowd together the remaining 'Recollections' of 1818[2].

[1] He might well conclude his poem thus:—
> 'Now with thee blended, Oxford, o'er me swell
> Some bitter recollections;—yet,—farewell!'

And so, exit Spy:—
> 'As one, not all unworthy,—but whose song
> Was right in motive, if in judgment wrong.'

[2] The Oxford papers of May 20 advertised in close sequence and in common connection with the coming Commemoration,—the Radcliffe

May 2. In a contested election for the Keepership of the Archives, the votes were for Cooke, C.C.C., 180; Bliss, St. John's, 122; Heyes, Exeter, 107.

In this year *Craniology* (since, I believe, called *Phrenology*), with a good deal to say for itself, but not enough to establish its claims and justify its pretensions, demanded to be admitted among the sciences.

At the same time, that pretty play-thing, called (as every pretentious thing is called now-a-days) by its Greek name, *a Kaleidoscope* (said to have been invented by Sir David Brewster), came into vogue, and found its way even into the drawing-rooms of our gravest dignitaries.

At the Commemoration *Ormerod* of New College gained and recited both the Verse prizes; soon after, while on a tour in Scotland, he was attacked by a fever, and died [1]. And so it often is; our *bright ones* vanish from us, like meteors, leaving us to plod on our way, made all the darker from the short-lived glow they had afforded us.

About this time Dr. Tatham, of Lincoln College, circulated a Letter on the Public Examinations, which concluded Sermon; Concerts on a large scale; a Sermon for the Dispensary, and '*A fine Turtle*, to be dressed at the Star Inn on the *Commemoration-day!*'

[1] Mr. Boone (Oxford Spy) wrote some very beautiful lines on Ormerod's early death; a few are here given:—

'Where is he,
Happy in well-earn'd fame so lately seen,
Now taught alas! how quick the loss may be
Of all that loveliest in our life hath been!
He snatch'd the cup of honour, and between
None came to dash it from him:—
And then, e'en then Death hover'd near, and laugh'd
As though there lurk'd some poison in the draught!'

I find the above statement is incorrect; Ormerod died, not in Scotland but in Wales, at Llandaff, and lies buried in the Cathedral church-yard.

thus: 'I am (it is known) a decided enemy to all *plucking;* the present system of Examination might pluck a Bacon, a Boyle, a Newton. Oh! the wonderful Examinations!!!'— 'Veri*tatem*[1].'

It had been thought a *great thing* when Miss George (a pupil of Dr. P. Hayes and a vocal performer at our Music Room), being a daughter of old George, the New College porter, was married (some years before this date) to Sir John Oldmixen[2]. But how did it end? They went to America, quarrelled and eventually parted. Lady O. (as her letters of 1818 informed her Oxford friends), by her musical talents, supported herself and a *young* family of *Old*mixens, while Sir John, being wretchedly poor, earned his own living as a market gardener[3]?

A.D. 1819.

[B.A. 225! M.A. 113. Hon. Degrees at Commemoration, 12.]

A *bonne bouche* is here presented to my academical readers; viz. a *portion* of a learned and playful paper by Mr. (now Dr.) Cotton, Archdeacon of Cashel (at the above date Under-Librarian in the Bodleian[4]).

---

[1] 'Veri*tatem*' was (he says) his family motto and heraldic pun.

[2] Who and what he was I do not 'recollect' to have heard.

[3] For a long time before 1818, when 'he ceased to occur,' there was an impudent fellow about the streets of Oxford who called himself 'The University accredited Guide.' Being dressed in (rather shabby) black and carrying a smart cane, he often took in strangers, and on parting would reject 5s., saying, 'Half-a-guinea is my authorised fee!' His lies were said to have been prodigious. Query: Would it not be a good thing if there were really 'accredited Guides,' well-informed men?

[4] I leave out some things rather pungent, but the remainder is given with the consent of the Ven. Archdeacon.

Eruditis Oxoniæ studia Amantibus, salutem!

Acerrimis vestrûm omnium judiciis permittitur Conspectus, sive Syllabus libri *breviter*[1] edendi, et è Prelo Academico, si diis (i. e. Delegatis) placet, prodituri; in quo multa scitu et notatu dignissima fusè admodum et liberè tractantur et explicantur.

Subjiciuntur capitum quorundam argumenta:

1. Ælfrædi Magni somnium, de Sociis omnibus Academicis ad Episcopatum promovendis[2]. Opus egregium, solertiâ plusquam Angelo-Maianâ nuperrime redintegratum.
2. Wiccamici publicis examinationibus liberi[3], sibi et reipublicæ nocentes.
3. Magdalenses semper ædificaturientes, nihil agunt[4].
4. Orielensibus, ingenio, ut *ipsi* aiunt, exundantibus, Aula B. M. V. malevolè denegatur[5].
5. De reditibus Decani et Canonicorum Ædis Christi, sive 'de *Libris* Canonicis.'
6. Respondetur serenissimæ Archiducissæ de Oldenburg[6] quærenti, 'Les Associés du College, che vous appellez "All Souls," à quoi s'occupent t'ils? Anglicè, What do the Fellows of All Souls do?'

---

[1] Nonne potius '*brevi*,' vir venerabilis?

'With suppliant smiles they bend the head,
While distant mitres to their eyes are spread.' (Byron.)

[3] New College had not then given up its privilege of examining its own men.

[4] A reproach long since removed.

[5] Oriel at that time (and even still later) was said to have coveted its neighbour's 'House.'

[6] See 'Recollections in 1814'—May 3.

7. E Collegio Ænei Nasi legati Stamfordiam missi Nasum illum celeberrimum, Collegii ἐπώνυμον, solemni pompâ Oxoniam asportant.
8. Petitur ne in posterum vox 'Wadham' (quasi 'Wod-ham' scripta esset) efferatur; præsertim cum istius vocis pronunciatio vel ex *cantilenâ* usitatissimâ satis innotescat[1].
9. Ex Societatibus cæteris ejectos Aula S. Albani pessimo exemplo ad se recipit[2].
10. De Golgothâ et Golgothitis[3].
11. Prælectores an prælectiones numero sint plures[4]?
12. De Academicorum in ven^{li}. dom. Convocationis sedentium pedibus igneo quodam vapore calefaciendis[5].
13. Magistri in Congregatione *necessariò* adsistentes more Attico τὸ τριώβολον recipere debent.
14. De Bibliothecario et ejus adjutoribus.
Bibliothecarius. 'Quid agis, Ricarde?' *Ricardus.* 'Nihil omnino, domine.' *Bibl.* 'Quid et tu, Thoma?' *Thomas.* 'Ricardo, domine[6], præbeo auxilium.'

[1] 'In Charles's reign one Dr. Badham
A quondam Tutor of Coll. Wadham,' &c.

[2] St. Alban's Hall has long since ceased to be a 'refugium peccatorum,' and now educates about fifty of its own Commoners.

[3] A name formerly and irreverently given to the old Hebdomadal Board.

[4] The question in later days (from the increase of Professors and the thinness of their classes) has sometimes been 'an feles an mures sint hodie plures?'

[5] It has often been asked, 'Why this was not done when the adjoining Divinity School and the super-incumbent Bodleian were warmed?' The only answer given has been, 'that if the Convocation House were made more comfortable, debates, already long enough, would never end.' [A few years later, however, the experiment was made.]

[6] I have presumed to Latinise this No. 14, which in the original is given in English—'Dick and Tom,'—and is indeed an old joke.

15. An Procuratorum pedissequi ritè nominentur 'Bulldogs?'

16. De Passere, intra Templum B. Mariæ concionantibus obstrepente, per Statutum coercendo.

  ὦ Ζεῦ βασιλεῦ, τοῦ φθέγματος τοὐρνιθίου.—Aristoph.

17. Probatur Bedellum Academicum, vero et genuino sensu, quartum esse Prædicabile Aldrichianum; quippe qui comes adsit Vice-Cancellario 'omni, soli et semper.' Doctissimus tamen Higgenbroccius *Differentiam* potius esse putat[1]. Nec errat forsan vir clarissimus: si enim Collegii cujusvis Præfectum (Genus) rectè dividat Bedellus adstans (Differentia), fit illico *species* optata,— Dominus scilicet Vice-Cancellarius.

Omnes igitur, qui famam aut Academiæ aut suam salvam esse velint, moras excutiant, bibliopolam nostrum integerrimum præstò adeant, symbola conferant, dent nomina.

Oxoniæ, Id. Febr. MDCCCXIX[2].

The beginning of 1819 produced a weekly (and weakly) Oxford paper, called 'The Undergraduate,' which, like many other similar attempts made since then, was soon discontinued. A very different and talented production appeared at the same time; viz. Whately's 'Historic Doubts relative

---

[1] Cujus hæc sunt verba,—

  'Bedellus est de *Vice-Cancellarii essentiâ*,
  Nec potest dispensari cum absentiâ;
   Nam sicut Forma *dat esse* rei,
   Sic *esse dat* Bedellus ei.'

[2] The 17 clauses here given are less than half the original MS., which contains 40. Perhaps however too many are here introduced for *modern* ears and eyes.

to Napoleon Bonaparte,'—a clever, but elaborate *jeu-d'esprit*, which alarmed some slow, matter-of-fact people.

Early in this year the High Street was lighted with gas, as an experiment; it was, of course, a most successful one, and all Oxford was on foot to witness it.

In March, Oxford, and Balliol College in particular, lost a valuable man, who had done good work for the University, —Dr. Parsons, Bishop of Peterborough and Master of Balliol.

In the same month, a subscription was raised for rebuilding Carfax Church; Dr. Tatham, of Lincoln College, offered £100, on condition 'that a tower were built in imitation of that at Great Malvern!' The old tower, however, was not meddled with, and the Doctor kept his £100[1].

May 7. Dr. Gauntlett, Warden of New College, was appointed a Prebendary of St. Paul's by his nephew, Dr. Howley, then Bishop of London! It was, I suppose, *honoris causâ*, —as the Stall had not, like a Canonry, much emolument attached to it. It furnished however an instance (probably the first instance) of a new kind of *nepotism;* or rather *avunculism*, i. e. *nepotism inverted!* An uncle getting preferment from a nephew!

In the spring of 1819 appeared a silly sort of *anomalous* vehicle, called a *Velocipede*, in which the motion was half riding and half walking; it had *a run*, but turned out to be *no go*. The only *gentleman* I ever saw venturing to use one (and that round 'the Parks') was a Fellow and Tutor of New College; his name, curiously enough, was *Walker!* When he *dismounted*, he exclaimed (like the Irishman who

---

[1] A tower like that at Malvern, with its open battlements and richly ornamented outside, would, no doubt, *look well* against the western sky; but unless the body of the church corresponded with it (as is the case at Malvern) it would have been quite anomalous.

took a *ride* in a bottomless sedan chair), 'Well, if it were not for the fashion, I would as lieve walk.'

In June, in the Commemoration week, the sum of £185 10s. was collected at the doors of St. Mary's, after the Radcliffe Sermon[1].

This summer was disgraced by riotous meetings, 'Orator Hunt,' as he was called, being the arch demagogue. At a monster meeting near Manchester, the Yeomanry-Cavalry were unhappily carried away by their zeal and loyalty, and several people were stricken down or trampled to death.

During some alterations this year in St. Mary's Church the coffin of Dr. Radcliffe was discovered on disturbing the pavement; no monument[2] or tablet, not even an engraved slab, having been dedicated to the memory of this great benefactor, or to mark the spot where he was buried.

A. D. 1820.

[B.A. 199. M.A. 163. Hon. Degrees at Commemoration, 15.]

During severe weather in January the large sum, raised by subscription, was turned to good account; employment

---

[1] *Now*-a-days (in 1860) it is a great thing to get £40 or £50. But *then* it was thought a part of the duties of the week (or, in fashionable language, 'quite the thing') to attend the service. [N. B. This Sermon was finally dropped in 1863.]

[2] As he was buried near the north entrance, just facing his *Library* (or rather what used to be his Library*), might not the idea be borrowed from St. Paul's (as to Sir Christopher Wren) and the simple words be inscribed on a tablet, 'Si monumentum quæras, (not 'circumspice' as there, but) *respice?*'

* 'The *building* itself was too heavy to move
By those who are fond of such larks;
Or else a new wonder one day it might prove,
And settle plump-down in the Parks.'

was found for men (otherwise out of work) in the construction of some of those foot-paths by the road-side which now form our *constitutional* walks, and a permanent benefit was derived from the passing visitation.

Jan. 10. A considerable part of old Magdalen Hall was burnt down, an incident which (as there was no loss of life) no one lamented, as it was the first step towards its entire removal. The members of the *adjoining College* certainly did not bewail the fire and its consequences. It was, like all such College-fires, the result of carelessness in the putting out, or rather the *not* putting out, of candles. The fire broke out in the night, and was first observed by the guard of a passing mail-coach, who gave the alarm [1].

March 23. In Convocation, *a Term* (to be claimed for *any subsequent Degree* by any one then on the books) was proposed to be granted as a compliment to his Majesty George IV on his accession [2]. Being rightly considered as a doubtful good, it was strongly opposed, but carried [3].

The paucity of University incidents in this year is made up for by painful reminiscences of extraneous and political events.

The early days of the new reign [4] were unhappily marked by a conspiracy, called, after a leading member, the *Thistle-*

---

[1] It was said that one gentleman, having been pulled out of his bed, as the flames were bursting into his room, rushed back, crying, ' For God's sake, let me save my Aristotle!'

[2] Or, as it was expressed in unnecessary and scarcely true terms of adulation, 'to record the grateful sense, entertained by the University, of the many acts of favour and munificence which his Majesty has been pleased to confer upon it.' The '*grateful sense*' perhaps was like the Irishman's idea of gratitude, viz. ' a keen anticipation of future favours!'

[3] A similar *bonus* (si bonus fuerit) has not been since proposed.

[4] Which, in fact, was hardly a new reign, as being only a change of title from that of ' George Prince Regent' to that of King George IV.

wood Conspiracy. The *first* object proposed was to assassinate the Ministry! what the *next* step would have been happily was not known, for the sudden and determined manner in which the police[1] (the bravest of whom was at once killed) burst in upon the assembled conspirators crushed the affair at once. A month afterwards Thistlewood and five others were hanged.

Hunt's trial and sentence to imprisonment were followed by those of Sir Francis Burdett[2]; and that, as it made him a '*political martyr*,' naturally led to his election for Westminster.

Manchester and Glasgow were scenes of riotous meetings; and, to crown the whole, what was called 'the Queen's business,' or, in other words, 'The *Delicate* Enquiry[3],' caused the intended coronation to be put off. On the breaking down of the trial (in November of this year) an attempt was made by the mob at Oxford to produce a *forced Illumination*. It was however put down with a high hand by the authorities, and the good feeling of the respectable inhabitants. The same

---

[1] 'Bow-street Officers' they were then called.

[2] Sir Francis, though not an Oxonian, was no stranger to Oxford; he for some time occupied a house there, Lady B. being a patient of Mr. Grosvenor, a surgeon who had gained a wide-spread reputation by a persevering system of *rubbing*. Sir Francis was a frequent guest at Dr. Routh's, who had an affection for Whigs as well as wigs, and did not object to a *little ultra* in both respects, in the person of Dr. Parr.

[3] After a lengthened and painful exhibition, this, which was called a 'Bill of Pains and Penalties,' broke down. The quasi-verdict of 'Not proven' (to borrow a Scotch Law-term) was hailed as a triumph, the trial and its excitement having lasted for months. As to further details of those disreputable proceedings (so different, thank God! from the Court-life of our Victoria), I may adopt the notorious words of an Italian witness on that occasion, 'Non mi ricordo,'—they do not come within my 'Reminiscences.'

riotous attempt was made at Cambridge, but was crushed chiefly and irregularly (with the connivance of the magistrates) by a self-constituted body of 600 Undergraduates!

May 3. The foundation-stone of (new) Magdalen Hall was laid, on the site of Hertford College, by the Vice-Chancellor, Dr. Hodson.

In June, at the Commemoration, Dr. Crotch's fine Oratorio of 'Palestine' was performed in the Theatre, conducted by himself. The friendly meeting of the poet and the musician (Heber and Crotch), as they complimented each other between the acts, in the area of the Theatre, was observed by the audience and hailed by a hearty round of applause.

In this summer Mr. Dornford of Oriel and Mr. Henderson of Brasenose, in ascending Mont Blanc, with a scientific party, had the horror to see their three guides swept away by an avalanche. After vain efforts to save them, the party returned to Geneva (as the papers might well say) 'in a state of consternation.'

In Sept. Dr. Routh, being in his sixty-sixth year, married a lady, through whose conjugal care he lived to see his hundredth year.

A.D. 1821.

[B.A. 221. M.A. 145. Hon. M.A. at Commemoration, 2.]

At the last day of Lent Term it had been customary for the Junior Proctor to deliver a Latin speech, upon Aristotle and Logic, to the 'Determining Bachelors,' in the Theatre. This year the Junior Proctor (J. Bull, Ch. Ch.) was spared the ceremony[1], there being no longer any 'Determiners' to address.

[1] The only wonder was, that the antiquated forms of 'Determining' and 'Lent Exercises' had not ceased much sooner, after having been brought, for twenty years, into contact with the realities of the Public Examination, the dead with the living.

I may be excused (as looking forward possibly to something of the sort, 'Deo volente et Academiâ consentiente,' for myself) if I admit 'apud nos Oxonienses' the following Reminiscence of a liberal act in our sister University : 'Cambridge, May, 1821, Mr. Beverley[1], the senior Esquire Bedel, was allowed by the University to retire *with the full emoluments* of his office, in consideration of his long services and advanced age.'

In January of this year, a respectable and wealthy Oxford tailor, Mr. Speakman, was discommoned in the Vice-Chancellor's Court 'for having sued a Member of Convocation (for a debt) in the Courts of Westminster-Hall.' He appealed to the Court of King's Bench, but the privilege of the University Court was still allowed. He retired from business, having well filled his pockets by his former gains.

Oxford has its *Logic Lane*[2]; it once had its *Divinity Walk*, which branched off from Cheney Lane (or the old London Road) towards Shotover. There was a traditional story of its being haunted by the ghost of a young girl *killed and buried* there by an Academic.

---

[1] This Cambridge Esquire Bedel is not to be confounded with R. M. Beverley, Esq., who in 1833 published, in a 'Letter to the Cambridge Chancellor,' a gross and exaggerated account of Cambridge in his day. He was well answered by more than one Cambridge Tutor, and proved to have considered his own unhappy experiences *in a bad set* as a fair representation of the whole body.

[2] M. Aubrey in his 'Oxonii dux poeticus' (see 'Recollections' for 1791) accounts for the name of *Logic* Lane, by referring to a tradition, 'that undecided disputes or argumentations in the Schools were occasionally transferred by adjournment (a sort of 'Probo aliter et alibi') to this Lane, to *fight it out* with the argumentum baculinum. It more probably took its name from *Aristotle's* Hall, which formerly stood there. How Logic Lane intruded itself here I cannot tell; this notice of it however, though unconnected with what went before or what follows, may help to illustrate the Lane as *a mere passage* to something else.

At a sale of Mr. Christie's, this year, the *original paintings* by Sir Joshua Reynolds[1] for New College Chapel-window sold as follows:—

	£	s.	d.
Sir Joshua and Mr. Jervas as Shepherds	430	10	0
Peasant girl and children with a torch	420	0	0
Shepherd's boy and dog	630	0	0
St. John and Lamb	183	15	0
Charity	1575	0	0
Faith	420	0	0
Hope	682	10	0
Temperance	630	0	0
Justice	1155	0	0
Fortitude	735	0	0
Prudence	367	10	0
Total	£7,229	5	0

This summer the Lord Chancellor was created *Earl* of Eldon, and his brother, Sir William Scott, so long Member for Oxford, was made Baron Stowell!

May 5. Bonaparte died at St. Helena.

The Long Vacation of 1821 was enlivened by a contest (carried on in rather *a bitter spirit*) for the vacant seat for the University, on the elevation of Sir William Scott to the peerage. The competitors were, Mr. Heber and Sir John Nicholl; Heber had 612 votes, Nicholl 519.

In December a more vulgar kind of contest took place, and, like the preceding, in rather *a bitter spirit*. In our *Oxford* contests the real combatants never appear on '*the stage*,' but in this the poor combatants knocked each other

---

[1] My friend, Dr. Bloxam, tells me that the *principal scene* of the Nativity was burnt at the fire at Belvoir Castle in 1816; he refers me to Dibdin's 'Northern Tour,' vol. i. p. 66.

about for an hour or more. At the end—when it was nearly *all up* with one of them—the *chances* were described, in the emphatic language of 'the ring,' as '*Christ Church* against *New Inn Hall.*'

A.D. 1822.

[B.A. 246. M.A. 146. Hon. Degrees at Commemoration, 5.]

Jan. 18 died Dr. Hodson, Principal of Brasenose, and Regius Professor of Divinity, of whom some particulars are given in another Chapter.

Oxford, this year, contributed liberally to the subscription which was raised for the ' Distressed Irish.'

It was stated in the Oxford Herald, of October 19, in this year, that ' Formerly *Undergraduates*, as such, did not wear silk-tassels to their caps; but before they were authorised by Statute to do so, the Undergraduates of Balliol applied to the then Master to be allowed the privilege, enjoyed by Bachelors of Arts. ' Gentlemen (replied the Master), be in no hurry,—you shall all wear them *by degrees.*' Dr. Leigh's Mastership was of the unusual length of fifty-nine years, i. e. from 1726 to 1785.

In the Commemoration week of this year the Crown Prince of Denmark, with his Princess, visited Oxford. As he was travelling *incognito*, he declined a Degree in the Theatre, though both he and the Princess sat there during the solemnity; having been conducted thither from the Star Hotel by the Vice-Chancellor and Proctors. A diploma Degree of D.C.L. was afterwards decreed and sent to his Royal Highness.

The following rather serious *jeu-d'esprit* was circulated in the Michaelmas Term of 1822, and by no one so readily and good-humouredly as by the subject of it, Dr. Buckland, who in his Lectures often showed that he enjoyed a good joke, even at his own expense.

EPITAPH—(*by anticipation*).

'Where shall we our famous Professor inter,
  That in peace he may rest his bones?
If we hew him a rocky sepulchre[1],
  He'll rise and break the stones,
And examine each stratum that lies around;
For he's quite in his element underground.

'If with mattock and spade his body we lay
  In the common alluvial soil,
He'll start up and snatch those tools away
  Of his own geological toil.
In a stratum so young the Professor disdains
That imbedded should lie his organic remains.

'But expos'd to the drip of some case-hard'ning spring
  His body let stalactite cover,
And to Oxford the petrified Sage we will bring .
  When he is incrusted all over.
There 'mid mammoths and crocodiles high on a shelf,
He shall stand as a monument rais'd to himself[2].'

A.D. 1823.

[B.A. 267. M.A. 187. Hon. Degrees at the Commemoration, 3.]

In January appeared a poem entitled 'Oxford,—*an Eulogistic Satire.*' It has left no remembrance of its existence,

---

[1] Something like this was actually done, when the lamented Professor's body was laid in a grave *hewed out of the solid rock*, at Islip, six miles from Oxford.

[2] This *jeu-d'esprit* is given by Miss Whately (with three additional stanzas) as the production of her father the Archbishop.

except that the title, being a contradiction in terms, at once deterred sensible people from perusing it.

Not only had the Public Examination now become, after twenty years' trial, a settled 'Institution' with its increasing numbers of First Classes, and even of 'Double-Firsts,' but a necessary though melancholy consequence had equally become an 'Institution,' viz. the rejection of *non-satisfactory* candidates, as the Examination Statute tenderly describes them. The term however by which their *status academicus* has been for some years expressed, viz. '*pluck'd men*,' was said to have *originated* from some such incident as this[1]. The Clerk of the Schools was one day sweeping out torn papers and worn-up *pens or quills*, and, being a wag, cried out to a passing friend, 'See what sport *we* have had to-day! the feathers of the *geese we have plucked!*'—and so the 'animal bipes, implume' of the Schools obtained a name, and, as the numbers increased, a *sort of class*.

One obvious effect of the increase in these failures soon began to show itself in the cool manner in which they were met by the unplumed individuals and their sympathising young friends; so that at a wine-party, after drinking the health 'of those gentlemen who had *satisfied* the Examiners,' it was no uncommon thing to propose that 'of the gentlemen who had *not satisfied* them!' The speech of thanks thus

---

[1] It would be more correct to say, that the term 'plucking' (sometimes called deplumation) was then *revived* rather than *originated;* for (as has been mentioned in Chapter II) the practice and the term were known, though very rarely applied, under the old system of Examination. The term also has been connected with the power possessed in Congregation of stopping Degrees (or, what is the same thing, the Grace) by either whispering a Non-placet into the ear of the Proctor, as he passes, or 'per aliquod signum externum,' which *signum* is traditionally said to be, the *plucking* or twitching the procuratorial velvet sleeve *en passant*.

elicited was generally the most amusing and often the cleverest of the evening; for plucking in most cases is the result of idleness rather than want of ability.—N.B. The term 'being plucked' has (among the *young men* at least) yielded to that of '*being ploughed*,' possibly from having confounded in their German lessons *pflügen* and *pflücken*[1].

June 14. Dr. Thompson, Principal of St. Edmund Hall, was succeeded by the *Rev. H. Wheatley*, a Fellow of Queen's, and formerly Proctor. The appointment to the Headship of the Hall seems at that time to have been (like that to the College Livings) a matter of succession by seniority. Mr. Wheatley died very soon after; probably he was never fully and formally admitted, for his death took place, not in the Principal's Lodgings, but at the *lodging-house* nearly adjoining. In the list of Principals given in the 'Oxford Calendar' Mr. Wheatley's name is altogether omitted!

August 26. *Rev. C. Atterbury*, senior Student of Ch. Ch., was crushed to death by the upsetting of a Birmingham coach. Riding on the box of one of Costar's coaches had been for years his favourite enjoyment, indeed on that very journey he had, after much wrangling, induced a fellow-traveller to give up to him, as an established claim, the seat of honour and (as it turned out) of death[2]. Mr. Atterbury,

---

[1] It is said that the clever book entitled 'The Art of Pluck,' instead of being looked upon as a *jeu-d'esprit* (rather a *grave one* certainly, like most academical ones), is often *seriously studied* by the young freshmen, on the same principle as they read the early experiences of Mr. Verdant Green.

[2] He used to be called 'Costar's right-hand man,' and would frequently go down the whole line to see that 'all was right.' He did not take the reins himself, but his hobby was to see the working of a well-appointed coach and to sit behind a fine 'team,' skilfully handled. This taste did not vulgarise him, for he was a perfect gentleman; indeed Costar's *coachmen* were themselves men of good manners and respectable

however, did not neglect his clerical duties, and on the *preceding* Sunday he had preached at St. Mary Magdalen parish Church (of which he was the Vicar, and where he was highly esteemed) on the text, 'Set thy house in order; for thou shalt die and not live.'

But to pass on to other 'Recollections,' and less grave topics. Many talented writers, formerly of Oxford, have introduced Oxford reminiscences into their books, but none of them more successfully than Lockhart, formerly of Balliol, and Sir Walter Scott's son-in-law. One of the best descriptions of an Oxford Gown and Town Row appeared this year in his novel, called 'Reginald Dalton.' The account of the '*kill* and wounded' ends thus: 'Long shall be the faces of Pegge, Wall, and Kidd [Oxford physicians] as they solemnly walk their rounds to-morrow morning; long shall be the stately stride of Ireland, and long the clyster-pipe of West [Oxford apothecaries]; long and deep shall be the probing of thy skilful hand, O Tuckwell [an eminent surgeon]; and long shall all your bills be, and long, very long ere some of them are paid[1]!'

The Oxford Herald, in this autumn, gave a long poem

---

characters. I may here add an interesting communication from a clergyman, a D.D., of great learning and piety: 'I attended the death-bed of a man, who was brought to serious thoughts by Mr. Atterbury's death so immediately after having preached on that text, which he was giving out when my informant dropped into the church out of mere "far niente."' N.B. It is stated in the 'Alumni Westmonasterienses' that he was driving at the time.

[1] Within my recollection surgeons were liable to be admitted 'ad practicandum' in Convocation, and the fee paid by them on the occasion was stated in the then used Table of Fees, though struck out at the late revision of fees. I remember three or four of them (Stephens and Swift of the number) being called upon (and obeying the call) to be formally admitted and paying their fees. The experiment has not since been repeated.

'On the Boar of Shotover,' from a pretended old MS. of the seventeenth century. The student, with his Aristotle in his hand, sees the boar approach with open mouth:—

'He seiz'd the clos'd volume, text, comment, and note,
  And thrust it afar down his ravening throat!
The wild monster started, and tore up the ground,
  Shriek'd, panted, and toss'd the white venom around.—
His bowels within him, they heav'd and they heav'd[1],
  He groan'd and he retch'd, and he yell'd, and he strain'd;
Recoil'd, stretch'd his jaws, yet was nothing reliev'd,
  The obstruction still firm in his thorax remain'd,' &c. &c.

A. D. 1824.

[B.A. 239. M.A. 191. Hon. D.C.L. at Commemoration, 3.]

The days of Lotteries[2] were not yet quite ended; you could not open your letters of a morning without receiving a most tempting circular, 'to take advantage of possibly the last opportunity of gaining a large fortune at a small risk.'

---

[1] All this amplification, clever as it is, falls short of the old, simple way of telling the story, with its touching climax: 'Swallow that, if you can,' (cried the unarm'd student, thrusting his Aristotle down the boar's throat). 'Græcum est,' cried the boar, and expired, foaming at the mouth;—for he found Aristotle (as many other throats had done and will do) too hard for him!

[2] A still worse feature of the times (in brutality at least) was the frequent occurrence of prize-fights, or pugilistic contests. At one of these disgraceful scenes, in 1824 (credite posteri!), a Viscount acted as umpire for one combatant and a Baronet for the other. The latter (and probably the former) had tried the studies of Oxford for awhile, but, being out of his element, left it with the cry, or at least the sentiment,—

'Farewell, stupid Oxford! away I must scud;
As for *study*, I ne'er could get farther than *stud*.'
[An old Eton pun.]

You could not walk in the streets of Oxford without seeing the walls covered with 'Lucky Numbers' sold by *Goodluck* and Co.

Jan. 14. Died at his rooms in Magdalen, Dr. Shaw (or '*Shavius doctissimus*' as the German critics called him). He had been Fellow of the College for many years, and was a fine sturdy specimen of the *strong-headed* Fellows, who used to live and die within their College-walls. He was a scholar, and in early life had edited a Greek author (Apollonius Rhodius), but was said to have taken a disgust at the pursuit, offended probably by impertinent or even pertinent criticisms. He had a brother, likewise a Dr. Shaw, and a naturalist; but he used to speak slightingly of him, as 'my *scientific* relation! that is, my *cockle-shell* brother[1]!'

June 24. St. John Baptist's day. The University Sermon was as usual preached in Magdalen College *Chapel;* and as we passed from the President's Lodgings into the dark antechapel, we looked with rather longing eyes to the old stone pulpit, and thought of the sermons thence delivered to a

---

[1] Dr. Shaw, as Shavius, had not such good reason to dislike his Latinised name as Dr. Monk (alias Monkius) had. I have been asked by an old Magdalen man why I have not given some description of '*the giants* of Magdalen at that time.' My answer is that I do not (and did not) think they were giants *out of the Common-room*. Even in that respect they were much calumniated; they only did what was done elsewhere in the days of early dinners and long sittings. Of the three persons named by my friend, one certainly had nothing of the giant, being a little, 'tityre-tu-tottery' man, with tell-tale red circles round his eyes, and persevering (when the wind was not in the east) in his daily walk to Jo. Pullen's tree. The second was a quiet, amiable gentleman, worthy of the family he belonged to. And the third was only a giant as being tall, and reading occasionally in chapel with what might be like to an elderly giant's voice, deep and trumpety, but of the cracked-trumpet order!

congregation seated *al fresco*. On this hook I may hang a traditional story of the middle of last century:—

'In 1750, or thereabouts, a *Dr. Bacon*, Fellow of Magdalen, preached on St. John Baptist's day from the stone pulpit, surrounded (in imitation of St. John preaching in the wilderness) with a forest of *green boughs*, and the ground strewed with green rushes. This combination of names and things led to a joking question that ran through the University, "How did you like Maudlin Greens and Bacon?"' Query: Had the ridicule then thrown upon the *open-air* ceremony anything to do with its discontinuance, and the adjournment to the *College Chapel?* Or did the falling off in the congregation (till it literally realized the 'Vox clamantis *in deserto*') suggest the wisdom of discontinuing an experiment unsuited to our uncertain climate? When we learn that President Harwar died, in 1722, in consequence of a cold caught during his attendance at the Sermon, on St. John Baptist's day, may we not wonder that this open-air ceremony was continued till 1766? Query the last: Why has not *St. John Baptist College* long since relieved Magdalen by claiming the Sermon on *St. John Baptist's day?*

A. D. 1825.

[B.A. 283. M.A. 194. Hon. D.C.L. at Commemoration, 4.]

Feb. 1. In Convocation, the University seal was affixed to an instrument releasing the Mayor, Bailiffs, &c. of Oxford from the ceremony of the *Dies Scholastica*, the observance of which had been imposed for 'the slaughter' in Edward III's time. This act of Release[1] was conducted under the auspices

---

[1] Some of the accompanying indignities (e. g. the appearing *with ropes round their necks*) had long before been discontinued, and now at length

of the Vice-Chancellor, Dr. Jenkyns, who did the thing most graciously. The City (as well it might) 'returned the warmest acknowledgments to the University for this act of grace[1].'

The *ceremony* thus abolished was this: At a fixed hour on the stated day (i. e. the anniversary of '*the slaughter*' which took place on the 'Dies Scholastica'), the Vice-Chancellor, the Proctors, the Registrar, and the Vicar of St. Mary's awaited (in the chancel of St. Mary's) the coming of the Mayor and Bailiffs with so many of the citizens (or freemen) as would make up the required number of sixty-three, said to have been the number of 'scholars' slain in 1354, when 'the gutter of Brewer's or Slaughter Lane[2] ran with academic blood.' The Vice-Chancellor was seated under the organ, a corresponding seat was taken by the Mayor; the Vicar and Proctors, with the Registrar and the Bedels, were within the Communion-rails; the citizens took the seats on either side the chancel, and then *the Litany* was read by the Vicar (originally, i. e. in Roman Catholic days, the 'raw,' so long *established* and painfully *kept open*, was to be entirely healed.

[1] This *gracious act*, however, was not quite unexpected or *un-extorted*; for the citizens in the preceding November had resolved, 'That it will be advisable for the Mayor and Bailiffs to abstain from attending at St. Mary's Church on the Dies Scholastica.' Then followed a little coquetting. The University, i. e. the Hebdomadal Council, suggested that the City should formally *request* the cessation of the ceremony; and the City duly and humbly requested its discontinuance.

N. B. There had always been *an alternative*, in the shape of a considerable sum to be paid as a fine by the Mayor. I do not *recollect* that this was paid more than once, and that was by Richard Cox, Esq., Banker.

[2] Hearne says that Brewer's Lane was not called Slaughter Lane 'from the Scholars being killed there,' but 'from the slaying of cattle there,' as a place 'removed from the body of the University.' (Bliss's Reliquiæ Hearnianæ, ii. 236.)

there were *Masses* read for the souls of the slain), after which sixty-three pence, generally in small silver coins, were presented by one of the Bailiffs, and received and carefully counted (at the rails) by the Senior Proctor. The City procession then retired (exchanging bows with the Vice-Chancellor as they passed his seat) and the pence were distributed, the larger share to the Vicar, the rest among the Bedels.—As it was not a pleasant business for the citizens, the University authorities had often to wait awhile before the exact number of sixty-three citizens could be collected; the chief number consisted of Members of the City Council (or 'Chamber' as it was then called), who attended out of respect to the Mayor; but the inhabitants of the neighbouring houses, being freemen, were generally called upon at the last moment to make up the deficiency; for the name of each citizen, composing the required number, was carefully taken down by the University Registrar and the Town Clerk, and presented to the Proctors.—Sed de hac re jam bene præteritâ satis superque.

And so, to pass 'from grave to gay,' I quote

AN IMPROMPTU

On Miss Stephens's Visit to Oxford in 1825, and the performance of her favourite Song.

'If high above were heard that pray'r,
"O take me, angels, to your care,"
Those spirits, captur'd by the strain,
Would call their sister back again.'

In this February a periodical, called 'The Oxford Quarterly Magazine,' appeared as a candidate for public support; but, like other abortives, it did not survive. A sharp critique from a sort of *Saturday Review* was supposed to have fallen like a red-hot shot into the *Magazine*, and at once *blew it up*.

Feb. 23. An alteration was made in the Examination Statute. For some years four Examiners had done all the work in Classics and Mathematics; *now* there were to be nine Examiners, six for Classics and three for Mathematics. Previously there had been only two Classes,—the second Class being virtually divided into two by an arbitrary line [1]; *now* there were to be three Classes, nay four ;—the *fourth* being expressed only by the *total number*, without the names of individuals.

In March died the amiable and learned ' Peter Elmsley,' as every one used to call him ; and it may be remarked, by the way, that when a man is thus *familiarly* designated, it is not from any of the familiarity which borders upon contempt, but that which springs from love and generates kindly admiration. Dr. Elmsley has been more than once mentioned in these ' Recollections.' He would have rejoiced in his last hours had he been told of what I have next to mention.

In April a new stimulus was given to scholarship [2] by

---

[1] A very strange and awkward contrivance,—for instance, when a young man candidate for an appointment, might have to describe himself as ' Mr. So-and-so, *Second Class under the line* !' It was well said of such a status (in words borrowed from Aldrich's Logic):—

'Nomen habet nullum, nec, si bene colligis, usum.'

Aut aliter.—' Your case, Sir, is hard, neither leo nor pard ;
But how would you have yourself reckon'd ?
To call you a " Third " would be false and absurd,
But indeed I can't call you a Second."'

[2] Or, in the words of the endowment, ' to classical learning and taste.' Dr. Ireland, Dean of Westminster, was a Servitor of Christ Church. In the strong language of Professor Rogers, ' he had owed

Dean Ireland's foundation of four Scholarships[1]. Indeed, this year (1825) seems to have *rained* endowments on our ever-thirsty but productive soil. In May, H. Drummond, Esq., of Christ Church (the eccentric Member for Surrey), founded and endowed the Professorship of Political Economy; and Dr. Ellerton, of Magdalen, endowed with twenty guineas a-year a Theological Essay.

In other respects also (i. e. not strictly academical) golden showers descended upon Oxford and its immediate neighbourhood; and who, after the following statement, can say that the men of this date were not liberal? In this year three subscriptions were simultaneously going on, and produced for the County Lunatic Asylum £13,500; for building St. Clement's Church £4,300; and for repairing St. Thomas's Church £700;—in all £18,500.

A visitor to Oxford at the Commemoration of this year wrote to the Oxford Herald an effusion of delight, and apologized for his raptures by quoting (or intending to quote) 'the versatile and courtly Horace:' 'Dulce est decipere (*sic*) in loco!'

June 30 died Dr. Burton, Canon of Christ Church[2], an amiable, 'gouty, un-influential old gentleman, who had held the Canonry for many years, and whose death opened a vacancy for Dr. Buckland.

his education to the coarse beneficence of that kind of dotation, and repaid thousandfold the advantages he had received.' (Education in Oxford, 1861.)

[1] One Scholarship to be filled up every year. And a splendid list of distinguished names has since marked the value of the endowment.

[2] This Canonry,—having been, during Dr. Burton's long tenure, distinguished by gossip and sober whist on the Doctor's part, and by crowded routes and blue-stocking coteries on Miss B.'s, and having in Dr. Buckland's time been more celebrated for geology than theology,—has since been judiciously attached to the Archdeaconry of Oxford.

Oct. 6. A Mr. Mulock (sometimes called *Moloch*) began to preach at some conventicle in Oxford, and having caused several men to leave their wives, the women of St. Thomas's parish very naturally took alarm. Mulock was roughly assaulted, and he and his followers were hunted and dragged in the mud, till they took refuge in the Town-hall yard[1].

A.D. 1826.

[B.A. 205. M.A. 166. One Hon. D.C.L. at Commemoration.]

Jan. 25. *Richard Heber*, who had for some years represented Oxford University in Parliament, 'being under a cloud,' retired from public life. The 'cloud' was (we all believed) a gross calumny; but always a shy, proud man, he could not face it, and resigned his trust. He was succeeded by a good man and excellent County-magistrate, Mr. Estcourt (formerly Gentleman-Commoner and then M.A. of Corpus), who was soon found to be 'valuable in Committees of the House,' but, like Mr. Heber, no speaker.[2] While Alma Mater was anxiously looking for some proof

---

[1] In connection with this occur the following lines in the Oxford Herald of that date:—

'You may well take refuge within the Town-hall,
For 'twixt Mulock and Moloch the odds are but small;
To Moloch, more mild, men offer'd the child,
To Mulock they sacrifice mother and all.'

In the obituary of the same paper occurred this *affecting* paragraph: 'On Saturday last died, of a deep decline, the "Oxford United Debating Society!"' This Society was, I believe, a *City* Debating Club; the *University* 'Union' had only just come into existence.

[2] So that if Oxford had *votes* in Parliament, it certainly had no voice, as far as regarded one of its Representatives; but then it had, in its other, Sir Robert Peel!

of her new Member's talent and fitness to represent her, she had the satisfaction of learning that he had successfully moved for 'a Bill to regulate Ale-houses[1].'

April 24. A Master's Degree *by Diploma* was conferred on *Blanco White*, in consideration of his recent and able exposure of Romish errors and corruptions in a series of pamphlets, having himself been for many years a Roman Catholic priest in Spain. As a Master of Arts, thus adopted, he became a member of Oriel, and was several times called on to preach in the University pulpit; his Orders as a priest being, according to the liberality of our Church, at once recognised. His sermons, though not powerful, were interesting from the frequent and touching allusions to his former position and his gradual convictions[2]. Alas! how sad was the termination of his career! how little did Oxford think that the adopted champion of our Church would soon after openly become an Unitarian, and at last die an unbeliever in Christianity! But so it was, according to the old rhyme:—

'From believing too much, how sad was the fall,
Till at last he believed in just nothing at all!'

[1] As far as Oxford *University* was concerned, this Bill might have suited Dean Aldrich's time, when it was said (or rather sung),—

'There's ne'er a man will leave his can
Till he hears the mighty Tom!'

[2] Blanco White was a man of superior intellect, great acquirements, and refined sentiments; he was also a most finished player on the violin, but being of a highly nervous temperament, he could very rarely be persuaded to touch the instrument in company; if he joined in a quartette, it was on the condition of 'no party, no talking.'—It is worth remarking how many men of note and celebrity, besides *Blanco White*, were (about the same time) members of Oriel Common-room,—Copleston, Whately, Arnold, Newman, Pusey, Jelf, Hampden, J. Keble, two Wilberforces, Geo. Denison, &c., &c. In June of this year the members

A liberal subscription was raised this year in Oxford, in aid of the distressed workmen connected with the failing manufactures in the North of England.

At the Oxford City Election in July, Mr. Hughes Hughes, once the popular candidate, was defeated by Mr. Langston, who kept his seat till his death. Few places were said to be more venal than Oxford City before the Reform Bill extended the suffrage to the non-freemen householders. The lower and more numerous class of freemen (whether under the Blenheim dynasty or in the subsequent interval) liked a change of man, throwing away the old favourite as a boy does the orange *he has sucked.* Election-squibs were issued in abundance, but most of them *appropriately* signed at the bottom of the page, ' *Trash*, Printer.'.

The autumn of 1826 brought to Oxford the sad news that in the preceding April Bishop Heber had been found dead in his bath, from a (supposed) attack of apoplexy.

of Oriel held a great Jubilee meeting to celebrate the fifth Centenary of their Foundation. Mr. John Hughes's song, ' Floreat Oriel,' was highly spoken of; his clever *jeu-d'esprit* about Miss Ellen Douglas and Gaisford is too long and too personal to be introduced here. I must, however, give the second verse as a specimen; it is in the metre of the Boat Song in Scott's ' Lady of the Lake : '—

' In Greek I believe I must utter my passion,
   For Greek's more familiar than English to me;
And Byron has lately brought Greek into fashion,
   There's some in his "Fair Maid of Athens."—Let's see:
      Pshaw! this vile modern Greek
      Won't do for me to speak;
Let me try, Ζωή μου, σας αγαπῶ.—
      No, I don't like the tone,
      Come, let me try my own,
Κλυθι μου, Ελενη, σου γαρ ερῶ.'

N. B.—The *jeu-d'esprit* found its way into ' Blackwood' before 1820.

Alma Mater had grudged her favourite son to India, and had sent him out with a prayer (not, alas! to be granted) 'Reddas incolumem, precor!'

A.D. 1827.
[B.A. 262. M.A. 178. Hon. D.C.L. at Commemoration, 5.]

The Anatomy School at Oxford was, at this date, generally supplied with 'a *recent subject*' from one of the London Hospitals (when they could spare one), or with an unclaimed body (sometimes a black man or woman) from some London Workhouse. These bodies were mysteriously conveyed by night to the School at Christ Church near 'Skeleton Corner,' as a part of the College, between the Anatomy School and the Kitchen, was then appropriately called. Two Undergraduates of Christ Church, having heard one day of such an arrival, walked into the Anatomy School when the Professor, protected by an outer covering suited to his employment, was busy in preparing for his lecture. 'I say, old fellow,' said one of the youths, taking the Doctor for a servant of the establishment, 'let's have a look at your blackie; we are come to take an autopsis.' He soon, however,

('Improvisum aspris veluti qui sentibus anguem
Pressit humi,'—)

found that he had 'caught a Tartar,' and would, with his companion, have been unceremoniously expelled by the indignant Professor, had they not escaped by a hasty flight[1].

[1] The supply of 'subjects' was not, I imagine, increased by the influence of the *example* set to the profession by a London surgeon, *Mr. Ellerby*, who, dying about this time, directed by will that his body should be conveyed, immediately after death, to the Anatomical Theatre; bequeathing (after dissection) his heart to one anatomist, his lungs to another, his brains to a third!

Feb. 17 died Dr. Hall, who had been *translated* from the Deanery of Christ Church to that of Durham.

In this Lent a general cry was raised in Oxford against the old custom of holding the University Sermon at St. Peter's Church on Lent Sunday afternoons; i. e. of appointing *attractive* preachers in a church of very limited accommodation. The required reform was soon to come.

Oxford was about this time edified by the publication of a 'Narrative of a Visit to Oxford, paid by the Lord Mayor of London,'—'written,' as the title further informed us, 'in commemoration of the event, by his Lordship's Chaplain. 'What a pity,' every one said, 'that the University was not aware of the honour till after the occurrence!' and 'that the Long Vacation should have been chosen for his Lordship's arrival,'—'in a carriage, too,' as his Chaplain relates, 'drawn by his own four horses, with his wife (the Lady Mayoress), his Chaplain, his coachman, and lady's-maid!' The visit was, no doubt, all right and proper,— possibly enjoined upon a Lord Mayor, now and then, as 'Curator of the Thames;'—the striking feature was the writing and publishing of a really *serious account* of the journey[1].

July 22. A strange blunder was committed by holding a *Congregation* in *Vacation* time, for the purpose of admitting a new Pro-Proctor, a Congregation in Vacation being at least against the spirit of the Statute 'De Congregationibus.' It was soon found to be a mistake, but one which could not be corrected till the following 10th of October, when the said Pro-Proctor was duly admitted, not having presumed to act.

---

[1] Had the said Chaplain been a wit, he might have made the narrative an amusing and interesting affair, and produced a book worthy to be placed on the Bodleian shelves with other valued Itineraries.

At the beginning of Michaelmas Term, 1827, in consequence of the great alterations going on at St. Mary's, the Vice-Chancellor was *authorised by Convocation* to transfer the University Sermons and Services to some other church; and on the 27th of October 'the thanks of the University were voted in Convocation to the Dean and Chapter of Christ Church, for the offer of the cathedral[1].'

Dec. 10. It was ordered by vote of Convocation that 'the Lent and other Sermons, hitherto preached at St. Peter's-in-the-East, should be transferred to St. Mary's;' the Statute 'De Concionibus' was altered for the purpose.

A.D. 1828.

[B.A. 299. M.A. 162. One Hon. D.C.L. at Commemoration.]

March 1. St. David's day. Up to this time (perhaps I should rather say, *down* to this time) it was customary, on St. David's day, for the Welsh members of Jesus College to *walk the High Street*, wearing a *leek* attached to the tassel of their cap; an usage, I believe, now nearly discontinued[2], or confined to the walls of the Welsh College.

March 2. St. Mary's Church was re-opened, having been closed for eight months. The seats had been newly

[1] Arrangements of this sort are more quietly and with less ceremony settled now-a-days (e. g. in 1860) between the Vice-Chancellor and the Dean, without troubling Convocation or the Chapter.

[2] This year (1828) as a Master of Arts of that College was *doing his duty* to the Principality with a leek in his tassel, a boy innocently (?) ran up to him, crying, 'Please, Sir, somebody has been sticking an *onion* into your cap.' 'Thank ye for nothing,' was the testy reply. Dr. Fowlkes, the Principal of Jesus from 1817 to 1857, made a point (like his predecessor, Dr. Hughes) of 'doing the High with a tremendous leek on his cap.'

arranged, the galleries enlarged, a stone-fronted organ-gallery erected in the place of a shabby old wooden one, and the pulpit, removed from the middle of the church, restored[1] to its *old* place against one of the pillars on the south side.

March 3. By a vote of Convocation the form of '*creating* Sophs' (which was done by a Master of the Schools laying an 'Aristotle' on the head of the would-be Soph, and saying, 'Creo te Sophistam Generalem') was annulled. 'All Undergraduates of two years' standing, having passed their Responsions, are to be considered Sophs[2] without any formal ceremony.'

In this spring it was recorded, as a remarkable instance of rapid travelling, that a coach went from London, through Oxford, to Cheltenham (100 miles) in nine hours and ten minutes; and that it was expected that the distance from London to Birmingham, through Oxford, would soon be done in thirteen hours and a half!

'Mrs. Ramsbottom,' the funny 'correspondent' of the 'John Bull' newspaper, succeeded in spelling *Oxford* with-

---

[1] The pulpit was placed exactly where an older pulpit had stood (from which Cranmer preached his last touching sermon, i.e. a *recantation* of his *recantation*). This is proved by the strong staple, *still remaining*, from whence it was partly suspended. The new pulpit is well conceived and skilfully constructed; the one which it superseded was a large wooden tub or box upon four pillars or posts, with an ugly sounding-board resting (apparently in a very unsafe way) upon two slender, ordinary posts at the back of the pulpit.

[2] The retention of the term 'Soph,' or Sophist (like the terms 'Responsions' and 'Masters of the Schools'), savours of times gone by and exercises discontinued; it was probably retained (like those others) out of consideration for the Statutes of some particular College (Exeter, for instance) where persons eligible for certain Fellowships were required to be 'General Sophists.'

out one of its component letters,—thus: 'Mr. Fulmer is going to *Hawks-phut* next Term to be made a Doctor of laws.' What follows is so amusing that it must be quoted: 'He says he shall be away only two days, but I doubt its being over so soon, because he himself told me it must be done by *degrees*. After he is made a Doctor he says he means to practise; but I told him I thought he had better practise *first*. A friend of his came here to see him from Hawks-phut College, who I thought was a clergyman by his dress; but I found out, by what Mr. F. told me, that it was an old lady in disguise,—for he said she was *Margaret* something, and went so far as to call her a *Divinity*.'

June 22. By a vote of Convocation 'the *two Schools* of Geometry and Medicine' were permanently annexed to the Bodleian Library, i. e. the *two Rooms* so denominated in large letters over their respective door-ways.

Same day, the annual salary of the Pro-Proctors was raised from £50 to £80; and that of the Keeper of the Archives from £40 to £100 [1].

In this summer died at Ch. Ch. Dr. Nicoll, Professor of Hebrew, who is spoken of largely in another Chapter. A volume of his sermons (not of a very remarkable character) was soon after published by subscription, in aid of a fund for his widow and family.

In this year there appeared (monthly) a literary and antiquarian periodical, called 'The Crypt;' some of its articles were severe against Oxford, but Oxford still exists notwithstanding such sharp attacks. 'The Crypt,' like most

---

[1] This salary of £100 was, some years later, raised to £200. When it was only £40 a-year it was generally considered more of a sinecure than it became in Dr. Bliss's time.

of the 'forlorn hopes' which have assailed our battlements, has itself fallen, and lies ἐν κρύπτῳ, on the shelf.

In 1828 I had a correspondence (as the University Coroner) with the *Berkshire* Coroner, who, notwithstanding previous remonstrances, had held an inquest on an Academic; it ended with his acknowledgment of being in the wrong and his promise that he would not again interfere with the University privileges. The University Coroner claims to act 'intra quatuor Hundreda proximè adjacentia.' The Hundreds are Wootton, Ploughley, Bullingdon in Oxon, and Horner in Berks.

A.D. 1829.

[B.A. 282. M.A. 206. Hon. D.C.L. at Commemoration, 5.]

The Proctors of this year, Messrs. Round and Thorp, not choosing to pay (as their predecessors had done) two Chaplains of New College for chanting the Latin Litany at St. Mary's, *read* it, though contrary to Statute as well as custom. To speak more correctly, they intended and attempted to *chant* it, but, breaking down at the outset, proceeded to *read* it in (what was meant to be) unison; as they diverged more and more from each other, the effect was anything but solemn[1]. Two men may *chant* well together, but it is next to impossible for them to *read* well together, even for a few sentences, much less the long Latin Litany. Query: Does it not sound very odd, that in the same Latin Service (as printed by the University for St. Mary's Church)

---

[1] The old Statute gave no option—'solenniter et devote *cantent*:' the recent Statute gives it, '*cantare aut legere* teneantur.' Later Proctors have had no such difficulty; *intoning* has become indeed so *fashionable*, that if they could not chant themselves, they have had no difficulty in finding *volunteer* chanters among their clerical friends.

we should have to say 'Miserere *nobis*' in the Litany and 'Miserere *nostrûm*' in the Communion? What authority is there for the former, except that of *ancient* usage? But is the Church's usage as ancient as Cicero? and on such a point is *its* authority to be compared with *his?*

Feb. 5. After a vote in Convocation against the 'Roman Catholic Claims,' a Letter was read from Sir Robert Peel, offering to resign his seat for Oxford, on the ground that he, as a Minister, had recommended to his Majesty *an Adjustment*[1] of those Claims. He had changed his opinions, but the majority of his Oxford constituents had not changed theirs; his resignation was, of course, accepted, and Sir Robert Inglis was invited to succeed him, to occupy though he could not *fill* his place. Peel however was again nominated, a great number of the voters (myself amongst the number) being unwilling (as was the case long after with respect to Gladstone) to part with our Alma Mater's most distinguished son[2]. On the 26th of February the University Election began, and, at the end of the polling (which was kept up for two days), Inglis had 755 votes; Peel 609.

Feb. 9 died Mr. Crowe, the Public Orator, aged eighty-three. He was succeeded by Mr. Cramer.

In this month my early friend, *John Matthias Turner*, a humble native of Oxford[3], was appointed Bishop of

---

[1] '*Adjustment*' was not quite an honest term, as it really and simply means only an '*arranging*' or '*methodizing*,' whereas it was intended by Sir R. to be an *acknowledging* and *granting* of such claims.

[2] Though, like other forward sons, he thus declared himself to be wiser than his parent.

[3] As a Servitor of Ch. Ch. he had challenged and gained the Honours in 1804. He entered at fifteen, having had no other instruction but at the school of Mr. Hinton, a learned and highly-respected dissenting minister in Oxford.

Calcutta. Like most of the Bishops whom we at first sent thither in rapid succession, he soon sunk under the effects of the climate upon a constitution never very strong and quite unfitted for such an experiment.

March 2. The Marquis of Chandos presented to the House of Commons a Petition 'against further concessions to the Roman Catholics,' from certain *Bachelors of Arts and Undergraduates* of Oxford, amounting to upwards of 300 names. Such a thing from persons *in statu pupillari* was till then unheard of; it was however very naturally followed by a Counter-petition from young men of the same standing;—but a Proctor, wishing to stop this irregular sort of demonstration, demanded the Petition at the shop where it was placed for signature, and carried it off, signatures and all, under his sleeve[1]!

April 2. A contest for the Anglo-Saxon Professorship took place between Mr. Walesby and Mr. Moberly; the former had 147 votes, the latter only 64. Mr. W., a clever but indolent man, never did anything as Professor.

In this spring scarcely anything was talked of in Oxford but 'The (so-called) Catholic Relief Bill,' which was at length carried even in the House of Lords by a majority of 105. On that occasion *Dr. Lloyd*, Bishop of Oxford (Sir R. Peel's former tutor), took lessons of his pupil, and,

---

[1] This spirited proceeding was thus versified:—

'We Proctors and Pros, being deadly foes
  To boys' unsanction'd exhibition,
Both pro and con do seize upon
  And hereby quench your sage Petition.

'And if you ask, why your fine task
  Thus finds itself in sad quandary,
You have, dear boys, with all your noise,
  No *voice in statu pupillari*.'

in supporting the Bill, was reported to say that 'he did not conceive the invocation of saints to be superstitious[1]!'

Our country at this date had no reason to be proud of its social condition; duels were by no means rare,—even the 'iron Duke,' our future Chancellor, had not *the courage* to refuse a challenge. In this case happily no harm was done;—I suppose they took care to *shoot wide*[2]. All the duels, however, were not equally bloodless.

Early in 1829 appeared (and, after a number or two, disappeared) a weekly periodical called 'The Oxford Literary Gazette.' The only *reliquiæ* of it I find in a memorandum of one of its statements: 'That a German Botanist named Schulte, who had visited Oxford in 1824, asserted in a work of his that our Botanical Garden is frequently *flooded knee-deep above the plants*[3]!'

In this summer, by the great exertions of the then Proctors (Messrs. Round and Thorp), the University Police was placed on a more effective footing.

In July, among the Hon. D.C.L. at the Commemoration, were SIR EDWARD PARRY and SIR JOHN FRANKLIN, fine, noble-looking men. Mr. Claughton, of Trinity, had the good fortune to recite his English-Verse Prize, 'On Arctic Discoveries,' before them. They were greatly moved by the poem, and especially by the hearty application of the leading points made by the whole assembly.

July 6 'the good *John Duncan*,' of New College, married

---

[1] Did he believe that they (the departed saints) could *bear* our invocations, or *grant* them? and if not, would not invocation be both idle and superstitious?

[2] Query: Had Lord Winchelsea shot *the Duke*, could he have survived the infamy?

[3] Its position is indeed ill-chosen; but its weak points have been long since raised and protected by embankments. Such an inundation as Herr Schulte mentions is not likely to recur.

and left Oxford; his brother, Mr. Phil. Duncan, succeeded him as Curator of the Ashmolean Museum, and there (and elsewhere) carried on the good work which his brother had begun. Hearne, speaking of the Ashmolean Museum in his days, says: 'Fifty pounds a year being settled on the keeper, 'tis designed to be a perfect sinecure, and nothing to be done for the honour of learning, unless he have a strange inclination thereto.' This crabbed antiquary, who had a good word or kind thought for no one who was not, like himself, a devoted Jacobite, gives some amusing notices of Oxford in the early part of last century, e.g. 'Pan-cake bell rings for dinner at ten on Shrove Tuesday.' This custom being soon after dropped, Hearne gravely says, 'When laudable old customs alter, 'tis a sign that learning dwindles.' It is to be supposed that he saw some connection between pancakes and learning! 'Some time ago,' he says, 'Merton Walks were so thronged on Sunday evenings as to become scandalous and cause the gate to be shut; the assemblies were transferred to Magdalen College Walk, which is now (1723) strangely filled, just like a fair.'

At the Stafford Assizes, in this summer, Mr. Mulock (of Oxford notoriety[1]) was convicted of shameful calumnies on honest, well-meaning men, once his dupes and followers.

In the 'Library of Entertaining Knowledge,' (in the number for this year) the following Oxford anecdote is appropriately given under the head of 'Pursuit of knowledge under difficulties:'—'*Dr. Prideaux*[2], afterwards Bishop of Worcester,

---

[1] Mentioned above in 'Recollections' for 1825.

[2] He might well be enrolled in the list of 'Devonshire Worthies,' for he not only became a Fellow of the College (where he had 'performed servile offices, while he prosecuted his studies at his leisure hours'), but was elected Rector in 1612; subsequently he was appointed Regius

having been born of poor parents, began his Oxford career as an assistant in Exeter College kitchen, but *worked* his way up, till he became a Fellow of the Society.'

October. At the Oxford City Sessions a woman was deservedly punished for 'plucking a live fowl!' An Oxford paper remarked that '*plucking alive* is a well-known practice in the University *in a place opposite the Pig-market.*'

Late in Michaelmas Term died a well-known University character, William Dodd, commonly called '*Billy Dodd*,' the half-witted *Clerk of the Schools*. The following lines[1] had appeared in the Oxford Herald a short time before:—

BILLY DODD'S LAMENT;

Or, Farewell to the Schools.

'Farewell thou dear scene of my glory,
    Farewell to my bands and my gown!
Ah! witness how much I deplore ye,
    Ah! see the big tear-drops run down.

'Adieu all ye Greeks and ye Latins,
    Dear Logic, adieu to thy rules!
No more, as the bells call to Matins,
    Your Billy shall open the Schools.

'No more in my snug little corner
    My dear *pocket-pistol* I ply;
Than Billy sure none is forlorner,
    Dear closet, dear pistol, good-bye!

Professor of Divinity and Canon of Ch. Ch. In due time he became Vice-Chancellor of Oxford, and eventually, in 1641, Bishop of Worcester! But those were troublous times; dying in 1650, he left nothing to his children but 'pious poverty, God's blessing, and a father's prayers.'

[1] That he *deserved* some memorial may be assumed from the fact that one of the proposed Chapters in Mr. Cotton's *Jeu d'esprit* (given above, in the 'Recollections' of 1819) was headed (though I there omitted it with many others) 'De Dodd.'

'There's an end to my fee for Testamur,
    (Dear youths, how I joy'd in your luck!)
The heavier fee from the lamer,
    The heavier still for a Pluck.

'Ungown'd and discarded I wander;
    All wasted my once chubby cheek;
On death by starvation I ponder,
    For what's forty shillings a-week[1]?

'In strange tones, like an ancient professor,
    Old Blenkinsop[2] calls me away;
While Dicky, my sage predecessor,
    Shakes his keys and reproves my long stay.

'Our ghosts shall all sit as a quorum,
    And anxiously wait twice a year
Till the "Ordo Examinandorum"
    And the Class-paper duly appear.

'As wise then as pundit or brahmin
    We'll argue the pros and the cons;
E'en Examiners we will examine,
    And search out the brains of the dons.

'Meanwhile I must try and dispose of
    (At what little profit I may)
My hoods, and my gowns, and whole rows of
    Umbrellas that fell in my way.

[1] He had been pensioned off at 40s. a-week; his place having produced not less than £300 a-year, in great part from traditional, unauthorised fees.

[2] Blenkinsop, father and son, were successively Clerks of the Schools; the son was, like Dodd, half-witted. Such men would not do now for the increased and responsible duties of the post, in connection with the Examinations, and so well discharged by Mr. Parker. It was a former Clerk of the Schools, named West, on whom (in allusion to his traditional blunder in announcing the statutable end of Disputations or Exercises pro gradu) Thos. Warton wrote the following epitaph :

'Hic jacet et tacet Thomas West,
    Cujus tempus *præterlabitur est*.'
See 'Recollections' for 1851, 2nd page.

'I must sell all my logical questions,
  The sweepings and dregs of the Schools;
They may still suit some sluggish digestions,
  And appear something clever to fools.

'Besides, there's my "Law-disputations[1]"
  And "Arguments," bare as you please;
They have served for some six generations,
  But without them they'll get no degrees.

'Time has been when, somewhat elated,
  I reckon'd on honours myself;
Nor fear'd I that, thus under-rated,
  Poor Bill would be laid on the shelf.

'By the glories of Athens and Roma!
  By those statues I leave with a sigh[2]!
I hop'd still to get my Diploma,
  And be dubb'd *Dr. Dodd* ere I die'

A.D. 1830.

[B.A. 291.   M.A. 179.   Hon. D.C.L. at Commemoration, 3.]

In the early part of this year[3] two attempts to improve

---

[1] It is a fact that before the recent Statute, which appoints a real, bona-fide *Examination* for the degree of B.C.L. (and has woefully diminished the number of Law degrees), the only Exercises consisted of a repetition of a set of *worn-out* Arguments in Dodd's possession. The *unreal* title also of S.C L. (which had been much abused) has been made *real*, being allowed only to *examined* persons,—I should rather say, 'persons who had *successfully passed* an Examination;' for there is a story that an S.C.L, of the old Statute sometimes described himself as an 'Examined Student,' reserving the fact of his having *failed* till farther enquiry!

[2] The 'Pomfret Statues' were at that date placed in one of the Schools, under the care of the Clerk of the Schools.

[3] This year began with very severe weather; it was not till Feb. 8 that the frost broke up, after forty days' continuance, during the latter part of which coal was sold in Oxford at 5s. the cwt.

the Examination Statute failed, by aiming at too much at once. The Statute of 1825 therefore remained in force,—till the Michaelmas Term following, when a fourth class was added,—with a fifth class, of which only the total *number* was to be given.

June 25. George IV died, as the doctors said, 'of a diseased organization of the heart[1].' Fate was busy at this time with the bearers and wearers of sceptres and crowns; in August, Charles X of France was deposed, and Louis Philippe became, by acclamation, not exactly King of France, but 'King of the French[2].'

July 19. An address of condolence, and also of congratulation, from the University of Oxford, was presented to King William IV. The Chancellor, Lord Grenville, being unwell, the Vice-Chancellor, Dr. Jones, read the address and presented the Delegates with much dignity.

At the beginning of September, the enforcement of the Otmoor Inclosure Act was resisted by the people of that neighbourhood; thirty rioters were escorted to the Oxford jail by a small force of Yeomanry-cavalry; but as they were being thoughtlessly conducted through the great crowd assembled at St. Giles's Fair, the Oxford mob pelted the Yeomanry with such violence that the prisoners were allowed to escape[3], instead of being lodged in the County jail.

[1] That disease was generally supposed to have been, *in some shape or other*, of long standing.

[2] Apparently but a nice distinction without a difference, but really expressive of his being an *elected* king.

[3] This naturally caused some alarm at the 'Horse-Guards,' and a company of the Guards was despatched to Oxford; at Oxford, however, that *unpremeditated* local riot had not attracted much attention or produced any anxiety. Indeed the Bill against the *Oxford* rioters was ignored by the Grand Jury at the following Assizes.

By-the-bye, is it not a fact that those new enclosures and embankments on Otmoor have caused *more frequent, sudden,* and larger floods at Oxford? Certainly Dr. Buckland used to assert, in his lectures, that a great mistake, in this respect, was made in the Otmoor Inclosure; for, instead of bringing the superfluous water (as now) by the *circuitous* bed of the Cherwell *into the Thames at Oxford,* it ought to have been (and might just as easily have been) carried *directly* into the *Thame-river* and so into the Thames several miles below Oxford[1].

Sept. 14. Poor Alfred Bennett, Mus. Bac. and Organist of New College, was killed by the upsetting of an overloaded coach, on his way to Worcester Music Meeting. He was a talented musician and excellent teacher. His body was brought back to Oxford and buried in New College Cloisters. A tolerably large subscription was raised for his young widow and infant son.

German at this time began to be more studied than it had been. Mr. Bramsen, for many years a teacher of German in Oxford, sent to a German University and ('by return of post') got his Diploma as a Doctor of Philosophy! He was an amiable old gentleman, but, as being a professed 'diner-out,' he was called by his pupils 'Dr. (or Herr) Speisen-sie.' On his tombstone (in St. Mary Magdalen Parish Churchyard) he is grandly called 'a traveller in three quarters of the globe!'

Michaelmas Term, 1830, was the period of 'Swing' riots, machine-breaking, and rick-burning. The University authorities were alarmed, special constables were sworn in,

---

[1] Imperial Rome is said to have done the same sort of thing (but by design) in turning the waters of the Chiana from the Tiber into the already overcharged Arno; thus producing frequent and disastrous floods about Florence.

and 300 cavalry sent for,—the latter chiefly for the protection of the surrounding country. No actual riots ensued. The burning of thrashing machines was made a subject of playful wit at Eton:—

> 'Dr. Keate, Dr. Keate, there's distress in your beat,
>   So the suff'rers assert, great and small;
> And 'tis plain to be seen that your *thrashing-machine*
>   Has something to do with it all.'
>
> *Dr. K.'s Reply.*
> 'My pupils perhaps have deserved my hard raps,
>   As you, Sir, may soon understand;
> But this cannot apply to my system, for I
>   Do the whole of my *thrashing by hand.*'

In November, the Provost and a deputation of the Fellows of Queen's College presented an address to Queen Adelaide, who, as *Queen-Consort*, was a sort of Patroness of their College.

I can hardly bring myself to credit the possibility of such remissness as I find stated in a memorandum *in my own writing*, 'sed litera scripta manet:'—'Oct. 8, 1830. The Vice-Chancellor was re-admitted for his third year,—not one of the Pro-Vice-Chancellors, nominated by him, being present at the ceremony!' Oct. 18, being St. Luke's day, one of the nominated but *not yet admitted* Pro-Vice-Chancellors went to St. Mary's as Vice-Chancellor, afterwards matriculated one or two young men, and was about to commit a delinquent to prison, when luckily the inchoate nature of his authority was recollected, before he had actually *committed himself!* Surely we all (even the accurate Registrar) must have been walking in our sleep! What a subject was here offered to a *Terrae-filius*, if such a character had then existed! On this personage (the old Terrae-filius) Huber says, 'he certainly possessed a sort of official and statutory authority.' His antiquity is undoubted, but he never could have had a *statutable* appointment. It was rather a traditional, assumed privilege, connived at, like that of a Court-fool (Huber's comparison), for its witty, fearless sallies, and, though liable to abuse, often valuable as a rough vehicle of criticism[1], and relieving the dull and formal exercises of the Act. As a vestige of the traditional character of the Terrae-filius in Oxford, I *recollect* in my early days to have heard the term applied as a reproach by an angry man to a still more angry woman, 'O you scold! you *terry-phillis!*'[2].

[1] Si quis erat dignus describi—
—multâ cum libertate notabant.

[2] That the Terrae-filii and their assumed privileges were generally popular, or at least connived at, seems to follow from the following extract from Anthony Wood, vol. iii. p. 684:—

'It was proposed by the Vice-Chancellor (in July 1658), that the Terrae-filii (whose office was considered a scandal by the "self-styled Godly") should be taken away. The House seeming generally to cry "Non," he required the Masters to *divide* (i. e. to go to different sides of the House). A scrutiny being called for and others making a ridiculous matter of it, the Vice-Chancellor was in a manner forced to set (sic) down and meddle no more in the matter.'

Wood here certainly speaks of their 'office,' but the terms which he applies to it and the story he here relates hardly justify the notion of a real University appointment.

CHAPTER VI.

'Gaudent praenomine molles
Auriculae.'—*Horace.*

Recollections of Professors.

Dr. Hornsby was rather a monopolist of academical appointments, being (I suppose from the short supply of mathematical and scientific talent in the University) made Savilian Professor of Astronomy in 1763[1], Radcliffe Observer in 1772, Sedleian Professor of Natural Philosophy in 1782, and Radcliffe Librarian in 1783; all of which offices he held till his death in 1810. It was in the last-mentioned character that he came into Convocation in 1808 (or thereabouts) brandishing the large key of the Radcliffe Library[2], in the lower or ground part of which building it was proposed in Convocation to deposit the collection, called the

---

[1] Dr. Hornsby was eulogised by that hard hitter, Dr. Tatham (in his Address to Convocation in 1810), for his Lectures as Sedleian Professor; he calls him 'the eye of Oxford,' and says that his average Class was about forty.

[2] In those days the term 'Radcliffe Library' included both the books and the building. The question here however referred to the building.

'Pomfret Statues,' then filling one of the Schools[1]. When the question was formally proposed, 'Placet ne vobis' &c. Dr. Hornsby rose and spoke to the following effect: 'Insignissime Vice-Cancellarie—*meum* est Bibliothecam Radcliffianam custodire; mihi *non Placet* statuas istas, vel potius Statuarum fragmenta et reliquias, intra fores nostras admittere. Ne tamen verba mea vel tempus vestrum, Academici, diutiùs absumam, ecce, quæso, *clavem* quam gero et per quam Veto quod nunc est propositum.' As he, of course, spoke with the approbation and authority of the Radcliffe Trustees[2], there was at once an end of the matter. 'Solvuntur risu tabulæ'—Convocation was dissolved!

This conduct of Dr. Hornsby (which I witnessed myself) does not quite harmonise with what is stated in the Report

---

[1] The Pomfret statues, to which the University (or rather the encroaching Bodleian) grudged the occupation of one of the Schools, were accommodated in the Randolph or University Gallery about forty years afterwards, with all their interesting deficiencies. No. I. naso caret; No. II. truncus merus, &c. See Catalogue, formerly kept by the Clerk of the Schools.

[2] Amid recent changes no one, I think, has asserted that *Dr. Radcliffe ever contemplated* the possibility of removing the books to be purchased with his money from the noble building he raised to receive them But after the recent incursions we have witnessed upon bequests, foundations and benefactions, 'nil admirari' is become more and more the 'res una solaque' for an old man's comfort. He may amuse himself for a while by falling back upon his '*Recollections;*' but, among other new lessons which he has to learn, he finds it no easy matter to disconnect the books, &c. from the building, and to learn to call that noble building (or even a portion of it) the '*Camera Radcliffiana !*' Dr. Radcliffe's name will still be gratefully retained at his Infirmary and his Observatory; the patients of the former will hardly be transferred to the Museum for the convenience of medical students and lecturers; and the grand instruments of the latter could not well be attached to Professor Donkin's diminutive observatory. Indeed, the University has no control over the Observatory, its Observer, or its instruments.

of the University Commission (p. 115), upon the authority (apparently) of Dr. Ingram's Memorials of Oxford (vol. iii. p. 12), viz. that Dr. Radcliffe contemplated his 'Library' (i. e. the building) ' as a *bequest to the University* of Oxford:' and again, ' This was the view taken by the Trustees *on the completion* of the "Library," on which occasion the Duke of Beaufort, in behalf of himself and the other Trustees, *formally delivered* the *key to the Vice-Chancellor*, for *the use of the University*.' Clearly the Vice-Chancellor, i.e. the University, had lost all hold of the key in Dr. Hornsby's time[1].

Dr. Randolph of Christ Church, after holding in succession one or two other Professorships[2], settled down in 1783

---

[1] A piece of Oxford gossip may be subjoined, which once interested and amused the University from the prominence of some of the dramatis personæ. Dr. Hornsby's daughter Arabella was of a good figure, and attracted notice as she rode out, regularly attended by a smart-looking, well-mounted man-servant. After *riding out* for some time followed by the *groom*, she chose to *ride off* with him as her *bride-groom*. The incident however did not end here; it happened that a Fellow of Brasenose (who from a peculiar gait or make was called in his College ' Dr. Toe') was an admirer of this spirited young lady. His supposed disappointment at her escapade elicited the following *jeu d'esprit* from the ready pen of Reginald Heber, then an Undergraduate of B.N.C.

> ' 'Twixt *foot*man John and Dr. *Toe*
> A rivalship befell,
> Which should be the favour'd beau
> And bear away the *belle*. [Miss Arabella.]

> ' The Footman gain'd the lady's heart,
> And who can wonder? No man;
> The *whole* prevail'd against a *part*,—
> 'Twas *foot*man versus *toe*-man.'

[2] He was elected Professor of Poetry in 1776, and appointed Professor of Greek in 1782.

on the Regius Professorship of Divinity, which he held with the Canonry of Ch. Ch. and for a time the Bishopric of Oxford; he was afterwards translated to that of London. I remember Dr. Randolph as a preacher and a lecturer in Divinity[1]. Those lectures were then given late in the evening, by candle-light; one effect of this (and not a very surprising one, considering the hour, the subject, and the audience) was, that many of the class slept through the lecture, waking up now and then at the sound of a Greek quotation; e. g. 'The question still recurs' (snuffing his pair of candles by turns) 'πόθεν τὸ κακόν; πόθεν τὸ κακόν; whence came evil?' Attendance, not attention (and that very irregular attendance), was all that was required to obtain a certificate to be presented to some bishop for ordination. The lecture was neither accompanied nor followed by any questioning or examination. Notes were supposed to be taken, but there was no inspection of note-books, nor a single remark at the close of the 'sleep-compelling' ceremony, no personal questions or special class. In short, the only things really carried away by the majority of the class, were the Syllabus given to each one at the commencement of the course, and a formidable printed list of authors recommended for future reading, presented at the close of the lectures.

Things are differently and better conducted now, and indeed have been for many years past; the lectures are not *post-prandian*, or at a time when dry theology and solid food cannot well be digested together, when the brain and the stomach cannot be made to work simultaneously.

---

[1] Though I had just been elected to the *lay* office of Esquire Bedel, I attended Dr. Randolph's lectures, thinking I might subsequently change my views and take orders,—not indeed with the aspiration of becoming a bishop (like Beilby Porteus) after carrying an Esquire Bedel's staff, but from an old hankering after a Minor-canonry.

A more personal interest too is taken in individual pupils, and a special course provided for the more earnest and more advanced students. Dr. Lloyd (afterwards Bishop Lloyd) took the lead in these improvements, and he was well followed up by Dr. Burton[1].

Sir Christopher Pegge, M.D. and Regius Professor of Medicine from 1801 to 1822, was an accomplished, gentlemanly person, of a noble appearance and courteous manner. He ought indeed to have 'set up his brass-plate' in London and near the Court and the West End; especially as he had professionally to run a hopeless race against two Oxford physicians, Dr. Wall and Dr. Bourne, in greater practice than any two have since been at the same time. Dr. Pegge, however, had the advantage of a Christ Church connection as well as the recommendation of an Oriel Fellowship; and having gained (probably through the former) the Regius Professorship as well as Lee's Lectureship in Anatomy, he succeeded generally in attracting a numerous class. It was then thought not *to be the thing* to leave Oxford without attending one course of these lectures, and the propensity to hard reading *for the Schools* had not yet set in so strong as to leave no spare time for other pursuits[2]. Dr. Pegge got

---

[1] They were indeed two most valuable men, and if God's inscrutable providence had spared them longer to the University and the Church, other persons, of deeper feelings perhaps but of weaker judgment, would probably have been *kept in check*, and their piety and zeal, their industry and talents might have been employed in showing the superior claims of our own Protestant Catholic Church to a Scriptural, Apostolic, and even Patristic basis, in comparison with the ambitious pretensions and exclusive claims of Papal Rome.

[2] Sir Christopher was a very ready, fluent lecturer, as I can vouch from having attended more than one course by his express invitation. 'Mr. Cox,' said he, 'as Esquire Bedel in *Medicine* I consider you *free of*

himself knighted; not that it gained him more patients, any more than the wig, the large turned-up hat, and the gold-headed cane which, when only twenty-five years old, he assumed, because it was the traditionary custom (or rather costume), and because his rival Doctors (much older than himself) had done the same[1]. Some wag of the day, himself, it is to be presumed, being healthy and therefore hard upon Doctors, said of

The Oxford Medical trio.

> 'I would not call in any one of them all,
> For only "the weakest will go to the *Wall*;"
> The second, like Death, that scythe-armed mower,
> Will speedily make you *a peg* or two lower[2];
> While the third, with the fees he so silently earns,
> Is "the *bourn* whence no traveller ever returns."'

Dr. White, Professor of Hebrew from 1802 to 1814, had been a noted Oriental scholar and Arabic Professor nearly thirty years before he succeeded to the Hebrew Chair and its accompanying Canonry at Christ Church. His Bampton Lectures, in 1784, made more stir than usual, not simply

---

the School, and as Coroner you ought to know something about these matters.'

[1] Dr. Kidd, his successor as Regius Professor, a man in all things straight-forward and anti-humbug, was the first Medical Doctor in Oxford who rejected the wig and large-brimmed hat, and never, I believe, carried a gold-headed stick.

[2] Or again—

Circe, alias Sir C.

> 'Like Circe *Sir C.* can prescribe a mixt cup,
> But mixtures Circeian beware to drink up.'

because they were good, but because it oozed out that, in writing them, he had received help from a dissenting minister[1]. We may conclude, however, that the *help* was not such, either in its nature or extent, as to injure the Lecturer's reputation for honesty or scholarship, or he would not have obtained his *subsequent* better preferment. He was a man confessedly devoted to his studies, 'et totus in illis,' and often so abstracted as to give occasion to amusing stories. Ex. gr. When residing as a Fellow at Wadham he undertook to serve a friend's church and to ride a friend's horse to Kidlington. The Doctor, who had seldom sat in a saddle before, managed, with quiet assistance from the groom, to mount, but after a mile or two he thought it would be more *comfortable* to walk. He accordingly dismounted and hung the horse's bridle upon his arm. On his approaching Kidlington turnpike the following short dialogue took place,—the gate being closed:—

Dr. W. Holla! Master gate-keeper, why don't you open the gate for me?

Gate-keeper. Open the gat! why, maun, you must be beside yourself.

Dr. W. Open it, I say, sirrah! immediately, and don't keep me and my horse waiting here.

Gate-keeper. Haw, haw, haw,—that's a good 'un. You and your horse! donna you think that side-gat is big enough for *you* to pass through? and as for your horse,

---

[1] A Mr. Badcock, who subsequently conformed to the Church of England. See Blackwood's Edinburgh Magazine, No. 181. Dr. White also received assistance in his Bampton Lectures from Dr. Parr. Dr. Bloxam writes to me: 'I have before me in MS. a copy of a most indignant letter from Dr. Parr to White on the subject. He was kept in ignorance of Badcock's help.' He adds, 'The whole story is told in Dr. Johnstone's Life of Parr.'

I can't see nothing like one, unless it be that there bridle on your arm !

Dr. W. Dear me! how can it be? what has happened to the poor creature? Sure enough, here is the bridle, but what can have become of the horse?

Deep in thought about 'crooked letters,' the Doctor had not felt the gradual slipping off of the bridle from the head of the animal, which was found quietly grazing on the roadside a mile behind !

It was not till 1802 that Dr. White was made Professor of Hebrew and removed to Christ Church from his house in Broad Street. About seven years afterwards, in his old age and when he was suffering from the gout, he and his wife (also a great invalid) were one night put to a sad trial and alarm by the breaking out of a dreadful fire[1] in a set of rooms adjoining the Hebrew Professor's Lodgings, in Tom Quadrangle. The flames soon spread to their abode, and the old, infirm couple were taken from their beds in the midst of the night and removed to a place of safety. By great efforts the fire was extinguished, but not before several sets of rooms and a part of the Professor's house were destroyed or injured. It was an awful but beautiful picture, presented by the calm moon hanging over the tower or turret at the south-west angle (as viewed from the street), while the flames streamed out of the windows.

Dr. Abram Robertson was Professor of Astronomy and Radcliffe's Observer from 1810 to 1827, having previously (i. e. from 1797) been Savilian Professor of Geometry. He came early in life from Scotland to Oxford, where he arrived with empty pockets. My authority for most of these parti-

---

[1] This fire, I think, happened in 1809.

culars is (or rather was) the late Mr. (or, as he was latterly called, Dr.) Ireland[1], who, in spite of his name, was a *Scotchman*, and Abram Robertson very naturally called upon him, as his countryman, for help and advice, when the following dialogue took place:—

Mr. I. What brought you to Oxford, young man?

A. R. I thought, Sir, the air of Oxford was impregnated with Greek, Latin, and Mathematics[2], and that I could easily get employment, at least in teaching the latter.

Mr. I. Well, young man, I suppose you don't expect to live upon this Oxford air, or to be engaged as a teacher without introduction?

A. R. No indeed, Sir. University pupils, I know, are not yet to be expected by me; I have tried already to establish an evening school for young mechanics, but, I find, they spend their money and their evening-hours otherwise than their likes do in Scotland.

Mr. I. What then is your object in calling upon me?

A. R. To apply for your place as servant, and assistant in the shop at leisure time.

Mr. I. Well then—but what do you say is your name?

A. R. Abram Robertson, Sir.

Mr. I. Well Abram,—I'll try what you can do;—but mind, I must have work for my wages.

---

[1] *Mr. Ireland* was a well-known Oxford apothecary;—for there were apothecaries in Oxford then, though they are now an extinct species of the medical tribe. I believe Mr. Ireland obtained a Doctor's Degree from a Scotch University on his retiring to Headington, where at the age of eighty he set up his brass-plate as Dr. Ireland.

[2] By-the-bye, this is more in Mr. Ireland's florid style of talk than in that of the future Professor, who, though full of Mathematics and not ill-stored with Latin and Greek, was always dry and slow, but never poetical.

So the engagement was made;—and now comes the pith of the story. 'One day' (said Mr. Ireland, a boasting, pompous sort of man, from whom I have heard the account more than once), 'one day, when the now eminent Dr. Baillie, then a Student in Medicine at Oxford, was dining *tête-à-tête* with me (Abram being employed at the sideboard), our conversation took a mathematical turn, and we were discussing a problem in Euclid. The topic being somewhat dry, we called for more wine. Abram seemed deaf and abstracted, so that I had to repeat the call, with a reproof for inattention. On the following morning, on being remonstrated with, he artlessly replied: "Well, Sir, if ye wad ken the truth, I was deep in that problem, but had nae courage enoof to tell ye, that ye were baith quite wrong." Finding on further conversation the mathematical talent so decided, I lost no time (continued Mr. Ireland) in making known the fact, and soon obtained for Abram a Servitorship at Christ Church.'

Mr. *I.* (and in his stories it was always *I*) ever afterwards considered himself his patron[1]; from being a Servitor he became a Chaplain at Ch. Ch., biding his time, under the better patronage of Dean Cyril Jackson, until a Savilian Professorship, or something of the sort, should become vacant and (in the then scanty supply of mathematical talent in Oxford) *fall into his mouth.*

While thus waiting and working in private tuition at Ch. Ch., he, as B.A., in 1782 obtained the Chancellor's Prize for the English Essay 'On Original Composition.' At length, in 1797, he was appointed Savilian Professor of

---

[1] And in truth he might well be so considered, for he put Abram's foot on the ladder on which he mounted to his subsequent preferment and distinction.

Geometry, and in 1810 Professor of Astronomy as well as the Radcliffe Observer[1].

Professor Robertson was married, but had no family; his wife died many years before him. At the Observatory he lived in a very retired manner, being taken care of by an old housekeeper, whom, just before he died, he calmly instructed 'how to treat his corpse, to tie up his chin, to lay him out,' &c., &c. !

Dr. Philip Hayes, Professor of Music, comes next in my Recollections; but before I speak more particularly of him, I will say a few words on Heather's Professors generally. William Heather, himself a Doctor of Music, stands in good company in the list of the Public Benefactors of the University: e. g. 'William Heather, Mus. Doc.,—Edward Earl of Clarendon,—King Charles I,—Archbishop Laud,' &c., &c. All his Professors, from 1620 to 1797, appear to have been organists (excepting perhaps Dr. Wilson in 1653). In our own times, Sir H. Bishop, knt., was appointed out of regard to his deserved popularity as a composer: at all events, he was a professional musician, i. e. one who *lived* by music[2]. His successor, Sir F. A. G. Ouseley, is a singular exception, being a baronet, a clergyman, and an M.A. as well as a Mus. Doc. My present business, however, is not

---

[1] I do not mean to say that he was 'the eminent mathematician, who read Joe Miller *straight through* and then observed that it was a very *desultory composition;*' but I have seen him silently and slowly putting together (secundum artem mathematicam) the particulars of some witty story or anecdote which had been told, and when every one else had forgotten the subject, ejaculating 'Yes, indeed; that's vary good, vary !'

[2] With all his fame as a laborious and successful composer (certainly the most successful and talented of English dramatic composers), he is said to have died in poverty and distress.

with him, nor his brilliant pianoforte-playing, nor his interesting lectures, nor his talented Musical Exercise, of an oratorio character, but with the *greatest* musician of his day (in point of size and weight), *Dr. Phil. Hayes*, who succeeded his father, Dr. William Hayes, as Professor in 1777, but was very inferior to him as a composer. Like his father, he was not only an organist but a monopolist of organs, being at once Organist of New College, Magdalen, and St. John's, besides St. Mary's as University Organist; like his father also in another respect, he never, I believe, gave any lectures as Professor[1]. How he and his assistant could discharge all these duties seems a puzzle; but it is in some measure explained by the fact that the services were at different hours. In the morning, New College at 8, Magdalen at 10; no choir service at St. John's. The p.m. service at Magdalen at 3.30; New College at 5; St. John's at 6.30.

In addition to his Oxford duties, generally discharged by deputy, the Professor also held the (apparently) incompatible appointment of 'Gentleman in the Chapel Royal,' St. James's, in fulfilment of which duty, when he occasionally went up to London, it was said that he regularly took two places, one on either side the coach[2]. There was indeed no end to the stories of him and his good-nature. One of them I must record:—

On the occasion of a visit paid to Oxford by George III,

---

[1] I remember being taken to his house, in my very early days, *to have my voice tried;* he had been for many years remarkable for his state of obesity, and I have not forgotten the awe I felt at the huge *projection* over the keys of his harpsichord, contrasted with his delicate, small hands, and accompanied with a soft, velvety voice.

[2] 'What's the name of that *double passenger?*' enquired one of his fellow-travellers of the coachman. 'O, Sir, that's the famous Dr. Phil. Hayes.' 'Dr. *Fill-Chaise*, you mean,' was the touchy reply.

the Doctor, after playing the organ at Magdalen Chapel, was hurrying (as well as he could hurry), full-dressed, in his cocked hat[1] and silk gown, up Queen's Lane to pay the same compliment to the Royal party at New College. Panting for breath from over-exertion and excitement, he called out to a country fellow, whom he saw approaching, 'Friend, pray lend me your arm a little way.' 'Yes, your Majesty, by all means,' replied the simple rustic, who had heard that the King was in Oxford and fancied this *great man* must be he.

In the obituary of the Gentleman's Magazine for 1797 occurs this notice:—'March 19, died, in his 58th year, Philip Hayes, Professor of Music, Oxford, and Mus. Doc. in 1777. He had just come to town, in order to preside at the ensuing festival for "The Musical Fund;" he dressed himself in the morning, to attend the Chapel Royal, St. James's, but suddenly showed symptoms of approaching dissolution and expired a short time afterwards. Dr. Hayes's remains were, on the 21st, interred in St. Paul's Cathedral, where a musical funeral-service was performed.'

Dr. Hayes was succeeded, as Professor, in 1797, by *Dr. William Crotch*, a real musical genius. It appears, from an account of him as a 'musical prodigy[2],' that he was born at Norwich in 1755, and that at the early age of $2\frac{1}{2}$ years he began to play 'God save the King,' at first with one hand, but soon after with both, on an organ built by his father[3].

---

[1] The three-cornered cocked-hat was at that time a part of the full dress of lay academics of some standing, with ruffles at the wrists, lace frills, silver buckles on the shoe and at the knee. It was over-done, but certainly gave a gentlemanly appearance. This *dressiness*, however, was not confined to members of the University.

[2] In the Gentleman's Magazine for 1799, abridged from Dr. Burney's longer paper in the Philosophical Transactions.

[3] 'At a very tender age (says Dr. Burney) he could transpose into the most difficult keys whatsoever he played.'

For several years 'Little Crotch' exhibited his powers, both in public and in private parties, as a Musical Wonder. He seems to have soon settled down in Oxford, with a view, probably, to the musical honours and appointments which he afterwards obtained there, and where he found friends and patrons. At a very early age he was appointed Organist at Ch. Ch.; and at Dr. Philip Hayes's death he was made Organist at St. John's College and at St. Mary's, as well as Professor of Music. He was a married man, of a religious turn of mind, and of quiet, studious habits. He had also a natural taste for painting, and amused himself in the production of many paintings and drawings in all styles. I remember seeing him at work upon a portrait[1] of himself very like and well executed in oils.

After several years of residence Dr. Crotch left Oxford, either from a dislike to Oxford society (though he never mixed much in it), or induced by London attractions, lectureships, and a lucrative engagement at a large establishment, or Ladies' School. He retained, however, his Professorship till his death. He ran down indeed to Oxford on the day of the Encænia, or Commemoration, when he received Lord Crewe's benefaction of £30 for playing the organ at the entrance[2] of the procession into the Theatre,

[1] I believe his portrait is still in the possession of the Lock family. He was left-handed, and not only handled his brush in painting, but also his bow in playing on the violoncello, with his left hand: in this latter performance, of course the strings of his instrument were reversed. On the organ, in days when pedals were scarce, his left hand was of course very effective.

[2] The grand, voluntary performance of 'God save the King [Queen]' by the whole assembly (one of the finest expressions of loyal feeling that can be heard) had not become an established custom in Crotch's time: the entrée was then accompanied by the 'March in Scipio,' or something of the kind. The *interludes* also were more or less audible, and

and short interludes between the ceremonies and recitations.

Dr. Crotch did indeed visit Oxford at an Installation, when he had to set an Ode to music, and on two occasions to conduct the performance of his fine Oratorio of 'Palestine.' This noble composition, with his volume of Anthems and two or three pleasing and clever glees[1], placed him at the very top of recent English composers. He never, however, courted popularity, and his 'Palestine,' not being published in score, has little chance of being, as it deserves to be, reproduced in Oxford and elsewhere[2]. The recent Musical Statute (of 1858) has imposed the *necessity* of a terminal lecture, Heather's small endowment of £12 a year (or thereabouts) being raised to £100, exclusive, I believe, of Lord Crewe's donation mentioned above.

Of the Professors of *Modern History* I have a faint recollection of *Dr. Nowell* and of his passing his *later years* very quietly (partly at St. Mary Hall, of which he was Principal, and partly at his pretty house overlooking the lock at Iffley), after having added, in his own person, one incident to the history he *professed* to teach: I allude to the fact of his sermon, preached before the House of Commons, having been condemned by the House and ordered to be burnt[3]!

not (as of late years) drowned by the *rough music* and discreditable *performances* of the 'gallery.'

[1] And most especially his two grand motetts, 'Methinks I hear' and 'Mona on Snowdon calls.'

[2] His course of lectures (given in London rather than Oxford) was on 'The Styles of Music,' and on the 'Rise and Progress of the Art.' His work, 'Specimens of Music,' in 2 vols., forms a valuable selection from the early masters; his other compositions and publications were never popular.

[3] This sermon, preached in 1772, was full of high Tory sentiments;

Dr. Beeke, who succeeded Dr. Nowell as Professor of Modern History in 1801, had the reputation of being an elegant scholar, and generally commanded a respectable attendance at his terminal lecture given in Oriel College hall. He died, I think, Dean of Bristol.

Dr. Nares, who came next in order (being appointed in 1813) held the Professorship for twenty-eight years. He seemed to take his professorial duties rather easy, not always (when he did come up from his living) attracting an audience, though he was an accomplished scholar, a perfect gentleman, and an amusing writer. He was the author of a clever, witty story, entitled, 'Thinks I to myself,'—a book very popular at the time, and full of dry humour and satirical pleasantry. His connection in early life with Blenheim has been mentioned elsewhere.

But what a name comes next in the list of the Modern History Professors! that of *Dr. Arnold!*

'Ostendent—hunc tantùm fata, neque ultra
Esse sinent.'

I am not going, however, to say more than a few words of one whose Life has been written *con amore* (as such a Life ought to be written) by his pupil, Dean Stanley. My 'Recollections' of him are confined to the two periods of his connection with Oxford: the first was in 1815, when, fresh from gaining his splendid First Class, he read his Prize Essay from one rostrum and C. Giles Daubeny[1] read his from the

---

he was thanked by the House and requested to print it; but, under the influence of a turbulent factious spirit the vote of thanks was afterwards expunged; the burning is, I think, doubtful.

[1] These two distinguished sons of Alma Mater, who may be said to have done much towards the introduction of a new and better state of studies in Oxford, had been brought together, as it were, to close, with decency and honour, the studies and peculiarities of the older system;

opposite one; the other period was when, in 1841, he returned to Oxford as Professor of Modern History, about (as we all hoped) in a lengthened professorial career to confer more on Alma Mater than anything she could offer him. Never, I believe, was expectation raised higher than it was at his delivery of his Inaugural Lecture; nor was that expectation disappointed: the assembled audience, too numerous for the usual lecture-room in the Clarendon, adjourned at once to the Sheldonian Theatre[1]; where he kept them entranced by his earnest manner and interesting matter. The younger academics heard him with delight (no *compulsory* attendance was here required), and the older ones submitted readily to learn history anew under the teaching of this new and talented master. The few subsequent lectures which Dr. Arnold gave were attended with equally flattering circumstances; but, alas! he was not allowed to follow up the high subject he had undertaken. In the following year (1842) he died!

Dr. John Sibthorp, Professor of Botany (successor to another Dr. Sibthorp, who had held the appointment for thirty-seven years), was appointed in 1784, and held the office till 1795. He built what is called 'Cowley House' (being in the parish of Cowley), merely separated from the Botanic Gardens by a meadow and a stream. It was said that he intended it as a residence for his successors[2]; the gift, how-

---

inasmuch as they served together the office of 'Collectors,' then held *for the last time*, in connection with the worn-out and exploded Lent Exercises of the 'Determining' Bachelors in Arts.

[1] A *move* more common in later days of excitement and female audiences, but a rare and therefore more striking compliment then.

[2] The house in which Dr. Daubeny resided was built (or rather added to the old lecture-room) by himself. But his outlay has been

ever, was never made. The house is said to have been built of bricks made of the clay upon the spot. Dr. S. in some measure spoilt its arrangement and proportions, in order to accommodate a fine staircase and some large windows which he had purchased at the pulling-down of Lord Abingdon's house at Rycot, near Thame. The building itself certainly has no pretension whatever to external beauty, notwithstanding its fine situation : Dr. Sibthorp, nevertheless, the admirer of his own creation, appears to have thought otherwise; for he is reported to have asked the Dean of Christ Church for a Studentship for one of his family, on the ground of having built 'so beautiful and classical a terminus to the vista of the Broad Walk!' 'A Studentship!' (replied Dean Cyril Jackson); 'My good Sir, I will give you *two* if you will be so kind as to pull it down again.'

Dr. S. never felt such a '*stinger*,' except perhaps when, as he was lecturing upon nettles (having several specimens and species carefully laid out upon his table), he said, 'Now, gentlemen, we all know, from our childhood, that some of the nettle-family have a *powerful pungent property;* others a less powerful, less pungent property; and others again none at all, or next to none. Now, to begin with the last species, this you see' (suiting the action to the word) ' may safely be drawn through the hand, thus '—some wicked wag, while the Doctor's back was turned, had impudently changed the order in which the specimens lay, or the Professor had unwittingly laid a trap for himself. The effect may be imagined! This story, I confess, is told of other

---

followed by so many occasional sums voted by Convocation that the whole building will, of course, be permanently attached to the Professorship. Dr. Tatham, in 1807, says that within his recollection the Botanical Professor had a class of sixty. The Chemical Lectures too (he adds) were well attended.

Lecturers, and the practical joke may have been repeated elsewhere.

Of *Margaret Professors of Divinity* my 'Recollections' take in Dr. Randolph, Dr. Collinson (both of whom have been spoken of elsewhere), and Dr. *Timothy Neve*, Fellow of Corpus, afterwards Chaplain of Merton and one of the early Bampton Lecturers. It is to be presumed, therefore, that he had had some reputation as a theologian, though his day was gone by when I recollect him. He had a daughter who was considered a belle, at a time when Oxford could not boast so many young ladies as it does now (1860); and his wife (afterwards for many years his widow) was a gay old lady, living in Beam[1], or Biham, or Bohemian Hall, opposite Merton College Chapel, where she boasted that her drawing-room (not a very large one) had often accommodated seven card-tables!

Dr. Faussett, Margaret Professor from 1827 to 1853, is of almost too recent a date to come within the scope of these Recollections; but as he is so intimately connected with what are now become historical transactions (quoad Academiam et Ecclesiam), I venture to attach him to the list of Margaret Professors here noticed. He had (what was considered) the *good fortune* to have a Canonry of Ch. Ch. attached (by a recent arrangement) to his Professorship, instead of a Prebendal Stall in Worcester Cathedral: this was in 1840. Perhaps I ought rather to have said 'he had the *misfortune*,' since this change brought him to reside in Oxford at a time of great excitement and commotion in the theological circle of the University.

[1] 'Beam' was perhaps the English pronunciation of *Böhm*, i. e. Bohemian. I naturally take an interest in the old house (or Hall), having spent many of my early years in it.

He was himself rather a warm controversialist, having for some time changed his style of sermons (which in his early days, when he was a Select Preacher, were quiet, well-written discourses) into warm attacks upon Romanists and 'Romanisers.' It was in this spirit that he called upon the Vice-Chancellor (in 1843) to form a Court of six Doctors in Divinity to sit in judgment on Dr. Pusey's famous sermon. The enquiry (as every one knows) ended in suspending Dr. Pusey from preaching before the University for two years; but some few wise men then, and many more since, were of opinion that more harm than good followed from the sentence.

The intercourse of Christ Church dignitaries at that time, and for some years after, must have been rather awkward and uncomfortable, when Dr. Pusey, Dr. Faussett and Dr. Hampden met, at least, in the same Chapter-house, and ministered in the same Cathedral services!

I have to record my 'Recollections' of only one more Professor, but that one was, to all who knew him, a very interesting character:—

Alexander Nicoll, D.C.L., Professor of Hebrew and Canon of Christ Church from 1822 to 1828. The early death of this talented Professor and amiable man was deeply felt throughout the University; leaving, as he did, a young wife and a family indifferently provided for, and closing prematurely the distinguished career that seemed marked out for him by his rare faculty of acquiring languages. Alexander Nicoll came from Scotland at a very early age to be matriculated upon a Glasgow Exhibition at Balliol College. I have heard Mr. Cheese, then a Fellow of that College, say, that on entering the College-gate one day, he observed a youth 'standing by a trunk, and shedding tears.' On accosting him, he found he had been 'dropped at the College-gate' (as he said) 'just like a portmanteau,' when even the porter was absent, and 'not a soul at Oxford caring for or knowing of his existence.' Under this impression of utter loneliness, he confessed that he had been momentarily overpowered; a few kind words soon raised his spirits, and his ingenuous, handsome countenance and modest manners very soon gained him friends.

Discouraging as such a commencement might at first appear to him, his subsequent course at Oxford was as rapidly prosperous as it was thoroughly deserving of success. His Class at the Public Examination (in 1811) was only 'a Second,' but the Classics and Greek Philosophy were not his particular line. Languages, as such, soon absorbed his attention; and his early acquirement not only of Oriental languages, but also those of Northern Europe, soon marked him as a prize for 'the Bodleian,' where, as a Sub-librarian, he worked in his proper element, acquiring knowledge and gaining reputation, till the promotion of Dr. Laurence to the Archbishopric of Cashel vacated the Regius Professorship of Hebrew. Oxford did not then abound[1] with Hebraists, and Nicoll, who was hardly thirty, 'was of course too young to be thought of as a Canon of Christ Church,' to say nothing of a Professorship generally held by scholars of long standing. He himself (as it soon appeared) was the last person to think of such a possibility. In this unconscious, humble

---

[1] Query: Did it ever? does it now? Will the Magdalen Exhibitions of £10 a year (!), founded by Dr. Ellerton, ever produce a supply? In my younger days it was said, that the first question of Dr. Blayney, the then Professor, to any one who called to request permission to attend his lectures, was, 'Pray, Sir, are you a man of *letters* (i. e. do you know your alphabet?), or of *words* (i. e. can you read Hebrew?).'

state of mind he one morning received a letter by the Post, with a large seal attached to it, in which he read something to this effect: 'Dear Sir, having been well informed of your singular fitness for the Regius Professorship of Hebrew, now vacant, I am authorised by his Majesty to offer you that appointment, with the accompanying Canonry at Christ Church. I am, &c. &c. LIVERPOOL.'

The story goes on thus:—Perfectly convinced (from his modest estimate of himself, as well as his high estimate of such a post) that some impertinent person had played an elaborate hoax upon him, he kept the letter in his pocket for several hours, quietly resuming his place in the Bodleian, and determined not to gratify the hoaxer by getting himself laughed at. After awhile, however, he was induced (quite in confidence, and sure of not being quizzed in that quarter) to produce the letter for the amusement, at least for the opinion, of a trusty friend. That friend, having had more experience than Nicoll, and having also a far higher estimate of his fitness, at once saw that it was no hoax[1], but a genuine letter from the Prime Minister. Of course, the flattering conviction of the fact was, after awhile, admitted, and the gracious offer gratefully accepted. And so, to every one's delight, as well as astonishment, the humble Scotch Exhibitioner of 1807 became in 1822, per saltum, Hebrew Professor, with all the honours, advantages, and responsibilities belonging to the appointment.

In that office (it is scarcely necessary to add) he was still, during the few years allotted to him, the same modest man,

---

[1] I have lately been told that this story (which I have always believed to the letter) was—not contradicted but much modified by Dr. Nicoll's father-in-law, Mr. Parsons. At all events, 'se non è vero letteralmente, è almeno ben trovato.'

the same earnest student. I once heard 'Peter Elmsley' say in his emphatic and Johnsonian manner, in answer to a remark on Nicoll's modest bearing,—' Sir, he is not modest, —he is modesty itself!'

Comp. Martial's

'Non vitiosus homo es, Zoile, sed vitium.'

CHAPTER VII.

'Paulo majora canamus.'—*Virgil.*

Recollections of Heads of Houses.

BEFORE I particularise individuals among Heads of Houses of a now remote date, I must state the very solemn idea suggested to Oxford natives *of that day* by the title, much more by the sight and presence of one of the *Heads of Housen*, as the citizens then called them. In the first place, they (with a few exceptions) wore the large cauliflower wig [1], which was worn for a long time after by the bishops. In

---

[1] *Parody on* '*Three poets in three distant ages born.*'

'Three diff'rent wigs, by diff'rent wearers worn,
The Judge, the Don, the Canon did adorn:
The first was flowing, dignified, profound;
The second bushy, cauliflower'd, round;
The third was scratchy, one-curl'd, close, embrown'd.
But all the three to Parr's the palm did yield,
The Cambridge $\begin{Bmatrix} \text{Mega-thauma} \\ \mu\acute{\epsilon}\gamma\alpha\ \theta\alpha\hat{\upsilon}\mu\alpha \end{Bmatrix}$ beat the field;
The eyes of barbers could no farther see,
To form that fourth they join'd the other three.
So compar, impar, dispar all combin'd
To weave a wig fit emblem of the mind;
Imposing, showy, pompous, grandiose,
Brow-beating now, and now again jocose.'

the next place, they seldom, if ever, appeared abroad out of their academic costume, super-induced on a cassock,—many of them sitting in it during the day. It was traditionally said, that when a portion of Queen's quadrangle was burnt down, the then Provost, on being called up with the cry of 'Fire,' calmly stopped to put on his gown, cassock and bands, before he descended to see 'his Troy in flames[1].'

One striking peculiarity of their position was, that as soon as a Fellow had become, by election, the Head of his College, he was at once, as one of the 'Dii majorum gentium,' cut off from equal intercourse with his Fellows in the friendly society of the Common-room, and forced, nolens volens, into the terminal routine of 'Cod's-head and shoulders' with his brother Dons[2]. Of course on these occasions the entertainment was of the best; but there was little attempt at grandeur, no elaborate variety 'in vino et cibo.' On blank days (that is, days on which there was no Dons'

[1] Something like this took place at Magdalen more recently on the alarm of 'Fire' at the Hall, then adjoining the College. But it is to be remembered, that probably no other dress was so nigh at hand

[2] Heads of Houses were wont to proceed to the Degree of Doctor, as a matter of course, till Mr. Sneyd, Warden of All Souls, set the example of doing without it. It has been supposed, that the old title of the University. 'The Chancellor, *Masters*, and Scholars,' points to an earlier time and practice, and that the Degree of *Doctor* was not known till the time of Henry II, 1154. So at Cambridge, at the earliest periods, the Senate consisted of the two houses of Regent and Non-Regent Masters; *Doctors* being frequently called also Masters. (Historical Account of Cambridge by B. D. Walsh, M.A. 1837) The term 'Don' will not, I trust, give offence,—as it is here and elsewhere honestly used, not merely for the sake of brevity (though that is worth consideration), but in the reverential sense which, as applied to Heads of Houses, it certainly had in my early days. Latterly indeed it may, in some degree, have changed its meaning and lost some of its weight, when applied by Undergraduates to a very young and rather assuming Tutor.

M

dinner) the recently elected Head took his solitary meal, often repining for the cheerful society of 'the lower House.' As this state of things was not likely to continue without some effort to improve it, the Don soon introduced a Donna;—and the College soon found that it had a biceps government.

Some Heads indeed persisted in remaining bachelors, gradually settling down under the worst of all tyrannies[1], that of their *old servants*. One or two married 'rather beneath them,' as the phrase goes; the ladies whom the others married were content to lead a dull quiet life, seldom cheered by a family of children, both parties at the time of marriage being generally rather advanced in years. The ladies, of course, were 'prima donnas' in every sense but the usual, that is the musical one; but their gaieties seldom went beyond the regular dinner-party, with its subsequent rubber:—no musical parties (Mrs. Marlow's excepted), no conversaziones, no throwing open a suite of rooms, no 'tableaux vivans,' no being 'At Home,' in the modern sense of the phrase, no private theatricals, no croquet parties.

But to come to individuals.

My first 'Recollections[2]' in connection with Heads of Houses begin with my early patron *Dr. Routh*, who suc-

---

[1] Sometimes called a *dulocracy* (δουλοκρατία). 'Terræ Filius,' (vol. i. No. 13), always, of course, to be read 'cum grano,' gives an amusing paper on this subject. 'There ever will be (he says) insolent *slaves*, kept to domineer over their masters' clients, and sometimes *over their masters themselves*.'

[2] I might say my *last* as well as my *first*; for as he lived to his hundredth year, he survived by twenty years the latest of those Heads whom I have presumed to comprise in this Chapter. 'Si tamen ad centesimum vixit annum, senectutis eum suæ non pœnitebat.'

ceeded *Dr. Horne* as President of Magdalen. I was too young to have *known* anything of Dr. Horne, though his name was familiar to me in such phrases (then 'in ore virûm volitantia') as, 'True as George Horne,' 'Sweet-tempered as George Horne,' and the like. His daughter also (familiarly called, at least in Magdalen, Mary Horne) was still spoken of as having been 'the Oxford beauty,' whose admirers would hang about the College entrance, for the chance of seeing her pass from the President's house (or 'lodgings' as such houses are, not very reverentially, called) to the College chapel[1].

My 'Recollections' of Dr. Routh and Magdalen College begin in 1794. For many successive Gaudy-days I saw him seated in the chair of state[2], made from the famous Magdalen oak. So great was the impression made upon boyish minds by his awful wig, his over-hanging eyebrows, and solemn carriage, that though he was then only a little more than forty, he seemed to me and my schoolfellows nearly as old as he eventually lived to be[3]. His introit

[1] Dr. Horne was a frequent preacher before the University, but his sermons, though interesting and marked by his own sweetness of temper, do not exhibit him as a great theologian. He was the Bishop who, in reply to the enquiry of George III, 'Who, my Lord, are these Scotch Bishops, who have appealed to me for help? I know nothing of them;'—answered, 'Please your Majesty, they are far better Bishops than my humble self.'

[2] The last time Dr. Routh sate in that chair (about fifteen years before his death) he choked very badly at dinner, and, being alarmed, rushed out of the hall; retiring with the Vice-President into the Common-room, he was frightened on vomiting what seemed to be blood. He was re-assured, however, by Mr. Booth, the Vice-President, exclaiming (on due examination), 'Only a little currant-jelly from the venison, Mr. President!' He assisted at the Examination for Demyships next day.

[3] It may be mentioned as a remarkable result of his long Presidency,

and exit at chapel were very peculiar, owing to his gliding, sweeping *motion*, I can hardly call it *gait;* for he moved along (as the heathen deities were said to do) without seeming to divaricate or take alternate steps. This effect was of course partly produced by his long gown and cassock. His gestures during the service were remarkable, his hands being much in motion, and often crossed upon his breast. His seat or pew being large and roomy, he was wont to move about in it during service, generally joining aloud in the responses, but without any relation to the right tone.

It may be satisfactory to curious posterity to know that one at least of Dr. Routh's prodigious *caliendra*[1] was actually sent by Dr. Daubeny to be immortalised by submission to the petrifying spring at Knaresborough; it was deposited in Dr. Daubeny's collection.

Of *Dr. Dennis*, President of St. John's, who died in 1795, I have no personal recollection, but I remember the strong sympathy excited for his widow, a highly respected and amiable lady, who having lived for some time after his death in good style in Holywell Street, was at length completely impoverished by a spendthrift son, a clergyman and a Master of Arts! He, as the phrase is, soon 'went to the dogs;' his mother became a resident in the Widows' College at Bromley.

Dr. Fothergill, Provost[2] of Queen's (who died in 1796),

---

that he, who appointed me to be a chorister at Magdalen, did, *very many years* afterwards, give a similar appointment to my *grandson!*

[1] Dr. Johnson, famous for his own wig, says that 'wig' is *contracted* from 'periwig!'—adding, however, the derivation of the latter from 'peruque.'

[2] Dr. Fothergill had been an influential Head of a House, and, as Vice-Chancellor, was instrumental in conferring the Doctor's Degree, by

I merely recollect as a gaunt, solemn figure, who, at a regular hour of the day, with a long-tasseled cap, a large wig, unusually broad bands, and a particularly broad sash, used to come down the steps of his College gate-way, to take his accustomed walk, *followed* by his quiet-dressed wife. I say emphatically 'followed,' for even at setting-out they generally appeared in that order, the distance rather increasing during their walk; in reference to this they were called by the wits of the day 'Orpheus and Eurydice[1].' The old Provost was succeeded by Dr. Collinson, whom I have mentioned in Chapter II.

Dr. Hoare, Principal of Jesus College (who died in 1802), was for many years only seen as he took his drive, carefully wrapped up, in his carriage;—it could not properly be called '*taking an airing*,' for the windows were always scrupulously closed. Under this management, however (perhaps because of it), he lived to a great age, and might have lived still longer but for an untoward accident. He had a pet tom-cat, which enjoyed the privilege of living in his master's study, of sleeping on his best leather-bottomed chair, and usurping the warmest berth on his hearth-rug. Unfortunately, one day the old Doctor, in seating himself, placed a leg of his chair upon one of Tom's legs,—and,

---

diploma, on Samuel Johnson, in 1775, Lord North being then Chancellor of the University.

[1] The *nick-name* suggested these saucy lines:—

Orpheus and Eurydice.

'If you'd have no more strife,
Keep aloof, my good wife!
You can do, when you please, as I bid, I see;
Now we're both of one mind,
(And I won't look behind,)
I'll be Orpheus, and you'll be Eurydice.'

being quite deaf, was unconscious of the pain he was inflicting, till the cat in its agony seized upon the Doctor's leg, and scratched it violently. The wound, thus caused, would not heal, and he died after lingering some days[1].

Dr. Hoare's successor, as Principal, was *Dr. Hughes*, a hearty, rough old gentleman. In the office of Pro-Vice-Chancellor he ventured once (and only once) to officiate in conferring Degrees. His peculiar pronunciation of the Latin forms tried the gravity even of the Deans and Regent-Masters; e. g. '*Aygo* admitto *tay* ad gradum,' &c. Unhappily in his old age, and with confirmed old-bachelor habits, he was *persuaded* to marry the sister of another Head of a House; the honeymoon was scarcely over when he betook himself alone to London, and going to his old Coffee-house, put a pistol to his head, and *made a vacancy* at Jesus College (in 1817).

Dr. Phineas Pett, Principal of St. Mary Hall (who died in 1830, as a Canon of Christ Church) had had the good fortune to be tutor to George Canning when a Christ Church Student. Dr. Pett resigned St. Mary Hall in 1815. He was for many years highly respected as Archdeacon of Oxford[2], and was said to have declined a bishopric offered to him through the interest of his former pupil. I remember

---

[1] A resident Welsh bard was supposed to have struck off a Lament, part of which (in English) was to this effect:—

> 'Poor Dr. Hoare! he is no more!
> Bid the harp-strings of Cambria mourn;
> The Head of a House died the death of a mouse,
> And Tom must be hang'd in return.'

[2] The Archdeaconry of Oxford, to which a Canonry of Christ Church is now attached, had then, I believe, no emolument, except the small Incumbency of Iffley, near Oxford, the revenues of which barely paid the officiating Curate.

calling at Dr. Pett's to receive Mr. Canning's fees for his Honorary D.C.L. Degree, conferred in the Theatre at Lord Grenville's Installation in 1809, and was struck with admiration at his handsome features and fine head. Those features, however, took rather a glum expression at having to 'fork out' (that, I believe, is the proper term) the sum of ten guineas[1].

In connection with Dr. Pett and St. Mary Hall, I may as well mention his immediate successor, *Dr. Dean*, who, after being for many years Fellow and Tutor of Brasenose College, Public Examiner, Proctor, &c., carried with him to the Headship of the Hall a high character for scholarship. He was one of the then few remaining speakers in Latin in Convocation; his witty application of a line from Juvenal, on a repeated attempt of the Hebdomadal Board to force a disputed statute on the reluctant House of Convocation,—

'Occidit miseros crambe repetita *Magistros*,'

has since been *sported* in Convocation and Congregation, till it has become stale. Dr. Dean died in 1833.

His successor, *Dr. Hampden*, will require a separate Chapter, when I come to the date of his controversy, or rather his persecution (in 1836). Nor could I in a few lines do justice to Dr. Hampden's successor at St. Mary Hall, my valued, kind-hearted friend, *Dr. Philip Bliss*, whose place in

---

[1] This fee for the Honorary Degree, till lately paid by the recipients of the honour (who often made wry faces at being called upon to pay solid money for the unsubstantial compliment), is now very properly paid by the University; it is reduced, however, to *four guineas*, with the prospect (at the death or resignation of two University officers, 'qui nunc sunt') of being reduced to the presentator's fee of two guineas.

[N.B. One of the two (myself has since vacated (in 1866), so that another reduction of a guinea has been made.]

Oxford, in business, in society, and in antiquarian pursuits, it will take more than one man to fill up.

Dr. Wills, Warden of Wadham (who died in 1806), had the reputation of being very close and rigid 'in re pecuniariâ.' He might be seen, on a summer's day, working with his hay-makers in the Warden's Close[1], quite in earnest, and in his shirt-sleeves,—his coat hanging on a hurdle. He saved money however (as appears from the fact of his name being added to the list of the University and College Benefactors), for the benefit of others. He considerately left a pension for two *superannuated* Fellows[2]. This pension, I believe, was only once enjoyed by a quondam Fellow, a Mr. Williams. We may presume that this particular endowment (being no longer, in consequence of recent alterations, required) is appropriated to other College purposes.

Of *Dr. Chapman*, President of Trinity (who died in 1808), I can say nothing, because I recollect nothing,—except that he was a tall, dignified Head of a House. Like his successors

---

[1] This *Close* has since been taken into the Warden's garden and inclosed with walls; in Dr Wills's time it was partially open to view, as being only protected by a hedge and a ditch; an intervening space, between the ditch and the close, being let out to a market-gardener.

[2] The Fellowships of this College, according to the old statutes, expired after being held about twenty years! that is, just when the income and other College comforts were most wanted. This by a recent enactment has been wisely altered, and the Fellowships, like those of every other College, are now tenable for life. In connection with superannuated Fellows I may add from Huber (i. p. 203), and quoted by him from Hearne and others :—' The supplementary statutes of Oriel provide that the Fellows should resign their Fellowships upon obtaining a benefice elsewhere, or *when twenty years had elapsed without their obtaining any*, since such a case must pre-suppose that they deserved none, and had employed their time improperly.'—N. B. It is not clear from the printing, whether the concluding sentence is a continuation of the statute or Huber's inference.

at Trinity, he seems to have preferred a quiet, easy life. He did not disturb that quiet, like *Dr. Ingram*, by engaging in any literary production[1], but in his Vice-Chancellorship he received a Royal visit.

Dr. Nathan Wetherell, Master of University College (who died in 1808), accumulated preferment and enriched a large family. A man who, as he did, reached the top of his Society, obtained a Deanery (that of Hereford), and lived to see three or four of his sons Fellows of different Colleges, and one of them on the road to high legal honours, must have been a talented as well as a fortunate person. As Vice-Chancellor, he laid the foundation-stone of the Radcliffe Observatory; he also inaugurated the opening of the new Market in 1772, and speculated successfully in Oxford Canal Shares[2].

[1] Dr. Ingram's work, 'Memorials of Oxford,' requires no eulogy of mine; being well known not as 'My *little* Work' (as he used modestly to call it in his annual speech at New College Gaudy), but as the valuable and well-illustrated result of much labour and research.

Dr. Lee, his successor as President of Trinity, is mentioned in my 'Recollections' of Vice-Chancellors.

Dean Aldrich of Christ Church is supposed by Warton to have designed the original plan of Trinity Chapel, though Sir Christopher Wren had something to do with it. It was more admired formerly than it is now; its fame (like the smell of its cedar wainscoting) is gone off. Of that wainscot Warton wrote, 'Halat opus Lebanique refert fragrantis odorem.' ('Hexam.' on Trinity College Chapel.)

[2] A critic (in the 'Atlas' of November 20, 1868) gives the following lines *as a proof* that 'Dr. Cyril Jackson was not (as I have said, and I believe correctly) averse to a mitre:'—

'Says Cyril to Nathan, just walking by Queen's,
"My very good friend, we are both of us Deans,
And Bishops may possibly be."
Says Nathan to Cyril, "I certainly shall
Bestow all my care on my little Canal,
Leaving you to look after the *See*."'

Of *Dr. Cleaver*, Principal of Brasenose College, and for some years also Bishop of St. Asaph, I have rather more to say, as may well be expected concerning one who introduced lawn sleeves into the 'Lodgings' at Brasenose and into the Hebdomadal meeting, having held the Bishopric and the Headship together till his death. Of course he wore a wig[1], as one of George the Third's Bishops as well as Head of a House, and being a tall man, with good features and stately gait, 'he looked' (as the old Brasenose porter used to say) 'quite the Bishop.' The *effect* too was not a little increased by a habit of walking with both his hands upon his chest, and those hands, as in the portrait, made conspicuous by gloves of bright *Bishop's-purple*.

The fortunes of Dr. Cleaver presented a striking instance of two things: (1) Of the importance of little things (for instance, a casting-vote) in forming the turning-point of great consequences; (2) Of a man's being benefited, promoted, and enriched, in spite of himself, and contrary to his own wishes and intentions. It was in this way.

In 1768 Mr. Cleaver, being then a Fellow of Brasenose, offered himself as a candidate for the office of Librarian to the Bodleian, and was opposed by Mr. Price of Jesus College. The contest was so close, that, after a long polling in Convocation, Mr. Price was elected by *a majority of only one vote*. Mr. Cleaver and his friends, of course, greatly lamented the result; but he was not left long to repine at what he considered a great misfortune. He did, what many

---

[1] Deighton's picture of him, intended, of course, as one in a series of 'Oxford Caricatures,' was really an unexaggerated representation, allowing for a little extravagance in the colouring. The same may be said of his Bishop Parsons,—both being excellent likenesses.

BISHOP CLEAVER.

a man had better have done who has sat down[1], contented with academical success in honours or income, for the rest of a long dull life,—that is, he looked beyond Oxford and Brasenose for occupation and preferment, and found both in the Buckingham family (then in the ascendant), in which he became a tutor, and from which he eventually obtained a bishopric.

Had he succeeded to the place of Librarian, he would probably have ended his days (as old Mr. Price did) in superintending the countless volumes of the Bodleian[2]. Mr. Price held the office forty-five years, having lived to be a very old man. His successor, Dr. Bandinel, reached his eightieth year, having scarcely begun to enjoy the well-earned pension on which he retired from the Proto-Bibliothecarian duties of forty-seven years[3].

But to return to Dr. Cleaver, the peg on which this digres-

---

[1] Making Oxford his little world, and viewing everything through the medium of a College and Common-room atmosphere... Dr. Cleaver in after-life might have said, 'Had I been elected Librarian, I should never have been a bishop,'—as Dr. Prideaux a hundred years before had said, in reference to a still greater rise, 'If I had been made parish-clerk of Ugborow (my early object of ambition', I had never been Bishop of Worcester.'

[2] By-the-bye, that moth-like living in the close air of a Public Library seems by no means to tend to shorten life, either in a case like Mr. Price's, in whose time no attempt was made to warm the place, or in that of Dr. Bandinel, during whose time, after several experiments (which either fell short of success, or went too far), the Library was at length effectually warmed, and more attention paid to air and ventilation.

[3] I was going to say 'forty-seven years' *work*,' but was checked by the 'Recollection' of a *jeu d'esprit* by Dr. Cotton of Christ Church (himself formerly one of the Sub-librarians) which was printed for private circulation, and of which the greater part is given in my 'Recollections' for 1819.

sion has been hung,—and again merely to append to his name and College one more 'Recollection' in the form of another digression. Dr. Barker, his predecessor as Principal of Brasenose, died in 1785, and tradition, Collegiate or Academic, has handed down nothing concerning him. In fact, I only mention him in order to connect him with a respectable old man of the name of Barker, who lived, as I remember, in a small house[1] in what was then Cat (or St. Catherine's) Street; that old man was butler of Brasenose, and (I was always told) brother to the late Principal, Dr. Barker. Such family anomalies were not so uncommon in Oxford some few years ago as they are now.

The year 1809 (in which Dr. Cleaver died) took from us, by his resignation and retirement into his 'otium cum dignitate,' a great and distinguished character, *Dr. Cyril Jackson*, Dean of Christ Church. At all events he was, both in and out of Oxford, a very influential person. He had the great credit of assisting largely in the important task of

[1] That house, with several others adjoining, was pulled down to make room for Dr. Macbride's house, as Principal of Magdalen Hall, in 1822. What I have here called Cat Street, or St. Catherine's, is probably what Antony Wood calls School Street, or Shydiard Street, i. e. Vicus Schediasticorum. This in the English translation of Huber is called 'the Street of *short-hand* writers.' Were they not rather (as in the Psalms) '*ready*-writers,' i. e. copyists, necessarily employed before printing existed? The term 'schediastici' (from the Greek root $\sigma\chi\epsilon\delta o\nu$, propè) would be more literally translated 'writers *at hand*,' than '*short-hand* writers,'—who (*if their art then existed*) would rather have been called brachygraphers or tachygraphers. [I have since met with the following statement:—'Plutarch says of Cicero that he dispersed about the Senate-house several expert writers, whom he taught to make certain figures, and who put down all that he said in little short strokes, equivalent to words.' Guardian Paper.] Hearne thinks 'that Schidyart Street (as he spells it) was Shieldyard Street, where shield-makers formerly lived.' There was also a Hall called Shield Hall.

framing the 'Public Examination Statute,' which has done so much towards raising the character of the studies of Oxford. His own College (or rather his '*House*,' as he always correctly called it) probably never stood so high before. He took care to keep up a supply of clever tutors, and patronised industry and talent among his Chaplains, Commoners, and Servitors, as well as his Students. He had a wonderful tact in managing that most unmanageable class of Undergraduates, Noblemen[1]. Even there he could distinguish and vary his treatment according to character; e. g. having one day overheard one of that class call out to his compeers, 'I say, who will go anywhere and do anything?' he at once advised his removal from Oxford, to do something, or anything, or nothing *somewhere else*. Certainly there was a much larger show of *gold tassels* in his time than at any period since[2].

[1] Perhaps a good deal of that management consisted in letting them manage themselves, or what is called 'giving them their head.' It is but justice to Christ Church to say that in the then low state of our Public Exercises, the *private Examinations* at Christ Church had attained considerable efficiency under Dean Jackson's superintendence.

[2] The recent statute, which enables Noblemen to decline the privilege and costume of their rank, may certainly lead them to study and live like other young men 'by falling into the ranks;' it may also save them from being '*pillaged* and *preyed upon*' (*out of College* at least); but they might have been allowed, nay, required (spectaculi causâ and in return for this indulgence) to appear in their splendid gowns and caps in the Theatre at the Commemoration and on Royal visits. I may here mention, in the chain of my 'Recollections,' the customary attendance of the young Noblemen at St. Mary's in their full dress-gowns, at what were called the 'Court-days,' their servants robing them at the church-gate, and, after sermon, unrobing their impatient young masters. Those Court-day services and sermons have been authoritatively discontinued, excepting those on her Majesty's Accession. The rich gowns, however, and their wearers do not *show* on that occasion: loyalty now-a-days does not like display and ceremony.

He was all but idolised by Christ Church men, and the fact of their setting up his ponderous statue (I will not say to be worshipped) in the Cathedral is a standing proof of some such feeling [1]. One thing is certain, that 'Christ Church pride [2]' and Christ Church exclusiveness never ran so high as they did *regnante Cyrillo*. It was notorious that the young men of Christ Church (sufficiently elated by their position and numbers) were discouraged from forming acquaintances out of their own Society, and that no one was allowed to read with a private tutor of another College.

Of University sermons at Christ Church in my Undergraduate days I have but little recollection; I quite well, however, remember that the Dean's sermons were always well attended. Nor do I forget the apparent zest with which he *smacked his lips* (a peculiar action of his), as he once enunciated his text (first duly given in English) in what he called upon us to observe as '*the almost classical* Greek of St. James' (i. 8), Ἀνὴρ δίψυχος ἀκατάστατός ἐστι ἐν πάσαις ταῖς ὁδοῖς αὐτοῦ, 'A double-minded man is unstable in all his ways.' This was, I think, in 1803 [3].

---

[1] *Apropos* to statues (and Christ Church statues in particular) I may here introduce the leaden one of Mercury, which stood (on one foot) in the middle of the Tom-Quad. fountain, and was the subject of many practical jokes among the Undergraduates of the College. When the fountain was frozen over, Mercury sometimes appeared in the morning curiously adorned and arrayed. When however, on one occasion, the 'Messenger of the gods' left his pedestal and attached himself to the Dean's knocker with a saucy epistle in his hand, he was condemned as a nuisance, and sent to the plumber's to be melted down into some humbler but safer form.

[2] As it was *then* commonly called and classified at the head of various shades of Oxford pride.

[3] It was said that his brother, Dr. William Jackson, in an University sermon at Christ Church, gravely remarked (on some doctrine or other), 'St. Paul says so and so,—and *I partly agree with him!*'

The Dean and his brother, Dr. William Jackson, had each a share in the early education of George IV, and his brother the Duke of York. When offered a bishopric again and again, the Dean was reported to have added at last to his repeated 'Nolo episcopari,' 'Try Will,—he'll take it;' and so 'Will' did. Assuredly the royal pupils did no credit, nay, must have caused many a pang to the brother-tutors. Cyril Jackson was often called 'The Great Dean,' in comparison (it may be presumed) with some small ones before him. In the following little scene, however, he does not appear so very great:—

SCENE, Tom Quad. Time, 10 A.M.

Dean. 'Get on faster, can't you, Mason; we are late.'
Verger. 'Please, Mr. Dean, we are in very good time.'
Dean (after a few steps, as slow as ever). 'Get on, I say, Mason, you old fool.'
Verger. 'Old, if you please, Mr. Dean, but no fool.'
Dean (apologetic to the old Verger). 'Well, Mason, don't be affronted; but you must allow, you are the first of your family that ever wore a gown.'
Verger. 'No indeed, Sir, not by a good many.'
Dean. 'How so, Mason?'
Verger. 'Why, Sir, my mother wore one, and my grandmother too!'
(Tintinnabulus cessat; introit Decanus; Virgifer victor evadit.)

Dr. Jackson, after resigning his Deanery in 1809, lived in perfect retirement at Felpham, close to the sea, near Bognor. I once had the great pleasure of finding him there, having walked over from Littlehampton for the chance of seeing him. He was sitting very much as he is represented by his statue[1], but, of course, without the paraphernalia of his

---

[1] And by the fine painting of him (in the hall of Christ Church), from which Chantrey modelled the statue.

Doctor's gown and large wig. He was simply dressed as a fine, venerable old man, without anything decidedly clerical in his appearance; his large Oxford wig was replaced by a very simple, one-curled, *brown wig*, which was surmounted by a large, broad-brimmed, black straw-hat. He conversed with me for some time, showing a lively interest in the state of things at Oxford; I shall not soon forget the impression made by that interview. As he thus sat on a chair, placed for him near the edge of the low cliff and facing the sea, with his hands (one of them holding a golden snuff-box) clasped upon the top of his walking-stick, he looked greater and grander than I ever thought him (in his greatest and grandest days), when walking stately in 'Tom Quadrangle,' every cap (as was then the custom) being off the head, even of Tutors and Noblemen, while he was in sight[1].

Dr. Hall, who succeeded Cyril Jackson as Dean[2] of Christ Church in 1809, was a very handsome, clever man, and had been a distinguished tutor; he was a good preacher and a Bampton Lecturer. Having subsequently exchanged the Deanery of Christ Church for that of Durham, he was

---

[1] The only exception, curiously enough, applied to the Scouts, who were ordered by him to wear (and to *keep on*) a leathern fur-cap while in the quad., because he one day mistook and addressed a good-looking member of that class as one of his Undergraduates. Dr. Tatham, who was always opposed to Dr. Jackson, writes bitterly of him in one of his addresses to Convocation, in 1810: 'The great Choriphæus [of the Exam. Statute] is fled from the field of action; he has left a few sugar-plumbs (*sic*) which he could not take himself, in the mouths of his foremen.'

[2] I do not pretend to know what Dean it was, who (on receiving a civil but rather silly note to this effect, 'The *Dean of Oriel* presents his compliments to the *Dean of Christ Church*, and requests'—so and so) replied, '*Alexander the Great* sends greeting to *Alexander the copper-smith*, and'—so and so.

cut off by death before he had had time to benefit by the change.

Dr. Samuel Smith, the next Dean of Christ Church (in 1824), though an aboriginal Christ Church man, never seemed quite at home in his position; he was indeed highly respected, and under his Deanship Christ Church was not so stiff-starched as it had been; but (as the result showed) it was not a case of 'the right man in the right place.' At the end of seven years a negotiation[1] was successfully carried out, and Dr. Smith gave up the Christ Church Deanery and succeeded to the 'Golden Stall' at Durham; exchanging, that is, with Dr. Gaisford, who was supposed to long, not so much for the Deanery of Christ Church (which in twenty-four years of subsequent experience he found it hard work to manage), as for the Curatorship and use of the Bodleian Library and the superintendence of the University Press. And so, Oxford had the advantage of welcoming its great Greek scholar to a *permanent* residence,—the Regius Professorship of Greek[2], with its £40 a year, being now compensated by the £2000 of the Deanery.

---

[1] How such a *negotiation* is managed, and by whom, nobody (at least among the uninitiated) ever knows; it would seem to be done by a sort of Ministerial hocus-pocus, and *dealing out the cards* afresh. In other professions it would be called 'chopping and changing;' but when good comes of it (as it did in this case) who has a right to complain?

[2] Dr. Gaisford had already held that Professorship for twenty years; —he never indeed gave a single lecture, but satisfied his own conscience and (it seemed) the requirements of others, by his labours in connection with Greek authors. He had always a large *private* income, so that he could not, like Goldsmith's parson, be said to be

'passing rich on forty pounds a year.'

Dr. John Smith, Master of Pembroke College[1] (1796 to 1809), was distinguished among the 'Heads' of his day by having been a traveller, though I never heard that it was to any great extent. At all events, it was then confessedly rare in his class even to have 'crossed the water.' Dr. Smith never published his Travels, but he was said to have exercised so largely in society what is called 'the traveller's privilege' in relating and *embellishing* the stories of his travels, as to have gained the *sobriquet* of 'Sinbad the Sailor.'

Pembroke College, in size and appearance and as a place of education, was humble indeed in comparison with what it has become since Dr. Jeune became its Master.

---

[1] Until Pembroke College was, not many years since, new-fronted and enlarged, it was not very distinguishable from the old adjacent Almshouse, which gives a decent lodging (with a small weekly payment) to a half-dozen old men, whose qualification is to have served in the army. Some forty or fifty years ago the Christ Church Chapter, to whom the patronage belongs, resolved upon pulling down the building, which had been neglected, and was certainly in a disreputable state. *Notice to quit* was accordingly given to the occupants, whose number had been suffered *to die off*. One of them, however, a fine old Scotchman, named Carrick (who, after serving in the army, had been the old drill-sergeant of our Volunteer Corps), coolly resisted the Notice, reminding the Chapter that he held his place from the same source and by the same tenure* as they held theirs. The old Sergeant gained the day, and the Christ Church authorities wisely gave up the destructive for the restorative process. A building which was rapidly going to decay was made not only a comfortable asylum for the old almsmen, but *externally* as respectable a building as some of our Colleges and Halls.

* Peshall in his History of Oxford says, that 'Henry VIII, taking upon him to perfect Wolsey's College, settled also the number of almsmen to be 24, and each of them to have £6 pr. ann.—which,' he adds, 'continues to this day,'—i.e. 1775.

Dr. Berdmore, Warden of Merton College (from 1790 to 1810), led a very quiet, gentlemanly life in his fine old College, which was becoming, in his Wardenship, yearly more and more, not a provision and permanent residence for ecclesiastical students (as the Founder intended it), but a pleasant, occasional resort, a kind of Club-house (as All Souls had already become) for men of good family, with now and then a dash of military titles[1]. Dr. Berdmore himself was an estimable man. In the days of his predecessor, Warden Barton (a notorious punster[2]), he had been the subject of a practical witticism. Dr. Barton gave a dinner one day and invited Mr. Rook of his own College, Mr. Crowe of New College, Mr. Woodcock of Christ Church, and Mr. Partridge of Brasenose,—who, according to express invitation, were punctual at 5 o'clock. 'Well, Gentlemen,' said the elaborate wit, 'I think I have got almost "all the birds of the air," but we must wait a little for one *bird more.*' Mr. Berdmore had been purposely invited at 5.30[3].

Dr. Berdmore undertook the office of Vice-Chancellor, but gave it up after a year's trial, preferring (it may be pre-

[1] One Fellow died quite recently, having been for some years a General in the army.

[2] Punsters, or word-torturers, have never been wanting in Oxford. 'Terræ Filius' in 1726 gives what he calls a 'Supplement to the Oxford Jests,' and concludes with the following: 'The Rev. Dr. *Delaune* having lately preached an excellent sermon before the University against Hoadly the Bishop of Bangor, a Christ Church man observed, "that the Doctor was to be applauded; for (added he) the Bishop ought to be *de-lawn'd.*"'

[3] 'So, gentlemen, I hear that you are thinking of putting up an organ in our chapel,' said the same Warden to his Fellows; 'and if you do, I beg leave to say, "I'll *put a stop* to it."' N.B. This was not the College which having suppressed its choir at the Reformation and

sumed) his wonted ease to public duties. Things were lax enough at Merton in his days, but they became worse in those of his successor, Dr. Vaughan. The *ghost* of Walter de Merton might well be said to have appeared in the College; but whether it did or not, something of his *spirit* returned when Merton produced (or adopted) such men for Fellows as Messrs. Denison, Hamilton, Adams, Hobhouse, &c. Backed by their energy, Warden Marsham, a family-man as well as a man of family, in a few years saw his College restored to a state and reputation which, as the original pattern-College, it should never have lost; he has seen it become not only a valuable school of education by the election of first-rate men as Fellows and Tutors, but also a nursery for studious theologians and active parochial clergymen. May it so continue!

Dr. Ford, Principal of Magdalen Hall and Professor of Arabic, died in 1813, having been Principal twenty-five years. He had been Professor before he was made Head of the Hall, and was considered a good scholar[1] in that department. He did not, however, give many public signs of it while living, and left no proofs of it behind him. Having married a lady nearly connected with the then Bishop of Hereford, he was promoted to a Canonry in that Cathedral. Both the Doctor and his Lady were shrinkingly

---

transferred the fund from the chapel to the hall, was said 'to dine every day on its choristers.'

[1] Oriental learning (we are told) fell into disrepute after the Restoration; Pococke, the first Laudian Professor, fell ill at Oxford. The Arabic Professor at Cambridge, Dr. Castell in (1666), one day, *in a pleasant mood*, is said to have stuck this Notice on the School-door, ' Prælector linguæ Arabicæ cras ibit in desertum.'

shy, and of rather an un-English appearance. On one occasion, however, he was said to have exhibited English pluck and feeling, when he roughly turned out of his house a conceited young Curate of St. Peter's-in-the-East, who (without any previous acquaintance) called one morning on the Doctor and offered himself to him as a son-in-law, on the ground that 'Miss Ford had for some time *looked favourably* upon him at church[1]!'

Dr. Eveleigh, Provost of Oriel (who died in 1814), was a truly venerable 'Head;' very imposing in appearance with his large wig, his slow and solemn gait, his mild but rather melancholy countenance and his gown and cassock which he constantly wore. He had the reputation of great piety, and lived to see his College arrive at the highest pitch of reputation and success, in the persons of the Fellows (the 'cream of the University') and of the class-men who were the pupils of those Fellows. Corpus gave up to Oriel its best Scholars, Magdalen its Demies, and Christ Church its distinguished

---

[1] The Doctor's daughter was young, very pretty, and too modest and shy (like her parents) to have given cause for such impertinence. That Mrs. Ford was rather an odd character may be inferred from a little domestic incident, thus related to me by a gentleman: 'I was,' he said, 'one day in the market-place in the town of Ledbury, waiting to see the Oxford and Hereford coach change horses; and as I came up to the Inn-door, whom should I see suddenly drawing back into a corner of the coach but my friend, Mrs. Ford! Notwithstanding her evident wish not to be noticed, I looked in and said, "Dear me, Mrs. Ford, can it be you *returning* to Hereford, which you *left* but yesterday for Oxford? What *is* the matter?" "Oh!" she answered, "I am travelling *quite incog.*; please don't say at Oxford that you saw me,—for I am going back *upon the sly*, to fetch *all* my keys, a whole bunch,—which I unfortunately left behind at Hereford."'

Servitor[1], Mr. Davison, to swell the galaxy of talent and scholarship, which by this very process left other Colleges in comparative obscurity. Mention has already been made of the honourable fact, that Dr. Eveleigh shared with Dean Cyril Jackson and Dr. Parsons the labour of framing the first Public Examination Statute. He married the daughter of a former Provost, Dr. Clarke, and left one daughter, well provided for. Dr. Eveleigh was succeeded in the Headship by a great man (academically speaking), Dr. Copleston, afterwards Dean of St. Paul's and Bishop of Llandaff[2].

Dr. Isham, Warden of All Souls (from 1793 to 1817), was a fine, venerable-looking man[3], and that without the aid of a wig. He did not trouble himself with any academical matters beyond those of his own quiet, aristocratic College. That quiet repose was indeed striking and melancholy to any one who ventured within All Souls quadrangles;—there being no Undergraduates within the walls, except three or

---

[1] One Christ Church Servitor, *John Matthias Turner*, who 'gained the Honours' in 1804, was advised by the Oriel authorities not to offer himself (as he had intended) for an Oriel Fellowship, ' because his mother, a widow, *was in business* at no great distance from the College!' He consequently extended his views *beyond Oxford*, and, after an honourable career in private tutorship at Eton, went out as Bishop of Calcutta, where he died after a short episcopate.

[2] Dr. Eveleigh is further mentioned (in the chapter ' De Bedellis') in connection with the Terminal Latin Litany and Holy Communion.

[3] The portrait of him, hanging in the hall of his College, will testify to that;—being a good painting of a fine old man. All Souls College has of late undergone such changes of a serious kind, that it may well have dropped the absurd annual ceremony called ' The Mallard.' Hearne says, ' All Souls "*Mallard*" was kept as usual,—i. e. with a supper, and drinking all night,—and singing " The song of the Mallard!"'

four Bible-clerks, who were expected to eat their commons quietly, speak (when they did speak in the quadrangle) under their breath, and get a Degree *as they could*. Dr. Isham, like Dr. Berdmore, *tried* the office of Vice-Chancellor; but gave it up (as Dr. Berdmore had done) at the end of one year[1]! I have nothing farther to say of this fine, old, gentlemanly Head of a House, except the fact (which might in some measure account for his high bearing) that he was born, bred, lived, and died in the atmosphere of academical dignity; not only having lived to become the Warden of All Souls, but having been born, and, as it were, apprenticed to the business, in the 'Lodgings' of his father, Dr. Euseby Isham[2], Rector of Lincoln College;—a coincidence (or rather a sequence) which perhaps had never occurred before, except in the case of Dr. Samuel Fell, Dean of Christ Church in 1638, and his son Dr. John Fell, Dean in 1660.

Dr. Samuel Gauntlett was Warden of New College from 1794 to 1822. Of him, as my own Warden and kind patron, I must be allowed to write at some length. He was elected Warden, though the least popular of three candidates at the time of his election. After repeated meetings of the Fellows and as many unsatisfactory scrutinies (kept up till the last day, on which, if no election were made, the choice would have lapsed to the Visitor), the supporters of Messrs. Le Mesurier and Sismore, finding they could not gain the required

---

[1] And yet the duties of the office, towards the close of the last century, were not half so laborious as they have since become.

[2] Hearne tells us that this Rector of Lincoln, in *his early days* of Headship, told him 'that a fair offer of marriage had been made to him'—by a lady; and that his answer ('which he read to me') was 'that at present he was not inclined to alter his state of life.'

majority of the Fellows then present, finally voted for a third man, Dr. (then Mr.) Gauntlett, that they might at least disappoint their opponents' candidate. The event showed that, in spite of themselves, they had chosen the best man. He was indeed no great scholar, beyond the usual standard of Winchester men. Of his rivals, Mr. Le Mesurier was the most talented, and had taken orders after practising some years as a barrister[1]. He subsequently (i. e. in 1807) preached the 'Bampton Lectures,' and his discourses were, at least, remarkable for a vehement antagonism to (what for many years was called) 'Catholic Emancipation;' a vehemence which gained for him the patronage of the Bishop of Durham. Mr. Sismore retired upon a Fellowship at Winchester, which he held to extreme old age[2].

But to return to Dr. Gauntlett. On his election to the Wardenship he assumed 'the *big-wig*' (though of a moderate size[3]), and with his quiet and rather solemn deportment, looked, as he stood statue-like in the chapel, the beau-ideal of a Warden[4]. The only difference at morning and at evening service was, that at the latter the statue had a slight

---

[1] A transition more easily managed, and therefore more frequent, in those days than now.

[2] As a proof of a strange and perverted taste, it may be mentioned that the fine oak roof in the hall of New College was taken down, and a flat plastered ceiling substituted for it, near the end of the last century; and that Mr. Sismore to his dying day used to boast of his share in the work. 'Sir,' he would say, 'that elegant improvement was made " me consule"—when I was Bursar!' Seventy years afterwards a noble roof of oak was replaced.

[3] And that wig in his latter years gradually diminished in size.

[4] It used to be said, that he fixed his eyes on a particular stone of the chapel pavement on entering his stall and never removed them till the service ended. It was often found, however, that he did see what was passing, and very sharply too.

glow[1] on its face which was wanting in the morning. He was a fine, well-built man, indeed a good type of the then Oxford dignitary. His attendance at chapel was most exemplary; not because he liked choir-service or understood choral music (for he had no ear or taste for either), but because he was the only disciplinarian there in those lax times.

Dr. Gauntlett's knowledge of business and his attention to the management and improvement of the College estates were duly appreciated by the Society, and were attended with a great improvement in the value of the Fellowships[2]. The Warden was no theologian, but he sometimes took his turn to preach at St. Mary's.

After he had been Warden about twelve years, he bethought himself of marrying. Indeed his home and table must have been very solitary, as he had lost his old friends and cotemporaries in the College, and, except at an annual dinner, rarely invited any of the Society to his table. Having screwed up his courage to the change, he called to mind (it was said) an 'old love' in the person of a widow lady, the sister of one of his former cotemporaries[3]. Being himself a sensible, straightforward person, and judging the lady

---

[1] This glow (it is fair to add) was only the natural and genial accompaniment of a *post-prandian* chapel-service. [The dinner-hour then was 4.30 and the Service was at 6 p.m. The earliest College dinner-hour which I remember was at Christ Church, *at* 3 *p.m.*, where there was also a show of supper at 9. But that dinner-hour gradually became later, as the meal was often an unfrequented ceremony; and the hall supper, which had been for some time represented by a Servitor carrying up a single dish, was discontinued.]

[2] This improvement was not confined to the Warden's endowment and the income of the Fellows, but was liberally extended to other members of the Society.

[3] That cotemporary, Mr. Yaldon, was the last of the old set of

(from his former knowledge of her) to be the same, he is said to have written his proposal in a brief epistle, requesting a speedy answer—*Yes* or *No*. The answer in the affirmative duly arrived; the wedding soon took place; and New College (I may say Oxford society generally) received in Mrs. Gauntlett (accompanied by an amiable niece) the valuable addition of a most kind-hearted, unaffected lady. Being herself genial and hospitably social, she soon made her husband, to a certain extent, the same.

Warden Gauntlett, during his Headship of 27 years, though an occasional attendant at the Hebdomadal Board, and likely enough to have spoken his mind there with sturdy honesty, never gained any notoriety out of his own College [1]:

Fellows who (not liking the then newly-introduced luxury of Turkey carpets) often adjourned to smoke their pipe in a little room opposite to the Senior Common-room, now appropriated to other uses, but then kept as a smoking-room. Had he lived *to our days* he might have company in his ' cloud-compelling ' enjoyment (as Dr. Parr called it); though he would find his favourite bowling-green now turned into an archery-ground.

It was in the time of Warden Coxhead (Hearne tells us) that a door was made out of his Lodgings into the Lane—' a thing,' he adds, ' much taken notice of!'

[1] Indeed it was *then* a striking feature of that College (Warden, Fellows, and Scholars) to shut themselves up very much within their own Society, not troubling themselves with other bodies or taking much interest in University matters. This was chiefly, though not entirely, the natural result of their clinging proudly, but not wisely, to their privilege of *private College Examination* for the Degree of B.A. An auxiliary cause was the habit of treating each other and thinking of each other as still school-fellows, if not school-boys. Having then no Commoners (and only an occasional Gentleman-Commoner), and moving all pretty much in the same Winchester *groove*, they did not keep pace with the stirring improvements in the education and studies of the place. The *Wykehamical pride of scholarship*, excusable in former days, was now satisfied with an occasional prize for Latin Verse.

nor did he make any effort to rouse his Society from the lethargy that was spreading through it, or to sweep away the cloud which was yearly growing darker and thicker by comparison with the atmosphere without, which was becoming brighter and clearer. There was plenty of *Classical scholarship* in the College, perhaps more than in most other Colleges at that time; but there was nothing more, except in name. It required, therefore, more stirring energy and a higher appreciation of science than Dr. Gauntlett possessed, to work a change and free his College from the fetters of its cherished '*privilege.*'

That privilege had been properly given to Wykeham, because his College, with the previous advantage of his famous School, then stood much higher in grammatical and classical knowledge (the only knowledge then valued) than the rest of the University. But now a change had come over the studies of Oxford; the Tutors of the other Colleges had awaked from their slumber. But the state of things remained unchanged at New College till *Warden Shuttleworth* (Dr. Gauntlett's successor)—himself a man of talent, with a philosophic mind and a vast fund of general information—succeeded in rousing his College to the necessity of a change, and persuaded them to drop their privilege and *go into the Schools* for a Public Examination [1].

---

[1] The privilege of taking the Degree without '*Supplicating* the Grace of the House' (as men of other Colleges do) is still retained in the case of Scholars or Fellows of New College,—having, I suppose, never been *formally relinquished*. Indeed the *privileged* Examination was never (quoad Academiam) FORMALLY relinquished: the only change was, that about 1838 New College men quietly put down their names (like other men) in the Examination List, and went into the Schools to get their Testamur. The wisdom of evading the 'Supplicatio' after dropping the *essential* privilege of a private Examination (with which it was origi-

Dr. Gauntlett, however, quitted the scene before any such '*innovations*' were introduced. But it is time to end this long Reminiscence of one to whose patronage I have been so much indebted.

Dr. Winstanley was Principal of St. Alban Hall from 1796 to 1823, during which period it could hardly be called a place of education, there being seldom more than a couple or two of members resident at the same time, and they generally Gentlemen-Commoners, in statu (sed non ætate) pupillari. Dr. Winstanley early in life married a daughter of Mr. Blenkinsop, Clerk of the Schools, and by so doing vacated a Fellowship in *Hertford College* of the value of £15 a year! 'Hertford College!' (an Undergraduate will say); 'Where in the world is that?' I answer, 'It *is* nowhere, but it once actually *was*, and stood where Magdalen Hall now stands, but on a somewhat smaller scale.' At the beginning of the last century *Hart Hall* was rather flourishing *as a Hall*, but it had the misfortune to get an ambitious man, Dr. Newton[1], for its Principal. He must have been an influential as well as an ambitious man, to succeed, as he did, in getting his Hall changed[2] into a College. Of course

nally coupled, and of which it was the crown and supplement) is not very apparent.

[1] Hearne says, 'The four Fellows were endowed by Dr. Newton (commonly said to be *founder-mad*) with £60 among the four.' See Dr. Bliss's Reliquiæ Hearnianæ, p. 844.

[2] On this weak peg (Hertford College) I venture to hang rather a long note (and that a tardy one) on a question already settled and about a name already given. I cannot, however, withhold the expression of wonder that the building in honour of the venerated John Keble should have been called a *College* and not a *Hall*. 'Keble College,' I allow, sounds better (by a quasi alliteration) than 'Keble Hall;' but is it, in the usual meaning of the word *at and in Oxford*, really what it is called?

he was required to endow it, which he did by founding three

Out of Oxford any large building or Institution, where numbers are *collected*, may be (and in very many instances is) called a College; but *at Oxford*, where the distinction between a College and a Hall has always been so decidedly marked and kept up, is this tacit assumption quite fair and honest?

It is well known that many of our Colleges (e. g. University, Balliol, and Oriel) grew out of Halls; and by what process? By incorporation, Statutes, and endowment. Tutors or Teachers became Fellows, Students became Scholars, Scholars looked forward to Fellowships, Tutors to a College living, and all were kept in order by a body of Statutes. *Our Halls*, as distinguished from Colleges, are placed under the governance of the University by what are called the 'Statuta Aularia;' will the Keble Institution, by calling itself a *College*, be exempt from that superintendence? Or am I writing in the dark, while all the time a code of Statutes is prepared, Fellows and Scholars are to be elected and endowed, and preferment or retiring pensions to be provided for worn-out Tutors? I hope it may be so.

Pembroke and Worcester are Halls expanded into Colleges; but in becoming so they started with a goodly array of Fellows, Scholars, and some (though at first not much) Church patronage in prospect. Even when Hart Hall set up to be Hertford College, Dr. Newton not only gave it a code of stringent Statutes, but also, to constitute its collegiate character, endowed it with a small body of Fellows. It was done, indeed, ineffectually, and no wonder it came to nothing.

All this, and more than this, has possibly been weighed and considered by the managers of the Keble Fund, but this question has never, I believe, been *publicly* ventilated ; certainly not a word on the subject was uttered at the grand meeting in our Theatre in 1867. Like every one else, I contributed my mite, this scruple not having then occurred to me. Keble College will be 'Keble College,' and will do its work, I trust, in a manner worthy of its name; but still—

> There's a difference not small
> 'Tween a College and a Hall,
>   And I'll tell you the reasons why;
> A Hall has got no Fellows
> ('Tis an organ without bellows),
>   And that is one reason why.

or four Fellowships with an annual income of £15[1]. Even

> Then its Tutors' stinted number,
> Whom so many will encumber,
>   Is a second good reason why;
> They'll be cheer'd by no Foundation,
> No *domus*—no expectation
>   Of a *living* before they *die*.
>
> The claims then are but feeble
> Of the building rais'd to Keble,
>   (That name so great and so high!)
> Though rich in worth and knowledge,
> A *Hall* is not a *College;*
>   And these are the reasons why.
>
> In science, knowledge, art,
> A *dwarf* may take his part,
>   But no *giant* is he, though he try;
> Whate'er its title, strive there
> To keep that name alive there,
>   And ask no further reasons why.

---

[1] Dr. Newton had three successors, Dr. Sharp, Dr. Durell, who held the office of Vice-Chancellor (never obtained by Dr. Newton), and Dr. Hodgson, on whose decease no one would accept the poor Headship*, with its beggarly foundation,—loaded, too, with absurd oaths and impracticable duties. Mr. Hewett, one of the Fellows, constituted himself Vice-Principal;—a solicitor, named Roberson, introduced himself and his family into the Principal's 'Lodgings,' at first by sufferance, on the plea of keeping the place decent, but not long after assumed a quasi 'right of possession,' with no one to say 'Nay.' Emboldened by his example, other persons took possession of rooms, and strange characters they were;—as if being 'half-cracked' were a qualification for admission! In short, it became such a nuisance, that the University authorities assumed the power of shutting up poor Hertford College. Indeed, a

---

* In most Colleges in Oxford it is said that a Headship is equal (in emolument) to three Fellowships: according to this standard the Headship of Hertford College would be £45 a year! To this, however, would be added a varying profit from the rent of rooms, never very numerous,—the best of them forming the Principal's Lodgings.

that small number was seldom filled. After Dr. Winstanley no names occur but those of two Fellows, named Hewett and Carpenter, clever, odd men, but both considered to be '*half-cracked*.'

But to return to Dr. Winstanley and St. Alban Hall. He had been Camden Professor of Ancient History ever since 1790, and at the death of Dr. White (who held the Hebrew Professorship with the Laudian Chair of Arabic) Dr. Winstanley (in 1814) succeeded to the latter also. That he discharged the duties of his two Professorships we may take for granted; the fact that he ever had a class does not come within my 'Recollections;' but I do remember that, though himself a remarkably plain, pur-blind old man, he had a daughter with a lovely face, classic features, and a *perfect figure* [a 'syllogism in A.A.A.' an eminent logician called

part of it,—a lath and plaster building (of considerable height and containing at least a dozen sets of rooms),—fell down one morning with a great crash and a dense cloud of dust. In one of those sets *Charles Fox* had resided, and from his window would sometimes address an Oxford mob*;—so at least it was traditionally affirmed in Hertford College. Next to shutting up the late College, came the idea of disposing of its site and ruins; and this was soon effected by giving them up to Magdalen College, as a place to which that Society might (by obtaining an Act of Parliament) transfer *old* Magdalen Hall, which had long been found to be 'nimium vicina' to the College. This was carried into execution in 1822, and the *new* Magdalen Hall now stands and flourishes where the ambitious but weak Hertford College had sunk into early but utter decay. No heir-at-law claiming the property, the little chapel and some sets of rooms were given up to Magdalen Hall; and what is called 'The *Hertford* or University Scholarship' was founded (in 1834) with the remaining money, by Letters Patent from the Crown, to whom it had lapsed.

* I think that the author of the Oxford novel, 'Reginald Dalton,' goes too far in speaking of a tradition, that 'Fox jumpt out of that window to join a Town-and-Gown row!'

her]. The old gentleman's heavy form and seeming dulness were forgotten by the side of the elegant daughter, who regularly walked out with him.

The house or 'Lodgings' in which they resided at St. Alban Hall formed but a poor *family*-dwelling; and though it served pretty well for Dr. Winstanley's immediate successor (the learned, amiable, but *unmarried* '*Peter Elmsley*[1]') during his short residence of only two years, it was condemned and replaced by a new house by Dr. Elmsley's successor, Dr. (afterwards Archbishop) Whately.

The Camden Professorship seems to have had a prescriptive connection with the Headship of St. Alban Hall in the persons of Dr. Winstanley, Dr. Elmsley and Dr. Cardwell, who for many years gave lectures in that character. It is sad, while writing this (in 1861), that I should have to add his name to the number of those whom death has taken from Oxford in the midst of their usefulness[2].

[1] Dr. Elmsley, after many years' absence (during which he had gained the highest reputation as a Greek scholar), found himself quite in his element on his return to Alma Mater, her libraries, her learned press, and her literary society. He at once won all hearts by his kind manner and charming conversation. Unfortunately, from neglect of exercise and from studious habits in the midst of good living, he had become excessively corpulent. He died in 1825, having held the Headship of the Hall and the Camden Professorship but two years.

[2] With Dr. Cardwell was supposed to expire an office (that of 'Secretary to the Chancellor of the University') which had no apparent duties and was without any statutable recognition; but which, from *traditionally allowed* fees (from Chancellor's Letters in connection with M. A. Degrees), had been worth considerably more than £300 a year. In the New Table of Fees (drawn up in Michaelmas Term, 1855) the office was so far recognised as to *limit* the payment of the fees 'Secretario, qui nunc est, Cancellarii,' that Secretary being Dr. Wynter of St. John's.

N. B. This nominal office has since been revived; the income, however, is limited to £100 a year, and granted to the Secretary of the *Chancellor* 'qui nunc est,' [eheu! qui fuit—Oct. 1869.]

Dr. Blackstone, Principal of New Inn Hall, after holding the Headship for thirty-seven years as a perfect sinecure (himself generally non-resident, without a single member on the books but himself), at length in 1831, after repeated and strong hints, both public and private, resigned the appointment. He was a layman and a lawyer; nay, the Vinerian Professor of Common Law. He resided in a large house close to Woodstock, where he transacted the business of law-manager and adviser to the Duke of Marlborough, and curator of the vast property. Dr. Blackstone was, no doubt, a good lawyer and an accomplished man; but he seems to have supported his reputation pretty much on being the son of the great lawyer and writer upon law, Sir Wm. Blackstone. Like him he had been — 1st, Fellow of All Souls; 2ndly, Principal of New Inn Hall; and 3rdly, Viner's Law Professor; in which last character Judge Blackstone had delivered the course of lectures which are said to have formed the basis of his famous Commentaries.

Dr. Blackstone, on resigning the Hall, was succeeded by *Dr. Cramer,* who laboured hard to make it a place of education. He actually built a few sets of rooms, and one large room to serve (like that at St. Alban Hall[1]) for chapel,

[1] This complication has been since corrected at St. Alban Hall by the erection of a pretty little chapel; but not (it is said) without getting into a new complication, the chapel, small as it is, being partly (I suppose inadvertently) built on ground belonging to Merton College, which seems to be only waiting for a pretext to absorb the little Hall on condition of building it elsewhere.—[A small chapel has lately been added to New Inn Hall also.]

The close connection of the following anecdote with the locality of New Inn Hall tempts me to borrow it from Sir Travers Twiss's ' Life of Lord Eldon,' vol. i. p. 87:—' I had a walk one day in New Inn Hall garden in company with Dr. Johnson, Sir Robert Chambers (then Principal of the Hall), and some other gentlemen. Sir Robert was

hall, and lecture-room. From his connection with Ch. Ch. (where he had been Student and Tutor) he was, for a time, supplied with some of their overflowings, in the shape of *fast* (and sometimes *slow*) men, who wanted severally either more liberty or more patient help than Ch. Ch. Censors could afford to them; both of which were supposed to be found in a Hall[1]. New Inn Hall seems never to have been a very flourishing place; and as for making money there by *recoining* the dross from other Societies, the very thought reminds one of the use which Charles I made of this very Hall when he established in it a *Mint*, supplied by the plate *sent thither from the Colleges* to be melted down and *new cast* into coin for his Majesty's service.

Dr. Cramer was Public Orator as well as Principal of the Hall. His learned book upon Ancient Italy, with its elaborate maps, remains as a proof of his scholarship; it was, however, sixteen years before he was promoted to a better and more dignified post, by his appointment to the Deanery of Carlisle; and when now fairly on the road to still higher preferment, his earthly career was stopped by death.

gathering up snails and throwing them over the wall into his neighbour's garden. The Doctor reproached him very roughly, and stated to him that this was unmannerly and unneighbourly. "Sir (said Sir Robert), my neighbour is a Dissenter." "Oh! (said the Doctor) if so, Chambers, toss away, toss away as hard as you can."' It is to be hoped that the pious Lexicographer was more than half in jest.

[1] Now and then too a plucked-man was admitted, who wished to rearrange his ruffled plumage, and, having 'learnt his lesson better' in this 'locus pœnitentiæ,' to *try again*. I believe it is a rule at most of the *Colleges*, that if a young man fails twice in the same School, he is expected to *leave;* with, of course, a ' bene decessit,' i. e. a *good riddance*. I once heard a benevolent lady, under a strong sense of pity for unsuccessful examinées, express a wish that she was rich enough to endow a special Hall or College, to be called Dull-boys' College or Try-again Hall.

Dr. Tournay was Warden of Wadham from 1806 to 1831. On the death of Dr. Wills he was said to have been *invited*[1] by his Society (where he had been Fellow and Tutor) to return to them as Warden. It was considered to be a good and judicious choice, as he had private funds, good connections, and an active, stirring mind, with a knowledge of the world picked up beyond the College walls of Oxford. Wadham certainly made a start under his government, which it has since well maintained. The Warden's 'Lodgings' are so implicated with the architecture of the College (which, simple and unpretending, consists of large but low rooms, with small windows), that even Dr. Tournay, with all his zeal for improvements and his readiness to find funds, left them much as he found them. Indeed, as a *Bachelor Head* he had ample accommodation,—much better certainly than the set of rooms over the College gateway, which, it is said, were assigned by Dorothy Wadham to the first Warden, and intended for his successors. Dr. Tournay[2] having a great taste for landscape-gardening, soon attacked what was then a close or field, extending from the College to the Parks, and, at a considerable expense, formed the beautiful and extensive grounds and garden which are so well kept up by his successor[3]. I have spoken of Dr. Tournay as

[1] This sort of amiable arrangement does not very often occur at the filling-up of a Headship. Such matters are, of course, generally kept secret (at least for a time), and, *after* much and earnest competition, an unanimous election is reported. A single vote, however, is said to have turned the scale now and then.

[2] One of Warden Tournay's first improvements (and a very great one it was) consisted in the entire removal of an ugly, damp sort of terrace (partly surrounded with a wall and scrubby trees) in front of the College,—resembling, but upon a smaller scale, that which is still in front of St. John's College, and, in proportion, narrowing the road.

[3] One striking feature of the garden was entirely created by Warden

a bachelor, i.e. an unmarried man; and, in fact, he could not, according to the College Statutes, be otherwise. Though founded *after the Reformation* (viz. in 1613), celibacy was imposed upon the Wardens[1]. Against this narrow-minded restriction Warden *Tournay* undertook a generous *tourna-ment*. I say '*generous*,' because I believe that he never intended himself to introduce a wife into his Wadham Lodgings, even if the oaths on which he had been admitted did not exclude him from the privilege.

As the Heads of the old foundations had been relieved from a compulsory celibacy by Act of Parliament (or at least by a Protestant construction of the '*priesthood*' in which they were included), the same power was sought for and obtained by the Warden of Wadham. In order, however, to do the thing quietly, as well as effectually, the permission for the *future Wardens* to marry was said to have been tacked on, as a 'rider,' and passed through Parliament as an appendage, to an Oxford *Turnpike Bill!* Dr. Tournay declined the office of Vice-Chancellor, confining his public services to the duties of ' Curator of the Public Walks.' In that character, riding about on his pretty cob, he planned and superintended the formation of several of the road-side walks (now so valuable for our Tutors' 'constitutionals '),

---

Tournay, viz. the long terrace-walk on the east side, on which, till his health failed him, he was often seen taking his walk.

[1] As an *after-thought*, according to traditionary report, and because the *first* Warden would not respond to Dorothy's wishes to be the first *Wardeness*. She had survived her husband, Nicholas Wadham, and had full powers as co-foundress. However this may have been, in her anxiety for the purity of one sex and her jealous distrust of the other, she enacted that no females were to be suffered in the College: the laundress was not, on any account, to advance with her linen-baskets beyond the College-gateway!

THE UNIVERSITY COURT. 197

and particularly the pretty, winding path up *the back* of Headington Hill[1].

Dr. Tournay resigned the Wardenship in 1831, and resided in St. Giles's Street for several years before his death, which took place after a few hours' illness at Peterborough[2].

[1] On this occasion the joke was applied to him which many years before had been applied to the Rev. 'Jo. Pullen' (when he planted the elm-tree, still called by his name, and formed the foot-path up *the front* of the same hill), viz. 'that he had made a way [away] with the public-money.' Mr. Pullen's name was Josias, not Joseph. Pullen's foot-path was made by a general subscription in 1740.

[2] As a concluding note on *Heads of Houses*, it may be observed that they had not always such an appropriate room as what is called 'The Delegates' Room' to assemble in. Laud fitted up for them (and for the University Court) what is called the Apodyterium. *Where* they met (*if they did meet as a governing body*) before that, is not, I believe, known. They had individually, in their respective Colleges, what a Cambridge wag called 'a *Commination* Room,' in which Undergraduates were received to be reprimanded. As a proof that Heads of Houses formerly considered themselves to be a separate class, it was said that one of them was one day thrown from his horse in St. Giles's Street, and that as he lay on his back he cried out to an Undergraduate, who ran up to help him, 'Sir, I won't trouble you; I see the President of St. John's coming, and he will raise me up.'

CHAPTER VIII.

'Majus opus moveo.'—*Virgil.*

Recollections of Vice-Chancellors.

THE list of Vice-Chancellors in the 'Oxford University Calendar' begins with Dr. Landon in 1802. Surely it might just as well have been commenced at as early a period as that of the Chancellors, High Stewards, Heads of Colleges, and Professors. This might have been done (and in future Calendars may still be done) at the expense of a little research into the University Archives[1].

I have a faint reminiscence of Dr. Isham (of All Souls)

---

[1] Since this remark was written that omission has been amply filled up in Messrs. Parker's Ten Year Book, the list of Vice-Chancellors there commencing in 1568. As the subject of Chapter VII was introduced by an expression of the writer's deep reverence and respect, so the heading of this Chapter seems to suggest still greater caution in approaching such high-fenced ground. As however the latest of the individuals here mentioned is separated from us (at the time of writing this) by an interval of *thirty years*, the statement of a few 'Recollections' during thirty or forty years *before that interval* may well be allowed,— honourable as they are to their memories; especially as they are associated with much that is academically interesting and historically important.

and Dr. Berdmore (of Merton) successively filling the Vice-Chancellor's seat at St. Mary's, each for one year only,—towards the end of the last century, between the Vice-Chancellorship of Dr. Cooke[1] of Corpus and that of Dr. Marlow, whose quadriennium of office began in Michaelmas Term 1798. My first *clear 'Recollection'* of a dignified person, walking behind gold and silver staves, begins with Dr. Marlow, passing with his full attendance to read the Riot Act (or, at least, to be present at its reading) on Carfax, on occasion of what were then called 'bread-riots[2].' My next recollection of Dr. Marlow, as Vice-Chancellor was on my being matriculated at his Lodgings early in 1802. Before and after his Vice-Chancellorship (for the Vice-Chancellor is exempted from his preaching-turns as Head of a House) Dr. Marlow's sermons were considered sound and earnest discourses; but *they* alone were not thought to have gained for him his Stall at Canterbury. The University of Oxford had then the good fortune to have a Prime Minister (the Duke of Portland) for its Chancellor, and the four-years' Vice-Chancellorship was often followed by promotion to a Stall or a Deanery. Mrs. Marlow (for the transition from

---

[1] I had, of course, no official connection with Dr. Cooke, excepting, once (and in an irregular way) when, in the Long Vacation of 1806, or thereabout, no Vice-Chancellor or Pro-Vice being to be found, *we of the Staff* got 'old Dr. Cooke' to fill the Vice-Chancellor's seat at St. Mary's! though in strictness he had no more *right* to sit there than any other Doctor. Dr. Cooke was then, and for many years afterwards, highly respected; his little parlour at C.C.C. was for a long period the regular place of meeting for the County Magistrates on Saturdays;—the 'County Court' with all its conveniences having then no existence.

[2] I had often seen tumultuous proceedings in our Oxford Streets, at first political and revolutionary; latterly, in connection with the high price of bread, when a mouldy loaf was carried about upon a pole, and the bakers' shops occasionally cleared out by *non-paying customers*.

Don to Donna is easy and natural) was very musical, and as she sometimes entertained persons of first-rate musical talent as her guests, it was a great treat to be present at her musical parties. She was a good, kind-hearted woman, and did a great many kind and liberal things both at Oxford and at Canterbury; but, from an unfortunately stiff carriage in society, she was sometimes styled 'the Duchess of Freezeland.' On becoming a widow, she retired to private life at Bath, where for some years she was better understood and more justly appreciated[1].

Dr. Landon, Provost of Worcester College, succeeded Dr. Marlow (in 1802) as Vice-Chancellor. Indeed, they were old friends and brother sportsmen (as far as shooting went to form that character), and occasionally, in autumn, doffed their don's robes and donned their shooting-jackets[2]. Dr. Landon was a handsome, burly man, with a remarkably fine, rich-toned voice and impressive manner. Indeed, he

---

[1] As has been said elsewhere in these 'Recollections,' the wives of all the Oxford *dignitaries* were not necessarily *dignified*. One individual certainly was not, who, intoxicated by her elevation, wrote thus to her cousin in the country-town she had left: 'La! my dear, don't talk of what we were at ——; at Oxford, I do assure you, *we* are *little kings and queens*!'

[2] But not 'upon the sly,' as was said of Dr. Holmes; who having acquired a taste for shooting while Fellow of New College, sometimes *took a day* at Stanton Woods, when Canon of Christ Church. Unwilling to shock the starch-stiffness of the Christ Church of those days (i.e. about the end of the last century), he would walk up Headington Hill with his gown, &c. over his shooting dress, [there were no Hansom cabs at that time], and under the shelter of Jo. Pullen's tree (ulmi sub tegmine grati) put off the canonicals, take his gun, hat, and dog from a servant in waiting, and trudge on to the forest. Whether he reversed the ceremony on his return, and marched down the hill to the tune of 'cedant arma togæ,' the story does not say.

had been musically as well as classically educated in the Cathedral School at Worcester, and could take his part, as a very effective bass, in a glee or madrigal. I used to wonder that, when Vice-Chancellor, he never *chanted* the latter part of the Latin Litany at St. Mary's [as the late lamented Dr. Williams did in 1856 and 1857], but conformed to the custom of *reading* it, established by non-musical Vice-Chancellors[1].

I received my gold staff from his hands on being elected

---

[1] I do not presume to say much of our *Chancellors*. During my first three years of office the Duke of Portland was Chancellor; but, though his *name* rang in my ears every Degree-day in what were called 'Chancellor's Letters,' and in the Bidding-prayer on Sundays at St. Mary's, my eyes never had the satisfaction of seeing him. He did not often visit the University.

Lord Grenville, his successor, was the proudest-looking man I ever saw; indeed he seemed cold and unbending even to 'great people.' At the exciting occasion of the grand assemblage of 'Crowned Heads' at Oxford (in 1814), when, as Chancellor, he had in some respects *to do the honours*, his bearing was less gracious and more starched than that of our Royal Visitors[*].

Not so the Duke of Wellington, who, with so much to be proud of, never seemed to know what pride was. Lord Grenville looked as if he could not laugh (or, at least, thought it infra dignitatem Cancellarii); the fine old Duke seemed always ready for a laugh. 'Mr. Vice-Chancellor,' he said, one day, as we were waiting at St. James's for a summons to her Majesty's presence, 'sit down, sit down; the rule at Court is *to sit when you can;* you're sure to have plenty of standing;'—and he laughed heartily as if he felt he had said a good thing. And so indeed he had. But such familiar talk and natural carriage would have been out of character in Lord Grenville.

The Earl of Derby —— Sed de vivis, quamvis facile et jucundum loqui, melius et tutius est tacere.—[Alas! though since dead, he still lives and will live in Oxford memories. Oct. 1869.]

[*] 'I recollect (says Lord Eldon) Mr. Pitt saying, with some indignation, he would teach *that proud man*, Lord Grenville, [in the formation of his Ministry in 1804,] that he could do without him.' (Twiss, vol. i. p. 449.)

Esquire Bedel in March 1806; and during the remainder of his Vice-Chancellorship formed one in the procession which (when Beaumont Street did not exist) had to grope its way from Worcester College to St. Mary's or to Convocation (even on the Commemoration-day) through 'Gloucester Green' (then the *acknowledged* site of the pig-market) and down the whole length of 'Friar's Entry;'—and this, at the risk of being besprinkled by trundled *mops* in those straits of Ther*mop*ylæ (as we always called them), of stumbling over buckets, knocking over children, of catching the rinsings of basins, and ducking under linen-lines suspended across from the opposite houses. This is no exaggeration of the state of things, 'quæ—ipse miserrima vidi,' and which could not always be passed through salvâ dignitate. No wonder that saucy Undergraduates of other Colleges sometimes spoke of Worcester College as *out of Oxford*, before Beaumont Street was formed.

Dr. Landon sometimes preached at St. Mary's, and I find in an old memorandum-book the following passage from a sermon of his: 'In all matters of *worldly* wisdom pretensions to extraordinary powers and new discoveries are generally regarded with doubt and suspicion. The exact contrary to this is the case with respect to religious knowledge. To start some new opinion or to assume a strikingly different manner from that of the established clergy is a sufficient lure for the gaping vulgar. This indeed has been confessed by one of the leaders of the Dissenters. Though the ministers of the establishment (he says) should preach like angels, they would excite but feeble interest among their flock; but tell them " yonder is a man preaching on the tops of mountains," and they will run in droves to hear him [1].'

---

[1] This is very like what Dr. Johnson said of Whitfield: 'His popu-

Having, after his Vice-Chancellorship, obtained a Stall at Norwich (afterwards exchanged for the Deanery of Exeter), Dr. Landon, for awhile, divided his time between his College and his Cathedral duties. Unfortunately he broke one of his legs, or received some injury which caused permanent lameness; and being thus altered from a fine, erect man (the beau-ideal of a dignitary), he seldom left Oxford, and was seen there only when taking an airing in his carriage. He died in 1839.

Dr. Henry Richards, Rector of Exeter College [1], was the next Vice-Chancellor to Dr. Landon. He held the office but one year (1806), having (as is elsewhere mentioned) caught a cold, from which he never recovered, on attending a Grand-Compounder's procession. As he died while in office, he was buried with much pomp in Exeter College Chapel. He was rather a rough, undignified person, and his domestic arrangements were not (it may be supposed) of a very refined character, he having married a daughter of a former cook of the College [2].

larity, Sir, is chiefly owing to the peculiarity of his manner. He would be followed by crowds were he to wear a night-cap in the pulpit, or were he to preach from a tree.' (Boswell.)

[1] Not to be confounded with Dr. J. Loscombe Richards, subsequently Rector of the same College.

[2] The taste for marrying a College-cook's daughter was not confined to Dr. Richards; the Head of another College did the same, or nearly the same. What the *Professors* of those days did in that way I do not recollect; a deputy-Professor, who afterwards rose very high on the Episcopal Bench, was said to have married a milliner at Woodstock. No doubt his lawn sleeves were well looked after. Dr. Nares too went to Woodstock for a wife, but she (as if to adjust the Professorial balance) was a Duke's daughter! Dr. Richards, during his short tenure of office, had occasion to go up to St. James's with an Address; in 'A Companion to The Guide' (published in 1806) there is a Latin

Dr. Parsons, Master of Balliol College (from 1798 to 1819), succeeded to the office of Vice-Chancellor (in 1807) earlier than he expected, but at all points well prepared; being highly qualified for the government of the University and for presiding over its counsels. He was a good scholar and an impressive preacher, though he did not preach often; above all, he was thoroughly conversant with University matters, having been for several years the leading, or rather the working, man in the Hebdomadal Board. Indeed, he had the great merit of elaborating the details of the Public Examination Statute at the end of the last century. His subsequent promotion to the Episcopacy of Peterborough was considered as the well-earned reward of that his great work. Dr. Parsons had also the credit of laying the foundation of that collegiate and tutorial system which Dr. Jenkyns afterwards so successfully carried out, and which bears such good fruit at Balliol under Dr. Scott. Although one of the chief authors of the great reform (the Examination Statute), Dr. Parsons fought manfully against 'innovations.' On the 'Catholic Emancipation' question, which was annually stirred up and petitioned against in Convocation, he sturdily declared that 'his opinion on the question was not in the least influenced by the eloquence of Dr. Copleston or the rhetoric of Dr. Hodson.' Like many other D.D.'s of that

poem called 'Syllabus Pietatis Oxoniensis,' in which occurs an account of a Delegacy to the King, e. g.

> 'Jam sumus en! Londini,
> Parate paulum vini;
> Haustu medico vini sumpto,
> Omnes togas induunto.
> Magister Vice-Can. præcedit,
> Et coram rege versus legit.'

I have only this short extract; but if it were all like this, the *poem* does not appear to have deserved even this 'Recollection.'

period, Dr. Parsons was very often interrupted in his official duties by attacks of the gout[1], when he was nursed by a good wife (an Oxford native, like her husband), who long survived him.

It is an incident, or rather a co-incidence, worth remarking, that while Dr. Parsons was Vice-Chancellor of the University, his brother, Mr. Herbert Parsons, the highly-respected Banker, was the Mayor of the City; he declined the offer of a Baronetcy which was pressed upon him. Dr. Parsons, after holding the office of Vice-Chancellor three years, was (in 1810) promoted to the bishopric of Peterborough, retaining with it the Headship of Balliol College[2].

Dr. Cole, Rector of Exeter, was the next Vice-Chancellor (in 1810). From his rubicund face and rotund figure he was considered,—at least in the young men's gallery in the Theatre,—to be like his *royal namesake*. In fact, he had served for some time as a chaplain in the Navy, and under excitement (even in a certain solemn place[3] of meeting) he was said to have occasionally enforced his sentiments by the introduction of strong, nautical language. Having held

---

[1] Those of the dignitaries who kept off the gout, did so by a regular jog-trot ride (sometimes called a 'bile-trot'); but Dr. Parsons was never seen on horseback.

[2] Before we take leave of Balliol, let me observe that a tradition existed in Oxford in my early days, that the handsome portrait of Devorguilla, the co-foundress of the College [in the Bodleian Gallery], is not genuine, but that the wife of an Oxford tradesman sat for it in the last century. That of the founder labours under a similar suspicion. Who indeed would vouch for the genuine character of half the portraits in the Picture Gallery?

[3] It was indeed whispered that in that solemn place disputes would sometimes run very high. Constituted as the new Council now is, there is no fear of undignified explosions or jarring personalities.

the Vice-Chancellorship (a *ship* which, with able support, he steered very successfully) for the full period of four years, Dr. Cole was succeeded by Dr. Lee.

Dr. Lee, President of Trinity, went through his quadriennium of office (from 1814 to 1818), like his predecessor, in calm, easy-going days, and in an amiable, unobtrusive manner;—so unobtrusive indeed, as to leave no prominent incident on my memory[1]. In his private and College life he was highly esteemed: he also played a steady second-violin part in a quartett. Before he became President he had long resided on an incumbency at Ipswich, and was married to a native of that town.

Dr. Frodsham Hodson, Principal of Brasenose College, who, in 1818, came next as Vice-Chancellor, was in many respects a superior person. He had long been known as a first-rate College Tutor and Public Examiner, with the rare advantage of a good figure, handsome countenance, and a winning address. He was a devoted supporter of the ·Grenville[2] and Buckingham party; indeed he was mainly instrumental in bringing in Lord Grenville as our Chancellor (in 1808) in opposition to Lord Eldon. Under these circumstances it was no wonder that the family exerted their interest for Dr. Hodson's promotion; he held the Vice-

---

[1] It may seem somewhat strange that my 'Recollections' of so amiable a Vice-Chancellor should lie thus 'in a nut-shell;' but academical and other matters just then flowed on very smoothly, and he was not a man to disturb that flow for the sake of excitement or notoriety.

[2] Lord George Grenville had recently been a member of Brasenose, not indeed having distinguished himself there; unless it were by that fantastic taste in dress, of which Deighton's caricature (called 'A View from B.N.C. Gateway') was a very slight exaggeration.

Chancellorship only two years; during which, however, his courteous manner gained him 'golden opinions[1].'

Dr. Hodson was appointed Regius Professor of Divinity (on Dr. Van Mildert's promotion to a bishopric), with, of course, a Canonry of Christ Church, as an appendiculum; and ,strange to say (at least it was then thought strange[2]). he was allowed to hold that appointment with that of Principal of Brasenose College; where he still continued to reside.

The office of Vice-Chancellor Dr. Hodson at once resigned, in order to devote himself to the new studies and duties to which he had been appointed. That he would soon have mastered those studies and discharged those duties with advantage to others and honour to himself, his fine abilities left no room for doubting; but he had scarcely entered upon them and their responsibilities, when a sudden, internal illness (brought on, it was supposed, by a complication of causes[3]) carried him off, in 1820; i. e. only two years after the appointment, which was to have been the stepping-stone to a bishopric.

It was impossible for any one to discharge the duties of a Vice-Chancellor more graciously and considerately than Dr. Hodson did. Even a reproof he administered with an evident recollection of the wise rule 'suaviter in modo.'

---

[1] From all, that is, but some few 'old stagers,' who affected to doubt his sincerity, feeling perhaps his gracious bearing to be a reproof to their own stiff carriage.

[2] Dr. Prideaux held this Canonry and Regius Professorship at the same time with the Rectorship of Exeter College for many years.

[3] Such as, new studies, rival professorial and collegiate claims, family anxieties, high living and neglect of exercise; he had a numerous young family of daughters, and it was a pleasing sight to see them clinging to him as he left home for Convocation, when he would gently shake them off, with 'Away, ye dear little incumbrances!'

On his going up to Court with an Address, as Vice-Chancellor, I heard[1] him remind Sir Robert Peel (at St. James's) of his having examined him for his Degree,—adding, 'My fellow-examiners accused me of flattering you, or, at least, putting a bad pun into your mouth,—when I selected, for your vivâ-voce construing, the passage in Virgil—

'Referes ergo hæc et nuntius ibis
Pelidæ genitori,' &c.

Dr. Hall, Master of Pembroke College, on his being admitted Vice-Chancellor (in 1820), gloried not a little (in his Latin admission-speech) as being ' primus, qui *fasces* in Collegium suum introduxerat,' i. e. the first Vice-Chancellor whom Pembroke had produced. Indeed it had not, since its foundation in 1624, figured much in the University annals; sharing, perhaps, in the difficulties which seem to have attended ambitious Halls[2], which aspired to become

---

[1] On the authority of a lady, a niece of Dr. Hodson, I here state, first, that his Christian name of Frodsham was not derived from any *personal* connection with a place so called in Lancashire, but simply from his grandfather having married a Miss Frodsham, of Elton Hall, in Cheshire; secondly, he was not born at Frodsham, but at Liverpool, where his father was Rector.

[2] Pembroke College was originally Broadgates Hall. As to Dr. Johnson, its most distinguished alumnus,—'stat nominis umbra;' his career there was short and unsatisfactory. Proud as he was poor, he had no right to complain (if indeed he ever did complain) that he was not fostered or appreciated; that he then deserved more favour than he received by no means appears, and his visits in later life to Dr. Adams, the Master, at least showed a reciprocal regard between him and the College which he had left without a Degree. His Degree of D.C.L. was sent to him by Diploma in 1775, after he had become famous. Dr. Moore, Archbishop of Canterbury at the end of the last century, was, I believe, an alumnus (if not a servitor) of Pembroke.

Colleges. Of late years, indeed, it has effectually recovered from the possible effects of such a transition-state, and has grown, in size and still more in reputation, into one of our most successful and influential societies. But, to return to Dr. Hall, as Vice-Chancellor; he held the office the full time (four years) and glided through it so quietly (at the same time most amiably and considerately) that my memory (as in the case of Dr. Lee) brings back to me nothing particular of his administration. He had an interesting family, and the close of his Vice-Chancellorship seemed to be hailed by him as a happy restoration to a fuller enjoyment of domestic quiet and collegiate duties.

Dr. Jenkyns, Master of Balliol, who succeeded Dr. Hall as Vice-Chancellor (in 1824), was a very different sort of person from his predecessor, as my 'Recollections' may help to show. Dr. Jenkyns had already, in the space of five years[1], shown great skill in raising the character of his College, and during thirty more years of his government he saw it gradually reach that high position, which the throwing open of the Fellowships and, in great measure, the Scholarships

---

[1] At his first starting as Master, his watchful enforcement of discipline was thought to be carried too far; indeed saucy Undergraduates of other Colleges twitted the Balliolites by asking when the board with 'Dr. Jenkyns's Academy' painted on it was to be placed over Balliol gateway. The good sense however and tact of his excellent staff of Tutors soon produced a right understanding between the Master and the young men; the latter were allowed the natural vent for their youthful spirits, while the former adopted that excellent suggestion to parties necessarily yoked together:—

'Be to my virtues very kind;
Be to my faults a *little blind.*'

In other words, 'govern, not only *agendo*, but also by *non*-agendo.'

first enabled it to obtain. Dr. Jenkyns became Vice-Chancellor much younger, probably, than any one who had held the office before him; and, from an over-anxiety to enforce discipline in the *Masterly* way he had been used to in his College, he became at the first an unpopular Vice-Chancellor. In the Convocation House, on Degree-days, his manner, in his anxiety to enforce order, was *not conciliatory*, and some of the deans and regent-masters returned his *attentions* in a manner which was annoying to him. A better feeling, however, soon followed as he was better understood, and order[1] was certainly better observed than it had been.

It seemed to be the bias of Dr. Jenkyns's official mind to overdo rather than leave anything undone: even in the streets, on his way to and from St. Mary's, he was not content with being Vice-Chancellor, but would also do the Proctors' work. Ex. gr. On a Saint's day morning, meeting

[1] If the want of order in the Convocation House was trying to Dr. Jenkyns in his days, how would he be astonished could he see *Candidates* for Degrees entering the House before they were formally *led in* by the Yeoman Bedels (i. e. before their *graces* are past),— nay, taking their seats side-by-side with the deans and regents;—' as if (he would say) they were going to overawe the House, and get their Degrees by a *minatory* rather than a *supplicatory* process.' It is curious to trace the *progressive* intrusion of candidates for Degrees. Formerly they were left to cool themselves in what was vulgarly called the ' Pig-market,' i. e. the covered but windy space that runs along the east of the Divinity School. There is a traditionary notion, that they stayed there till they were called, in order to give any tradesman an opportunity of demanding payment of unsettled bills, with the threat of stopping their Degree. They next took possession of the Apodyterium, as a place of refuge from external annoyance, and close to the final scene of action; a farther step (and one easily taken in these days of Undergraduate self-will and unrestrained action) placed them within the walls and on the seats of the Convocation House!

near St. Mary's a young man with his books and papers under his arm, he stopped him with the question, 'Pray, Sir, whither are you going?' 'To my private tutor's, Sir, for a lecture[1].' 'Then, Sir, you will come into church with me, and after sermon tell your tutor from me that he should not only not keep young men from church, but should also come himself.' 'If you please, Sir, I shall lose my *hour*, for Mr. ——'s morning is quite filled.' 'Well, Sir,' concluded the Vice-Chancellor,—his natural good-temper (for he was naturally kind and good-tempered) returning,—'You may go this morning; but give my message, and—another time' (smiling pleasantly) 'don't *meet the University authorities* if you can avoid it.' He was, indeed, an excellent and conscientious Vice-Chancellor, thoroughly conversant with the Statutes and University matters, and deservedly possessing much weight in the Hebdomadal Council. The promotion to the Deanery of Wells was universally considered his due, and especially appropriate as it did not separate him from his beloved College[2]. He was so averse to change and innovations, that his death, in 1854, might be considered a merciful escape from the pain of witnessing the sweeping alterations which the last few years have wrought.

The above lengthened notice of one Vice-Chancellor will leave the less room for his two successors, Dr. Jones and

---

[1] N. B. Private Tutors had not yet become 'Coaches.'

[2] The inscription at the entrance of the newly-built Chapel of Balliol College is strongly expressive of the great esteem in which Dr. Jenkyns was held. As a preacher before the University he was certainly 'parcus et infrequens.' He had an annual preaching-turn as a Head of a House, but I do not remember his using it more than twice; and on both occasions, but at some interval of time, he preached the same sermon, or rather lecture, on the same text, 'Owe no man anything.'

Dr. Rowley, concerning whom, indeed, there is but little left on the 'retina' of my memory.

Dr. Jones, Rector of Exeter College, like the preceding Rector, Dr. Cole, had been for some time, I believe, a Navy chaplain, and, like him, retained a slight 'smack' of that service. He had, however, returned to College early enough to act, for some years, as College Tutor and as a Public Examiner in 1812, 1813, and 1814. Dr. Jones became Vice-Chancellor in 1828, and held the office through the usual τεσσαρεία, discharging its duties with quiet self-possession, though sometimes fretting a little under its increasing weight and constant interruptions. He lived in calm, easy-going times (academically speaking), and was not himself likely to stir up any agitating questions.

Dr. Jones, though in ordinary circumstances plain, if not rough, in the routine of public business, could, on solemn occasions, bear himself with much dignity. He survived his Vice-Chancellorship six years, and died in 1838, while on a tour in Scotland. He was buried at Oban, where he died.

Dr. Rowley, Master of University College, came next[1], in the order of Vice-Chancellors, in 1832. By dint of hard work and steady application (with a strong head and a sturdy will), he had worked his way up from the bottom to the top of the College-ladder; that is, from being Bible-clerk to become the Head of the Society. He had well

---

[1] And comes *the last* of those Vice-Chancellors who are included in these 'Recollections;' not that I *forget* the many kindnesses and the unbroken series of favourable consideration shown me by those who have succeeded him; but because the list of names is of too near and recent a date to be adequately or safely followed out.

earned his Fellowship by gaining (in 1803) what were then called 'The Honours,'—the result, that is, of an almost encyclopædiac Examination, which existed (for five years) till, in 1807, '*Classes*' were introduced.

Dr. Rowley married and had a family, living generally in a quiet, domestic manner; working hard, at his leisure hours, in his garden, and taking long country-walks. On becoming Vice-Chancellor he could no longer (from the constant interruptions and engagements incident to that responsible office) either practise horticulture or escape often into the country. This change was said to have told unfavourably upon his constitution; he held the office, however, the usual four years, and he had rather a trying time of it, including the Installation of the Duke of Wellington, whom he entertained at his 'Lodgings,' and prompted[1] in the Theatre. He died, after a short illness, at the end of the Long Vacation of 1836,—a week or two before the day on which he would have resigned his office.

Dr. Rowley had been throughout his official life what he had shown himself in his early years—a steady-working man; going cheerfully through anything and everything that came to him in the way of business. He was, during as well as before his Vice-Chancellorship, unaffectedly plain and straightforward in his intercourse with every one. He was never, I believe, known to preach, at least before the University; and though a sound scholar, it did not follow that he was a profound theologian. Piety, I fully believe, was not less real then, though it was less demonstrative than now.

[1] 'Where are we now?' said the Duke audibly, and more than once, to the Vice-Chancellor at his elbow. 'Oh! I see, Placetne vobis,' &c.

CHAPTER IX.

'Mecum loquor hæc, tacitusque recordor.'—*Horace.*

Recollections of Proctors.

HAVING presumed to report my Reminiscences of Vice-Chancellors and Heads of Houses, it would seem a 'descensus facilis' to the velvet-sleeved supporters of University discipline—the Proctors. But as some animals conceal formidable talons under velvety claws, so these wearers of velvet and ermine are really the more formidable in proportion to their shorter official life, a single year[1]. What Heads of Houses, as such, have nothing to do with, and what Vice-Chancellors do not generally feel called upon to notice, the Proctors, young men[2] and fresh to their work,

---

[1] It used to be said that a Proctor had to do that in one year which a Vice-Chancellor had to do in four; viz. three months to work his way up to the full swing and consciousness of his authority; six months in the unchecked exercise and enjoyment of it; and again three months to let himself down softly and gradually to his former level as an ordinary M.A.

[2] Before the Statute of 1856, Proctors were 'Masters of Arts from four to ten years from their Regency;' the chances then were that a Proctor would be under thirty years of age; but now that the tenth year from the Regency is extended to all but the sixteenth, this *description* of Proctors may not always apply.

are expected to scrutinise 'per se aut per deputatos.' They are supposed to be ubiquitous as well as omniscient: no Convocation, no Council, no meeting (nay, no night-row in the streets) can go on well without them. If, however, they are at any time exhausted, or indeed, for any sufficient reason, are absent, they have each two pros, who can supply their place, except at the Council[1]. With any *recent* Proctors, however, I have here nothing to do, but shall only stir up my 'Recollections' of a very few and those of remote date.

The year 1800 had *Mr. Tench* of Brasenose, and *Mr. Wood* of Ch. Ch., as Proctors. The latter, a distinguished mathematical Tutor and Censor, carried his censorial ideas of power and discipline too far, and rushed into a problem which he found difficult to solve; i. e. he involved himself, and with himself the University, in a squabble with the City, by carrying off to the *Castle* (as was the practice in those

[1] In the Cambridge Statutes the Proctors are called the 'oculi Vice-Cancellarii;' and though not so in the letter, they are really so in spirit at Oxford; nay, they are his hands and his feet, especially in the exercise of the Watch and Ward, which he annually commits to their care. We are historically told that in 1234 this charge was in the hands of the Town, but, from neglect, was transferred to the University authorities. The riot and slaughter of Dies Scholastica in 1355 caused Edward III to grant the University still greater powers.

Within my recollection the Pro-Proctors were wont to walk round St. Mary's on a Sunday when the University Sermon was about to commence, to prevent loungers outside and *to see* young men *into church*. This practice, in Hearne's time (i.e. at the beginning of the eighteenth century), was, he tells us, once productive of an extraordinary effect. 'The Proctors, during a sermon at St. Mary's, *saw* some young scholars *into church;* their rush into the gallery frightened the congregation, who, thinking the church was falling, dispersed in confusion.'

Again,—' At a University Lent Sermon in St. Peter's-in-the-East an alarm was caused by some boys throwing stones down from the tower on to the roof. Preacher and all rushed out.'

days when there were no Police-rooms) a quiet, but stubborn, old man, who refused to 'go home' at the Proctor's bidding, at the close of a *Gown and Town row*. Legal proceedings against the Proctor followed; but the case being *claimed* by the University to be decided in its own Court, the poor townsman relinquished any further proceedings.

The other Proctor, Mr. *Tench*, was at once pronounced to be *an odd fish* when he 'came up,' after some years' absence from Oxford, wearing a vulgar-looking, powdered, one-curled wig, speaking with a strong Lancashire dialect, and reading with a voice of thunder: indeed his enunciation of the oaths and exhortations on Degree-days was an awful infliction on the drum of one's ear. At the end of their official year these two gentlemen, like most of their predecessors and successors, fell back quietly and peaceably into their former privacy[1].

In 1801 the Proctors were *Mr. Faber* of Lincoln, and *Mr. Nott* of All Souls College. It was a remarkable coincidence that each of these gentlemen, during a part of his year, preached the Bampton Lectures in his Proctor's gown.

[1] The calm and quiet manner in which the Proctors generally return to their respective Colleges, on resigning their office, exhibits a very different state of things compared with the stormy days of former times, especially of the sixteenth century (i.e. 1520), when (we are told) in consequence of the riots and factions of '*Grecians and Trojans*,' in which the then Proctors were officially involved, leave was granted to the Senior Proctor 'to wear a dagger for his defence for two years following his year of office.' There was also another division into opposite factions of Northeners and Southeners (as the Americans would call them), and the two Proctors, being generally representatives of them, must have had enough to do to keep the peace between the '*Nations*,' as these factions affected to call themselves. It is perhaps a remnant of those stormy days, that the *going-out* as well as the *coming-in* Proctors are, on the first-day of Easter Term, escorted in procession to their Colleges.

Mr. Faber (long after known in controversial theological literature as 'George Stanley Faber') delivered in 1801 a course of lectures, the substance of which he published under the title of Horæ Mosaicæ. They had at least the two usual features of the Bampton Lectures, that of length and dryness[1]. It was apparently in a spirit of emulation that Mr. (afterwards Dr.) Nott undertook to write his Bampton Lectures on the heels of his learned colleague. All that I recollect of them is that they were short. It has been only now and then that we have had Bampton Lecturers who, while they exhausted their subject, did not also exhaust their audience.

Mr. Rodd of Exeter College, Proctor in 1802, was, of course, soon found, or at least (joci causâ) *said*, to be a disciplinarian worthy of his name; but being yoked with a quiet, steady-goer, Mr. Wetherell of University, he soon settled down into the jog-trot pace, which best suited quiet days and smooth well-beaten roads. A curious train of thoughts is annually suggested on the Commemoration, as to the fact that the then present grave Doctors and Masters (so obviously annoyed by the tumultuous behaviour of the juniors) were probably among the noisy boys of *their day;* and, vice versâ, that those youngsters, who are now using or rather abusing the privilege of their Saturnalia, will, in a few years, change places; and from the area or the rising semicircle look up to the noisy gallery with a scowl of disapprobation and deprecation.

The year 1803 had for Proctors *Mr. Broughton* of New College, and *Mr. Michell* of Wadham. The former, my

---

[1] Several Bampton Lecturers of recent date have been well attended throughout; in remoter times it was almost a matter of course that the first lecture commanded a tolerably full church, but the subsequent lectures were addressed to a gradually diminishing audience.

old tutor in logic and ethics, was more of an artist[1] than a logician, scholar, or philosopher. As *Proctors* they left little or nothing to 'recollect' out of the beaten track; they lived in jovial times[2], and went pleasantly with the stream. Mr. Michell was one of the Public Examiners when I *went up*[3] for examination in 1806, and his favourable opinion then formed (for we were strangers to each other) caused him to invite me to become a candidate for the office of Esquire Bedel in Law, as a successor to his Wadham friend, Mr. Hall (then promoted to the Divinity Staff). I obtained the appointment from Convocation, and so became a fixture for life in Oxford.

In 1804 Messrs. (afterwards Drs.) *Ellerton* of Magdalen, and *Barnes* of Christ Church, were Proctors. The former was my old and excellent Master at Magdalen College School; he was a good Latin scholar (as his speech on going out of office proved), but in Greek he was not thought profound. He subsequently became (as the Oxford Calendar will show) a Benefactor (on a small scale) by founding a Theological Prize Essay, and, conjointly with Mr. Pusey and his brother Dr. Pusey, a Hebrew Scholarship. He also endowed with £10 a year two Hebrew Exhibitions for Magdalen Demies. Dr. Ellerton for some time importuned the University authorities to accept a sum for a prize for Elocution. The difficulty of adjudication, as well as the smallness of the offer (a feature belonging to all his endowments), caused

---

[1] Mr. Broughton published a Tour (in England) well illustrated by his own drawings.

[2] The political horizon was indeed cloudy and threatening, for the war with Bonaparte broke out afresh in the July of 1803; but the atmosphere of the Oxford Common-rooms was nevertheless of an enjoyable character.

[3] Or '*went in*,' as it is *now* expressed.

his proposal to be declined. His colleague lived to an advanced age amongst us, esteemed and respected, as a Canon of Ch. Ch.

In 1805 the University had as Proctors two very handsome and gentlemanly men, *Mr. Clare* of St. John's, and *Mr. Vaughan* of Merton College. The former, *Mr. Clare*, after his quiet year of office, being no longer *clarus*[1], subsided into an incumbent on a good living, with the prospect of still quieter years. *Mr. Vaughan*, his colleague, subsequently became Warden of his College.

One of the Proctors of 1806, *Mr. Marshall* of Balliol College, managed, somehow or other, to make himself unpopular with the Undergraduates, who said 'he *out-marshaled the Marshal.*' At the close of the ceremony, on the Commemoration-day, as he was retiring at the tail of the Procession across the area of the Theatre, a well-aimed orange[2] ('credite posteri!'), thrown from the gallery, struck him forcibly on the face. In the confusion of the general

---

[1] Or '*egregius*,' the epithet by which the Proctors are Convocationally addressed.

[2] The Proctors appear to have been always more or less subject to rough treatment from individuals who had probably incurred their castigation. 'In 1603' (we are told in the 'Oxoniana'), 'one of the Proctors, Mr. Dale, was a *large man*, but his colleague, *Mr. Laud*, was a *little man*' [though afterwards, as the famous Archbishop Laud, and in a different sense, a *great man*]. 'On going out of office, Dale was hissed and hooted, and still more his brother Proctor. A wag, on the occasion, said of Dale that he had no right to complain, as he had discharged the office "cum *parvá laude.*"'

Perhaps the now hackneyed pun, as applied to the Proctors' annual exit from the Theatre, '*laudatur ab bis,*' had its first application on the occasion here mentioned. We may remark, too, that the 'going out of office,' here alluded to, was in the Convocation House, and the 'hissing and hooting' probably on leaving it. The Sheldonian Theatre was not built till 1669.

exit it was impossible *from below* to detect or mark the daring delinquent;—those *above*, of course, would not betray him. The gross affair was hushed up:—

> 'Incertum, quâ pulsa manu, quo turbine adacta;
> Nec se (Marshalli) jactavit vulnere quisquam.'

But the recorder (not necessarily the laudator) 'temporis acti' must not run the risk of being himself '*proctorised*,' by going any farther in the list of Proctors; interesting as it is, to one of long standing, to recall their memory, as they *then*[1] came on in the vigour of manhood, and to follow them and see some of them being, or having been, men of distinction (Copleston, Rigaud, Shuttleworth, Hussey, Longley, among the 'have-beens;'—Symons, Lightfoot, and Liddell, among 'those that be'), but by far the greater number subsiding into respectable retirement after their one year of academical power and distinction; each of them clinging fondly, if not proudly, to the recollection of that year and of the events which passed '*me Procuratore*.'

Some of the duties of the office were formerly more trying, and, to quiet, refined men, more disagreeable than they have become since the institution (about the year 1829) of an enlarged and effective [2] 'University Police.' The night-walking (at least the worst part of it); the searching of ill-famed

---

[1] I emphatically say '*then*,' not only in antithesis to their individual subsequent history, but in reference to the Statute of 1856, which may occasionally introduce older Masters into the Procuratorial Chairs: better perhaps for council, but worse for action! Recent and modern times have never given occasion to record anything like what Hearne asserts of his day, i. e. in 1723:—'On Sunday last (he says), being Coronation-day, Mr. Streat, of Merton, then Senior Proctor, and his Pro, Mr. Briton, were with others at a tavern at an unseasonable hour. The Vice-Chancellor *walked* that evening, and going into the tavern dismissed them all forthwith.'

[2] *Effective*, at that date, before the town of Oxford extended so far.

houses; the hunting-up, and sometimes the running-down, of those unhappy persons whom Proctor Ellerton, in his 'dying-speech [1],' called 'pestes noctivagæ;' the being called out, sometimes *called up*, to put a stop to a row resulting from protracted wine-parties:—such duties as these often deterred quiet, nervous men from undertaking the office when it came to them. But the University has never wanted the necessary supply of energetic, conscientious persons to support its character and discipline in this responsible office.

By way of compensation for the 'disagreeables' above-mentioned, the Proctorship was wisely surrounded with honour, invested with patronage, and endowed with a liberal income. The honour and the patronage, of course, attracted most,—some few, probably, urged by the pressure of some still unsettled bills of their Undergraduate days, and the sense of the 'res angusta domi,' were influenced by the prospect of a year's liberal income [2]. Till the year 1829 the Proctors had been (by a long-standing traditional abuse) the recipients, in equal shares, of Dr. White's £100 per annum [3], bequeathed by him in 1621 to pay a *Professor* of Moral

---

[1] i. e. his speech on *resigning office*.

[2] At that time, and for many years afterwards, that income was made up from several sources, but depended principally upon fees from Degrees; so that, on entering upon the Proctorship, it was a common practice to wish the Proctors 'a quiet year and plenty of Grand-Compounders;' nay, I believe it was the *standing toast* at their first dinner.

[3] How such a practical catachresis really originated, and came to be openly and annually repeated, it is difficult to imagine. It was whispered, however, in 1828, that the ghost of Thomas White, D.D., the founder of the *intended* Professorship (certainly the donor of the £100 misappropriated for two hundred years), began to *walk* near the precincts of the Delegates' Room, crying, 'Where is my Professor? What is done with my hundred a year?'

Philosophy! It would almost seem to have been done as a *practical* joke (though a strange and discreditable one), founded on the idea of the Proctors being very often called upon to *lecture* a 'compulsory' audience of young men on *moral* subjects! At all events, the conscience of the University, stirred up perhaps by the scruples of high-principled Proctors themselves (such, for instance, as 'Charles T. Longley, Ch. Ch.,' and 'Andrew Edwards, Magd.,' in 1827), awoke to a sense of the abuse. The Proctors' income was raised by an equal sum, through a vote of Convocation, and the Moral Professorship *made a reality* in 1829, by the appointment of William Mills, B.D., of Magdalen College, a most amiable man and a scholar of high reputation, who, alas! died too early for Oxford, and especially for Magdalen School and College, which were justly proud of him[1].

But to return to the Proctors (of whom and of 'Recollections' of whom I here take leave); their annual income has, for some years, been the fixed sum of £350.

[1] The tenure of this Professorship was limited by the Founder to five years (an absurd arrangement, and one which probably led to the misapplication above detailed, from the want of proper applicants); and although Mills was followed by a brilliant list of successors (such as W. Sewell, Stocker, Johnson, Liddell, and Wilson), little impression could be expected, even from them, during so short a tenure.

By an order of the Queen's Council, in 1858, the Chair may be held for life (as voted previously in Convocation); and the stipend has been raised by the University. Mr. Wilson of Corpus was *re-elected* in 1858, on this new arrangement.

CHAPTER X.

'Haud ignota loquor.'—*Virgil.*

Recollections of University Characters.

ONE of my earliest official 'Recollections' is connected with the name of *John Price*, B.D., of Jesus College, who was the Bodleian Librarian for forty-five years, i.e. from 1768 to 1813[1].

---

[1] In Chapter V some particulars have been given as to Mr. Price's election (after a close, neck-and-neck contest) in preference to Mr. (afterwards Bishop) Cleaver;—a decision which, as is there shown, the unsuccessful candidate had no reason to lament. Not that it follows that Mr. Price would have been a bishop, and Mr. Cleaver have continued Bodley's Librarian till his death, had the election been reversed. Mr. Price, no doubt, had his *bookish* recommendations, and therefore, very luckily for both parties, was fixed in his proper place, moved in his proper element, and throve on the close air of the Bodleian. The Bodleian is here referred to as it was in Mr. Price's time, when its atmosphere was either close or cold, and, for a great part of the year, both. Things are vastly improved of late in that venerable place in this and many respects. [How simple must have been the state of things when the University Library was contained in the structure *over the Divinity School* in 1480! How sad to think that before the end of the reign of Edward VI that small collection of books was dispersed, and that at the close of the sixteenth century the University had no Public Library at all. The very bookshelves were sold and the walls

It does not appear that he ever did or wrote anything 'memoriâ dignum peculiari;' but, at all events, he possessed a first-rate quality in a Proto-Bibliothecarius, that of being always at his post,—and this when no attempt had been made, or even thought of, to warm the Library and make it really a place of comfortable study, instead of a very rare resort for a hasty and unsatisfactory reference to damp books with chilled fingers. The absence of a fire-place, chimney, stove, or flue in the building would by itself show that a fire *by day* was as much forbidden by implication, as it was literally and elaborately forbidden for any one (even ipse Bibliothecæ Custos) to introduce '*per noctem*, funale, lychnum, lampadem, lucernam aut quodvis *luminare* accensum.'.

From 1806 to 1813 I was officially brought into contact with the Librarian, and on two different occasions: one was at the end of each Term, when I paid him the fees, then appropriated to his office, from Degrees, especially from Grand-Compounders. On that occasion, if I did not find him in his Bodleian 'sanctum' or closet (for age was beginning to tell upon him), I paid him a visit at his little tenement in St. Giles's, a small and humble dwelling, where he lived in the plainest style, attended by a single domestic '*who did for him.*'

The other occasion was the 'deductio a domo,' or the attendance on the Grand-Compounders' procession from the respective Colleges to the Convocation House. This procession was *headed* by Mr. Price (or a deputy), not how-

left bare. (Hallam's Lit. Hist. ii. 358.) That Bodley *built on* to the Divinity School (more than a hundred years later) is sufficiently evident from windows, buttresses, &c., now inclosed, but originally external.]

ever as Librarian, but as the '*Capellanus*[1] Universitatis,' or University Chaplain; a character which appears to have been always involved in that of the Librarian. We find no mention of the office in the University Statutes[2]; indeed, the Statute De Bibliothecario and his qualifications did not *expressly* require that he should be in Orders. It might seem to be *implied* in the old Statute (lately very much compressed), which, while it forbade his undertaking the cure of souls, 'nisi in beneficio prope adjuncto,' suggests the inference that he was nevertheless to be in Orders.

It is a fact, however, that the Librarian, as Capellanus, not only attended and led the above-named procession (for even Dr. Bandinel, Mr. Price's successor, did so till the procession was discontinued in 1817), but also that, in Roman Catholic times[3], the Capellanus on those occa-

[1] 'The office of University Chaplain, attached to that of the Librarian, was instituted by Letters Patent of Edward I for the saying of daily masses for the souls of the Benefactors of the then Library.' (Peshall).

[2] It existed, however, in the Table of Fees for Degrees (lately superseded) in connection with the Grand-Compounders' procession.

[3] The same things of course took place at Oxford and Cambridge respecting this silver cross in the trying times in the middle of the sixteenth century. At Cambridge it was the duty of the 'Capellanus Universitatis' to carry this cross in processions 'per se vel per aliam honestam personam,'—'to have *the care of the University Library*, chalices,' &c. A silver *cross* (Dr. Hook tells us) was borne before Augustine at Canterbury, '*the crucifix* not being then known.' For myself, I confess that the procession had lost much of its imposing effect from the absence of the 'large silver cross,' and that the Capellanus, walking at the head of the procession without it, and having really nothing to do there (except to earn his fee, which was a considerable one), always appeared superfluous and unmeaning. We are told that in 1278 one of the many Jews then resident in Oxford tore the cross from the hands of the academic bearer and trampled it under foot! The University, as a mild punishment, obliged the Jews to make a heavy silver crucifix to be used in processions like that above-mentioned. (Huber's English Univ.)

sions bore on his shoulder a large silver cross. At Cambridge (and doubtless also at Oxford), in the short reign of Edward VI, the cross was sold; but alas! for the

> 'Nescia mens hominum fati sortisque futuræ; . . .
> . . . tempus erit, magno cùm optaverit emptum
> Intactum.'

Edward's brief reign soon came to an end, Popery was again in the ascendant, and 'bloody Queen Mary's' still shorter reign was long enough to cause the purchase and use of another silver cross,—itself to be finally laid aside 'in good Queen Bess's reign!'

While on the subject of changes, I must be allowed to take leave of the Librarian, Mr. Price (of whom I have no farther 'Recollections'), and to mention a few things in reference to the Library and Librarian, as matters of curiosity. 1st. Until Dr. Bandinel's time (when the Statute was altered) the Librarian could not marry[1]. 2ndly. That which used to be called 'The Bodleian dinner' at the Vice-Chancellor's, with its attendant ceremony[2] (on the Bodleian

---

[1] The old Statute ran thus respecting the Librarian:—'Nexu conjugali solvatur,'—intending, it is presumed, that he should be *free from* the nuptial tie, not *freed* from it, as the word 'solvatur' might rather mean; and then came the reason, very unscrupulously expressed,— 'conjugium enim domesticis plerumque negotiis sic abundat, ut otium suppetere non possit sui copiam in dies singulos exhibendi.'

[2] The ceremony alluded to was this: the Yeoman Bedel in Arts went in 'inter epulandum' and presented a pair of gloves ('chirothecas') and ten shillings to each of the Regius Professors and the two Proctors, in consideration of their trouble in the visitation or inspection. At the same time forty shillings extra were given to each of the Proctors 'ob fidelem *clavium* custodiam.' These keys belonged to a mysterious 'ferrea cista' with three several locks, each lock having a double key, 'for the safer keeping of the Library moneys.' The Proctors and the

Visitation-day), has been discontinued. Of course Bodley's funds furnished to the Vice-Chancellor something more than. an *honorarium* for the dinner; but the recent Statute has unmercifully swept away this English (and not un-academic) way of doing honour ' viro isti incomparabili (in the words of the old Statute), bonarum Literarum Patrono et Mæcenati divinitùs nobis concesso, Thomæ Bodley, Equiti.'

As an appendix to this long gossip 'de rebus Bodleianis,' a few lines may be borrowed (from the 'Oxoniana') of a Macaronic Poem by Peter Allibond, who had been a chorister and took the degree of B.A. as a Clerk of Magdalen College, and who died in 1658. The poem (rather a long one) is entitled ' Rustica Academiæ Oxoniensis nuper Reformatæ Descriptio:'—

> 'Conscendo orbis illud decus
>   Bodleio fundatore;
> Sed intus erat nullum pecus,
>   Excepto Janitore.
> Neglectos vidi libros multos,
>   (Quod minime mirandum)
> Nam inter bardos[1] tot et stultos
>   There's few that understand 'em.'

Vice-Chancellor had charge of these keys, which indeed were reckoned amongst the '*Officii Insignia*,' and handed over from the old Proctors to their successors at the time of their admission to office in Convocation. Whence those Library moneys arose, and how they were applied, is now, of course, unknown. Those strong, old chests had their day, but they naturally led to an unproductive accumulation of specie, unwieldy in the handling. Old Hearne declares that 'a Bursar of Merton died from bursting an internal blood-vessel, in lifting a bag of silver of 600 lbs. weight!'

[1] *Bardos*, synonymous with *tardos*, and formed from βράδυs, slow, dull-witted.

(From the Bodleian the poet goes to St. Mary's, and there)

> 'Procuratores sine *clavibus*[1]
> Quærentibus ostendas,
> Bedellos novos sine *stavibus*[2]
> Res protinus ridendas!'

And so for many stanzas proceeds Mr. (or Dr.) Allibond[3]. The recent abrogation of obsolete or impracticable Statutes struck out the 'ferrea cista' of the Bodleian Library, but spared the 'Communis et magna cista, ferreis laminis circumdata et *quinque seris* obfirmata,' for the safe keeping of *all and single the revenues of the University*. The *five keys* to the *five locks* are still enjoined to be kept respectively by the Heads of Magdalen, Merton, Corpus, and New College, and the Dean of Christ Church. This venerable iron chest still exists, and in good preservation, in the Bursary of Corpus College, but it is a very long time since it was used or even opened. The University, as represented by its Vice-Chancellors, has long known how to make a better use of a large sum than keeping it locked up under five different keys. Query: Does it still contain any of the 'jocalia' (jewels) and the 'vasa aurea et argentea, si quæ fuerint,' which used to be therein 'in tuto reposita?'

---

[1] The *claves* or keys of the Bodleian 'ferrea cista' mentioned above, and formerly carried by the Proctors' man (with other insignia officii) in a bag.

[2] The *staves* were probably (if not previously concealed or even buried) melted down into money. Indeed there is a tradition among the Bedels that the old staves were buried in the Dean's garden at Ch. Ch. by the spirited Mrs. Fell, and were either never dug up or so injured by their long interment, that at the Restoration a new set of staves (those now in use) was introduced. One of the old staves, very inferior in size and make to the more modern ones, still exists (I believe) somewhere among the 'jocalia' of the University.

[3] The poem was republished in 1834 with many curious notes.

The *Rev. William Crowe*, B.C.L., Public Orator for forty-five years (i. e. from 1784 to 1829), and formerly Fellow of New College, was in many respects peculiarly qualified for his office; being gifted with a fine, rich, powerful voice, master of good Latinity, and that aided by the 'ore rotundo' pronunciation of the Winchester School. Thus endowed, Mr. Crowe always commanded respectful attention in the Theatre at the Commemoration; and, though no great divine, he always attracted a large congregation at St. Mary's, where he was a frequent preacher[1].

It was remarkable in Mr. Crowe, that in the rostrum of the Theatre and in the University pulpit (and especially in his addresses to Royal visitors,—as, for instance, to the galaxy of Royalty in 1814) he was grand, dignified, and impressive; while in common discourse his speech and manner were rather rustic, if not coarse, having (if one may so say) a strong smack of the tone and spirit of Socrates, or rather Diogenes, or other talkers still more βαναυσίκοι. His talk too on political subjects was that of an ultra-Whig, almost a republican, though he had the tact not to let this bias affect his public addresses[2],—so, at least, as to offend

[1] Mr. Crowe was decidedly a '*character*;' indeed there would be no difficulty in adding to the small number which this Chapter contains. The University in his day had not yet been smoothed down into a level uniformity in manners, costume, phraseology, &c.; it therefore really contained individuals of distinctive, characteristic qualities. This remark, however, will apply to English society generally, though not so strikingly.

[2] These addresses, or orations, were of course in Latin (some of them he published); and being set off by his imposing manner, an occasional sentence, rather strongly seasoned, only sounded the more classical;— passing perhaps for a quotation from Cicero or Livy. Mr. Crowe occasionally (but not as Public Orator) read a course of lectures on *Architecture* in New College hall; they were tolerably well attended, though he did not profess to go deep into the subject.

the loyal mind of Oxford. His elegant but short poem called 'Lewesdon Hill,' proved him to be a real poet; and consequently his opinion, in deciding the Prize Verse compositions, had always great weight with his brother judges.

Mr. Crowe's income was never large, his College living being under £300 a-year, and the Public Oratorship less than £100[1]. Under these circumstances he never went to the expense of keeping or hiring a horse or carriage for his frequent journeys to Oxford from his living in Wiltshire; even in his later years he walked the whole way, not scrupling in hot weather to carry his coat, hung upon a stick, on his shoulder[2]. On these pedestrian journeys he had not a very clerical appearance; and it happened one day that the late Lord Abingdon in his early days, while following the hounds, saw Mr. Crowe, in his walking costume, near a hedge; holding out a shilling, he called out, 'Here, old fellow, just hold back that branch, while I clear the gap.'

---

[1] Query: Is Anthony Wood justified in asserting (respecting the learned Dr. Hammond) that 'being made Canon of Ch. Ch., he became, *by virtue of that appointment*, Orator of the University?' If so, when and why did the connection cease? Was the Canonry of Christ Church ever *formally attached* to the Public Oratorship, or the latter to the former? Was not Dr. Hammond *elected* Orator by the University *after* he had become Canon of Christ Church by the appointment of Charles I, and not because of it or 'by virtue of it?' If our present Orator were to claim a Canonry, he might be answered as I was when, being Esquire Bedel in Law, I (though not in earnest) told Mr. Collingwood of the Clarendon Press that he had usurped an office (that of Archi-typographus) which, by the Laudian Statute, belonged to me. 'Sir,' said he, 'if you raise the question, I think you would find that you have got my office of Esquire Bedel in Law.'

[2] On his way he mixed freely with rustics and other casual guests at way-side houses of refreshment; and by talking with them, without ceremony, and by studying their mode of thought, he extracted from them their real sentiments, and sometimes original ideas.

The branch was, of course, held back ;—whether the shilling was picked up and pocketed, with the (un-intended) affront, the story does not say; the probability is, that it was. I had sometimes the honour of breakfasting with him in my early days at New College; for though an Incumbent, he kept a set of rooms (I can hardly call them furnished rooms) in College; on these occasions there was barely the addition of an egg to the usual buttery commons. From his frequent long walks, his habits of observation, and easy, familiar intercourse with farmers, artisans, and others, Mr. Crowe, among other kinds of practical information, had acquired a skill and tact in judging of timber; consequently he acted for New College as their *Woodman*[1]. In that character he attended annually at the marking of such trees as were of proper age and condition to be felled in the woods of Stanton St. John, when his judgment (as well as his *trenchant* manner of expressing it) was duly appreciated. I remember his preaching a sermon on 'the barren fig-tree,' when he strikingly reminded the New College part of his auditors of his office at the College wood, by the emphatic manner in which he every now and then thundered out, 'Cut it down.'

Mr. Crowe, as it may be readily supposed from what has been said, was not very attentive to externals, such as matters of dress; dining one day at Magdalen, he was asked by a friend why he appeared in his cassock as well as his

---

[1] The 'Woodman' was then, I believe, a regular agent of the College in connection with the bursarial department. It is recorded of his cotemporary, T. Warton, the Laureat, and the Historian of English Poetry, that he was (like Mr. Crowe) not averse from the company and conversation of persons of a mean rank and education, with whom he would sometimes drink his ale and smoke his pipe. I do not think however that Mr. Crowe (like T. Warton) ever attended at an execution, disguised in a carter's dress!

gown; 'Why, in truth (he replied) I have no cloth breeches in Oxford, so I put on these petticoats (which I keep here for St. Mary's) to hide my old leathern shorts[1].' I used to hear an anecdote told of the Public Orator, that, once when (acting for the Regius Professor of Law) he had to present (for an Honorary D.C.L. Degree in the Theatre) a foreigner who was a distinguished warrior, and had begun, as usual, ' Insignissime Vice-Cancellarie et vos egregii Procuratores, præsento vobis virum hunc bellicosissimum,'— on looking round to take his hand he found that the hero, attracted by something in his rear, had *faced to the right about!* The awkward incident was instantly and happily turned to rhetorical account,—' virum, aio, qui nunquam antea *tergiversatus* est.'

The ready wit, of course, told upon the whole Theatre, especially upon the gallery, while the distinguished general (also of course) took it all as a studied compliment to himself[2].

[1] Conversing one day with a friend about his family, he cheerfully observed, 'Well, you know; "God feedeth the young ravens," and so He will, I trust, the *young Crowes.*'

[2] I am bound to confess, that I have lately found this or a very similar story told of Dr. South in the Gentleman's Magazine. In conclusion of this Chapter, I may add that it would be very easy (though not advisable) to introduce other 'University characters,' both those of whom a great deal, interesting and amusing, might be said; and still more, those of whom some one thing or saying might be recorded, as for instance, 'Mr. S—l, of St. John's' invented a piquant sauce, still called by his name in the College kitchen!' But, 'non locus hic est pluribus umbris.'

CHAPTER XI.

'Semper ego auditor tantùm?'—*Juvenal.*

University Sermons and Preachers.

FEW persons probably have heard more sermons than I have; of course I shall be told 'that I ought to be, in proportion, the better for them;' I only rejoin, that I hope I am not the worse, *notwithstanding*, having conscientiously tried hard to consider it as a privilege, and not merely an official necessity.

During my Undergraduate days (that is from 1802 to 1806) I went to St. Mary's 'whenever a great gun' (as we called a noted preacher—not necessarily a *Canon*) was expected to fire away (as was then the wont) at a methodistical or a dissenting target. I heard also *Dr. Tatham*, Rector of Lincoln, preach his famous *two hours and a half sermon*[1], in defence of the genuineness of the disputed verse

---

[1] In the course of his argument, as he grew warm with his subject, he more emphatically than charitably wished 'all the German critics (or 'Jarman,' as he pronounced it) at the bottom of the "Jarman" Ocean.' In charity, I presume that he only meant their *writings*; and as neither Porson's cutting[*] and overpowering Reply to Travis, nor Turton's answer to Burgess, on the disputed passage, incurred the Doctor's imprecations, I presume they had not then appeared.

[*] I find, on inquiry, that Porson's Strictures on Travis's Letters on the disputed text, after appearing in the Gentleman's Magazine in 1788 and 1789, were published as a whole in 1790. Dr. Tatham preached his long sermon in 1802 or 1803. Burgess wrote to invalidate Porson's arguments after Porson's death, in 1808. Turton's Reply to Burgess followed soon after.

in St. John's first Epistle, 'There are three that bear witness,' &c. Long as the sermon was (and I have not overstated the time), few, if any, left the church till the conclusion[1]; so strangely attractive was the mixture of learning and coarseness. Some persons however had better have left him to his 'second hour-glass,' especially one old Head of a College, who was said never to have recovered from the effects of the long sitting.

Dr. Tatham had previously established his reputation by his Bampton Lectures, entitled 'The Chart and Scale of Truth;' but he scarcely ever resided in Oxford, preferring a rough country-life, farming his own glebe, and breeding (what he really prided himself upon) his own pigs[2]. Of course he seldom appeared at the Hebdomadal meetings; but when he occasionally *dropped in*, he produced an effect like that of a bomb falling inside a battery,—a panic and a hasty packing-up of papers ensued, a cessation of discussion, and postponement of 'the question,' with a whisper (it was said) of something about 'The devil over Lincoln[3]!'

---

[1] The conclusion was to this effect:—'I leave the subject to be followed up by the "*larned*" bench of bishops, who have little to do, and do not always do that little.'

[2] He was sometimes seen, on a market-day, opposite his College gate-way, mounted in a cart and helping to *land safely* a couple of fine hogs of his own breeding. In later life, indeed, though his fine countenance and bright eye never lost their expression of power and self-reliance, his costume and appearance were so suited to his favourite pursuit, that he was not very likely to be taken for a Doctor of Divinity and Head of a House.

[3] In 1810, Dr. Tatham *formally accused* 'the Board' of 'holding meetings in *an artful, collusive or smuggling manner*.' The Board, in June of that year, ordered a Case to be prepared for the opinion of Council, as to legal proceedings against the Rector, under thĕ statute 'De famosis Libellis.' Dr. Tatham defied them; 'I am one,' he said, 'with every one against me.' No action was brought against him. In

In Chapter IX some observations occur on the subject of the Bampton Lectures; a few more words may nevertheless be allowed here. The very idea of an individual occupying the University pulpit for *eight Sundays* in Term-time (there being not more than twenty-one or two *unclaimed* Sundays in the academical year), and that individual addressing a necessarily shifting congregation through three successive Terms, may well be called preposterous[1]. What is called

his latter years he resided entirely in the country; his College house (or lodgings) was locked up, not a servant living in it. As might be expected, the house-key was sometimes not to be found on his unannounced, flying visits. 'Never mind, John,' he would say to the College Porter, 'I can take my gin and water in the Common-room Man's pantry when I come in from the market.' He had ceased to attend the Hebdomadal Board, where he had long opposed the Dean of Christ Church and Dr. Parsons of Balliol in the construction of the Examination Statute. 'Give them (he used to say) more of Bacon and less of Aristotle: Dialectica here, Dialectica there, Dialectica everywhere!' At the end of one of his 'Addresses to Convocation' on this subject he writes, 'I have only to request that the old University Motto, " Dominus Illuminatio mea " be changed into

" Aristoteles tenebræ meæ." '

It seems to have been difficult to him to speak civilly of any one; for instance, he says of a learned Doctor of Divinity, 'One Vicessimus Knox, a specious but superficial writer, endeavoured to expose the University by publishing what he was pleased to call facts.'

' I call out (in 1809) the *dormant* Professor of Greek (Dr. W. Jackson) to discharge his public duty or resign. He might well say of himself, " I am a plain man, devoid of ceremony, blunt in my manner and abrupt in my expression." ' (See his Address to Lord Grenville in 1811.)

[1] The offer of such an endowment, if made now, would be rejected, or at least be modified, so as not to exclude other talented preachers, and prevent other important subjects from being ventilated in their season. What, for instance, can be more *unseasonable* than addressing *the last of eight lectures* (on what is called Commemoration Sunday) to a crowd of visitors, who have heard none of the previous discourses?

'The Preaching-turn' does not come round to a clerical M.A. early enough to prevent him (being tired of waiting for it) from removing his name from 'the books[1];' while, at the same time, and from the same cause, our *Select Preachers* have not a sufficient number of turns to work out their proposed subjects. The answer to all this is, of course, 'The University has accepted the Rev. John Bampton's bequest, nay, has enrolled his name as a *Benefactor;* we cannot therefore help ourselves.' But have not much greater invasions into Benefactors' wills and wishes been recently made? and, surely if the *wording* of the bequest is all that stands in the way of any modification or curtailment, a Convocational or even a Parliamentary remedy might be found[2].

Undoubtedly the 'High Church movement' (thirty-three years ago[3]) relieved the University pulpit, in general, from a succession of dry, cold discourses and occasional elegant essays. The re-action however went too far, and much too fast for the hearers; the changes were now rung on the

---

[1] This old custom of calling up preachers from the country, though pleasing in theory, is a failure in its results. Even when a clever man and good preacher comes up *to take his turn*, being a perfect stranger he attracts no juniors, and very few seniors, to St. Mary's. The days have long since gone by when it was felt to be a *duty* to attend the University sermons in compliance with the Statute.

[2] The remarks here freely made apply to the Lecturers generally, without any special reference; yet who can forget the choking effect of dry discourses, and what the common people call 'hard words?' The following specimen of sounding verbiage was noted down a good many years ago: 'A system thus hypothetically elaborated is after all but an inexplicable concatenation of hyperbolical incongruity!' Such sentences, delivered in a regular cadence, formed too often our Sunday fare, in days happily gone by.

[3] i.e reckoning from 1860, when this was written.

Church, the Sacraments, the Rubrics, the Duty of Fasting, and frequent Communion, topics which till then had been scarcely ever alluded to, certainly never enlarged upon. Now and then indeed, before that movement, we had had excellent sermons, but at very long intervals; 'Preaching-turns' having been eagerly obtained for such men as Rolleston of University and Miller of Worcester. But in general University sermons were attended by a thin and listless congregation. 'Select Preachers' did not yet exist, and consequently most of the un-accepted 'Preaching-turns' fell into the hands of some four or five residents, who were (not improperly) called '*hack-preachers*,' or 'Oxford hacks.'

On the rise of the High Church party we began to have, at least, better written sermons; 'Preaching-turns' were eagerly taken[1], and hack-preaching died out. Ever since that time (it must be confessed) the University sermons have greatly improved, being evidently written by the preachers of them, and producing an earnest attention from larger congregations. The appointment of Select Preachers soon began to improve and elevate the character and tone of sermons generally; a sort of emulation was thus excited, and the consequence has been that the goodly array of Select Preachers (ten in number) have scarcely had turns enough to answer their own requirements, or to satisfy the desire to hear them.

It was, it may well be supposed, a great relief (to the Vice-Chancellor and his attendants), when, in 1819, Dr.

---

[1] Before this time, if a preacher did occasionally take his turn and come up from the country, he was pretty sure to be a zealous, Calvinistic divine; and all the sermons of that school were as sure to express (earnestly but tediously) one and only one side of the Christian religion,—truth, but not the whole truth, and requiring generally more than an hour for its exposition.

Hodson being Vice-Chancellor, the Long-Vacation sermons were *entirely* done away with[1]; for if hack-preachers had filled the University pulpit too often in Term-time, they would, as a matter of course, get and keep possession of it in the Long Vacation. One of them was known to have preached over and over again (at successive intervals, and without any regard to times or seasons) a few well-written sermons[2] which he had obtained from a clever friend (a former Bampton Lecturer).

Another (and the 'hack of hacks') always *seemed* to preach the same sermon; whether it really was always the same 'Oxford hack' *with a new saddle and bridle*, or whether the sermons were successively the productions of an ill-stored mind, unconsciously repeating its own platitudes, was a question never quite determined.

A third sometimes boasted, that 'he was the best-paid preacher in the Church of England;—for he often got a guinea a head[3]!'

A fourth once edified his Long-Vacation audience with a discourse on the character of Abraham: (1) as a patriarch; (2) as the father of the faithful; and lastly, as a *country-gentleman!*

---

[1] The Long-Vacation sermons on Sunday afternoons and on Saints' days had been *experimentally*, and by way of a *feeler*, discontinued for about twelve years before.

[2] It did not much matter however that they were *well written*, as they were certainly so badly preached that few whole sentences could be followed; and thus the 'crambe repetita' passed unrecognised, except by the experienced and *long-suffering* ear of one who knew both the preacher and the writer.

[3] His preaching-fee being four guineas, and his academical hearers (exclusive of official persons) *only three or four!* The poor listeners had 'the tinkling cymbal,' and he the 'nummos in arcâ.'

It would hardly be believed, without the assurance of the fact, that a retrograde step on a path of such obvious improvement should have been attempted; that is, that after eleven years' release from that solemn mockery (an University sermon without the chance of an University audience), an effort should have been made (through the influence of Dr. Pusey) to restore the Long-Vacation morning sermon! It was however actually proposed in Convocation[1], June 25, 1830 (Dr. Jones of Exeter College being the Vice-Chancellor), and only rejected (in a thin, careless House) by a majority of three votes. I take to myself much of the credit of this rejection, by having *introduced*, in a printed circular, an anecdote, which I have since heard told *as a good story*: viz. that Lord Liverpool (the Prime Minister) was fond, as an Oxford and a Christ Church man, of running down to Oxford, during the quiet of the Long Vacation[2]. On the Sunday morning St. Mary's great bell naturally drew him to the University sermon, which, agreeably to the state of things above detailed, he found only puzzling from its inanity[3]. But this was not all; for it is said, that Lord Liverpool, on two successive summer visits to his Alma Mater, made the same Sunday experiment, which was followed by a similar, nay, the same result; for he recognised the same preacher, and, what is more, the same (or what appeared to be the same) sermon[4]! The circulation of

---

[1] It had, of course, been previously approved by the members of the Hebdomadal Board, scarcely one of whom would ever be present at such sermons.

[2] 'Inter silvas Academi quaerere verum,' or at least *otium*.

[3] It had however one merit, *brevity*; and his Lordship, safe in his *incognito*, retired with at least the satisfaction that he had not been preached at, as a former Premier, Lord North, was by an Oxford preacher.

[4] Now I do not vouch for this being a fact to *the very letter*; the story

this anecdote certainly had a telling effect, and the promoter of the retrograde movement, though backed by his then rising party, failed to re-impose the heavy yoke—even though (or perhaps rather, *because*) he offered to find a supply of preachers from among his friends[1].

That the proposed re-animation of a lifeless ceremony was wisely rejected has been thoroughly proved, not only from the fact that no like attempt has been made for now more than thirty years, but also from the increasing tendency in the University to make the Long Vacation a *reality*[2].

---

in its principal points had a good foundation of truth, and the occurrence was not only possible, but probable, from the fact that one particular preacher (whom I have called 'the hack of hacks') had managed almost to *monopolise* the Long-Vacation sermons.

[1] Certainly this very offer helped to defeat his object, and even roused a quiet and inactive man, Dr. Radford, Rector of Lincoln, to deliver a Latin speech against the measure in Convocation.

[2] In connection with this subject two hints suggest themselves: (1) that in the Long Vacation (of full three months) the Vicar of St. Mary's might be induced to fill the pulpit, vacated by the University preachers, and add a *parish sermon* to his Morning Service. [N.B. This has since been done.] (2) That Dr. Pusey might try his influence 'nearer home,' and persuade the Dean and Chapter of Christ Church to perform that duty in our Vacations which, as a matter of course, is performed throughout the year in other cathedrals; viz. to give on Sundays a full cathedral *Morning* Service (including a sermon by one of the Chapter, or an adequate representative) for the benefit of the inhabitants and visitors. Not only ought this to be done, but it also seems not unlikely to be done (after a while), since 'innovations,' in what was called 'unchangeable Christ Church,' have actually commenced under the auspices of Dean Liddell. Strangers coming to Oxford for the Sunday in the Long Vacation would not then have to ask, 'Where is the cathedral? and why do we not find *cathedral service* there, at the usual canonical hours? If Christ Church has been a *college* for *nine* months, let it, at least, be a *cathedral* for three.' [N. B. This also is now done by a full morning service: 1869.] The Evening Service, at 5 p.m.,

This subject cannot be better closed than by copying a memorandum which I wrote in 1819, when the Long Vacation sermon was formally discontinued: 'Query: How long will it be ere the same thing, or some portion of the same shall be done for the Christmas Vacation sermons?' a question which was at length answered in Michaelmas Term, 1859, when *most* of the sermons in the Winter Vacation were discontinued by a vote of Convocation.

From time immemorial the University sermons (with the view, probably, of keeping up the memory of the mother-church) had been preached in the Church of St. Peter's-in-the-East on the Sunday afternoons during Lent, as also on St. Peter's day. If the preacher was a man of note or of rising reputation, the want of accommodation was greatly felt as compared with that in St. Mary's. The Undergraduates and Bachelors sat in the gallery, the Masters in the body of the church, the Vice-Chancellor, Doctors, and Proctors under the north windows (the Vice-Chancellor's and the Proctors' pews may still be recognised by their size and position). Until 1822 (when the office ceased to exist)

has lately been numerously attended in the enlarged choir and transept. Dr. Corfe, the talented organist, has greatly improved and made the most of a limited choir; nor is he likely to be scolded as Dr. Crotch once was by Dean Jackson:

Dean (with his watch in his hand, but no music in his ear). 'Mr. Organist, you are over your time.'

Dr. C. 'Mr. Dean, only a few minutes.'

Dean. 'Only a few minutes, Sir, why, that's an age to an old man with rheumatism in his knees, and sitting under your noisy organ.'

N.B. The Dean's seat was then literally under the organ, which had not at that time been put aside. It is but fair to state that the Cathedral has *of late* been open on Sundays with a Morning Service and sermon also,—but at too early an hour. Even this is, I believe, only a Long-Vacation arrangement. In Term time the Cathedral again becomes a College Chapel.

R

the two 'Collectors,' as representatives of the 'Determining Bachelors,' sat in state in front of the gallery at St. Peter's, with a red velvet cushion before them to mark their place of honour. They were also conducted from their Colleges to church by a Yeoman Bedel borrowed from the Vice-Chancellor's staff; and, as their gown and sleeves were exactly like those of the Proctors, they were of course *capped* by the freshmen, to the amusement of other Undergraduates.

The only sermon connected with the 'Lent Exercises' and the 'Determining Bachelors' was one in Latin, on Ash Wednesday, at St. Mary's, and attended almost exclusively by the 'Determiners,' who wore their hoods and a lamb's-wool tippet or collar, and were addressed by the preacher throughout the sermon[1] as 'florentissimi Baccalaurei.'

When St. Mary's Church was re-opened in 1828, after a new arrangement of seats and pulpit, with new galleries and a new organ-loft screen, the Lent sermons at St. Peter's were, by a decree of Convocation, transferred to St. Mary's; a power was at the same time reserved to the Vice-Chancellor to give such turns in the Sunday-afternoon sermons, during Lent, to the Corpus men, as their Statutes require. For before proceeding to a B.D. degree their Statutes direct them to preach a sermon either at 'Paul's Cross,' London, or else at St. Peter's-in-the-East, during Lent. The former opportunity had long ceased with the removal of the Cross

[1] This sermon and the chanting of the Latin Litany in St. Mary's chancel at 8.30 a.m. every Saturday morning during Lent, were, of course, dropped when the so-called 'Determining' ceased in 1822. The attendance of Determiners at the Latin Litany during Lent was enforced by a roll-call after the service, and a fine on the absentees, levied at the College butteries by a Yeoman Bedel.

itself[1]; to preach therefore at St. Peter's had been adopted as the other alternative.

The University sermon on St. Peter's day, which had hitherto been preached by a member of University College, was, on the re-opening of St. Mary's (above mentioned), transferred, *sub silentio*, to the regular list of St. Mary's preachers: having been (it would seem) considered by the College as an onus rather than a privilege, it was suffered to lapse unclaimed. The College naturally might say, 'We preach, if we preach at all, at St. Peter's; but if you go, as you mean to go, to St. Mary's, you (the University) must find the preacher;' and so the University has done ever since. Query: Has the Corpus *claim* to a Lent Sunday preaching-turn ever been made of late years by the College, or thought of by the successive Vice-Chancellors in making out their list of 'Lent Preachers[2]?'

---

[1] The proverbial saying of 'robbing Peter to pay Paul' was thus reversed. It was in conformity with this College Statute that Hooker went to preach at 'The Cross,' when falling ill in London, he was there carefully nursed, and married the daughter of the woman who nursed him.

[2] In this Chapter, and frequently elsewhere, Dr. Pusey's name has been freely and openly mentioned; the obvious excuse for such a liberty is that he has for so many years and so decidedly acted an influential part in the shifting scenes of our Oxford drama, that it would be mere trifling and affectation to avoid the use of it by a clumsy periphrasis or a poor recourse to * * *. In fact, he may well be considered by this time as a *historical personage*, or at least a *public character*. I reverence him sincerely, though I do not always agree with him; and I hope he will forgive me for using the same freedom of speech on questions of academic interest which he used in the debates and printed circulars about the Statute 'De Bedellis.'

CHAPTER XII.

'Quò fessum rapitis?'—*Virgil.*

Recollections De Bedellis.

OF all my predecessors as Esquire Bedels, I am especially bound to mention *Nathaniel Cryne*, M.A.[1], of St. John's College, who bequeathed a small house in Cornmarket Street to his successors in the office of Esquire Bedel in Arts. This house was subsequently sold by the University authorities, and the sum of £400, the produce of the sale, was invested in the Funds, the Esquire Bedel in Arts for the time being, receiving the interest yearly, viz. £12, subject to income-tax[2].

I have often thought (when the *esprit du corps* was particularly strong upon me) that I would endeavour to make out from the University records a list of my predecessors, some of whose names might be worth recalling. Indeed,

---

[1] Mr. Cryne in 1745 left his books and MSS. to the University; they are kept apart, I believe, in the Bodleian.

[2] Query: As the office of Esquire Bedel in Arts will, by the recent vote of Convocation, expire with me or with my resignation, what will be done with the £400 and the dividends? Can the University legally appropriate the money to any other office or any other purpose?

the old President of Magdalen, Dr. Routh, once said to me, 'Yes, Sir, your staff has been held by many Fellows of Colleges and distinguished scholars; recently, Sir, as perhaps you know, by *Dr. Paget*, one of our Fellows.' In former years I have been hindered by other duties from such a task, and am now too indifferent to the subject to carry out the idea. I shall therefore confine my remarks to those who are within my personal *recollection*.

Mr. Matthews, M.A., of Jesus College, and Esquire Bedel in Divinity, died at an advanced age in 1806. Though a Master of Arts, he held the place of butler of his College! Whether he discharged the duties of the office in propriâ personâ or by deputy, I know not. At all events it may be considered as a proof of the simplicity of the times, or at least of that College. That he was highly respected, no stronger proof could be given than the fact that, of his three sons, one was a Fellow of Jesus (his own College), a second Fellow of St. John's, a third a Master Demy of Magdalen.

Mr. Matthews was succeeded as Divinity Bedel by *Robert Hall*, B.C.L., and originally Gentleman-Commoner of Wadham (whom I succeeded in 1806). Mr. Hall, having spent his patrimony, had been elected by the exertions of his Wadham friends to the Law staff, in 1793. Being no scholar, and having no particular pursuits, he gave way to an irritability distressing to himself and annoying to others. For several years he shut himself up (or, rather, was shut up by illness), his duty being performed and his staff carried by a non-academic nephew! Mr. Hall and I were at first good friends, that is, as long as I, as his successor, held the *Law* staff, which was poorly endowed. But when, nine years after, I succeeded to the more lucrative place of Esquire Bedel in Medicine and Arts, and the increasing numbers of the University improved my official receipts, Mr. Hall often annoyed himself by exposing an ungenerous envy. He died in 1832.

Mr. Rhodes, M.A. and formerly Fellow of Worcester College, was elected Esquire Bedel in Medicine and Arts in 1792. Though no longer Fellow, Mr. Rhodes lived, when I first knew him, in Worcester College. At the time when Oxford was high Tory and anti-Jacobin he had sympathized with the French Revolutionists, and occasionally spent the Long Vacation in Paris. He lived, when in Oxford, a solitary, unsociable life, but frequented the Bodleian for his amusement. His journeys to London (whither he regularly went to invest his money and receive his dividends) were always made on foot[1]. On one occasion he walked in from London unexpected by his scout; finding his rooms unprepared, he merely said, 'Never mind, John, I'll just take a turn round the Parks to take the stiffness out of my legs.' He does not appear to have turned his studies to much account. He was, however, a good scholar, and even ventured to publish a translation of Juvenal in verse! It is said to have been a very weak production; I never met with a copy[2], and in our many conversations he never alluded to what was, I suppose, a sore subject. The 'Edinburgh,' in reviewing (I think) Gifford's Translation of Juvenal, gives Rhodes's first line as a sufficient proof of weakness. Was not this like judging of a house by a single brick?

[1] What is here said of Mr. R.'s long walks might be said of many persons in those days of slow coaches. Porson, ' in his days of forced economy,' would sometimes walk the whole distance between London and Cambridge *in a day*.

[2] Since I wrote the above I have succeeded in finding a copy in the Bodleian under the heading of '*Juvenal*' in the Catalogue, and was surprised to find it a spirited, but *free* translation, with some sprightly notes.

Mr. Rhodes (who was also Proctor in the Court, University Coroner, and Clerk of the Market) was always punctual in the discharge of his official duties. His style of living was very peculiar; on one occasion, when I had to call upon him, I found him drinking rum and water, and enjoying (what he called his luxury) the fumes of tobacco, not through a pipe or in the shape of a cigar, but *burnt in a dish!* If this was his frequent custom, it is not surprising that he should be attacked by apoplexy, which soon ended in his death in 1815. He had saved, it was said, £10,000, which, as he died intestate, were claimed by a brother, a schoolmaster in Birmingham, who had never expected such a windfall.

Mr. Bobart, Esquire Bedel in Law, successor to Mr. Hall, had in early life been for three years a Commoner of University College, but never graduated. He was probably the only instance of a non-graduate holding the office of Esquire Bedel; nor was that the only drawback to his fitness for the appointment, for he was rather advanced in years. His claims, however, upon the University (or rather, on a party, and that an influential one) were peculiar, and require a detailed statement. His father and grandfather (I believe of German origin) had been connected with the Oxford Botanical Garden—the latter as Manager or Curator, and the former as Professor of Botany. That Mr. Bobart did not take a Degree in his early days was not from any deficiency in such scholarship as was required for a Degree at the end of the eighteenth century. Like some few individuals in the University at other and later times, he had acquired a taste for driving[1]; but, unlike

---

[1] A recent Bampton Lecturer, contrasting the present time with those of his early recollections, congratulated the University on the fact 'that the race of *Jebus* and *Nimrods* had passed away!'

those individuals, he thought he might as well make his favourite pursuit a source of profit. He therefore invested his patrimony in a four-horse coach, to run between Oxford and London, himself being the *auriga.* He kept up, at least, his acquaintance with Virgil, and was fond of challenging a freshman on his coach-box to '*cap verses.*' Many a youth was led, from this encounter, to argue, 'If Oxford coachmen are such scholars, what must the tutors and the heads be!' Poor Bobart was either very unfortunate on the road, or had lost much of his skill in driving, for twice, within a short period, his coach was upset, and he himself was, on each occasion, the sufferer by a broken leg. These accidents, however, gave a new and unexpected turn to his fortunes and occupations; first, they caused him to 'give up the reins;' and secondly, they induced several of his academic patrons (especially at Ch. Ch., headed by Mr. Goodenough, afterwards Dean of Wells) to bring forward 'the classical coachman' as a candidate for the office of Esquire Bedel! The strong feeling excited for him prevented any opposition, and, though rather advanced in age, he was unanimously elected on the death of Mr. Rhodes, above mentioned, in the year 1815.

He was a thoroughly respectable man and most exemplary in his private life and family duties. We did not meet much, except on duty, when we always (as he would say) 'ran our horses together very pleasantly.' It is but justice to him to record the following anecdote, not only as showing the man (and indeed two other good men besides), but as illustrative of the then state of things at Oxford, and especially at St. Mary's. We had been (as usual at the opening of Term), I think in 1838, to the Latin Litany and Sermon, and (as was then also usual) had left the church with the Vice-Chancellor, the Holy Communion (so solemnly required by Statute) *being omitted;*—none but the University officers having been present to hear a Latin sermon mumbled by a hack-preacher, and the solemn Latin Litany rattled through in a slovenly manner. On leaving church, Bobart met Messrs. Denison and Hamilton, Fellows of Merton (fellows too in many other respects, and afterwards successively Bishops of Salisbury). These good men, seeing Bobart in his official dress, and, like most other residents of the day, altogether forgetful of the solemn service, cried out, 'Hallo! Bobart, what's going on to day? where have you been with your staff?' 'Why, Gentlemen,' he replied, 'we have been where you, and such as you, ought to have been.' 'Ah, indeed! and where was that?' 'Where!—why, at St. Mary's Church; where, after Tallis's Litany, and a Latin sermon, preached to empty benches, the authorities turned their backs upon the chancel, and the Holy Communion was not administered, on the plea of "no congregation."' 'Well,' they replied, 'that is sad, indeed; it ought not to be; we take our share of the blame; and, be assured, this shall not happen again,—at least in our time.' Nor did it;—the next like solemnity brought together at least forty senior academic communicants;—and this, not merely 'exempli gratiâ' (as the Statute required of seniors), but as wishing to infuse new life into what had become a deadening, if not a dead ceremony. Nor up to this time (1861) has the attendance at Latin Litany and Communion very greatly (though it has in some measure) slackened. Indeed it has been an edifying privilege to see men of various and strongly-marked shades of religious opinion thus meeting at the Lord's Table. Convocation too since then has secured by a new Statute, De Concionibus, a better supply of Latin sermon writers.

But to return to poor Bobart (and what I am about to

add will explain why I call him *poor* Bobart);—anxiety for a numerous second family preyed upon his mind; his spirits sunk and his healthy religious turn became melancholy. His somewhat Calvinistic views threw a dark shade over his conscientious scruples; his mind gave way, and in a wretched moment he committed suicide.

In one of his brighter days Bobart had christened *Grand-Compounders* 'Mr. Cox's tulips[1].' As Grand-Compounders have become, since 1857, *an extinct species*, it is as well to add here, that, under the old system, graduating persons having £300 a year ('sive in agris, sive in pecuniis'), paid extra fees (e.g. £40 instead of £14 for M.A., and £30 instead of £7 for B.A.), were called 'Grand-Compounders,' and, as such, wore *a red gown* on being admitted to a Degree. Forty years ago a great deal of fuss and trouble was occasioned by a man's 'going out' as a Grand-Compounder. For instance, on the day preceding the Degree-day, he with his dean waited on the Vice-Chancellor and Proctors (at the Delegates' Room) to ask an extra Grace and request their attendance on the morrow. (This ceremony was called 'the circuit.') On the morrow accordingly,—whatever the distance and whatever the weather,—the Vice-Chancellor and Proctors headed a procession, consisting of the Grand-Compounder (who walked *capite aperto* with his presenter by his side) and the members of his College, cheered, on the way to the Convocation House, by the sound of St. Mary's bells. It was quite a show-spectacle for 'lionisers,' to see such a procession start from the Common-room at Christ Church (where, of course, Grand-Compounders were most frequent), the Noblemen in their purple

---

[1] It is singular that Meade, Milton's tutor at Cambridge, used to call the dandy Fellow-Commoners 'University *tulips*.'

and gold dresses, the Canons preceding them *within the walls*, but at 'Canterbury Gate' drawing back to give them precedence!

Grand-Compounders were comparatively *raræ aves* in former days, and almost confined to the aristocracy; but as the sons of commerce began to increase the number, such a ceremony would naturally be soon found burdensome and unsuitable to the times. Its discontinuance, however, was caused rather unexpectedly. Dr. Richards, Vice-Chancellor in 1806, on attending a procession of this kind caught a cold from which he never recovered. The Grand-Compounder's procession fell naturally into ill favour. But it was not wholly discontinued till 1817, and then only 'if not claimed.' It was not, however, claimed till 1853, when Mr. Baxendale of Balliol, being about to take the Degree of M.A. as Grand-Compounder, demanded a procession;— wishing (as it was said) 'to have the dance as he paid the piper.' The procession was not regularly *granted* to him, but as the Vice-Chancellor, Dr. Cotton, passed by from Worcester College with his procession, the candidate and all the Balliol men *joined on*, to the wonder and amusement of the lookers-on. This attempt, however, had its (probably intended) effect, and on the revision of the Degree-fees in 1855, 'novæ tabulæ' were drawn up and Grand-Compounders ceased to occur. For myself (whose interest in Grand-Compounders' fees was duly considered by a compensation in the new table) this cessation was a great relief; inasmuch as it had been a fatiguing as well as an unpleasant and responsible task, to extract an answer from each candidate for a Degree to three troublesome questions. First, 'How were you matriculated, as to your father's quality? Arm. fil.? Gen. fil.? or what?' each man's fees being accordingly, though slightly affected. Secondly, 'How many terms have you actually kept?—exclusive of the term in which you matriculated and this in which you graduate?' This again, though often, at the impulse or recollection of the moment, incorrectly answered, was to be considered in the fees. Thirdly (and in some respects chiefly), 'Have you any independent income, exclusive of University revenue?' (which was not reckoned). Ordinary Proceeders answered simply 'No,' and paid the lowest fees. If the answer was 'Yes,'— 'have you £300 a year of your own?' if 'Yes,' which was generally given with reluctance, sometimes extorted with difficulty and loss of time, ' Then you are a Grand-Compounder and your fees are so and so.' If under £300 a year and above £5, the proceeder was entered as Petty Compounder, and paid 10s. 8d. more than the ordinary proceeder. I should mention (to finish a story that will never have to be told again), that for the M.A. Degree (as also in the superior faculties) the farther question was asked of those who were in Orders, 'Have you a living rated at £40 a year in the Liber Regis?' (very few livings being rated so high). 'If so —you are a Grand-Compounder; if only £5 you are a Petty Compounder.' By the new table all this inquisitorial process is done away with; every B.A. pays £7 10s., and every M.A. £12, so that not only the paying of fees but the receiving of them is greatly simplified and expedited[1].

It is the painful consequence of an extended life and a long continuance in office to have to record the departure not only of cotemporaries but even of juniors. And not only juniors, but also (in my case) friends and pupils. I stand in this relation to two recent Esquire Bedels, both of them for many years my pupils at New College School.

[1] If any one should think the above account of Degrees, Processions, &c. prolix, let him compare it with that of Ayliffe, vol. i. p. 150 et seq.

Both of them were amiable, sensible, and modest; both of them, from perhaps the consciousness of a weak constitution, lived a quiet, unobtrusive life. *William Miller*, M.A., Esquire Bedel in Law, was succeeded in his office by *W. W. Harrison*, B.A. of Brasenose College, who will be distinguished, after my death or resignation, as the last of the old Triumvirate of Esquire Bedels. My other friend and former pupil, *Henry Forster*, Esquire Bedel in Divinity and M.A., who died in April, 1857, left no successor, his office having (by the recent enactment) expired with him.

I have somewhere read that Laud recommended that the three Esquire Bedels (not merely the Law Bedel as was provided but not enforced in the old Statute) should be employed in the University Press; if his advice had been taken, we should all have been *stereotyped!*

Members of Convocation will not object to an extract from a Latin speech made in Convocation by Dr. Ralph Bathurst, President of Trinity, on the election of an Esquire Bedel, on June 6, 1676. (See Warton's Life of Ralph Bathurst.)

'Qualis is esse debet, quem electuri estis, paucis exponam. Sit, opto, sobrius, sedulus, fidelis, obsequio dexter et præsens, specie habituque externo ad decorem virilem compositus; sit etiam negotiis tum intelligendis aptus, tum gerendis promptus et expeditus,—quique Academiæ nomine, si quando res postulat, ad magnates et Aulicos legati munere, si non honorificè at saltem non indecorè, fungi possit. Tales certè viderunt majores nostri, et supersunt usque hodiè reliquiæ veterum Bedellorum haudquaquam pœnitendæ; qui agiles et assidui officio suo etiam in provectâ ætate nullâ ex parte desunt,' &c.

On that occasion, *C. Minshull*, Fellow of New College, was

elected, 'unà aspirantibus Nic. Crutch, Coll. Ball. Socio et N. Violet in curia Cancellarii Advocato.'

Having obtruded much that is dull in relation to Esquire Bedels, I will relieve the subject with rather a livelier representation, in an extract from Percy's Ancient Poetry, vol. iii. p. 316: 'John Grubb, of witty memory in Oxford, 1688, in his second part of " St. George for England," speaks thus of a fat man :—

> 'He had a phiz of latitude,
> And was full thick i' th' middle;
> The cheeks of puffed trumpeter,
> And paunch of 'Squire Bedel !'

Percy's note on the last line is, ' men of bulk, answerable to their places, as is well known in Oxford.' Alas! that such a fine breed (fallen off, as we are, in fat and favour) should be doomed to become extinct !

Among former Esquire Bedels it would not be fair to leave out the laborious antiquary, *Thomas Hearne*, M.A., of St. Edmund Hall, who succeeded to the office of Esquire Bedel in Law, Jan. 1715, expecting (as had since Laud's time been the case) to be at the same time the Architypographus of the University Press. The Vice-Chancellor, however, ' chose, on his own authority, to separate the two offices, and set over the Press a common printer.' By the Statute De Typographis Universitatis (which has lately disappeared from the Statute Book) the Architypographus was to be 'Vir Græcis, Latinisque literis probè instructus et in studiis Philologicis versatissimus;' and as such he was to hold also the office of Esquire Bedel in Law. Hearne did not long hold the staff, thus separated from the Press,— he had made himself obnoxious by publishing Non-juror writings, and the Oaths of Allegiance &c. stuck in his throat. He fell back upon his office of Under-Librarian at the Bodleian; but even there his politics were turned against him. On being deprived of that post, he retired to a studious life in St. Edmund Hall. He was succeeded as Esquire Bedel by W. Mussendine, M.A. and Fellow of Magdalen College. (See a book in two vols. called 'The Lives of Leland, Hearne, and Anthony Wood,' published 1772.)

N.B. Cambridge did not (as Oxford did) originally possess its 'cherished *Triumvirate* of Esquire Bedels;' Mr. Walsh, in his 'Historical Account of Cambridge,' (publ. in 1837), says, 'The office of Esquire Bedel is one of the most lucrative and honourable in the University; anciently there were only two,—a third was instituted in 1556.' [In 1864 the number was again reduced to two; Cambridge having, in spite of a recent vote to the contrary, partially followed the example of Oxford.] The following are some of my predecessors in distant times.

1. Bedell Hall was bequeathed to the Poor Scholars in 1294 by Reynold de la Leigh, Esquire Bedel.
2. In 1533 E. Standish, Esquire Bedel, left several revenues for the maintenance of an honest, secular priest to sing for his soul and that of his mother, in St. Peter's in the East.
3. J. Doe (or Doo), Esquire Bedel—his epitaph is given by Wood, though it has disappeared (with many others) from St. Mary's; his arms were, 'A Bedel's staff, between two does' heads erased.'
4. In St. Aldate's Register occurs that of Mr. R. Peers, Student of Christ Church and Esquire Bedel, in 1690.
5. Holywell Church Register gives the names of Bernard Hore, Esquire Bedel in 1658, and of (a namesake of mine) Potten Cox, Esquire Bedel in 1715. (Peshall's History of Oxford.)

Of the *Yeoman Bedels*, in my long experience, I have little to say; they have been truly respectable men, though none of them more so than the present trio, Messrs. Pillinger, Harper, and Haines. The days are gone by when a Yeoman Bedel, after opening Convocation according to Statute, 'Intretis in Convocationem, Magistri, intretis,' used to think and say he had *intreated* the Masters. [Pillinger died since this was written.]

In 1806 there were two Yeoman Bedels respectively named Bliss and Wise, of whom saucy Undergraduates would sometimes say, 'Where ignorance is *bliss*, 'tis folly to be *wise*.' Wise indeed was not over wise; but Mr. Bliss was a respectable bookseller in a small way, and his father was assistant to Radcliffe's first Observer, Dr. Hornsby.

In connection with Mr. Bliss's name I may be allowed to introduce the following anecdote. About the year 1800 the performance of an Exercise in the Music School attracted a crowd at the entrance; the Proctors on trying to clear a passage, being somewhat roughly pressed upon, endeavoured to expel a young man, a son of Mr. Bliss (who was in attendance as a Yeoman Bedel). The young man resisted, and with some warmth of expression. The Proctors having *sat out* the performance, called upon Mr. Bliss to require his son to apologise or to do so for him. Mr. B. respectfully declined to do either. In our days of fair dealing and liberal notions it will hardly be believed that the father (under the threat of suspension on the day of 'deponing and resuming' the staves) was made to apologise for his son and himself in the Convocation House!

My *personal interest* in the subject of this chapter must plead my excuse for its length.

CHAPTER XIII.

'Fungar vice cotis.'—*Horace.*

Recollections from A.D. 1831 *to* A.D. 1836.

A.D. 1831.

[B.A. 280. M.A. 184. Hon. D.C.L. at Commemoration, 5.]

OXFORD at this time was partly supplied with water from the Isis; but the water-works by which it was thrown up were so constructed at *Folly* Bridge (as if the very name was contagious), that whenever the river overflowed (and that happens, as we all know, pretty often in autumn, winter, and spring) no water could be supplied to the town[1]!

Jan. 10. The notorious Carlile, on his trial for wicked and libellous publications, was appropriately defended by his friend, the 'Rev.' Robert Taylor, alias 'The Devil's Chaplain,' as he was called.

In this Lent (the forms and exercises of 'Determination' having been *intermitted*, a soft term for their *abolition*), the names and not the persons of the Bachelors of Arts, who

[1] This fault of engineering has been long corrected, and really pure water introduced from what is called the 'Rail-road Lake,' a piece of water formed from the springs on removing a large bed of gravel.

would have determined, were presented by the Deans of Colleges, in a special Congregation, in order to be Registered. So ended 'Determination,' which had become a farce.

'The granting of a Term,' which had taken place on the accession of George IV, was called for by some people to mark the beginning of William IV's reign; but having *then* been pronounced to be 'a doubtful good,' it was *now* pooh-poohed.

Feb. 6. Mr. Bulteel of Exeter College and Curate of St. Ebbe's (who afterwards seceded from the Church, or rather had his licence taken away by the Bishop for fraternising with Dissenters and preaching in their chapels[1]), preached, in his own turn, at St. Mary's, a sermon distinguished as well by its length as by a most violent attack upon the University, especially on the Heads of Colleges. He not only preached it, but also published it. Dr. Burton, Regius Professor, published a feeble answer, to which Mr. Bulteel replied. A 'Friendly Letter,' addressed to Mr. Bulteel, also appeared, but the 'lethalis arundo' still rankled; he had told the authorities some home truths (though bitterly overstated), especially as to the serious evil of giving Testimonials for Orders as a matter of course. The following are a few out of many dull lines that appeared in print in reference to this sermon and some contemporaneous radical movements in St. Ebbe's Parish :—

> 'From Priest to meanest pauper there
> Plans of Reform they're broaching,
> And ruthless prate of Church and State,
> "That ruin's fast approaching."

[1] It ended in his building a large chapel in Oxford, to which he for some years attracted a numerous congregation, who were called 'Bulteelers.'

> This dubbs the Doctors reprobates,
> That styles our Statesmen villains;
> Hard this one thinks, hard that one drinks,
> For ardent are their feelings!'

Mr. Bulteel pronounced the Bishop's act as to his licence to be that 'of an officer of the Church of Antichrist.'

Feb. 17. I held a most painful inquest on the death of *Lord Conyers Osborne*, second son of the Duke of Leeds and a Nobleman of Christ Church. Verdict, 'Death *per Infortunium*,' or 'Chance-Medley.' Lord Hillsborough [afterwards Marquis of Downshire, and lately deceased] gave the following evidence: 'About half-past eleven on the night of the 16th inst. I was running rather riotously about Peckwater Quad. with two or three young companions. The deceased (Lord C. Osborne) came out of his room, when I, wishing to save him from rough usage, forced him back into his room. A scuffle took place; the deceased, resisting my interference, struck me, and I struck him in the body, intending to force him into his chair.'

Being asked '*with what* he struck him?' '*With this*,' was the answer, and he held up his doubled fist! 'Observing,' he continued, 'that Lord C. Osborne sunk back in his chair and vomited, I became alarmed, and, after rubbing his temples with lavender-water, sent for Mr. Hitchings the surgeon.' Lord Osborne was a small, delicate man, Lord Hillsborough tall and powerful. Lord Hillsborough, after braving it out for a while, took his leave of Christ Church; *the blow* was indeed a heavy one to Lord C. Osborne's family.

This Christ Church inquest reminds me of a strange story told in a strange, cold manner by Horace Walpole (see his Correspondence with Sir Horace Mann, vol. ii. p. 344). 'April 10, 1747. We have some chance of a Peer's trial, that has nothing to do with the rebellion. A servant of a College has been killed at Oxford, and a verdict of "*wilful murder by persons unknown*" brought in by the Coroner's inquest. Those *persons unknown* are supposed to be Lord Abergavenny, Lord Charles Scott (second son of the Duke of Buccleugh), and two more, who had played tricks with the poor fellow that night while he was drunk, and the next morning he was found, with his skull fractured, at the foot of the first Lord's staircase. One pities the poor boys, who undoubtedly did not foresee the melancholy event of their sport.' Very true; but was there no pity for the poor man[1]?

Feb. 23. Mr. White, of Magdalen College, was duly chosen Proctor, but the *reporting* of his election to the Vice-Chancellor, as required by the Statute, *on the same day*, was forgotten and omitted. *On the 28th* the Vice-Chancellor, Dr. Jones, sent a note to the President of Magdalen to ask if any notice had ever been sent by the College, as he had received none. The President answered by apologising for the omission and informing him of Mr. White's unanimous election. This was followed by another note from the Vice-Chancellor, stating that he *had taken advice*, and in consequence considered that the nomination of a Proctor had lapsed to him, and that he had nominated a Gentleman of Magdalen Hall. The College of course felt indignant; though willing to make all due amends for the *ceremony omitted*, they were prepared to argue that it did not affect their real election, as the wording of the Caroline Statute seems to refer only to the case of a disputed, undecided election, whereas theirs was quite statutable and unanimous. Amusingly enough, it turned out that the Vice-Chancellor

---

[1] A pamphlet was published in 1747 in London, entitled 'A Letter to the Heads of the University of Oxford on a late very remarkable affair.'

himself, in correcting this error, had fallen into another, not having made his nomination '*intra triduum*' as required by the Statute! The Hebdomadal Board (on the 7th of March) rejected the claim still made by the College and referred the decision (as provided for by the Statute) to a Council, composed of the Vice-Chancellor and the two senior Doctors of Divinity[1], who settled the matter amicably by giving back the elective power to Magdalen College, who, of course, again elected Mr. White, who was duly admitted.

In March, Mathematics began *to look up* in Oxford, four Mathematical Scholarships, of £50 a year, being founded.

A great stir was made this year for Parliamentary Reform; Convocation, of course, carried a vote against it,—but with a decreasing majority.

In May, the Examination List began to exhibit a pretty large Fourth Class. In June a silver candelabrum was presented to Dr. Tournay by the members of Wadham College on his resignation of the Wardenship.

July 1. Died, at an advanced age and greatly respected, the *Rev. John Gutch*, who, as an antiquary, had laid Oxford under obligation by his edition of Anthony Wood's work. He had for several years received a well-earned pension from the University as former Registrar.

Sept. 30. Augustus Hare, of New College (the same *Augustus Hare* who, as Master of the Schools, examined *Cicero Rabbitts* of Magdalen Hall!) appealed against the election of Founder's Kin at Winchester and New College. Counsel were heard before the Bishop of Winchester and two Judges. Mr. Erle (afterwards Lord Chief Justice) asserted 'that there was not a drop of Wykeham's blood left in his so-called kin;'

---

[1] Or (according to another account) to the Vice-Chancellor, the Senior Head of a House, and the Senior D.D. Dr. Routh, being both, gave the Proctorship, of course, back to Mr. White!

and that a certain noble family had on *an unfounded pedigree* sent '*Founder's* kin to the School and College for several generations!' The Visitor, of course, *took time to consider*. But, I believe, nothing came of the appeal; nothing was done till it was done in earnest by the Commissioners in 1855.

Oxford must have been unusually unmusical at this period, as concerts at the Music Room were so thinly attended, though M^{de}. Stockhausen and Mr. Phillips were engaged, that the expenses were not covered by the receipts.

A.D. 1832.

[B.A. 277. M.A. 163. Hon. D.C.L. at Commemoration, 4.]

A Fellow of a College (who at this date drove a tandem) called his leader Xerxes, and his shaft-horse Artaxerxes, Being asked why, 'Our Tutor (he replied) used to tell us that Aristotle's Metaphysics were so called, because *they came after* (μετὰ) the "Physics;" so, my leader having, somehow or other, got the name of Xerxes, I (assisted by the groom) named his follower *Arter-xerxes*, or more correctly *Artaxerxes*.'

A testy Proctor, grieved at the frequent appearance of the above mentioned *tandem-driver*, as in his opinion setting a bad example to junior academics who were not allowed such a privilege, is said to have closed his remonstrances with a Ciceronian reproof:—'Quousque *tandem* abuteris patientiâ nostrâ!' He died from an upset.

In this year, Mr. Bulteel, 'the outcast minister of Christ,' as he called himself (and who has been mentioned already, at some length), published an account of his restoring three females (by prayer and intercession) from a state of bed-ridden helplessness, of several years' standing, to the power of walking. One of them (his wife's sister) had (he said) for seventeen years 'suffered many things of many physicians!'.

In the Public Examination, in Michaelmas Term, 1831, *Mr. Seymer* of Alban Hall, though blind from his birth, obtained a Second Class! Lord Grenville, our Chancellor, sent him a present of twenty pounds, as a sort of prize. It was said, by way of explanation of so great a feat under such circumstances, that Mr. Seymer had a clever, devoted sister who read with him. The Examiners gave him all possible help and kind consideration[1].

Feb. 7 died my old colleague Robert Hall, Esquire Bedel in Divinity. On his death there were four candidates for his staff: *Mr. Forster*, M.A. of New College, who had 105 votes; Mr. Dynham, B.A. of Magdalen Hall, who had 44; Mr. C. King, B.A. of Magdalen College, who had 20; and Mr. J. Cox, M.A. of Christ Church, who had 17 votes.

April 12 died Mr. C. Monk, B.A. and Fellow of New College. This gentleman, though only a B.A., was a senior Fellow when he died; his residence at New College had been cut short in a very singular and shocking manner. He was somewhere in the country, not far from Oxford, on a Sunday, and actually 'read the Service' in the parish church, not being in orders! This shameful act, of course, got wind; but those days of laxity were at least days of mercy, and he was allowed to hold his Fellowship on the condition of *his never residing*. This sort of connection continued for thirty years, and at his death he showed his love for New College, and (we may suppose) his gratitude

---

[1] N.B. In 1862 a pension of one hundred pounds was granted to him by the Crown 'for his contributions to literature, and his labours in educating the natives of India, in spite of his blindness.'

for the mercy shown to him, by leaving to the College several hundred pounds.

In this year the Rev. Daniel Wilson succeeded John Matthias Turner as Bishop of Calcutta; the successor (though apparently not of a strong constitution) made up by his long tenure of his sacred office, for the short episcopate of his predecessors, Middleton, James, Heber, and Turner.

The second reading of the *Reform Bill* was carried even in the House of Lords, by a majority of nine! The University petitioned against it to the last.

June 2. Mr. Robert Montgomery (formerly of Lincoln College), in advertising his new poem 'The Messiah!' (his *titles* at least were ambitious) added ' By the author of " The Omnipresence of the Deity!!"'—he could not I suppose screw up his courage to add 'and of " Satan;"' the climax would have been too shocking [1].

In June, the British Association held its meeting, for the first time in Oxford; at the conclusion, viz. on June 21, the Honorary Degree of D.C.L. was conferred on four of its distinguished members, one of the four being *Dalton*, a Quaker, who even appeared at St. Mary's in his Doctor's red gown [2]!

Oxford, in this July, was visited with many cases of

[1] Mr. Montgomery, being a clergyman as well as a poet, could not have been much flattered, or pleased, by Lady Morgan's flippant but characteristic account of an interview with him at a London party:—
' Then up comes Bob Montgomery, the poet,—he bows to the ground, —a handsome, little, black man. I asked him if he was Satan Montgomery,—and he said he was. So we began to be very facetious, and we laughed [concludes the unblushing ' Lady'] as if *the devil was in us!*'

[2] It is a curious fact, that Dalton had that peculiarity of vision called colour-blindness.

cholera, including forty deaths. A great cry was raised against that filthy stream, which empties itself into the Isis at Folly Bridge, and whose banks were lined with 'pigsties and other abominations.' The Christ Church authorities, however, succeeded in making the stream partially cleanse itself, by a system of *flashes* of water, and at a very great expense shut it out, at least *from the eye*, by carrying a wall along its course on the west of Christ Church meadow. Strict rules were enforced, pigsties were relegated to the suburbs, and a standing Board of Health kept a watchful look-out. St. Clement's also has its dirty stream, and the greatest number of cases (and fatal ones) occurred there and in that vicinity, especially at the house of the Common-room man of Magdalen College, on Cowley Road. The cholera carried off Mrs. G——, two grown-up daughters, and a maid-servant. Of the total number of deaths in July and August (viz. forty), twenty-nine occurred in St. Clement's[1].

Nov. 2. The Duchess of Kent and her daughter *Victoria* (then a girl of about fourteen) were received in the Theatre,

---

[1] It is very remarkable (we may well call it *providential*) that the cholera on its two appearances in Oxford broke out at the commencement of the Long-Vacation, and happily *went down* as the young men were beginning to *come up* for the Michaelmas Term. How much more serious were the visits of 'The Plague' in former times! One instance of this visitation was, curiously enough, attributed to a cause not likely to occur now-a-days: 'The plague, which made its appearance in Oxford in 1592, having been attributed to the crowding together of great numbers in *the Play-house* there, Orders were issued by the Privy Council to the Vice-Chancellor and Heads of Houses, desiring them not thenceforth to admit stage-players to come within the precincts of the University; and this, not only lest the Students should suffer in their health, but in their morals.' ('Instances of the Interference of the Crown with the Universities,' by G. E. Corrie, B.D., of Cambridge.)

fêted at University by the Vice-Chancellor, Dr. Rowley, and after being lionized by him, returned to Wytham, Lord Abingdon's place. In the Theatre the Vice-Chancellor read and presented an address, and the Duchess made a short reply; Sir E. Conroy, her Equerry, was made Honorary D.C.L. What a leaf might have been added to the address, could the Vice-Chancellor have foreseen what that 'young girl' was to be only five years afterwards! The royal visit was celebrated in a printed copy of Macaronic verses of considerable talent, and amusing by the exhibition of wit. They were attributed to Mr. Lowe, then a Commoner of University, afterwards Fellow of Magdalen, and a distinguished M.P. A reprint of the *jeu-d'esprit* has appeared this year (1861)[1].

---

[1] As the reputed author of this little absurdity has become a public character, and as its printer (with his sanction, we may presume) has republished it again and again, a few lines are subjoined for the edification of those who never met with a 'Poema Canino-Anglico-Latinum:'—

'Quid memorem quanto crepuit $\begin{Bmatrix} \text{the Theatre} \\ \text{domus alta} \end{Bmatrix}$ tumultu,

Intremuere scholæ, celsâ suspecta Cathedrâ,
Intremuit Christ-Church, tremuit Maudlenia turris,
Radcliffique domus, geminisque University portis.

. . . . .

Consedere duces et tum Vice-Chancellor infit.

. . . . .

Insequitur loud shout; loud-shoutis deinde quietis,
Kentea pauca refert, sed non et pauca fuerunt
Clappea, nec paucis se gratified esse fatetur
Curtseis, tanto mage gens perversa fatigat
Plausibus assiduis.

. . . . .

Alfredi tandem fessus domus alta recepit
Hospitio of the best, sed quod magis hearty voluntas
Commendat domini cum sedulitate feloum [fellows].'

A.D. 1833.

[B.A. 257. M.A. 184. Hon. D.C.L. at Commemoration, 1.]

Peter Maurice, D.D. of New College, published a book, entitled 'Popery in Oxford;'—except the fact of the *City* of Oxford electing, for their Member, Mr. Stonor, a Roman Catholic, in preference to Hughes Hughes (who, in the Oxfordshire dialect, was said to have been *hused*-up), Dr. Maurice had not then much ground for alarm. He afterwards claimed the character of a prophet, 'having (he said) foreseen the coming popery of the University, though then no *bigger than the palm of a hand.*' Mr. Stonor, at a public dinner, given to him in his own neighbouring town of Henley, boasted of his 953 supporters '*unbought, unbribed*[1], unprejudiced!' Sir Charles Wetherell failed,—for why? He gave Oxford citizens plenty of small talk, which cost him nothing, but nothing else, not even small-beer. It was at this City election that the Head of a College said to the College porter, 'I believe, John, you are a Freeman.' 'I am, Sir.' 'Then will you oblige me by voting for Sir Charles?' 'I thought, Sir, you *believed* I was a *Free-man!*' 'You are right, John, and I was wrong; go and vote for whom you please.'

An Oxford dentist, named Lukyn, about this time having had the good luck to operate successfully upon a Vice-Chancellor's ἕρκος ὀδόντων, asked and obtained the privilege

[1] In March, a Committee of the House (in the first Session of the Reformed Parliament) declared Mr. Stonor's election null and void, on the *ground of bribery*. Mr. Hughes recovered his place, against Mr. Townley, another Roman Catholic, and Mr. Donald Maclean, of Balliol, who was afterwards more successful.

of being matriculated. The consequence was, that wherever he could, in newspapers and by printed circulars, he was ever before one's eyes as 'Lukyn, the Matriculated Dentist,' accompanied, in smaller type, by a reprint of the Vice-Chancellor's acknowledgment of 'having been benefited by his skill.'

March 27. At a political dinner given to Mr. Maclean, the late unsuccessful candidate, his friend Dr. Marsham, Warden of Merton, concluded a capital speech by recommending the citizens of Oxford to elect, at a future opportunity, his friend Mr. Maclean, a First-Class man in the University Calendar, and thus 'add *your* solid pudding to *our* empty praise.'

A few *black sheep* (or rather wolves in sheep's clothing) made themselves unhappily conspicuous in the flocks of those days; none more so than a Dr. Free, who having been most deservedly deprived of his living (to which he ought never to have been presented)[1], coolly tried by law (pleading his own cause in formâ pauperis) to force St. John's College to reinstate him in his Fellowship (which had been filled up long before), or at least to receive and support him!

No appointment was made in 1833 to the Bampton Lectureship, the Lectures being suspended for two years, to enable the estate from which the Lecturer was paid to recover from some incumbrances.

May 1. The Oxford Convocation voted a petition against

---

[1] The painful fact is, that College testimonials and presentations to livings had been looked upon almost as *things of course*. The consciences of some signers (too many, if only a few) must have suggested a laxity which in turn they hoped to experience. It was no secret that in 1833 a Fellow of a College was presented to a College living, who had either notoriously kept a mistress, who bore him two children in a neighbouring village, or had been for some time married, without having resigned his Fellowship!

a proposed Bill to alter and amend the laws relating to the Temporalities of the Church in Ireland, on the principle 'paries proximus ardet—tua res agitur.'

May 13. A meeting was held in Oxford 'for the purpose of promoting a subscription for some mark of respect to the memory of Sir Walter Scott.' The Warden of Merton, Mr. Denison, and Mr. Mills were the chief speakers. The object proposed was 'to secure Abbotsford with its Library and Antiquities to Sir Walter's family.'

In June, a large subscription was raised for building a church near the new Printing-office (afterwards called St. Paul's); and at the same time a small subscription was begun, for bringing down a pure supply of water from a spring on Headington-hill (then running to waste), to supply St. Clement's with the pure element; the want of which had (it was reasonably supposed) contributed to the recent spread of cholera in that neighbourhood. N.B. Each of the public pumps in the streets of St. Clement's has ever since been supplied from that spring.

At the Commemoration, beside the £20 attached to the Newdigate Prize[1], the prize-man of this year, Mr. Graham of Wadham, received £10 from Mr. Vincent (and one hundred copies) for the copyright! Query: Has this arrangement been kept up? or were his verses, on Granada, better than usual? He had had the reputation of being a poet at Winchester School, and after his popular Prize-poem at Oxford he published 'A Vision of Spirits,' much praised for elegance, tenderness, and good versification. He died young.

---

[1] Without any reference to Mr. Graham's poem, which was above the average, we may quote Lord Macaulay's cutting saying, that 'prize oxen are only fit to make candles of, and prize poems to light them with!'

Oct. 7. Poor old 'Counsellor Bickerton,' a crazy but inoffensive character (mentioned elsewhere in connection with the late 'ruinous and offensive' state of Hertford College), after having disappeared for some years from Oxford, died near London in a wretched hovel, of apparent starvation, having been for some time imbecile in body as well as mind. He had money and some property, but had long lived in a dirty, solitary state.

Lord Grenville's death, in December, closed the academic year.

A. D. 1834.

[B.A. 298. M.A. 193. Hon. D.C.L. at Installation, 71.]

Jan. 14. A numerously-signed requisition was sent to the Duke of Wellington, inviting him to be our Chancellor; he accepted the invitation 'provided there was no opposition.' An attempt (in bad taste) was made to persuade Sir R. Peel to come forward. Of course he would not (not to mention other reasons for keeping quiet) oppose *The Duke*, who was unanimously elected Jan. 28.

Lady Morgan tells us, that on receiving the news of the Duke of Wellington's election to the Chancellorship of Oxford, the Archbishop of Dublin requested an audience of Lord Wellesley (the Viceroy): 'I come to demand a troop of horse, my Lord.' 'For whom?' 'For myself!' 'Oh, I see!' Pretty sharp quizzing that, as expressing Dr. Whately's opinion as to the fitness of the choice.

Feb. 13. In order to help the Vice-Chancellor to meet the expenses of the coming Installation, £200 were voted to him in Convocation.

'In this month Dr. Daubeny was elected Professor of Botany by the College of Physicians;—that College being then not such an unwieldy body as it has since become, and Oxford being, numerically, better represented than it is likely to be at a subsequent election.

March 21. A humble Petition was voted in Convocation (with only one non-placet), requesting his Majesty to withhold the proposed 'Charter to the University of London,'— at least under the projected form. All that one need say *now* is, that it was then quite natural in the old University, but not very noble, or very wise. Movements of this kind, if let alone, generally (in sensible England) rectify themselves; while opposition (especially from interested parties) only adds life and energy to them. Thus the *Reformed* House of Commons had soon a glut of the results in the persons of some of its newly-elected Members. When the House looked round its benches, and saw there such persons as Hunt (a demagogue and a blacking-manufacturer), and Gully (recently a celebrated pugilist, but in 1833—Gully, Esq., M.P.), this mode of representing the *people* soon brought about its own cure. Cobbett and O'Connell were (independent of talent) much better specimens; Mr. Hudson, 'the Rail-road King,' did not yet (politically) exist.

'The stewards of the Music Room' still took upon themselves the management and the responsibility of the 'Grand Concerts' given in the Commemoration-week. Of course they endeavoured to engage the great musical lion of the day, Paganini; but as he had the face to demand *five hundred guineas* for scraping his single string at the two Concerts, they very wisely did without him.

THE STEWARDS AND THE FIDDLER.

> 'Oxford its pounds might well afford
> For Lectures on the Monochord;
> To pay thee 'tis a diff'rent thing
> For scraping on your single string.
> At best 'tis but a wondrous trick,
> Thou master of the fiddlestick;
> And stewards wise are not such ninnies
> As thus to waste five hundred guineas!'

The 'Installation' of the Duke of Wellington, as might be expected, was a business of great interest and excitement. Convocations were held, on four successive days, in the Theatre, which on each occasion was crowded to suffocation. Complimentary verses were addressed to the great warrior, who seemed to find it warmer and harder work than the battle of Waterloo. Having to preside and to admit to Honorary Degrees (of which altogether there were seventy-one), he was occasionally choked and bothered by the Latin formulæ; turning round for help to his prompter, the Vice-Chancellor. His early Eton education however did him good service, and even Oxford ears were too much charmed by his manly, unaffected bearing, to criticise his Latin or detect false quantities. 'The many' did indeed 'rend the skies with loud applause,' and Oxford was in all its glory. This Installation was accompanied by the publication of a Satirical Poem, in six Parts, called (in allusion to Oxford, with its sombre garb, electing the soldier Duke for its Chancellor) 'Black Gowns and Red Coats,' by my lamented son George Cox, M.A., Fellow of New College, and Student of the Inner Temple. Its versification was allowed to be most exquisite. Who will grudge me the melancholy gratification of inserting here the following *prophetic* eulogy of Gladstone, with whom, being then a High Conservative, my son, an advanced Liberal, sometimes held an argument in the Oxford University Union :—

> 'Yet on one form, whose ear can ne'er refuse
> The Muses' tribute, for he lov'd the Muse,
> (And when the soul the gen'rous virtues raise,
> A friendly Whig may chant a Tory's praise,)
> Full many a fond expectant eye is bent
> Where Newark's towers are mirror'd in the Trent.
> Perchance ere long to shine in senates first,
> If manhood echo what his youth rehears'd,
> Soon Gladstone's brows will bloom with greener bays
> Than twine the chaplet of a minstrel's lays;
> Nor heed, while poring o'er each graver line,
> The far[1], faint music of a lute like mine.
> His was no head contentedly which press'd
> The downy pillow in obedient rest,
> Where lazy pilots, with their canvass furl'd,
> Set up the Gades of their mental world;
> His was no tongue which meanly stoop'd to wear
> The guise of virtue, while his heart was bare,
> But all he thought through ev'ry action ran;
> God's noblest work—I've known one honest man.'

A great stir was made, about this time, as to the admission of Dissenters to the University, and the non-subscription of the Thirty-nine Articles. But when at length such admission was allowed, few Dissenters took advantage of it; and when subscription at the first degree was made *optional*, very few hesitated to sign. As to the subscription at Matriculation, it was wisely remitted, if it were only to stop the

---

[1] The writer was then residing at Munich. The late Sir James Graham went still farther, when he predicted, twenty years ago, that Gladstone *would get himself turned out of Oxford, and lead the extreme Radical party in the House of Commons.*

mouths of Dissenters, or rather, of their advocates in the University.

Among the chief things which marked this year was the success which followed Dr. Daubeny's example and efforts in raising a subscription for the improvement of the neglected Botanical Garden.

In July, *Mr. Newman*, as Vicar of St. Mary's, refused to marry Mr. Jubber's daughter to Mr. Plowman, having learnt that she (a member of the Baptist congregation) had not been baptized[1]. The licence was altered, and the wedding took place, without difficulty (perhaps without enquiry), at St. Michael's.

Nov. 18. New College at length formally renounced its 'Exemption from Public Examination,' reserving, however, the privilege of graduating *without supplicating the grace* of Congregation; giving up the substance, and retaining the shadow!

A. D. 1835.

[B.A. 291.   M.A. 168.   Hon. D.C.L. at Commemoration, 2.
At the Queen's visit, 4.]

May 20. In Convocation, Dr. Rowley being Vice-Chancellor, a *strange measure* was proposed, viz. that instead of *subscription* to the Thirty-nine Articles at Matriculation, the 'juvenis matriculandus' should be allowed to say, 'I hereby declare my assent to the Articles, *as far as my knowledge of them extends!*'—deferring also the formal subscription to the taking of the first Degree. The result was very decisive: Placets 57, Non Placets 459.

---

[1] About ten years afterwards the same Mr. Newman so undervalued the baptism of our Church, as to submit to be *re-baptized* on joining the Church of Rome!

May 27. The sum of £1500 was voted in Convocation towards the erection of 'The New Church near the Printing-office,'—afterwards called St. Paul's, and to which a portion of the overburdened St. Thomas' parish was transferred.

In this and several preceding years '*knocker-stealing*' appears to have been considered a manly feat by certain Undergraduates. Stealthily as those brave youths prowled about for their plunder, yet now and then a bungler in the operation was pounced upon by a Proctor or a policeman; and then ample remuneration was made at the expense of this individual, who had to pay a fine equal to the cost of the knockers wrenched off in the two or three preceding Terms! My fine old brass knocker in Merton Street was a special object of desire and attack. Several times, late in the evening, have I rescued it just in time, on hearing the grating sound of a bar or poker. Several times also, late in the night, I was disturbed by the well-known sound at my street-door, and on my shouting out 'Police, Police!' away scampered the young peace-(if not house)-breakers. Christ Church fountain, on being cleaned out, soon after the cessation of this vile fashion, was found floored with knockers and broken fragments of sign-boards, ornaments, devices, &c., &c. They were probably two or three of these quondam Oxford noctivagous heroes, who, happening to meet in 1835 at Northampton, tried the experiment there, but not very cleverly; for being caught 'in ipso facto' their amusement cost them rather dear; they were called upon to pay the Court expenses, to make an apology in the local paper, to pay £20 to the Lunatic Asylum, and enter into recognisances (themselves and sureties in £20 each) to keep the peace for a year! In Guernsey this practice was rather too severely punished in the person of a young man, the son of a distinguished officer; 'he was arrested, tried before the

Royal Court, and sentenced for the crime of "brigandage" to one month's imprisonment, of which fifteen days should be solitary, on bread and water.'

Oct. 19. Queen Adelaide paid rather a long visit to Oxford—long, that is, compared with other royal visits, which have been generally but flying ones. It was thought somewhat 'infra dig.' that, instead of being received at the Lodgings of some dignitary, she should receive visitors at the Angel Hotel. There '*she showed* herself,' as she admired the view of the High Street from the balcony. A grand reception, however, was given to her in the Theatre, where our noble Chancellor, having come to Oxford for the occasion, read an address of welcome, to which her Majesty read 'a gracious reply.' Four of her train were made Hon. D.C.L.

The City after this claimed her attention, and there were great presentations and kissing-of-hands at the Town Hall. In the evening her Majesty, instead of being entertained, gave a splendid dinner to the Chancellor and other dignitaries, and concluded with holding a 'Drawing-room' at the Hotel. Very early next day her Majesty enjoyed a quiet stroll round Christ Church Meadow; and, after a long course of *lionising*, she came (at 2 p.m.) to Queen's College (a College especially under the patronage of Queens-Consort ever since Queen Philippa's time). In the hall she partook of a *déjeûner*, when the 'Queen's horn' was handed round, well filled with good beverage, the Provost giving out the old toast, 'In memoriam absentium, in salutem presentium.' The Provost also presented some of the College ale, with the remark that 'they had been brewers 500 years.' The Queen playfully, but gracefully, said she would '*smell* to it,' and so passed it on—' Primaque libato summo tenus attigit ore,' 'just kiss'd the cup and passed it to the rest.'

At night there were 'illuminations.' In the afternoon she departed, concluding one of those *Angel* visits which 'are few and far between.' Hearne tells us that Queen Anne visited Oxford in 1702. 'She *dined*,' he says, 'in the theatre [or *theater*, as he spells it], with her husband, Prince George. After dinner (when she was very merry and ate most heartily) she passed through the Ashmole Museum, and took coach!'

Nov. 18. The University received the large sum of £65,000, under the will of Sir Robert Taylor, formerly an eminent architect, to be applied (as it afterwards was, in conjunction with the Randolph fund) to the erection of the 'Taylor Institution.'

A.D. 1836.

[B.A. 268. M.A. 201. Hon. D.C.L. at Commemoration, 1.]

In January the University, and indeed the Church, sustained a great loss in the death of Dr. Edward Burton, Regius Professor of Divinity.

In February died Lord Stowell, the eminent jurisconsult, and brother to Lord Eldon. A poetical tribute to his memory ended thus:—

> '*Ossa* quieta, precor, tutâ requiescite in urnâ,
> Et sit humus cineri non onerosa tuo!'

Whether or not that prayer was granted, as to the urn, his bones and ashes, I know not. But now (in 1861) we have in Oxford not only *Ossa*, but Pelion, in the shape of his and his brother's colossal statues (by Nelson), which are deposited in the splendid and tasteful library of University College, built (at the expense of the noble family) as a kind of mausoleum in honour of the two great brothers.

February brought us intelligence of the death of another

sound theologian, Dr. Van Mildert, Bishop of Durham, who, as an Oxford man and a former Regius Professor of Divinity, might (as was said above of Dr. Burton) have helped to ward off the threatening storm which so soon after 'frightened Oxford from her propriety.' In this same month, Dr. Burton's post was filled up by the appointment of Dr. Hampden to be our Divinity Professor. 'Fons iste malorum,' said one party; 'Hinc illæ lacrymæ,' replied the other: but as a separate Chapter will be assigned to the 'Hampden Controversy,' it will suffice to express the conviction of many lookers-on, that jealousy, disappointed ambition, and despair of preferment (if he and his followers should block up the way) had nearly as much to do with the furious onslaught upon him, as zeal for orthodoxy or dread of lax opinions.

March 17. In Convocation a good many oaths were struck out of the Statute Book. It would seem as if our forefathers could not trust each other unless the 'Deus intersit,' and that often without any 'nodus vindice dignus.' At this date, a step was made so far in the right direction that more advanced graduates (it was thought) could safely be relieved from the frequent recurrence of these solemn adjurations; but the tender minds of the youngsters were not yet considered to be trustworthy, *unsworn*. The proposal, therefore, to annul the oath of supremacy at matriculation, and also the Bodleian oath (so absurdly elaborate) at graduating as B.A., was (but only for a time) rejected.

In this spring the branch-line from Oxford to Didcot was first projected; hitherto the Great Western at Didcot was reached by coaches, omnibuses, &c., as it had been (at earlier stages) first at Maidenhead and then at Wallingford station.

Oct. 28. Dr. Marsham, Warden of Merton, was nominated

a Pro-Vice-Chancellor, being a *layman*, a thing very unusual, if not unprecedented; some of the Vice-Chancellor's duties being strictly *clerical*, which he, as a Pro, could not discharge. Dr. Marsham, however, did not hold the office long.

November produced two singular works, 'The Art of Pluck!' and 'Oxford Night-caps'!!¹

Dec. 6. It was agreed in Convocation to accept the offer of an annual sum from the University Press, 'being a surplus over the expenses,' to be applied to the general fund of the University. What a famous milch-cow, that Press!

'Fontes perpetuos ubera *pressa* dabunt.'

A Charter was, at the close of 1836, granted by William IV to the University of London, with power to confer Degrees, &c.

Cambridge adopted a plan for what is there called 'the Previous Examination,' something like our Responsions or Little-go.

[1] 'The Art of Pluck' was by E. Caswall of Brasenose, now 'Priest of the Oratory' at Birmingham. 'The Oxford Night-caps,' a collection of Receipts for making Punch and other mixtures, was published by a literary Scout of Christ Church, named (or at least called) Cicero Cook!

CHAPTER XIV.

'Tantæne animis (cælestibus?) iræ?'—*Virgil.*

The Hampden Controversy in 1836.

IT was in 1836 (as we were told by Mr. Palmer, of Worcester College, in his 'Narrative[1]') that discussions (that is, private discussions) began to take place on the appointment of Dr. Hampden to the Oxford Divinity Chair; 'The Tract Association, as such, had only a share in the movement;' and, as Mr. Palmer was an influential member of that Association, we must, of course, believe him—though *what* share, or whether it was the lion's share, we are not informed. Now Dr. Hampden had preached his Bampton Lectures *four years before*, i.e. in 1832. The University authorities, nay, the University (as represented by the audience or congregation), had 'sat under' them, and no voice was raised against them, no doubt of their soundness was expressed. Certainly no public complaint was made respecting them, and it was not till 1836 that Mr. Palmer informed us that 'an admirable theologian agreed with him (Mr. Palmer) in thinking that their tendency was rationalistic.' Who that theo-

[1] 'Narrative of Events connected with the Publication of the *Tracts for the Times*.'

logian was he does not say, but it was probably Dr. Routh, President of Magdalen College. It was early in 1836 that Dr. Burton died, and 'in a few days,' Mr. Palmer says, 'we were electrified by the intelligence that Dr. Hampden was to be appointed to the vacant Chair.' To Mr. Palmer and his friends 'this measure seemed a *designed insult* to the University, and an attempt to force latitudinarian principles on the Church;' and yet, as the University had quietly sanctioned the printing and circulation of the Lectures (not a single voice of doubt or disapproval having been raised), how could the Premier (Lord Melbourne) be said to design an insult to the University by the promotion of one who had gained so many of its honours[1] and discharged its most responsible duties? The strong language, however, with which the appointment was hailed was quite in harmony with the acrimony of the period, an acrimony and a strength of language which the Tract Association, and Mr. Palmer among them, had ere long to complain of, when turned against the writer of No. 90. But to go on with 'the narrative:' the result was the formation of an Anti-Hampden Committee, which met at Corpus, *Mr. Vaughan Thomas* being the chairman.

'This movement,' Mr. Palmer says, 'was not guided by the Tract writers,' though he allows that, besides himself, Dr. Pusey and Mr. Newman were members of the Committee, who certainly were not likely to be merely *sleeping partners*, though their policy might be to let others fight ἐν προμάχοισι, or, at least, do the rough work as their pioneers. The first step (and a very cool thing to attempt) was to petition the Crown to recall the appointment! They

[1] Double First Class, Latin Essay, Public Examiner, Professor of Moral Philosophy, &c.

could hardly have expected to succeed, and had no right to complain of being *snubbed*, as indeed they were, by Lord Melbourne in his reply. With quite as little success (at first) they petitioned the Hebdomadal Board. 'Again and again,' says Mr. Palmer, 'our petition was rejected, and again and again we returned to the contest,' or what he calls 'this noble effort.' At length the *Board* suffered itself to be *boarded;* importunity prevailed 'to a certain extent,' and a vote of censure was proposed[1].

In a Convocation held March 22 the measure thus extorted from the Board was proposed, viz. 'That Dr. Hampden should be suspended from certain privileges and duties belonging to his Professorship,' (such as assisting in the appointment of Select Preachers). On this occasion (strange to say) the majority which (Mr. Palmer says) 'would have been overwhelming,' were prevented from giving their votes by the (rarely exercised) *joint veto* or non-placet of the two Proctors, Mr. Bayley of Pembroke, and Mr. Reynolds of Jesus College. The rage and disappointment expressed at this unexpected and unwise stratagem were prodigious and vehemently expressed. The Proctors indeed 'laughed in their sleeves,' but they had set an example which other Proctors could follow; and indeed their triumph was but short, for the first day of Easter Term was fast approaching, when they would go out of office. On that day, after the Latin speech of the retiring Senior Proctor (which, as might be expected, was very severe against 'Dr. Hampden's persecutors'), Mr. Vaughan Thomas would fain have inflicted upon the House, *more suo*, a lengthened oration (I beg his pardon, an 'oratiuncula,' as he more modestly than correctly called it, in its printed

[1] The Heads should have persisted in pleading that from the long interval elapsed since the Lectures were delivered, Convocation had 'placed itself out of Court.'

form), but he was at once stopped by the Vice-Chancellor with the information 'that the business of the day was strictly limited to the ceremony of the old Proctors' resignation of office and the new Proctors' admission.'

The speech, however, was not to be thrown away. Convocation, indeed, lost the 'vultum habitumque hominis,' his fine voice and powerful delivery, but it had the opportunity of reading and weighing deliberately the Latin oratiuncula, or little speech, of thirty-six closely printed pages! It must be borne in mind that Mr. V. Thomas was one of the old practised debaters in Latin (one of the lost academical species). After a hit at the late Proctors and their resignation of office, 'non sine maximâ bonorum omnium lætitiâ,' he went on, as if answering what he calls the 'furores, sævitiam, minaces vultus, insana judicia atque id genus opprobria superbæ Procuratoriæ.'—'Abrepta querimur suffragia, et jus deliberandi novis conditionibus impeditum,—curas querimur inanes et itinerum[1] longissimorum molestias, frustra susceptas. Mala hæc omnia, incommoda, injurias e potestate Duumvirali provenisse et piget et pudet.' He concluded his long and certainly learned address with a bold assertion that the Senior Proctor had been *prompted*, both in exercising his veto and in writing his speech: 'Viro egregio tum intercedenti, et postea convicianti ignoscendum est: non enim sponte suâ intercessit, *non e penu suo peroravit.*'

But, to recur to Mr. Palmer's 'Narrative,' he makes a distinction between what the Corpus Committee had desired (so, at least, he declares), and what was proposed in Convocation. 'Our desire,' he says, 'was that the *specific errors* advanced might be censured;—we did not ask for the censure of any *person:* the Statute proposed by the Heads of

[1] That is, the journeys of those who had *come up* to vote, as many had, from a distance.

Houses condemned Dr. Hampden without specifying his errors.' So much for the narrative of '*our* proceedings' and its disclaimer of *personal* censure!

A work, entitled 'Elucidations of Dr. Hampden's Theological Statements,' was thrown into the shade by Dr. Pusey's pamphlet, 'The Propositions, &c. of Dr. Hampden and his Opinions, drawn from his Bampton Lectures.' The statement of these 'Propositions' was well and strongly met (by Mr. Hayward Cox, I believe) by placing them, in their studied brevity, parallel with longer extracts, i. e. with the context, from which they had been torn. 'Allowing,' it was here said, 'for the important fact that the subject of Dr. Hampden's Lectures was "The Influence of *Scholastic Philosophy* upon the *Phraseology* in which Christian Doctrines were expressed," no charitable mind had a right (or would wish to have a right) to pick and choose parts of sentences and give them a colouring not belonging to them in their relative connection.' Take one example, out of many of these 'Propositions:'—

Dr. Pusey's Proposition.	Bampton Lecture, pp. 102–104.
'The whole discussion (on the Blessed Trinity) was fundamentally dialectic.'—*Bampt. Lect.* p. 104.	'The profane familiarity with which articles of the Trinitarian question are said to have entered into the every-day conversation of the times, characterises the general feeling on the subject, at a period when the spiritual polity formed the great commonwealth of the Roman world; and whilst Philosophy, regarded as identical with Theology, was essentially dialectical or colloquial. . . . . So great indeed were the impediments arising from the use of terms, where

the whole discussion was fundamentally dialectical, that the measure of accommodation between those who really agreed with each other, would probably have failed in any other hands than those of Athanasius.'

It would now (in 1861) be probably allowed that the above, and most of the other 'Propositions' then brought forward against Dr. Hampden, will not stand the test of this parallelism.

But, 'audi alteram partem;' the attacks upon Dr. Hampden's opinions were very naturally met by the publication of 'Statements' of his doctrine and teaching, taken from his published writings. Of these one may suffice, and that taken from his very Bampton Lectures :—

LECTURE VII.—' *Trinity in Unity.*'

' The only ancient, only catholic truth is the Scriptural fact. Let us hold that fast in its depth and breadth, in nothing extenuating, in nothing abridging it,—in simplicity and sincerity;—and we can neither be Sabellians, or Tritheists, or Socinians.'—*Bampt. Lect.* III. p. 289.

Dr. Hampden's 'Inaugural Lecture' as Professor was an earnest appeal to unprejudiced minds : of course it failed to move his determined opponents. Nothing could be fuller or more explicit than his declared support of all and each of the great doctrines of the Christian faith; nothing more touching and ingenuous than his confession, 'I will not pretend always to have stated my conviction in the fullest, clearest manner, so as to have avoided all possibility of misinterpretation,' &c. Notwithstanding all this, he was *twitted* with the question, ' Why don't you own your errors ? Why don't you recant ?' The only answer given, and that in the meekest manner, was, 'You have misunderstood me and misinterpreted what I have said.'

Bitter feelings, with bitter expressions of them in print, for some time marked these sad times. One anonymous pamphlet called the meeting at C.C.C. 'a hole-and-corner cabal,' and states that sixteen or seventeen of the persons *originally* there assembled seceded from the meeting with a declaration 'that it was a *dirty, personal affair.*' This was answered by another pamphlet in equally coarse terms, such as 'pure fiction,' 'mere invention,' nay, 'mendacity' and 'lying'!

May 5, 1836. The proposed measure against Dr. Hampden, which had been averted on the 22nd of March by the joint veto of the Proctors, was reproduced in Convocation, and (a change of Proctors having taken place) was carried by an immense majority. In an assembly of 568 (for voters came up from great distances) there were for the condemnatory decree 474, and against it only 94[1].

The following are *a few* of the many publications which followed this decision:—

1. A Letter, by the Rev. E. Churton, to the Writer (in the Edinburgh Review) of an Article headed 'The Oxford Malignants and Dr. Hampden.'

2. A Letter to Viscount Melbourne on Dr. Hampden's Appointment, by Rev. H. A. Woodgate.

[1] A great majority, certainly; but it was but the natural result of the then widely-spread *Tractarian* writings and of the *Tractarian organization* which (as we learn from Mr. Palmer's 'Narrative') had *preceded* this Hampden movement. After all, what were the 380 votes of the majority when weighed against the 3,000 members of Convocation who kept aloof (coldly, certainly, but still expressively) from such a proceeding? According to an *opinion* of Lord Campbell, Dr. Lushington, and Mr. W. W. Hull, the passing of this vote was illegal, as contrary to the Charter of 1636.

3. Remarks on the above Letter, by the Rev. Baden Powell.

4. Dr. Hampden's Introduction (75 pp.) to the Second Edition of his Bampton Lectures.

5. Strictures, by Mr. Lancaster of Queen's College.

6. By the same, An Earnest and Resolute Protestation against Dr. Hampden's Method of Theologizing.

This last work is accompanied by a correspondence (of 75 pp.) with some of the Oxford authorities, in connection with, and expressive of, poor Mr. Lancaster's trouble and indignation at *losing his preaching-turns* from Queen's College, in consequence of coarse invectives (e.g. 'that atrocious Professor,' 'that pestilent dog-matist,' 'that infelicitous theologian') hurled by him from St. Mary's pulpit at Dr. Hampden!

. P.S. 1868. It grieves me that his death has anticipated this vindication of Bishop Hampden. He has indeed been a quiet (nay, an inactive) Bishop, but his spirit was broken at the commencement of his episcopate by this Oxford persecution, and never seems to have rallied.

CHAPTER XV.

'If an historical sketch of the Tractarian movement be a desirable contribution to our literature, the free use of names is to be excused on the ground of necessity.'—*Oakeley's Preface to his 'Tractarian Movement.'*

The Tractarian Movement.

As early as 1833 (as mentioned above) the Rev. Peter Maurice had sounded the alarm respecting 'Popery in Oxford.' In 1836 he 'opened the war' in a lengthy pamphlet, in which he informs Oxford that, while slumbering at its post, notwithstanding his warning voice, his 'pastorale signum,' the enemy, whose approach he had marked *three years before*, had been steadily, if not stealthily, advancing their approaches; and that the 'Tract Association' had ever since then been in constantly increasing action. 'I come forward,' he says, 'not as *the man*, but because no one else better fitted will.' Dr. Maurice rather damages his claim to consistency by now admiring Dr. Hampden as an opponent to Tractarianism, whose elevation to the Divinity Chair he had so recently opposed and condemned. The pamphlet provoked no direct reply.

It was not, however, that Oxford residents or serious-minded men elsewhere were unobservant of, much less indifferent to, the movement—far, very far, from it. In truth, after a long period of coldness and all but deadness on Church questions, and a general neglect of Church privileges, the movement was hopefully watched by many who took no part in it, and hailed as a much-wanted *revival*, in the best sense of the word. There was a general acknowledgment that the time was come for the Church of England to 'show its colours'—to revive its claim to the title of Catholic and Apostolic. After being so *Low*, it was natural that it should become rather *High;* and there is no doubt that the movement, up to a certain point, was for good, and was looked upon by most men as a coming blessing. Prudent persons, however, without being cold while they kept aloof, both watched and prayed (what could they do better?)—watched the advances of 'the move,' and prayed for its safe guidance. Therefore it was, I think, that so little notice was taken (at least in any publications of a serious character) of the alarm which had been sounded. A somewhat irreverent *jeu-d'esprit*[1] did indeed appear in 1836 under the title and in the borrowed form of 'The Pope's Pastoral Letter to the University of Oxford.' Dr. Pusey replied in a very learned and candid 'Remonstrance,' with a 'Postscript' in answer to anonymous censures, especially to an article in the Edinburgh Review, headed 'The Oxford Malignants and Dr. Hampden.' The 'Malignants' were, of course, the Tractarian writers.

'Postscripts' indeed (not short and pithy like those proverbially attached to young ladies' letters, but long and laboured, after the fashion of Dr. Parr's Appendix to his 'Spital Sermon') became just now the prevailing mode of communication, as adopted by leading men. There was

---

[1] From the pen (I have been told, of the late Dr. Todd, of Dublin, who was then visiting Oxford.

a little, or rather not a little strategy in this; for in this way a book with an unpretending title, a 'Volume of Sermons,' for instance, or a 'Letter to a Young Student,' might find its way into a parsonage or any other house, and introduce with it (as the famous ram introduced 'his tail of ten yards and an ell' into the town of Derby) an appendiculum which the vicar or the paterfamilias might otherwise have shut out. Thus in 1837 the Rev. John Keble published a sermon on 'Primitive Tradition;' how long or how short that sermon was does not now matter, it was however long enough and strong enough to serve as a peg on which to hang a Postscript of 92 pp., together with No. 78 of 'The Tracts for the Times' of 120 pp. more, and containing an elaborate series of quotations from what he calls a 'Catena Patrum,' that is, English-Church Fathers, from Jewell down to Van Mildert; all of these extracts being (as he said) but expositions and comments upon the rule of Vincentius Lirinensis, 'quod semper, quod ubique, quod ab omnibus.'

It is not pretended here to sit in judgment on such productions as these, from the pens of able, good, and pious men, but only to record their appearance (and the use made of them) as proofs that matters were going to very great lengths. Indeed the favourable hopes of a safe and moderate, and therefore practicable, revival of Church principles were beginning to die away, after the bold avowal (in vain qualified by appeals to our English Fathers) that 'what we had thought to have been *gained* at the Reformation was *loss not gain*, and the sooner it was given up the better!'

May 20, 1838. Dr. Faussett's Sermon (at St. Mary's), which he published under the title of 'The Revival of Popery,' certainly opened people's eyes at Oxford to the impending danger, made many hold back who had almost surrendered their judgment, and, if it chilled some hearts, it excited in others a prudent caution. Dr. Faussett was an honest, out-speaking man, but hardly a match for his opponents; he was afterwards (i.e. in connection with Dr. Pusey's sermon and suspension) called a 'theological firebrand,' but the subsequent perversions proved that he did not over-state the tendencies and intentions of the Romanizers, and might rather have been called 'a *beacon-light.*'

Dr. Faussett's sermon produced 'A Letter' (of 99 pp.) addressed to him by *Mr. Newman.* It was a masterly argument, full of learning and large in quotations, but narrow in its view. The most striking feature of it was its proof of the ready fulness of Mr. Newman's mind, for (as appeared from its concluding sentence) it was *written in a single day!* Though strongly marked by his tendency to quiet sarcasm and the bias to Rome (whither he was going so fast), it yet contained beautiful as well as powerful passages, especially in relation to the real but spiritual presence in the Holy Communion. He affected to play with Dr. Faussett's statements with an air of conscious superiority in ability and in theological knowledge.

It would be an endless task to enumerate, much more to analyse, the numerous pamphlets, letters, sermons, remonstrances, remarks, strictures, and supplements of this period. To instance only a few:—

1. *Dr. Wilson's* 'Brief Examination of Mr. Keble's Sermon on "Primitive Tradition:"' its *brevity* was expressed in 69 pages! and Mr. Keble's *over*-statements were met by corresponding *under*-statements of the questions of Tradition and Apostolic Succession.

2. *Mr. Bricknell* published an argument to show that

Mr. Keble was pledged by his own words (in a letter to Judge Coleridge) either to resign his preferment, following that act 'by retiring into another diocese,' or, if *all* the bishops were agreed, 'to retire into lay-communion.'

3. *Rev. F. Merewether*, in his 'Strictures on the Sermons of Mr. Benson' (of the Temple), stated that he thought Mr. Benson wrong in insisting on 'The Bible and the Bible only,' while '*our* maxim [he speaks as a Tractarian] is the Bible as interpreted by the Catholic (especially by the Primitive) Church; this is our chart, our guide, our polar star.'

But there is no end of this; at least, there would be none, were we to go on with each publication, even thus briefly. The names of the writers must suffice:—Professor Scholefield, of Cambridge; Professor Baden Powell (in his work 'Tradition Unveiled'); Rev. T. Bowdler ('Quid Romæ Faciam?'); Rev. W. B. Barter; Hon. and Rev. A. P. Perceval; Rev. S. R. Maitland; Dr. Pusey (in a Letter of 200 pp. to the Archbishop of Canterbury); Rev. W. Gresley; Rev. W. Sewell; Bishop Copleston, two Sermons on Roman Catholic Errors; Dr. Symons, a Sermon preached at St. Mary's; Rev. F. Close, a 'Sermon against the Tractarians,' and another 'On the Tendency of the so-called "Church Principles" to Romanism;' Dr. Thorpe (in a Review of Mr. Sewell's Letter to Dr. Pusey), in which he says: 'Perhaps he [Mr. Sewell] is *designedly obscure*, on the principle inculcated by the Tract writers, to write mysteriously and to withhold a part of the meaning;' and he gives this quotation from the British Critic (then a Tract organ): 'The age in which we live is all light, therefore the Church is bound to be, we will not say *dark*—for that is a forbidding word,—but we will say, *deep, impenetrable, occult in her views and character.*'

The Rev. W. Palmer's 'Narrative of Events connected

THE TRACTS FOR THE TIMES. 293

with the Publication of the Tracts for the Times' (referred to in the preceding Chapter) requires more special notice. 'Our movement,' he says, 'consisted of two branches:—First, An Association, for the purpose of defending the Church, in her spiritual capacity, against the prevalent spirit of Latitudinarianism [this Association seems speedily to have come to an end]: secondly, the Publication of the Tracts.'

1. As to the Association. It began (in 1833) with Mr. Palmer and Mr. Froude of Oriel; and soon extended to Mr. Rose, Mr. Keble, Mr. Newman, and Mr. Perceval. A week's conference at Hadleigh (Mr. Rose's living) ended without any specific arrangements. At Oxford, by the autumn, 'Suggestions for the Formation of an Association' were printed and widely circulated; 'Expressions of approbation were received from the clergy in all parts of the country.' 'I went,' says Mr. Palmer, '(*as a deputation*) to Coventry, Winchester, and London,—and I returned to Oxford with a heart full of gratitude and confidence.'

2. The publication of the Tracts for the Times. These Tracts could not well be published by the Association; and, for a time, several of them were privately printed and dispersed amongst friends in the country. 'I confess,' says Mr. Palmer, 'I was rather surprised at the rapidity with which they were composed and published without any previous revision or consultation.' Mr. Palmer soon urged the necessity of appointing a 'Committee of Revision,' on finding that many objections were raised by the clergy against parts of the Tracts; his advice, he says, was not taken; he also found that 'there were material differences in his views and Mr. Froude's on several important points.' 'Mr. Froude occasionally expressed sentiments extremely unjust to the Reformers and injurious to the Church.' 'I accordingly ceased to take any active part in their proceed-

ings, or to be possessed of that intimate confidence with which I had previously been honoured.'

[The share which the Tract party had in raising the storm against Dr. Hampden has been already mentioned under the head of 'The Hampden Controversy.']

In 1835, formal meetings were held at Dr. Pusey's, forming a sort of theological society. Essays were read and discussion was encouraged, but afterwards discontinued. Some persons thought they were liable to the Statute 'De conventiculis illicitis reprimendis.' There was much at this time in the British Critic (the organ of the party) which savoured of sympathy with Rome and a spirit of discontent with the English Church.

Such, very nearly, was the state of things for four or five years, that is, till the Tractarian movement reached its climax (in 1841) by the publication of 'No. 90.' This Chapter being so lengthy, this topic will only incidentally present itself in subsequent 'Recollections.' In taking leave of Mr. Palmer, whose pardon is asked for the use I have made of his 'Narrative,' it is but just to say that he had always been considered a sound but rather high Churchman. He came to Oxford (for incorporation) a ready-made controversialist in Ireland, and at once proved himself a powerful antagonist to Popery, in the person of Dr. (afterwards Cardinal) Wiseman. In his observations on the 'Tendencies to Romanism' the same spirit shows itself, though modified and softened.

CHAPTER XVI.

'We see the past through the spectacles of the present.'—*Edinb. Review.*

Recollections from A.D. 1837 *to* A.D. 1840.

A.D. 1837.

[B.A. 279. M.A. 164. At Commemoration, 2 Hon. D.C.L.,
and 1 Hon. M.A.]

EARLY in this year there was a report in Oxford, which even got into the papers, that Worcester College was about to throw out a new front, and that £1200 had already been subscribed for the purpose by former members.

In this spring the English episcopacy received strength and ornament by the appointment of Dr. Denison to the See of Salisbury.

Oxford, at this time, had good reason to be proud of one of her most powerful and eloquent preachers. Mr. Hook (afterwards Dr. Hook[1]) had been for some time working and preaching at Coventry, when the Vicarage of Leeds became vacant. The wise people of the North sent a deputation to Coventry to hear Mr. Hook preach, as it were *on the sly*, or, more elegantly, *incog.* The deputation accordingly—

[1] Now Dean Hook. Why has he not become Bishop Hook ?

'Infert se sæptus nebulâ, mirabile dictu,
Per medios, miscetque viris; neque cernitur ulli.—
Dissimulant, et nube cavâ *speculantur* amicti.'

And well they might do so, lest the inhabitants should send them not to, but from, Coventry. The plan, however, succeeded; they came, they saw (rather they *heard*), they conquered; and the result of the visit was Mr. Hook's almost unanimous election to the valuable and important Vicarage. How successfully he there laboured for many years (for he was always a *working* man) is well known. How steadily he pursued his course through evil report and good report, and how generously he divided his huge parish into districts, with the sacrifice of half his income, is also well known and appreciated.

May 8. Lord Radnor withdrew his 'Motion' respecting the Universities, whose cause our noble Chancellor nobly defended.

Dr. Gilbert, as Principal of Brasenose, had for some time discouraged, if not prevented, his young men from attending Dr. Hampden's Divinity Lectures, on the ground of the Convocation's vote of implied censure; finding, however, that some of the Bishops (and in particular the Bishop of Lichfield, Dr. Butler) required a certificate of such attendance, Dr. Gilbert (in this May) withdrew his restriction.

In June, a Charter was granted to the University of Durham: Degrees were immediately conferred there.

June 20, died William IV: 'the sailor-king (as the papers had it) came to his final anchorage.' Victoria, his successor, had no fault attributed to her but her youth! An University address of condolence and congratulation was voted June 27, with a separate address to the Queen Dowager. A general election of course followed: in the Oxford *City* election, Messrs. Maclean and Wm. Erle (afterwards Chief

Justice) were elected, and Mr. Hughes Hughes was thrown out. Mr. Maclean was, after the usual fashion, carried home in a chair richly ornamented and borne on men's shoulders; Mr. Erle introduced a novelty (and an improvement), being drawn in a chariot by *four white horses*: a prognostic of his future career.

August 27. The authorities of Queen's College gave notice to the Master of the Grammar School at Hawkshead, in Cumberland, 'that, in consequence of the inadequate supply of candidates from thence, it was intended to extend the benefits of the Foundation (hitherto confined to Cumberland and Westmoreland) to other parts of the kingdom.'

In October died an old Oxonian, Sir John English Dolben. I remember his calling, a few years before, at my house in Merton Street, to see the room (a large laundry) in which his ancestor, Mr. J. Dolben[1], and a few others used to read the Prayer-book service when, in evil days, it was dangerous to do so. (A painting of his ancestor and two others, so engaged, hangs in Ch. Ch. hall.) The old gentleman, who was rather *tête-montée*, fell on his knees on entering the room, and in fervent language apostrophised his departed relative. Sir John's father, Sir William Dolben, on the old,

---

[1] Wood's account is as follows:—

'In December (1648) "Prayers according to the Liturgy" were taken away (by the Parliamentary *Visitors*) at Ch. Ch.—where they had been continued, in spite of the Visitors, till the Nativity. Afterwards certain divines of that House, namely, Mr. Joh. Fell, Mr. J. Dolbin (sic), Mr. Rich. Allestrey, &c., all lately expelled, set up the Common Prayer in the house of Mr. T. Willis, a physician, *against* Merton College Church,— at which place (admitting none but their confidents) were prayers and surplices used on all Lord's Days, Holy Days and their Vigils,—as also the Sacrament according to the Church of England administered,—continuing so till the Restoration of K. Charles II.'

established theory of 'once in for Oxford, always in,' represented the University in Parliament from 1780 to 1806.

In this Michaelmas Term, Oxford and Cambridge advanced *pari passu* in the way of reform, by substituting an Admonition from the Vice-Chancellor for the Oath taken at Matriculation. There was, however, a degree of inconsistency in the matter; for, though the Matriculation Oath (about observing the statutes) was abrogated, the Oath of Supremacy was still retained, by a majority of fifty-five votes in Convocation.

It will hardly, I think, be believed, that on November 21st it was proposed in Convocation that, on the beginning of each Term, the fine old Latin Litany (with its solemn music) should be not only read (i. e. not intoned), but read in English; and that a similar change from Latin to English should be made as to the Sermon (and, I presume, as to the Holy Communion). The proposal failed, as well it might, the votes being—Placet 81, Non-Placet 102. One would have expected that this decisive vote might at once have led to a revived attendance at, and appreciation of, this truly academic solemnity. But it did not; for it was not till 1839 that such a revival took place.

A.D. 1838.

[B.A. 255. M.A. 175. 1 Hon. D.C.L. at the Commemoration.]

The angry feeling occasioned in 1836 by Dr. Hampden's appointment to the Regius Divinity Professorship was kept alive, at the beginning of 1838 (as it had been more or less in 1837), by a series of lengthy anonymous letters (in the well-known style of the Rev. Vaughan Thomas), in which not only (though chiefly) Dr. Hampden, but Lord

Melbourne, Sir J. Campbell, and Dr. Lushington came in for a share of sarcasm. Indeed, what with Dr. Hampden's hard treatment and the Romanising of the Tractarians, Oxford at this time was by no means a bed of roses; it was rather a hot-bed of uncharitableness, of social distrust, recrimination, and discomfort. Even the unusually severe weather at the commencement of the year did not cool down some people. As usual, a large subscription was raised for the unemployed poor,—who did not benefit much by 'the sheep roasted on the frozen river, near Kennington!' It was in a later frost that some young men were driven in a 'char-à-bancs' on the frozen river between Iffley and Folly Bridge!

Jan. 13 died Lord Eldon, long an honour to Oxford and the boast of University College.

The propensity of our Undergraduates to *abbreviate* all academic names and phrases (as well as their hours of study and their Commoners'-gown) began to show itself about this period. 'Little-go,' the established but slang name for Responsions, was found too fatiguing, and so became 'Smalls.' The High Street, with all its beauty, was put upon short allowance, and became 'The High.' Of course, though somewhat later, Magna Vacatio became 'The Long,' and Moderations became Mods[1].

[1] By-the-bye, the term 'Moderations' is itself a misnomer; really and statutably it is 'The First Public Examination.' The Examiners for it being called Moderators (an old title connected with Disputations), the Examinations soon began to be called 'Moderations.' But altogether (without dwelling on the term Responsions and the probable reason for its adoption mentioned elsewhere) the nomenclature of our Examination system is clumsy and unfortunate; 'The *First* Public Examination' being really the *Second* (for is not what is called 'Little-go,' or Responsions, a bonâ-fide Examination?); and the *Second* or Final one (which, however, is not now the Final one) being really the Third.

This abbreviating process being applied to venerable Colleges (for instance, 'New College' is shortened into a monosyllable—' Are you going to New?') it is no wonder that the Halls should suffer in a similar way. I cannot bring myself to write the vulgarized form of St. Mary Hall; but in respect to another Hall, I would simply ask, which form of words sounded best to academic ears, as they were (in close contact) uttered on the top of a house-boat, by way of encouraging the crew of the last boat at the races:—

Senior man—' On, St. Edmund's, on.'
Fast man—' Go it Teddy! Go it Teddy'!

Is it not singular that Hearne, a member and for many years a resident in this Hall (and an antiquary), should assert (as he does, p. 234 of Reliquiæ Hearnianæ) that 'Edmund Hall took its name (not from St. Edmund, Archbishop of Canterbury, but) from an Oxford citizen, named Edmunds'? *St. Alban* Hall, we know, took its name from an Oxford citizen who, luckily, was called Robert de *St. Alban*.

March 17. A Petition of Convocation was voted to Parliament against the Didcot Branch-Railway to Oxford! The reasons given were—1st. That the existing means of communication with London were fully adequate! 2ndly. That greater facilities for that communication would be injurious to the discipline of the University!! 3rdly. That the works adjoining the river would cause floods by impeding the water-course!!! N.B. Since the Thame Branch was joined on there is some truth in this third reason.

March 20. A Petition to Parliament was voted in Convocation 'to preserve the Bishopric of Sodor and Man,' which by a previous Act had been prospectively condemned to be absorbed into that of Carlisle.

The scheme was relinquished and the separate See preserved.

March 24. Several alterations in the Statute 'De moribus conformandis' were proposed and approved; but one proposal, 'De ære alieno non contrahendo,' was rejected by 71 votes to 20. The Oxford tradesmen (it was said) had petitioned the authorities against the clause, as too stringent against *ticking* and sure to be evaded.

In this month the first steps were taken for a Boat-chapel, near the Oxford Canal; the plan originated with, and was carried out by, the excellent father of an excellent family, Mr. Ward, coal-merchant, who had found that the bargemen never did and never would present themselves *at a church* in their rough costume. 'It won't do for such as we!' They were quite '*at whoam*' in the barge.

In May, the attention of the University was invited to the formation of what was to be called 'The Oxford Apiarian Society!' It was got up in great form (with President, Secretary, &c.) by Mr. W. C. Cotton, of Ch. Ch. Rule 8 was —'To keep a garden for experiments on bees.' It did not last long, and ceased altogether on Mr. Cotton's going abroad.

June 9. In Convocation, a simpler form was substituted (not, however, as an oath, but as a declaration[1]) for the 'Bodleian Oath,' which had been hitherto taken on admission to the B.A. Degree, and which was properly thought too stringent and elaborate. As a proof of this, and as a matter of curiosity, I subjoin the abrogated oath which has disappeared from the Statute-book:—'Tu promittes (with the usual form of kissing the Testament) quod neque tu in

---

[1] The *Declaration* is simply this: 'Ego in Bibliothecam Bodleianam admittenduś, ex animo polliceor me libros cæterumque cultum sic tractaturum ut superesse quam diutissime possint, et quantum in me est, curaturum ne quid bibliotheca detrimenti aut incommodi capiat.'

persona tua aliquem vel aliquos libros surripies, permutabis, rades, obliterabis, contaminabis, aut alio quocunque modo detruncabis, abuteris, deteres aut imminues; nec alii cuiquam auctor eris horum quidvis perpetrandi,' &c.

June 28. The Coronation-day was marked in Oxford by a general, grand illumination. There was a talk of a dinner, to be got up by subscription, for the poorer inhabitants; but it was given up (it was said) on the wretched plea that our poor neighbours (*post prandium*) would be in too great a state of excitement for the quiet enjoyment of the illumination! Surely the effects of roast-beef, plum pudding, and a pint of ale, however strange to most of their stomachs and heads, would have evaporated in the interval between a one o'clock dinner and the eight o'clock lighting-up! The real truth was, more probably, that the question having been raised by the authorities (University and City), 'Dinner or Illumination,' the latter was decided upon as more expressive of loyalty. A great many people went up to London the day before the Coronation-day; indeed, 'beside the usual conveyances, *seven extra coaches*' started from Oxford for the nearest station, Didcot.

The year 1838 was especially marked by the persevering attacks and calumnies against Oxford by Lord Radnor, Lord Holland, and, occasionally, Lord Brougham; and this, when the University was steadily revising its Statute-book and removing abuses. The attempts made at this period to open Oxford to Dissenters were ingeniously attributed, by a writer in the British Critic, to the Hon. Degrees conferred upon Nonconformists at the meeting of the British Association:—'Those who were thus admitted "to gaze upon our treasures" (like those of King Hezekiah), learnt to covet a share, and naturally sought admission to a further taste of our good things.'

The first week in September is marked, at least by the *citizens* of Oxford, as the season of St. Giles's Fair. Falling, as it does, in the Long Vacation, it never possessed any interest for the University; but at Cambridge, even in Long Vacation, 'Stourbridge Fair' used to be (I know not whether it still is) a matter of great excitement,—the Vice-Chancellor, with full attendance, going to the Barnwell suburb to open the Fair by a solemn proclamation and other ceremonies, some of them connected with eating and drinking, and ending with theatricals! Before starting in procession, 'mulled-wine and cakes were presented and partaken of in the Senate House.' At the Oxford Fair a striking and picturesque group had been always formed by a large body of gipsies, men, women, and children, with their rough ponies and rougher donkeys; but this wild tribe was looked upon unfavourably by the City magnates, and the Mayor of this year (1838) issued an order for the positive exclusion of the gipsies from St. Giles's Fair. Pity for them, and early '*recollections*' of their fiddling, tumbling, stick-throwing, &c., &c., suggested the following lines, inserted in the Oxford Herald:—

THE GIPSIES' HUMBLE PETITION AND REMONSTRANCE.

Addressed to the Worshipful Mayor of Oxford.

'O Mr. Mayor, O Mr. Mayor!
  What have we Gipsies done or said,
That you should drive us from the Fair
  And rob us of our 'custom'd bread?

O had you seen, good Mr. Mayor,
  Our wond'ring, weeping, wailing band,
And marked our looks of deep despair
  When first we heard your stern command;

Could you have witness'd, Mr. Mayor,
    How young and old, and weak and strong,
Excluded, branded, cold and bare,
    We sat astounded all day long;

Your heart had ach'd, good Mr. Mayor,
    And felt that Gipsies too were men;
Then deign our losses to repair,
    Nor drive us thus to try the pen.

Alas! 'tis true, good Mr. Mayor,
    Our friend, Sir Walter Scott, is dead;
But Heav'n, that hears the Gipsies' pray'r,
    May raise another in his stead.

Dread not the name, good Mr. Mayor,
    No more the witch's pow'r we claim;
But still we are the Muse's care,
    And Oxford Poets guard our fame.

What place then so unfit, good Mayor,
    A war against our tribe to raise,
As that which lately filled the air[1]
    With Gipsy-lore and Gipsies' praise?

You welcome Lions to the Fair,
    Tigers and Monkeys, Punch and Fool;
Then suffer us, another year,
    To hold there our Gymnastic School.

Meanwhile farewell, good Mr. Mayor,
    Your frowns dismiss, resume your smiles;
We'll leave off cheating, take to prayer,
    And claim thy patronage, St. Giles!'

In November, 1838, a royal present was made to the University, and especially to the Bodleian Picture Gallery, in

---

[1] Vide 'The Gipsies,' Mr. Stanley's Newdigate Prize-poem for 1837.

the shape of two full-length, full-dressed portraits of William IV and Queen Adelaide, by Sir David Wilkie. Many persons thought them rather coarse, and over-done.

Nov. 22. The extreme High Church tendencies in a Romish direction (which under the influence of the Tractarian writers pained and disappointed many wise and good men) naturally produced a strong reaction in Oxford, and through Oxford throughout the kingdom. It was right and reasonable that our Alma Mater (the great majority of whose sons were in this, as in many former trials, true to their Church of England principles) should wish to show that she had not been influenced by the cloud that had hung over her. This healthy feeling found its expression in the erection of the beautiful cross and monument to the memory of Cranmer, Ridley, and Latimer. It was a noble proof (though a somewhat tardy one) that Oxford still cherished the memory of those great martyrs to the Reformation. The subscription was a very large one (£5000), and was raised with wonderful rapidity; out of it, besides the Martyrs' Memorial, was also built an additional aisle on the north side of Magdalen parish church,—to be called 'The Martyrs' Aisle.' It had been found impracticable to get a site in Broad Street, the actual scene of the martyrdom.

A.D. 1839.

[B.A. 264. M.A. 167. At Commemoration, Hon. D.C.L. 4, Hon. M.A. 2.]

Jan. 3. *William Miller*, B.A. of New College, was elected Esquire Bedel, as successor to Mr. Bobart.

Jan. 29. A power was given by Convocation to the Vice-Chancellor 'to *vary* payments by Members of the University, for the preaching tax, the tax for keeping up the fire-engines, the tax for the preservation from drowning' (i.e. for the boat and its keeper, 'old Charon'), 'and the tax for the public walks.' The *varying* consisted, I believe, chiefly in *reducing* them, as they had produced a surplus.

March 24. The proposal, in Convocation, to appoint two Prælectors, one in Grammar and Rhetoric, the other in Logic and Metaphysics, was rejected; the Placets were thirty-one, Non-Placets seventy-one.—Also 'a forced attendance on two courses of some one Public Lecturer' was rejected by a majority of fifteen votes.

May 13. The proposal for a Prælectorship in Logic was carried by twenty-seven to eighteen, the salary to be raised by a tax upon all persons under the degree of M.A.

May 21. A splendid reception was given in Oxford to the Russian Archduke Alexander [now, in 1861, the *Emperor Alexander II*] and the Prince of the Netherlands. Degrees by diploma were voted to the two Princes, and the Degree of Honorary D.C.L. was conferred on five of their attendants. To those who had seen Alexander I in 1814, and the tall Nicholas in 1817, the young Russian Prince did not appear so striking; the same might be said of the Dutch Prince. I had a little private transaction with the Russian Prince. Understanding that he was flinging about his money very liberally, I got my kind friend Mr. Lethbridge, of All Souls, one of the Proctors, to state to him (through a noble Lord, in attendance) the fact, that my late son, of New College, had left a translation of Dr. Otto's (German) History of Russian Literature; but that £50 would be required to induce a publisher (Mr. Talboys) to print it. The hint was most kindly and instantly taken, and the sum paid (through Mr. Lethbridge) to Talboys. The volume soon appeared, and I lost no time in transmitting a copy, handsomely bound, to the young Prince, through the Russian Embassy.

June 5. Mr. Michell was elected the first Prælector of Logic, against three competitors, Messrs. W. Sewell, Lancaster, and Wall.

June 6. The idea of a cemetery was first suggested in the City Council, and a committee was at once formed to carry out the idea.

June 12. At the Commemoration, *Wordsworth* was presented to the Honorary D.C.L. Degree; his reception was overpowering to others, though he stood it firmly, and apparently unmoved as one of his Westmoreland mountains. Keble, as Professor of Poetry, did him ample honour from the Rostrum. I was honoured by a call from 'the philosophic poet,' who was brought to my house by a friend to hear his little poem, 'She dwelt among the untrodden ways,' sung as it had been admirably set to music by Professor Donkin. Wordsworth remarked with regret that one stanza (which he directly repeated) had been omitted[1].

---

[1] About this time appeared a strange anonymous pamphlet (of seventy pages), entitled 'Oxford in 1888, A Fragmentary Dream*.' It was, as might be expected from its title, a rambling affair, beginning with a moonlight view of Oxford from the roof of the Radcliffe Library. Of course the dreamer sees great changes and innovations, in this jump of fifty years; e.g. 'a spacious, handsome edifice, styled "The British College,"—for the education of *all British subjects*, of *every religious sect;* and a second College for Diplomacy and Modern Languages.' Almost everything is quietly quizzed,—the then *unwarmed* Bodleian especially; —the want of pure water, fountains, &c.;—suggestions are given for purifying the western approach to Christ Church Meadow, and other parts of Oxford, where 'it might be said of the inhabitants, "Nasus illis Nullus erat!"' The following is a scene from 'the Dream:' 'Scarcely had "Orates" finished his sentence, when he beheld a thick volume of smoke pouring forth at intervals, and gleams of flame issuing from one

* Dr. Bloxam tells me that this 'Dream' was written by his (and my) friend Rev. Richard Walker, late Fellow of Magdalen College.

In July of this year a grand agricultural meeting took place in Oxford, which, though not academical, had several points of academical interest. (1) From the splendid *room* in which 2000 persons dined,—being none other than the quadrangle of Queen's College, covered over for the occasion. (2) From the fact of several academic speakers (the Vice-Chancellor, Dr. Gilbert, Dr. Buckland, and others) having addressed the company. The Vice-Chancellor, after some good observations in good English, said he would give the farmers a little Latin, 'Nihil agriculturâ melius, nihil *uberius*,'—translating it for them—'Nothing, gentlemen, (as you know better than I or Cicero), nothing is more *productive* than farming,'—(great cheers and hearty laughter).

of our principal colleges. The case was this: *Lord Boozy* had got drunk, and set fire to his bed-furniture, which finally caused the conflagration. The Head of the College, in agony, immediately rushed forth and ordered the wine-cellars to be strictly guarded ("ne *portum* occupet alter") and the statutes to be secured. Unfortunately, by some oversight, the valuable library and its invaluable MSS. were burnt to ashes;—but the wine was saved!—and the statutes'!!—The following improvements are enumerated:—

1. Trinity College garden laid out in the style of St. John's 'classical grounds.'
2. Balliol College front *made uniform*.
3. The balustrade round 'Tom Quad' removed.
4. The Cæsars 'capita illa horrenda' alongside the Theatre new modelled.
5. New College quadrangle gothicised to harmonise with the Chapel [supposed to have been *ungothicised* when the upper story was added to Wykeham's original building].
6. The fictitious portraits of college founders taken down; e. g. John de Balliol, really the portrait of an Oxford blacksmith, and Devorguilla, that of an Oxford apothecary's daughter.
7. The porch of St. Mary's, its twisted columns (that incongruous imitation of the baldaquin at Rome) swept away.

He particularly delighted the company by telling them that in a very few years Oxford would have a Professor of Agriculture or Rural Economy. Chevalier Bunsen also concluded his speech with a Latin verse :—

> 'Bella gerant alii, ter felix Anglia pacem !'

> 'From war though others ne'er may cease,
> Let happy England cherish peace !'

'Happy England,' however, was frequently at this time disturbed by Chartist riots at Birmingham, Newcastle, &c.

In August, the establishment of a Theological College both at Chichester and Wells, much wanted and wisely undertaken, was a strong reproof to Oxford, for sending forth her Bachelors of Arts (in general) quite ignorant of all that constitutes a theological scholar, and totally uninstructed in parish teaching and pastoral duties.

Oxford, in this Long Vacation, was enlivened by a 'Nuneham Regatta,' a Conservative festivity, at which Mr. Maclean (M.P. for Oxford City, and M.A. of Balliol) was the presiding genius, as well as the chief payer of the piper. I am tempted to introduce here a parody on Shield's famous song of 'The Gallant Arethusa,' in honour of the nine young gentlemen, natives of Oxford, who, as the crew of 'The Ariel,' carried off the chief honours of this regatta.

THE ARIEL'S CREW, SIR.

> 'Come every jolly rower bold,
> Whose heart is cast in honour's mould,
> While Nuneham's glories I unfold,
>   Huzza for the Ariel's crew, Sir.
> She is a vessel tight and brave,
> As ever skimm'd the ruffled wave;

Her lads are staunch to their fav'rite launch,
And when the race shall try our fire,
Sooner than yield we'll all expire[1],
    The dauntless Ariel crew, Sir.

' 'Twas in the Regatta she went out
In Nuneham's reach to cruise about,
Three rival boats, in show so stout,
    Bore down on the Ariel crew, Sir;
The Isis bold straight a-head did ply,
The sprightly Ariel seem'd to fly:
Not an arm, nor a back, nor a nerve did she slack;—
Though the foemen laugh'd and thought it was stuff,
    Knowing not the handful of lads how tough
        Were the dauntless Ariel crew, Sir.

' Eight strong-arm'd men on their oars did bend,
The stoutest Oxford Town could send;
We eight bold youngsters did contend,
    The plucky Ariel crew, Sir.
Our cockswain hail'd the Isis, " Ho," The Isis-men roar'd out
        " Hallo !
You'll ne'er win the cup, so you'd better give it up;"
" No, no," cries the Ariel, " that can't be,
    For I mean to lug it along with me,
        For the use of the Ariel crew, Sir."

' The race was off the Nuneham shore,
(Such a race as ne'er was seen before,)
We press'd them hard and beat them sore,
    The youthful Ariel crew, Sir.
And now we've beat the rival crew,
And shown what skill and pluck can do,
    Let each fill a glass to his fav'rite lass:
Here's a health to Maclean and Conservatives all,
    And may success and honour befall
        The lads of the Ariel crew, Sir !'

---

[1] ' Vitamque volunt pro laude pacisci.'

Dec. 5. The salary of each of the two Proctors (which had hitherto been fluctuating, as depending on the number of Degrees, and especially of 'Grand Compounders') was *fixed* at £350 for the year of office. I believe it was calculated on the average of the five preceding years, in which the income had been better than usual.

A.D. 1840.

[B.A. 254. M.A. 188. No Hon. Degree at the Commemoration !]

Jan. 10. The 'penny postage' came into action. It is surprising (now that we, in 1861, have seen its satisfactory results) to look back and observe how ungraciously this 'boon to families,' and especially to poor and middle class families, was at first received. It was unscrupulously denounced as 'that gigantic humbug,'—'the wise penny-postage scheme,' or the 'penny wise and pound foolish scheme,' while elaborate calculations of future losses to the revenue were widely circulated. A good deal of this obloquy and disparagement was, of course, to be put to the account of party and political influence. There had always been a local penny-post in Oxford, but who had ever expected to send a letter to John O'Groat's house for a penny?

At this period the country was still kept in excitement by Chartist disturbances. At Newport in Monmouthshire, a man of property, named *John Frost*, and others were tried for dreadful riots; 224 convicts on this charge, from different assizes, were transported to Van Dieman's Land.

Jan. 24. An attempt at law to stop the publication of the Magdalen College statutes by Mr. Ward of Trinity, failed on the ground that copies of the statutes were open to public inspection in the Bodleian Library, the British Museum, &c.

It is amusing, looking back from our vantage-ground in 1861, to see how jealously the College statutes were then watched and guarded (ab alienis saltem oculis), which only twenty years afterwards were so coolly *walked into* by an Act of Parliament, and so calmly surrendered by the Colleges. They are now probably laid by (in most societies) on some high shelf in the College libraries, to be referred to now and then as matters of antiquarian lore, or exhibited as curiosities along with Missals and Illuminated Manuscripts. Mr. Ward's publications of College statutes were English translations; an early death prevented his continuing this strange waste of time and labour.

Feb. 6. It was voted in Convocation that £80 should be paid annually to the funds of the Ashmolean Museum, on an understanding that all academics be admitted gratis. Previously to this, the payment of sixpence a head was expected, if not exacted, at every visit. A similar arrangement has since been made as to the Picture Gallery.

Feb. 10. An illumination took place in honour of her Majesty's nuptials. Unfortunately there was a bad spirit abroad at this time, and the lower orders of Oxford had not quite escaped its influence. The 'Gown' were of course demonstrative of loyal feelings; and collisions, with a good deal of shouting and skirmishing, took place in the streets of Oxford. The gutters, however, did not 'run with blood;' indeed, there was little more than the noise and show of fight. Here and there a blow was exchanged, and even a Master's gown did not protect its wearer from assault. One tutorial M.A. was roughly handled and went home with a 'black-eye;' a lotion and a draught were sent for, but unluckily the scout administered the lotion internally and bathed the blackened eye with the draught. What effect the latter had did not appear; but the lotion was (or might have been) *no joke*, though it was treated as one by an Oxford paper, in some lines, of which these are a sample; they were attributed to Mr. Lowe:—

> 'A stomach-pump was quickly brought and "all hands" set to work at it,
> And speedily they *cleaned him out!* let no man smile or smirk at it.
> His life was saved—but to this day (of that night's row the last trophy),
> That stomach-pump *sticks in his throat!* Thus ended the catastrophe!'

March 19. Prince Albert was made D.C.L. by Diploma[1].

June 1. The 'Great Western' was opened as far as Steventon (near Didcot), to and from which place Oxford passengers were conveyed in coaches, omnibuses, &c. By-the-bye, the carriage and its name 'omnibus' came into *use*

---

[1] In this March, the unfortunate and eccentric artist and painter, Haydon, gave a few lectures on High Art in the Ashmolean Museum. I well remember the striking effects he produced by a few strokes of chalk on a large black board, especially when, having spoken of the advantage of the study of anatomy in drawing the human form, and remarked that Sir Thomas Lawrence never placed a foot firmly on the ground, he sketched a pair of legs, the feet slightly on tiptoe, saying, 'I daresay you have all seen those legs.' A smile went round the room as we recognised those of the Prince Regent in the Theatre! Haydon was fêted by Dr. Daubeny at Magdalen, and was said to have been so pleased with the society of the Common-Room, that on coming away he exclaimed, 'Surely they are not the Fellows of *Gibbon!*' Haydon probably left a more favourable impression there than Porson, who occasionally visited Dr. Routh, sometimes dined at the Magdalen High Table, and drank wine in the Common-Room. He did not always make himself agreeable, and one evening was so rough and rude to one of the Fellows, that he (the Fellow aggrieved) on leaving the room, said to the Vice-President, 'Sir, I hope that the next time you introduce your *bear* here, you will have him *muzzled!*'

(penes quem norma loquendi est), like many other things and names, with the railroad. In the old coach time we had had 'sociables' (very like the omnibus) and clumsy vehicles called (as they really were) double-coaches; but the real *omnibus* and its rival *cabriolet* came into general use in connection with the 'ferrea strata viarum.' It was not likely that the drivers and cads would adopt such long names; they were therefore at once reduced to the monosyllables 'bus and cab.'

June 10. A vulgar fellow, named 'Oxford,' presented a pistol and fired at the Queen and her Consort. Happily neither this nor a second pistol-shot took effect, though the whiz of the bullet was heard by the Prince. The wretch ('twere profanation to call him by his name) was instantly seized, and on examination coolly said, 'he had been brought up to the *bar*—not indeed as a lawyer, yet something above a pot-boy.' An address was voted in Convocation to congratulate her Majesty 'on her preservation,' &c.

June 30. At the Commemoration this year there was not a single Honorary Degree, an unusual circumstance, though not unprecedented. Bishop Stanley, who came to hear his son's Essay, was well received in the Theatre, notwithstanding his politics. 'I expected,' he said, 'to encounter a pitiless storm,—but under my son's umbrella I got well through it.'

August 20. The members of Queen's College (Masters of Arts and upwards) assembled in Oxford to celebrate the fifth centenary of their foundation. Some fine specimens of hardy, rosy, old Cumberland clerks once more bestrode the High Street;—venerunt, oraverunt, ederunt, biberunt, dormiverunt, discesserunt. Mr. Barry, a former Michel Fellow (and who, as a Bible Clerk of All Souls, had '*gained the*

Honours' in 1803), delivered an eloquent oration on the occasion.

In this August died Dr. Woodcock, Canon of Christ Church, a large-hearted, excellent man. Having had the good fortune to be a cotemporary at School and College with influential persons, he had (though rather late in life) the option of several pieces of preferment. He coquetted for some time with the Deanery of Norwich, but at length decided for the less responsible Canonry at Christ Church. He was thought, however, to have made a wrong choice; for he returned, after a long absence, to find Oxford in a state of excitement, of revived theological study, and powerful sermons. His discourses, as Canon, at Christ Church were quite old-fashioned, with no pretensions to scholarship or originality, but with a frequent reference to 'our excellent Constitution in Church and State.' Some advantages, however, he had over some other Doctors; he was a fine, tall man, with a noble countenance and a voice like the lower notes of the organ tuba mirabilis. He and his family also contributed much to the spread of a more friendly and less starched intercourse in Oxford society.

Sept. 8. Dr. Shuttleworth, with the general approval of all Oxford men, was gazetted as Bishop of Chichester. Always a Whig (and not always a moderate one), he had been neglected by his party; luckily, perhaps, for his episcopal qualifications,—since, in the protracted interval of a 'longa expectatio,' he had sobered down in his political views and established his reputation as a theologian, as well as a wit and an elegant scholar. As Warden (though elected all but unanimously) he was not successful in his management of young men. Succeeding as he did to what had been a state of laxity, he was impatient of a state of transition and *gradual* improvement; his sharp manner was not conciliatory;

occasionally, when roused up from his studies by a call for enquiry or discipline, he was thought to treat this necessity for exertion as an interruption. Time, however, sobered him much in this respect, though being himself rapid in his conclusions, he did not easily make allowance for the slower conceptions of others.

Nov. 4. At the end of a *very long* sermon at Christ Church, a red-breast (probably the only untired creature in the Cathedral) began singing. The incident was thought worthy of poetical notice at the time; e. g.

> 'And well you might have deemed some angel there
> Hymning seraphic notes (for angels deign
> To hover in the sacred house of pray'r);
> But if an angel this, the guise he wore
> Of a lone red-breast!' &c.
> Dated Univ. Coll. (Query—F. W. Faber.)

This effusion reminded 'a learned friend' of a Latin poem addressed, 'Rubellioni ad Canonicas preces assiduo,' by Petrus Molinæus (A.D. 1626), beginning, 'Sacris amice cantibus, rubellio.' [N.B. '*cantibus*, not *concionibus* !']

CHAPTER XVII.

'Sirs, ye are brethren.'—*Acts* vii. 26.

Recollections from A.D. 1841 *to* A.D. 1843.

A.D. 1841.

[B.A. 279. M.A. 184. Honorary D.C.L. at Commemoration, 9.]

JAN. 1. Died Mr. Collingwood, the Superintendent of the University Press. It was a proof of the liberality of the University, that its chief printer was known to be a zealous Dissenter. He was an accomplished, amiable, and good man, as well as an excellent printer, in which character, from the liberal share of the profits granted to him by the University, he accumulated a considerable fortune[1]. His widow was his fourth wife; or, as he used to say, his 'fourth edition.'

In January of this year was formed 'A plan for a Benevolent Society'[2], for encouraging a prudent forethought

---

[1] The very type and paper in the hand and before the eyes of my readers call upon me to notice the noble use which his successor, Mr. Combe, has made, and is making, of his gains from the Clarendon Press, especially in the erection of the beautiful chapel (St. Luke's) attached to the Radcliffe Infirmary, and more recently of St. Barnabas' Church.

[2] This Association is still kept up (in 1861), and, being carefully superintended by some of the higher College servants, has been found to work very satisfactorily.

among an important part of our College Establishments, i. e. College Servants,—generally most improvident for themselves and families. By a small quarterly payment (with a little help from others) it was proposed to secure to them some slight provision when age or infirmity should disqualify them for their work.

The early part of 1841 produced a series of long and earnest letters ' On the *New* Opinions on Religious Matters' —by Mr. W. Sewell, Mr. Perceval, Dr. Miller of Armagh, &c. And in March attention was drawn to No. 90 of 'The Tracts for the Times' by a strong 'Remonstrance' addressed to the Hebdomadal Board, and signed by four Tutors, viz. Mr. Churton of Brasenose, Mr. Wilson[1] of St. John's, Mr. Griffiths of Wadham College, and Mr. Tait of Balliol. This was but 'the beginning of the end;' for it was soon followed by a 'Resolution' of the Hebdomadal Board in reference to No. 90 of the Tracts; 'That such modes of interpretation (evading rather than explaining the sense of the Thirty-nine Articles, and reconciling subscription to them with the adoption of errors they were designed to counteract) are inconsistent with the Statutes of the University, which require subscription to the Articles and the instruction of Students in them.' Mr. Newman at once avowed himself the writer of No. 90. Mr. Sewell lost no time in declaring the pain which No. 90 had given him, though he rather mystified his notions in the lengthy letters which he published; at all events, he did well in advising the

---

[1] Mr. Wilson little thought that his own writings would (in 1862) become objects of enquiry and condemnation. Indeed in joining in that Remonstrance he scarcely acted up to his own opinion, which I heard him enunciate in a sermon at St. Mary's, vlz. 'that Christ not only foretold but actually *intended* that divisions should arise in the Church; that the truth *required* to be thus elicited.'

discontinuance of the 'Tracts,'—too late indeed to stop the mischief done by them or check the ensuing controversy. It was something like the tardy wisdom of the boy Bill, who said to Tom (who had stuck several lighted matches into a rick), 'That'll do, Tom; don't let us waste our matches.' Many good and amiable men (true sons of the Church of England, who had found much in the Tracts that was excellent) would fain have stopped further proceedings against the writers of them. Certainly those writers (and Mr. Newman especially) had again and again pretty strongly declared their aversion to the tenets of Rome;—but what did the *event* prove? Having been disappointed in their hope (or rather their dream) of *assimilating* our Church to that of Rome, did not many of them go over to Rome? Great as was the respect entertained for their undoubted piety and learning, many good and pious Churchmen thought that they had neglected the blessed opportunity 'tantas componere lites,' by simply unfurling a banner inscribed with 'The Apostolic, Catholic, Reformed Church of England.'

Mr. Newman's 'Letter to the Bishop of Oxford' at this time was most touching in its submission; but, alas! how soon did he forget his own words:—' Our business,' he said, ' is with ourselves;—let the Church of Rome make itself (as we should try to make ourselves) more holy, more self-denying, more primitive,—it will come *nearer to us*, and will cease to be, what we one and all mean when we speak of *Rome*. To be anxious for a composition of differences is beginning at the wrong end.' And again: 'I think I can bear, or at least will try to bear, any personal humiliation, so that I am preserved from betraying sacred interests, which the Lord has given into my charge.'

Without being a 'Tractarian' I always thought we were under an obligation to the writers of the Tracts, for having maintained a greater reverence for our Liturgy, our Creeds, our Sacraments, and our Bishops; but that they wasted the great opportunity, brought about by themselves, of raising our low notion of what is meant by 'The Church,'—by shooting beyond the mark, and by forcing things (in some respects desirable) too far, too fast, and in too arrogant a tone.

Meanwhile Oxford, *as Oxford*, unmindful of such 'winds of doctrine,' calmly pursued its course in its usual generous spirit; witness the unanimous vote of £1000 for additional Colonial Bishops.

In this year, 1841, no Bampton Lectures were delivered; Mr. Wilberforce (afterwards Bishop of Oxford) had been appointed to preach them, but was prevented from doing so by a heavy affliction, the death of his wife. In some cases it might have been said, 'What a gain!' but in this particular instance we said, 'What a loss!' His Lordship perhaps is not sorry that he did not preach and publish eight sermons, or lectures, during such a disturbed state of the theological atmosphere.

May 20. Died the Rev. *Blanco White*, a name once held dear in Oxford[1].

June 24. *Mr. Sibthorpe*, Fellow of Magdalen, preached (before the University) and afterwards published a sermon of a very Popish tendency; and no wonder! for he soon after joined the Roman Church. But only for a while; for, after drinking of those muddy waters, he returned to the pure fountain of our Anglican and Apostolic Church, not having been able (it was said) to gulp down Mariolatry. It is but justice to add, that Mr. Sibthorpe was known and respected as a most excellent, pious man, but obviously more

[1] See more of him in 'Recollections' in 1826.

susceptible than stable. He had for some time held the Curacy of Kennington, near Oxford, and was then *followed* as a Calvinistic, Low Church preacher, and this after having had in his *very early* days at Magdalen a Romanising fit, which for a few days had imperilled his Demyship! He has for some years given (and is I believe still, in 1861, giving) a strong proof of his thorough *re-convictions* by his quiet retirement from all clerical duties, and a constant attendance in Lincoln Cathedral[1].

July. About this time Honorary Canons began to be appointed in the cathedrals where the number of actual Canons had been reduced. Some few years after, Honorary Fellows were tacked on to the list of actual Fellows in some of the Colleges at Oxford. On being asked the motive and the use of it, a Bursar of one of those Colleges answered, 'Why, don't you see? as "former Fellows" they often came to see us, and, of course, or at least from custom, *Domus* paid for their dinners, &c.; but now, as "Honorary Fellows," their names being replaced on the books, they battel as we do.' This bursarial speech was, of course, only half in earnest; but the other half would tell, both at College and at Chapter dinners. Honorary Canons have been called in at some cathedrals to make a show of keeping residence and filling a stall at the cathedral service, in the absence of all the regular Canons or Prebendaries.

In this summer we were tauntingly asked why Oxford was so slow in producing Doctors in Medicine—one or two in a year,—whilst the Senatus Academicus of Edinburgh could bring forth 103 M.D.'s at one litter. We could

---

[1] I have subsequently learnt that Mr. Sibthorp has again returned to the Roman Church, and according to 'The Catholic Directory' for 1869, is *attached* to St. Barnabas' Cathedral, Nottingham. Query: is he made use of there as a weather-cock?

only answer as the lioness did to the rabbit, 'But mine is a lion.'

Sept. 7. Dr. Pusey, in a letter (in which he cleared himself on the charge of having attended at Roman Catholic ceremonies), denied the charge (among several others) of 'professing to *adore* the *Eucharistic sacrifice* as identical with that which was offered on the Cross.'

The autumn of this year brought back to Alma Mater one of her brightest sons, Dr. Arnold, as Professor of Modern History. And one of her wealthiest sons, '*Robert Mason, D.D.*' (as he appears in the List of Public Benefactors, no other notice being taken of him elsewhere), poured into her lap £40,000 for the use of the Bodleian Library. Dr. Mason gave also as large a sum to Queen's College for the *immediate* creation of a modern library—so immediate, indeed, that a very limited time was allowed to the College thus to appropriate a bequest, which, if the time were exceeded, would (it was said) be transferred elsewhere. Dr. Mason must have been, notwithstanding his great wealth, a very quiet, retired sort of person, for no one out of his College (and very few there) had ever heard of him till his bequests were announced. He must, in some way or other, have attached a high notion to libraries and books, though he seems to have left no library of his own collecting. One of his books, at least, must have been above all price, viz. his banking-book.

At the end of 1841, a warmly-contested election loomed in the distance for the Poetry Professorship, vacated by J. Keble, whose ten years had expired. The candidates were Mr. Garbett and Isaac Williams.

A.D. 1842.

[B.A. 282. M.A. 163. Hon. D.C.L. at Commemoration, 2.]

Jan. 7 died Dr. Shuttleworth, having been Bishop of Chichester for the short space of a year and four months, scarcely long enough to be at all known in his diocese. Sobered as he was by age, qualified as he was as a theological writer to speak with authority ex cathedrâ episcopali, and talented above the ordinary level of English bishops, his death was a great loss to the Church, and was especially felt by his New College friends. It was amusing to read in the papers the many guesses at his successor, not one hitting on the right name, Dr. Gilbert. By-the-bye, it must be rather annoying (generally speaking) to have one's name thus *served up* on every one's breakfast-table, and yet nothing come of it. Some persons, indeed, may like to see their name in print, even though it may all end in smoke; a 'proximè accessit' (in later life as well as in Oxford Undergraduate life) may be acceptable among the 'solatia victo' in a race in which, though many run, only one is able to win the prize, 'victorque hominum volitare per ora.'

This year had begun in Oxford with a storm of angry words and a heavy shower of controversial letters in reference to the contest for the Professorship of Poetry between Messrs. Garbett and Williams, the Tracts for the Times being made to bear upon the question. The writers of those letters were Lord Ashley, Lord Dungannon, William and Roundell Palmer, Messrs. Golightly, Sibthorp, Bricknell, Seager, W. Conybeare, with a host of anonymous M.A.'s.

On the 20th of January, however, while every one was discussing the comparative merits of the two candidates, (one being decidedly a poet, certainly a scholar, but unfortunately a Tractarian; the other a clever man, a classical scholar and critic, but rather a Low Churchman), all the hubbub and all the discomforts of a contested election on a large scale were quietly put a stop to (pulveris exigui jactû) by a challenge to a comparison of *promised votes* from one side (Mr. Garbett's) and an acceptance of the challenge on the other; when, it being found that Mr. Garbett had 921 promises, Mr. Williams only 623, Mr. Williams at once retired from the contest. If no other party profited by the Garbett and Williams contest and the Tractarian controversy, the printers and booksellers certainly did. The air of Oxford was for a long while filled with pamphlets and other such missile weapons. At length, however, even Mr. Bricknell got tired of carrying on the controversy; at least, he found that others were tired, and demanded peace.

March 18. An address was voted to be presented by a delegacy to congratulate her Majesty on the birth of the Prince of Wales. Our noble Chancellor and the University Delegates had rather hard work to get through, for besides the address to the Queen, there was one to Prince Albert and another to the Duchess of Kent. The same ceremony had taken place on the previous birth of the Princess Royal; but, as her Majesty's family subsequently increased, the event became too much a matter of course to require the formal congratulations of the University.

In April, two additional Theological (Regius) Professorships were founded, with a Canonry at Christ Church attached to each (when they should fall in); one for Ecclesiastical History, first held by Mr. Hussey; the other for Pastoral Theology, held by Dr. Ogilvie. The University voted each of them an annual stipend of £300, to cease when the Canonries should become vacant. On the principle that *division of labour* is generally effectual in its results, this increased staff and classification of subjects were expected to raise the character of our theological school.

May 8. In Convocation the sum of £20 a year was voted to the Bodleian janitor, upon an understanding 'that, in future, any member of the University, either alone or with friends, shall be admitted to the Picture Gallery without payment, provided he appear in his proper academical dress!'—fees from strangers to be still allowed. Query: Was not that giving to the janitor, 'antro æternùm latranti,' a quasi Procuratorial power? That academics should *lionise* strangers (especially ladies) in their academical dress is, no doubt, very proper, and used to be considered as a matter of course; but in this, as in most other things, the rough freedom of the times shows itself.

In this year, 1842, the Prize for Latin Verse was not awarded! that is, not one of the few copies sent in was presentable in the Theatre. Tell it not at Eton, publish it not in the senior classes at Winchester! On second thoughts, if the talent of Latin versification is to be kept up, tell it and publish it there and everywhere.

June 7. After great and long excitement, Convocation (assembled in the Theatre, on account of the large attendance) had to vote upon the proposal of the Board 'to *rescind* the Statute of 1836,' which had deprived Dr. Hampden, as Regius Professor of Divinity, of certain privileges belonging to that office. After a protest from Mr. Sewell, a long yarn from Mr. Waye, and a strongly-seasoned Latin oration against the proposal from Mr. Vaughan Thomas, the House became impatient for the voting; there were given 219 Placets, 334 Non-Placets; majority against the proposal, 115.

So bitter was still the odium theologicum! so determined were Dr. Hampden's opponents to worry him, if not to death, at least to resignation; not seeing or wishing for the remaining alternative, viz. to hasten his escape from a bed of thorns to a bed of roses—from uncharitable Oxford to a comfortable bishopric!

About the same date the University and Rugby School sustained a heavy blow in the death of the good Dr. Arnold. He was loved and admired by many in Oxford, who could not keep pace with him in his *enlarged* views.

June 22. The drawings and designs by Raffaelle and Michael Angelo (since placed in the University Galleries) were secured to the University, chiefly by two acts of generosity: first, Mr. Woodburn, who had asked £10,000 for them, lowered their price to £6000 on learning where they would be deposited; and secondly, Lord Eldon (grandson of the Lord Chancellor) nobly presented £4000 for the purpose, £2000 being raised by a miscellaneous subscription.

Aug. 20. Dr. Cramer was appointed Regius Professor of Modern History in Dr. Arnold's place, relinquishing the Public Oratorship which he had held for thirteen years. In both offices he had to succeed very distinguished predecessors.

Dec. 1. A legacy was announced of £10,000 by Dean Ireland (already a benefactor to the University as the founder of the Ireland Scholarships) for a Professorship of the Exegesis of Holy Scripture, soon filled by Dr. Hawkins.

A.D. 1843.

[B.A. 282. M.A. 167. Hon. D.C.L. at Commemoration, 2.]

February. A Cambridge paper asserted that 'at the present day there exists, above the modern plaster ceiling in

New College Hall, the original carved oak roof, with the exception of the ends of the pendants.' This, however, is not correct to any extent. It is gratifying to learn (in 1861) that the College seriously intends to restore the rafter-roof; the plans and drawings are made, and a stimulus has been given by the offer of £1000 for the purpose from the Junior Common Room[1].

The early part of 1843 was marked by a great deal of bitter controversy, mostly in anonymous circulars or in the papers. One of the chief subjects of discussion was the *doctrine* of *Reserve* (sometimes called Economia and Phenacism) in the treatment of religious questions. It was consolatory, amidst all this agitation, to see sober-minded men pursue their even course as good and consistent members of the Church of England, and the great Church Societies doing their steady work and bearing their real testimony to the vital energy of our Church.

The question of raising a subscription for putting painted windows into St. Mary's Church was much discussed at this time, and even subjects proposed, but without any results. If it had been done, what havoc would have followed from the gas explosion in 1860! unless, indeed, the greater thickness of painted glass would have protected them, as it seems to have protected one of the Bartley memorial windows.

April 15. The 'assessment of the Colleges to the poor-rates' now began to be tried for, beginning with Exeter and Jesus Colleges,—a claim which the University, a dozen years afterwards, generously admitted and has since acted up to, to the great relief of the 'ingratæ urbis.' The University pays *one third* of each rate.

The Oxford Architectural Society was now beginning to

---

[1] This restoration has since been admirably effected.

rise into importance and increasing interest, bidding fair to rival the Ashmolean Society.

In May, Dr. Faussett called upon the Vice-Chancellor, requiring him to demand a copy of Dr. Pusey's University sermon, preached May 14, 1843, at Christ Church. The Vice-Chancellor, Dr. Wynter, being thus statutably called upon, appointed a Board of D.D.'s to examine the sermon; and this ended in Dr. Pusey's suspension from preaching before the University for two years. The principal charge against the sermon was said to be that Dr. Pusey therein taught the Real Corporeal Presence of Christ in the elements on consecration. Dr. Pusey of course protested against the sentence of two years' suspension, but gained nothing by his protest, or by his demand to be heard on 'definite propositions.' Without pretending to decide on such high points of doctrine, one cannot but assent to a remark made at the time, 'that Dr. Pusey was now made to wear the cap which in 1836 he had fitted on Dr. Hampden's head.' 'Quàm temerè in nosmet legem sancimus iniquam; cædimus inque vicem præbemus crura flagellis.' Dr. Pusey of course complained that he was not *heard*, not *present;* but surely he was present in his sermon, and that had been heard.

Mr. Morris, of Exeter College, preached at St. Mary's in Whitsun-week a much more objectionable sermon; but, being an obscure person (though a copy of his sermon was demanded by the Vice-Chancellor), he was left unmolested, to follow his obvious tendency to the Church of Rome, which he soon actually joined. In his College-rooms, during Lent, he was said to have carried mortification to an extreme, limiting his nourishment to a diet of split peas and warm water!

June 26. At the 'Commemoration' of this year, the Junior

Proctor, who had made himself extremely unpopular, was *paid off* by the Undergraduates with incessant and violent marks of disapprobation. If 'laudatur ab *his*' be indeed a proof of official merit, never did officer obtain so decided a *laudatio*. The expression of dislike, however, was carried to a disgraceful extreme, in manner and duration. After one burst of applause for the Vice-Chancellor, Dr. Wynter, one continued storm of yelling and hissing was kept up by the rioters. The Honorary Degrees (luckily only two) were conferred in dumb-show. The Creweian Oration by the Professor of Poetry, Mr. Garbett, was read, but not a word of it was heard. Tired out and disgusted (as was every one else not in '*the yelling-gallery*') the Vice-Chancellor dissolved the Convocation,—the Prize Compositions being left unrecited! This Convocation was also marked by another occurrence:—One of the two persons proposed for the Honorary Degree was Mr. Everett, the American Minister, who, it seems, had been an Unitarian preacher. Some over-scrupulous Masters of Arts[1] endeavoured to give

[1] The amusing author of 'Eothen' (in a note, p. 188) gives this whimsical account of Mr. Everett's visit to Oxford: 'An enterprising American traveller, Mr. Everett, lately conceived the bold project of penetrating to the University of Oxford, and this, notwithstanding that he had been in his infancy (they begin very young, those Americans) an Unitarian preacher. Having a notion, it seems, that the Ambassadorial character would protect him from insult, he adopted the stratagem of procuring credentials from his Government as Minister Plenipotentiary at the court of her Britannic Majesty; he also wore the exact costume of a Trinitarian, but all his contrivances were vain; Oxford disdained and rejected him (not because he represented a swindling community, but) because that his infantine sermons were strictly remembered against him: the enterprise failed.'—N.B. The wit or humour of this extract is not very apparent, nor is the principal statement, 'Oxford rejected him,' correct; 'swindling' should have been 'repudiating' (whatever that means in America); and as to the terms 'infancy' and 'infantine,' they are simply absurd.

a Non-Placet and demand a scrutiny, forgetting (1) the probability of exciting angry feelings in the mind of our 'Brother Jonathan' by this treatment of their ambassador; and (2) that an *Honorary* Degree requires no subscription to Articles, and has been conferred on all sorts of distinguished persons without hesitation or enquiry. Luckily the young men's noise rendered the Non-Placets inaudible to the Vice-Chancellor (I say 'luckily,' for how could a scrutiny have been taken in such a crowd and in such a tumult?). Mr. Everett was introduced and, being admitted in dumb show, took his seat among the Doctors. A small number of Masters of Arts afterwards protested, but of course to no purpose, except to extort a declaration from the Vice-Chancellor ' that neither he nor any one near him was made aware that a scrutiny had been demanded,' till the candidates were brought in for *presentation*, when it was obviously too late, 'Placetne vobis' having already been *put*.

This June was marked by a sad event, the death by drowning of Dean Gaisford's third son and Dr. Phillimore's youngest son, while bathing at Sandford Lasher Pool. Gaisford sank from exhaustion, fright, or cramp, in the rough water of the Lasher, and Phillimore went down while gallantly striving to assist his friend. Two monumental tablets were placed in Christ Church Cathedral, with an inscription by Dr. Gaisford on that of his son. There was also erected a memorial of them on the spot where they were drowned.

At the Henley Regatta, this June, the Oxford and Cambridge eight-oared boats being about to start, one of the Oxford crew was taken ill. The Cambridge men would not allow a substitute;—so 'the plucky seven' started, with all the odds against them, with four rowers on one side and three on the other ('*the bow-oar being vacant*'). To attempt the thing was audacious, to succeed in it (as the Oxonians did) was unprecedented in the annals of boating,—but 'possunt quia posse videntur.'

The Margaret Professorship is subject to the absurd form of re-election every second year; this year, 1843, there was a strong apprehension that a muster of hostile Bachelors and Doctors of Divinity (who are the electors) would attempt to negative *Dr. Faussett's* re-election. So strong a meeting, however, of his D.D. and B.D. friends and supporters attended, that the expected attempt was not made. Alas! poor divided Oxford[1]!

In July, the Vice-Chancellor declined to receive an Address (deprecating the proceedings as to Dr. Pusey's sermon), signed by more than 200 Members of Convocation.

In September, Mr. Newman resigned the Vicarage of St. Mary's and, with it, Littlemore Chapelry. His published sermons were not only unobjectionable, but excellent; his private teaching had long been distrusted, and pains had been taken at some Colleges to prevent Undergraduates from attending his Services, by making the College Chapel hour coincide with his Sunday Afternoon Service at St. Mary's. He was obviously preparing for a farther flight Romewards.

Mr. Garbett (in October) made a good remark in a published letter,—'that Romanism (*spontaneous* Romanism he calls it) would naturally arise from studying Scripture through the Fathers, instead of studying the Fathers by the light of Scripture.'

Nov. One of the earliest 'perverts' was *Mr. Seager*, of Worcester College. It was said that he went to Oscott 'for a literary enquiry;' that, after dinner, controversy was started by Dr. Wiseman, and was kept up till four o'clock

---

[1] Since 1858 the election is for life.

next morning, when Mr. Seager '*cried for quarter!*' Can we wonder that he, who thus rushed into the snare, should not have escaped? The account further added, that 'at 8 a.m. of the same morning he was baptized!' That act of baptizing converts from our Church is justly considered the most arrogant of all Romish proceedings; as ignoring our Church, our ministers, their orders and ministrations altogether. Only conceive such men as Newman, Manning, Oakeley, Faber, &c., thus renouncing, or rather denouncing, the Church of their fathers, and condemning, as *not Christian*, their own previous ministrations[1]!

While Oxford and the Church were thus kept *in hot water* by the Romanising Tractarians, Ireland was 'agitated' by O'Connell, and Wales by what were ridiculously called the '*Rebecca*' riots! The anxious state of things in Ireland may be understood from the fact that at this time 34,000 troops were kept there by Government!

---

[1] This act of re-baptizing is said indeed to be performed 'sub con-ditione,' but the insult and the humiliation are just the same.

CHAPTER XVIII.

'Conamur tenues grandia.'—*Horace.*

Proceedings as to Mr. Macmullen.

IN May, 1843, Mr. Macmullen, Fellow of Corpus, commenced an action in the Vice-Chancellor's Court against Dr. Hampden, Regius Professor of Divinity, for damages caused by his not being allowed (as required by the College statutes) to proceed to the Degree of B.D., or rather for not having been allowed by Dr. Hampden to argue on subjects of *his own choice*, as an Exercise for that Degree, in the Divinity School. The fact was, that Dr. Hampden, knowing, as every one did, Macmullen's Romish tendencies, required him to dispute on certain searching questions, and that he refused to accept them. By-the-bye, '*dispute*' was not the proper term; it was rather a 'dissertation,' to be approved or disapproved by the Professor.

June 21. The case of Macmullen *v.* Hampden was heard in the Vice-Chancellor's Court. The importance of the proceeding was at once shown by the introduction of regular 'Counsel' on both sides; a thing of rare occurrence, ordinary cases being conducted by the Proctors of the Court. Dr. Twiss appeared for the defendant (Dr. Hampden), and Mr. Hope, of the Chancery Bar (himself subsequently a 'pervert') for Macmullen. After a long, dry argument on both sides (the advocates sticking to the points of law, and cautiously avoiding all theological questions), the Assessor (of course) took time to consider the matter.

Near the end of Act Term notice was given that (as was allowed by the statutes) the cause Macmullen *v.* Hampden was transferred, by appeal, from the Vice-Chancellor's Court to the 'Delegates of Appeal in Congregation.'

In the following Term, November 29, Counsel were heard on the case before the Delegates of Appeal, sitting in the usual Court in the Apodyterium. After much talking and lengthened addresses (which actually lasted from 10 a.m. till 7 p.m.), the Court deferred its decision, taking more time to consider the arguments, &c. I

Jan. 4, 1844. The judgment of the Assessor, which had allowed *the libel* (on which Macmullen brought his charge against Hampden) to be good in law, was reversed by 'the Delegates of Appeal in Congregation.' The libel therefore, or charge, was dismissed. 'Solvuntur tabulæ!' But more work seemed to be cut out for the lawyers, in the shape of a further Appeal from the Delegates of Congregation to the Delegates of Convocation. This, however, was not followed up by the plaintiff, no difference of opinion being there to be expected. So Mr. Macmullen, who had brought the action for *the recovery of five pounds* (the ground of the action, as what he would have received extra from Corpus, if he had been allowed to graduate as B.D.), had multiplied his loss by expenses of many times that sum. It was believed, however, that his party did not leave him alone to pay his Counsel, while Dr. Hampden had to bear his expenses unaided.

April 18. Macmullen, having failed in his lawsuit against Dr. Hampden, submitted to resume his Exercises for the

B.D. Degree, but one of his two Dissertations was rejected by the Professor, on the thesis, 'The Church of England does not teach, nor can it be proved from Scripture, that any change takes place in the elements at Consecration.' Notwithstanding this rejection of his Exercise, Mr. Macmullen actually '*supplicated*' in Congregation for admission to the Degree of B.D., but on Dr. Hampden's informing the Vice-Chancellor and Proctors 'that the Exercise had not been duly performed,' the 'Grace of the House' was not conceded ('hæc gratia non est concessa').

May 24. The same attempt having been repeated by Macmullen, his 'Grace' was explicitly and finally refused, '*negata est*,' in Congregation. About the same time, Dr. Hampden, as Regius Professor of Divinity, was enjoined by the Hebdomadal Board to return to the form of 'Disputations' required by the letter of the statutes, as an Exercise for the B.D. Degree. This, of course, was hailed as at least a minor triumph by the Tractarian party, forgetting that this mode had been actually offered to Macmullen, instead of the 'Dissertations' which had been introduced by Dr. Lloyd, and continued by Dr. Burton.

June 5. Mr. Macmullen, having been allowed to do the required Exercises on a non-searching question ('an doctrina Romanensium de Purgatorio Sacræ Scripturæ contradicat?') at length took the Degree of B.D. He soon after this joined a strong party of his own way of thinking, in one of the churches at Leeds. What that 'way of thinking' meant, was at length fully shown; for, on the 9th of January, 1847, 'the *troublesome* Mr. Macmullen' (as the Oxford papers called him) was received into the Roman Catholic Church.— And there we may leave him, if not to do penance, at least to repent at leisure, and to feel (as other deserters like himself must have felt) how unimportant he had at once become.

But it is right to notice that this proceeding at Leeds, with other like things then and there going on, was said to have opened the eyes of Dr. Hook, who in the recent academic struggles had sided with the Tractarians. He was said to have acknowledged (in a letter to an Oxford dignitary) 'the pain with which he now thought of the part he had taken against the Heads of Houses'—'he no longer talked of "usurped authority," but from being a *protester* (against that authority) had become a *protestant*.' In his own language (as it was reported), 'he found that he had got a hornet's nest close to his garden gate.'

General '*Recollections*' resumed.

A.D. 1844.

[B.A. 289. M.A. 213. Hon. D.C.L. 13.]

Jan. 1 (1844). The question of a 'public cemetery'— that is, a burying-place open to all persons, of all creeds, or even of no creed—was discussed at a general meeting; when eight of the parochial clergy, who wished 'for the Church to bury its own dead,' left the room, on finding that their views and wishes were not favourably received by the meeting, who were for a general cemetery. For effecting this, however, nothing was done then or since; whereas the *Church view* soon began to show its truth and reality, by the successful efforts made for the acquirement and arrangement of the three parochial burial-places. These were soon consecrated, with their respective chapels, &c.;— but where is the 'cemetery?' There is something very pleasing and charitable in the idea, that 'all who call themselves Christians' should have one common κοιμητήριον, their dormitorium or resting-place, where they should lie down together, at peace in death, though separated in their lifetime, and awaiting their common resurrection; but in the *working it out* (as to officiating ministers, the rites and forms to be used, &c., &c.) difficulties and collisions would necessarily arise. At Weymouth there is a large cemetery, one portion of which (nearly the half) was set apart for Dissenters. Some feelings of annoyance may have been spared by this; but the comparison of the tombs, inscriptions, &c., is vastly in favour of the Church's dead, or rather the Churchman's honour for the dead. In Oxford the purchase of the burial-grounds by a subscription was soon effected,—indeed the site for one of them (Holy Cross) was *given* by Merton College;—they were to be 'for all persons, on the same footing as churchyards had been,' and 'for the use respectively of the adjoining parishes' to which they were allotted.

In February, a *musical mania* broke out and spread widely in Oxford, though it was not confined to Oxford. *Mr. Hullah's* system of vocalisation was supposed, after a few lessons, to make singers of all, both young and old! This 'hulla-baloo' first exhibited itself in Merton College hall, where there were at least seventy persons assembled, under the teaching of a Mr. May, Mr. Hullah's deputy. It was rather amusing to see Masters of Arts of long standing, who had never before shown either ear or voice, joining the class with their practice-books. It did not last long.

Early in this spring, with a view to raise the theological standard in Oxford, 'a voluntary examination' in Theology was instituted, with a great staff of Examiners;—but it did not work well. The annual notices and appointments have ever since taken place, with some slight alterations by way of attraction, but still it has excited no attention, and produced no fruit; none at least which the public ever heard of.

May 2. Some proposed alterations in Exercises for Degrees both in Law and Divinity were rejected in Convocation by very large majorities.

May 12. Mr. Garbett of Brasenose preached a sermon at St. Mary's, in which a busy member of Convocation (Mr. Knollis of Magdalen) thought he detected something heretical, and (as was reported) laid a charge before the Vice-Chancellor (Dr. Wynter); he however, having had enough of such enquiries, dismissed the *delator* with the remark, 'that he had observed nothing objectionable in the sermon,' unless (he might have added) it were its great length.

June 6. A plan proposed for the Taylor Institution was rejected; that for the Randolph Gallery was adopted. By-the-bye, the name of *Randolph* (somewhat ungratefully) seems likely to be lost in the title of 'The University Galleries.' It was hoped that the naked walls would soon be covered with pictures presented to the University; but Dr. Penrose's bequest of four or five valuable paintings has had as yet but few imitators. It will probably be a long time before Oxford can boast of a School of Art[1].

The branch railroad from Oxford to Didcot, so long in coming, came at last to a conclusion, or rather (*quoad nos*) a beginning; it was opened to the public on the 12th of June.

June 19. At the 'Encænia' (or Commemoration) of this year, the Undergraduates were admitted to the Theatre by tickets; what good that did, except to exclude any impudent *non-academic* from gaining admission by putting on a gown, did not appear. At all events, either from the sense of shame for the preceding years' gross misconduct, or from

[1] A practical School of Art has since been opened, but not in the higher sense of the term above intended.

the recollection of the serious consequences to one or two notorious rioters, or from the fact of there being no unpopular Proctor, their conduct was orderly and gentlemanly. Why should it ever be otherwise?

Aug. 25. Oxford was enlivened in Long Vacation by a visit of its Chancellor, 'the Great Duke,' with Prince William of Prussia, who, as a youth, had been made Honorary D.C.L. thirty years before, i. e. on the Royal visit of 1814. The scene must have revived in him many striking reminiscences of his father, of the Emperor Alexander, of Blucher, and a host of notables. The day was spent in *lionising* Oxford. The Prince returned to Prussia, eventually (after the incapacity of his brother) to become Regent, and on his brother's death, in 1860, King of Prussia, and father-in-law to our Princess Royal.

Sept. 25. The alarm was thus early sounded (as to the threatened opposition to *Dr. Symons'* nomination to the office of Vice-Chancellor) by a Notice issued by the Wadham Tutors, 'to Wadham men and others,' to be ready to support him on the 8th of October against this bit of spite on the part of the Tractarians, or (as in this case they must be called) Puseyites. They had never forgiven him for acting as one of the D.D.'s who sat in judgment on Dr. Pusey's sermon.

Oct. 8. The expected drama was carried into action,— and a wretched appearance was made by the party, headed by Mr. Ward of Balliol (himself so soon to be voted against in the same Theatre!). These 'perturbatores pacis' mustered only 183 votes against 883 supporters of Dr. Symons, leaving the unprecedented majority of 700! As a doubt was raised whether Convocation really could negative, or even vote upon the Chancellor's nomination, the retiring Vice-Chancellor, Dr. Wynter, granted the scrutiny under protest[1], or, as he expressed it, 'salvâ auctoritate et potestate Cancellarii.' Never did a party make a more wretched appearance (in the Theatre, where the Convocation was held) than did the minority on that occasion, 'pedibus eundo ad sinistram,' when facing the large majority 'ad dextram Vice-Cancellarii.'

It was reported; about this time, that the distinguished (Quaker) philosopher, 'Dr. Dalton,' was intending to bequeath £2000 to enlarge the resources of the Oxford Professor of Chemistry Subsequent reports informed us that Dalton, though always proud of his Oxford Degree, nevertheless so far changed his mind as to leave merely £100 to Dr. Daubeny for that purpose.

MR. WARD AND HIS BOOK. A.D. 1844-5.

Οἱ δὲ, καὶ ἀχνύμενοί περ, ἐπ' αὐτῷ ἡδὺ γέλασσαν.
Hom. Iliad II. 270.

It was very sad to witness, at this period, the unaccountable inconsistencies of good men on the brink of passing over to Rome, yet (like so many swallows, hovering about the roofs and towers of our churches, in preparation for their flight) still lingering in what they considered as 'a body that contained in it no outward marks of Catholicity.' Such was the position of Messrs. Newman, Oakeley, and others, at the time when Mr. Ward's 'trial,' or rather that of his book, 'The Ideal of a Christian Church,' was fast approaching.

---

[1] The event of this discussion showed that this caution was wisely taken; for Chancellor Wellington was not a man to be trifled with; and since then the nomination has been merely communicated and commended to favourable acceptance, but not submitted to the vote of Convocation. The Earl of Leicester, Chancellor of Oxford in 1569, took upon himself (says Wood) the right of naming his Commissary (or Vice-Chancellor) without asking the consent of Convocation.

Nov. 30, 1844. Mr. Ward was called before the Vice-Chancellor and asked, 'Whether he disavowed the authorship of the above work, or the sentiments contained in certain parts of it?' But he begged to decline giving an answer till he was informed what farther proceedings were intended.

The details of his 'trial' may properly be preceded by a few passages from his and other persons' pamphlets on the occasion.

An article of a powerful, argumentative character on his book, 'The Ideal,' &c., had appeared in the Quarterly Review.

1. Mr. Ward in a 'Reply' thereto, says, 'I concede that there are some of our formularies which I subscribe in "a *non-natural* sense;"' adding that 'he considers that *all*, who subscribe our formularies, subscribe several of them in a non-natural sense.'

At p. 36 of his Reply he speaks of 'those who, like myself, adopt the *whole cycle* of *Roman doctrine!*'

At p. 54 he speaks contemptuously of our Articles and formularies; as 'containing what certain bishops, three centuries ago, *considered at the moment* to be derivable from Scripture and antiquity.' 'What would be said,' he asks, 'if a Colonial bishop were to draw up a set of Articles and ordain no one except on condition of subscribing them? And wherein would this differ from what took place at the Reformation?' In the first place, the Reformers did not draw up our Articles, &c. hastily or 'at the moment.' In the next, their appeal to Scripture and antiquity led them to the real truths of Christianity, which Popery had departed from.

It may be true (as Mr. Ward asserted) that the Church of Rome imposes no *tests* (ex. gr. no Thirty-nine Articles) on its clergy, but does it not bind them hand and foot to the decrees of the Council of Trent, &c.?

2. Dr. Tait, in 'A Letter to the Vice-Chancellor,' remarked that 'It is but a few years since Dr. Pusey called for the revival of the old power of "Six Doctors," that he might overwhelm Dr. Hampden by the weight of their authority; and he is himself even now reeling under the blow which they have since dealt against him.'

3. A pamphlet by Mr. Norman gave a full statement of the charge against Mr. Ward and the Propositions to be made against him in Convocation. This pamphlet also gave the opposite opinions of Counsel as to the power of Convocation;—but ended by allowing it.

4. Mr. Hull (in his pamphlet) said, ' The vote or *privilegium* (i. e. private or special law) against Dr. Hampden was passed in 1836. In 1842 the Board endeavoured to repeal it, but the *Italian Band* was able to carry off the victory. It had first betrayed the Board to folly (i. e. to persecute Hampden) and then held them to it in their own despite.' ' Justice was outraged by the statute against Hampden, and Nemesis is probably at work for Mr. Ward's coming trial.'

5. Mr. Keble very warmly interceded for Mr. Ward in a short pamphlet, in which he strongly urged ' the injustice of charging with a breach of good faith so honest and straightforward a person.' All through his pamphlet, however, he kept out of sight the palpable foundation for the charge of *bad faith*, viz. the fact ' that Mr. Ward would still willingly continue a member of the University on the strength of his subscription made when he was (what he no longer continued to be) a faithful son of the Church of England.'

6. Dr. Moberly published a pamphlet, in which, being blinded by friendship, ' he could not admit the idea of " bad faith," because *he knows* Mr. Ward,'—and this when

Mr. Ward, while boasting of his belief in every article of *Popery*, would fain be a member of a *Protestant* University! Dr. Moberly seemed to forget that the 'Declaration' did not impute bad faith to Mr. Ward *at the time of taking his Degrees*, but to his wish *after Romanising* to enjoy an M.A.'s privileges in virtue of his *former* subscription. Dr. Moberly concluded with an unlucky but unintended pun, he hoped 'to have contributed to *ward* off danger from the University.'

7. Mr. Maurice in his pamphlet asserted (what no one else ever heard of) that first of all a Council of Doctors was appointed to sit in judgment on Ward's book; coolly observing, that 'he himself would rather be tried by such a court than by a miscellaneous *mob of gentlemen* from London clubs and country parsonages,'—i.e. Convocation! Mr. Maurice, like Mr. Keble, condemned the '*New Test*,' as it was well called, and which was eventually withdrawn.

8. Mr. Garbett in a lengthy pamphlet (which was really a powerful defence of our Church and its Articles) 'rem acu tetigit' in a single sentence: 'In what it proposes to do to Mr. Ward the University only proposes to withdraw those privileges, which were granted on an express engagement which he has broken.'

In explanation of the term '*The New Test*,' used just above, it must be added, that it was at first intended to subjoin to the charges against Mr. Ward this wordy Declaration: 'Nemini posthac qui coram Vice-Cancellario, utpote minus recte de Doctrina vel de Disciplina Ecclesiæ Anglicanæ sentiens, *conveniatur*[1], Articulis subscribere fas sit, nisi prius Declarationi subscripserit sub hac forma: Ego, Articulis fidei et Religionis subscripturus, profiteor hìc Articulis istis omnibus et singulis eo sensu me esse subscripturum, in quo

[1] Conveniatur—be *convened* or summoned.

eos ex animo credo et primitus editos esse et nunc mihi ab Universitate propositos, tanquam opinionum mearum certum ac indubitatum signum.'

This, as being virtually a New Test (and one liable to change with the *animus* of the imponents), was so strongly and generally disapproved, as soon as it appeared, that it was wisely withdrawn, leaving the personal question, regarding Mr. Ward and his book, to be voted upon on its own merits. But as if to make up for this withdrawal, a Vote of censure and condemnation on No. 90 of Tracts for the Times, was appended (rather hastily and injudiciously) to the votes concerning 'The Ideal' of Mr. Ward. This proposal was not approved of by the then Proctors (Guillemard of Trinity, and Church of Oriel), and, as they gave notice that they intended to exercise their *joint veto* upon it, attention was concentrated on the original propositions affecting Mr. Ward.

On the 13th of February, the area of the Theatre (where the Convocation was held) was crowded with Masters,—no one but voters being admitted. After the selected passages from his book had been read by the Registrar, Mr. Ward was allowed to read, from the rostrum, a lengthened defence in English. He did not appear at all distressed or excited by his position, but, in his usual, cool manner, *took it quite easy*. After a considerable time (either from being tired or, as was wickedly said, to read a letter from his sweetheart, brought to him by a friend) he begged for a short respite. The interval allowed by the Vice-Chancellor having expired, he resumed his defence and was listened to very patiently, though it was in most parts very dull.

When he had finished, Dr. Grant of New College proposed an amendment, which would have softened the censure very much; but the Vice-Chancellor would not allow of an amendment, as being quite an unprecedented thing in Convocation. The two questions therefore were successively put to the vote:—

Vote the first:—

For the condemnation of *the book*   777   ⎫
Against it 386   ⎬ 1163 votes.

                      Majority . . 391

Vote the second:—

For Mr. Ward's *Degradation* . . 569 ⎫
Against it . . . . 511 ⎬ 1080 votes.

             Majority only   58

This was a great falling off in numbers; but it was felt to be one thing to stigmatise a work, quite another to degrade and disfranchise the man.

On the third vote, i. e. for the condemnation of No. 90 (which really had nothing to do with the trial of Mr. Ward and his book), the Proctors (as above hinted), to the great disgust of the large assembly, threw their velvet sleeves over the *precious* Tract; in other words, they exercised their joint Non-placet.

> 'It seems no matter what a man believes,
> If he find shelter 'neath the Proctors' sleeves;
> When Proctors twain pronounce their potent Veto,
> In vain eight hundred Masters cry "Scrutinium peto."'

As might well be expected, a storm of indignation from disappointed voters followed the Proctors' *gagging;* but Mr. Ward was cheered by the Undergraduates (on his way to Balliol) 'as a *plucky fellow.*' Of course he protested and talked of further legal proceedings; whilst his friend (and fellow-traveller on the way to Rome) Mr. Oakeley claimed 'the right of *holding*, as distinct from *teaching*' (he being a clergyman, ministering in the Church of England), '*all Roman doctrine*,' and that, notwithstanding his subscription to the Thirty-nine Articles!

This exercise of 'the Proctors' veto' had been rarely, if ever, used, till it was introduced (in 1836) in the Hampden controversy, when it was soon found (i.e. in the succeeding year) that two parties could play that game, or (as the Welsh giant said to Jack the Giant-killer), 'her can do that trick herself.' With great efforts, and after a laborious correspondence, an Address, with the names of 800 Members of Convocation, was *got up* and presented to the Proctors, 'to thank them for having protected No. 90.' A great number certainly, and showing how widely the Tractarian influence had spread. But Oxford had at this very time more than 3000 Members of Convocation on the books.

To go on with the narrative. The above-mentioned Address naturally produced a counter-requisition, as numerously signed, to beg the Hebdomadal Board to persevere in the condemnation of Tract 90. During all this University hubbub, it was consolatory to find that the sun still continued to rise and set,—that Marshall's Concert was well attended, and that at least the citizens of Oxford enjoyed their Mayor's dinner; while those who sought other amusement found it in observing how complacently 'Counsel' had given (or rather sold) their '*opinion*' on both sides (pro and con.) as to the legality of the recent decision of Convocation; while Sydney Smith, tired of laughing at the follies of the world, finally took leave of it. And Mr. Ward, as if to settle the question of his holding his Balliol Fellowship after his 'degradation,' found consolation in the society of a wife. In a long letter, written in answer to comments made on his marriage, Mr. Ward disclaims having ever professed to lead a 'celibate life;' though he allows, or rather asserts it as 'a truth, even of natural religion, that celibacy is a higher condition of life than marriage'! This was obviously the expression of a Romanising bias[1]. On the 24th of April Mr. Ward, who had *face* for anything, actually presented himself (notwithstanding his recent '*degradation*') in a Master's gown in the Convocation House, where he actually gave a Non-Placet, at the formal reading of an ordinary Chancellor's Letter, and demanded a scrutiny,—not knowing or caring about the purport of the Letter (which was connected with an obscure individual's Degree), but wishing to assert his privilege, with a view probably to further legal proceedings. Of course no notice was taken of him or his motion; so having done this deed, he walked out[2]— not in a dignified manner, for to that, in his most palmy days, he had no pretensions. He actually began to take law proceedings, and in a month afterwards a *mandamus* was granted, requiring the University of Oxford to defend the proceedings of the 13th of February. This, however, was mere bravado, and ended in smoke. In the autumn of this year (1845) he did 'his own *quietus* make' by openly joining the Church of Rome. Even this he could not do quietly, but printed a long, flippant, and (for so clever a man) weak 'Justification' of himself, dated from Rose-Hill

[1] I have seen, with surprise, the same notion expressed very strongly in a book of Family Devotions by an honoured Bishop. Our Church calls matrimony 'holy;' where is celibacy so called?

[2] The authorities, thus insulted, were very lenient in not taking that opportunity of enforcing the ceremony detailed in the Statute 'De degradatione,' according to which, after the Vice-Chancellor's 'severa oratio,' 'unus e bedellis inferioribus singula gradus *sui* (*ejus*?) insignia, primò pileum, mox caputium, deinde capam, postremò togam detrahet, ac cum in modum, cunctis insignibus Academicis exutum et nudatum, e domo Convocationis *proturbabit*.'

(near Oxford), where for some time after his marriage he had made his bed of roses. But more than enough of the now '*W. Ward, Esq.!*' Of course there followed a few 'spent shots' both from him, dated from St. Mary's College, Oscott (whither, it is to be presumed, he did not take Mrs. Ward), and also from others. But by this final step (of joining Rome) Mr. Ward had lost all his importance, and I almost repent of having revived his claim to attention by this long account of his trial; but my 'Recollections' would not be faithfully reported by a shorter notice[1].

[1] If such was my feeling in closing the above Chapter of my first edition, how much more so must it be in 1869: when, the University (not however *as yet* the Fellowships nor the vote in Convocation) having been thrown open to all persons of all denominations, this account of Mr. Ward's struggle and defeat may well seem unnecessarily full and elaborate. My consolation must be, that it may be considered historically important.

CHAPTER XIX.

'From grave to gay, from lively to severe.'

Recollections from A.D. 1845 *to* A.D. 1850.

A.D. 1845.

[M.A. Regents, 198.   B.A. Determiners, 281.   Hon. D.C.L. at Commemoration, 3.]

THE following sentence is a specimen of Mr. Newman's mode of suggesting *loop-holes:* 'The Christian both thinks and speaks the truth, except when consideration is necessary; and then, as a physician does for the good of his patient, he will be *false*, or (as the Sophists say) *utter a falsehood!*'

In April, our respected representative, Sir R. Inglis, eloquently and manfully vindicated our University from the charges of Mr. Christie, a Nonconformist M.P. The time was not yet come, when a sweeping Commission, promoted by Alma Mater's own sons, would (as the phrase is) *ride rough-shod* through all restrictions of Founders' wills, statutes, and intentions.

June 5. Mr. Oakeley, seeing how things were going against him in the Arches Court, anticipated the sentence by resigning the ministry of Margaret-street Chapel. The sentence, however, was passed, and disqualified him from ministering in any church in the province of Canterbury.

In September, a sermon was advertised as having been 'preached in Holy Island by Mr. Knollis, Fellow *and Junior Dean* of Magdalen College.' What the simple people of Holy Island (or Lindisfarne) understood by that sounding title, no one can tell; even at Oxford it would hardly be used out of the walls of the particular College.—It was a good manœuvre when Mr. 'Mo. Griff.' of Merton caused the verger at Westminster Abbey to give a stall-sitting to himself and his friend Mr. R. of Lincoln College, by announcing him as '*The Dean of Lincoln*[1].'

The Ecclesiastical Court having, about this date, decided that *stone, unmovable altars* were contrary to rubric, Dr. Pusey, to comfort his followers, assured them, in a long letter, 'that there was no cause to grieve, since the *Eucharistic Sacrifice*, wheresoever and *whereonsoever* it was offered, is still the same;—that, in fact, the *sacrifice* constitutes the altar, whatever be the material or the name.' Of course, if this doctrine of the '*Eucharistic sacrifice*' be scriptural, that

---

[1] 'Mo. Griff.' was a well-known Oxford character, who, among other absurdities, dropped his real name Moses, and called himself the 'Rev. *Edward* Griffith,' by a sort of trans*mogrifi*cation. He was a decided misogynist, and would cross over or go out of his way to avoid meeting a party of ladies. He was often heard to say that he thanked God every morning for two things: 1st, that he was born a man, not a woman; and 2ndly, that he had never committed marriage. He was not always civil to males: e.g. on a Sunday morning he was walking (as he was wont,—for he abominated University sermons), to attend the service of his friend Dr. Ashurst at South Hinksey. 'Good morning, Sir,' (said a young clergyman who overtook him) 'we are both, I presume, going to Hinksey Church, whither I am going to supply Dr. A.'s place, he being unwell.' 'Sir,' (replied Mo.) 'I wish you good morning, I am going back to Oxford.'

would be quite correct; but is not such a notion both unscriptural and disparaging to our Lord's 'one [and *once offered*] full and sufficient *sacrifice*, satisfaction, and atonement?' We do not swear by Ambrose or Ignatius, though we reverence them.

Oct. 8. It having been announced, in a printed circular, that the Chancellor's nomination of a Vice-Chancellor, with the new form 'Assensum Convocationis rogo,' would be opposed, Mr. Eden of Oriel (who never wanted courage, though on this occasion he might fall short in discretion), cried out in Convocation 'Assensus non datur—Non-Placet.' The Vice-Chancellor, however (being satisfied by the 'legal opinions' communicated to the Board by the Chancellor), took no notice of Mr. Eden's Non-Placet. On this his second admission, however, to the office, as if to leave the question for further consideration, the words 'salvo jure Convocationis' were introduced. No subsequent question (as to the *nomination*) has since taken place; nor has the 'salvo jure' been repeated.

About this time, Mr. Dalgairns of Exeter College joined the Roman Church, and Mr. Newman, followed by his amiable pupil Christie, resigned his Fellowship of Oriel, previous to taking the same step. O Oriel! what a hot-bed of mingled talent, baneful and beneficent, has thy Common-room been! Happily, as is generally and providentially the case, the poison and its antidote were produced near together.

Mr. Hudson, commonly called (from his great success and influence in that line) 'The King of Rails,' or 'The Railway King,' entered his son, about this time, as a Gentleman-Commoner at Ch. Ch. It was a matter of course that the young man should be surnamed 'The Prince of Rails.'

A letter, this summer, from Dr. Pusey (in the 'English Churchman'), contained so much that was good and true and consolatory as to the Church of England (with 'the token of God's presence in it in the persons of Hooker, Andrewes, Laud, Taylor, Ken, and Butler'), that but for an elaborate '*Plan for Confession*, prescribed by him to a correspondent,' we might all join in the wish, 'O si sic omnia!'

One wonders what kind and amount of penance the Roman Church must have imposed on Mr. Newman for having, in his 'Lectures on Romanism,' called it 'crafty, obstinate, wilful, cruel, unnatural;' or 'as resembling a demoniac possessed with principles, &c. not her own;' and again, 'till God vouchsafes to restore her, we must treat her as if she were the evil one which governs her.' That her discipline with him was to be pretty strict and severe was shown by her requiring him to be *baptized* (like all other *Converts*) sub conditione on his admission. Father Dominick (a busy Roman-Catholic priest, at that time hovering about Oxford) might well say, 'I was almost out of myself with joy when, at Littlemore, Mr. Newman entered the room and, throwing himself at my feet, asked my blessing, and begged me to hear his confession and receive him into the Church!' By-the-bye, this Father Dominick was evidently a bit of a wag; witness the conclusion of his 'Reflections on *Littlemore*' in these words: 'O Englishmen, hear the voice of Littlemore! those walls[1] bear testimony that the Catholic is a *little more* than the Protestant Church, the soul is a *little more* than the body, eternity a *little more* than the present time. Understand well this a *little more* and I am sure you will do a *little more* for your salvation[2].'

---

[1] The *walls* here referred to were not so much those of the church there built, as those of an extensive building, *a quasi monastery* there constructed, at considerable expense, out of Costar's stables, and including a Tractarian press, &c. It has since *relapsed* to secular uses.

[2] The Quarterly Review (No. 232), in a long and friendly Article on

November witnessed a good deal of angry biting and snarling between resident Masters of Arts and clergymen at Oxford, who seemed to find a relief and satisfaction in exhibiting their irritability and mutual distrust in the public papers; firing, as it were, paper pellets, because they could not well shoot at one another in regular duel with loaded pistols.

Dec. 4. In Convocation, what was called 'The Convocation Tax' (originally imposed in 1798 in aid of the *Volunteer Corps*, but ever since 1802 applied to other academic purposes) was at length abrogated and remitted.

A.D. 1846.

[B.A. 256. M.A. 224. No Hon. D.C.L. at Commemoration.]

The clerical atmosphere of Oxford was still disturbed; Mr. Golightly endeavouring to stir up 'the Board,' or rather the Vice-Chancellor, to call upon Dr. Pusey to sign the Thirty-nine Articles before he resumed his place in the University pulpit on the 1st of February. The Vice-Chancellor, Dr. Symons, for very good reasons, declined to require the ' subscription.

One of the saddest instances of Roman perversion at this time was that of the amiable and talented F. W. Faber of University. Not content with his own desertion, he, in a truly proselytising spirit, carried over with him several of his parishioners, particularly two boys, or lads of his school or choir, who had been especially entrusted to him by their

---

Newman's 'Apologia,' notices the singular contrast between him in his early days (in 1828) as a subscriber to the 'Record' at its first start, and the Newman received into Papal Communion at Littlemore, in 1845, by 'a remarkable-looking man, evidently a foreigner, shabbily dressed in black.'

father. He had the hardihood to say, in reference to this *kidnapping* (in a lengthy letter to the Editor of the 'English Churchman'), 'As a Catholic, I believe that these youths, *being out of the Church*, were, with their convictions, out of the pale of salvation.' Well might the Editor reply: 'Had Mr. Faber been told by his bishop five years ago that he would be guilty of such conduct towards the sons of a poor man,'—and (the Editor might have added) would justify his conduct by such a reason,—' he would have replied in the words of Hazael, " Is thy servant a dog, that he should do this thing?"'

Feb. 1. Dr. Pusey again preached before the University (after his two years' suspension), and to a crowded, anxious congregation. If, however, they, or any of them, expected anything of a personal or even controversial character, they must have been greatly disappointed. He quietly took up the thread of his argument (which, like himself, had been so long *suspended*) in some such words as these :—' When Almighty God, for secret faults which he knew in me, allowed me to be deprived of my office as a preacher, I was endeavouring to mitigate the stern sentence attached to a Christian's sins, by pointing out the mercy of God; which met the penitent with means of salvation and the earnest of pardon,' &c. He then went on with his subject, as if nothing had happened to interrupt him, and preached a luminous sermon (an hour and a half long), in which even the most watchful critic could hardly have pitched upon anything that was not good and orthodox. Something very like this is recorded of Louis Ponce de Leon, a theological professor at Salamanca, who, in 1572, was imprisoned (by the Inquisition) at Valladolid, for having translated (not published, nor even printed) the Song of Solomon into the vernacular. After languishing in prison five years, he was allowed to return to Salamanca and resume his Chair. Every one expected that at his first lecture he would enter upon the tale of his wrongs; but he gently raised his hand, looked earnestly round, and amidst the deepest silence began:— ' My friends, as I remarked when we last met here,' &c.; and so continued the subject which had been so long and so cruelly interrupted.

March. An earnest enquiry was set on foot, at the suggestion of a number of zealous and distinguished persons (Charles Marriott taking the lead), and a committee made a report as to building a College, or enlarging some existing College, for the express accommodation of students on a *more economical* plan of living. It was well intended, but being ill-timed, nothing came of it.

May. A certain College was said by the Oxford tradesmen ' to have set up the grocery and confectionery business,' by the agency of two College servants. Some jealous tutors of other Colleges had sneeringly called it a trading College before this, from the business-like manner in which it *turns off* so great an amount of B.A.'s. But does not the same character proportionably belong to all Colleges?

This year (1846) has left little to recollect and to record in connection with Oxford. Controversy had worn itself out; the *ferrea via*, or railroad, notwithstanding the Bishop of Exeter's warning about speculating in shares, attracted even the clergy more than the *via media*. Instead of High Church, Low Church, or Broad Church, they talked of high embankments, the broad gauge, and low dividends: Brunel and Stephenson were in men's mouths instead of Dr. Pusey or Mr. Golightly; Mr. Hudson was in the ascendant instead of Dr. Faussett; and speculative theology gave way to speculations in railroad shares.

A.D. 1847.

[B.A. 256. M.A. 224. Hon. D.C.L. at Commemoration, 2.]

Jan. 23. It was gratifying to read, in 'A Letter to a Friend,' the following words, forced from the good 'John Keble' by reports of his 'Romanising:'—' The truth is (and I thank God for it), that I feel daily, more and more, how impossible it would be for me, *either to unchurch the Church of England*, or to *assent, as a matter of faith*, to the Roman *Catholic terms of communion.*'

March 4. Regulations, &c. for the 'Taylor Institution' were voted in Convocation: £400 per annum for a Professor of Modern European Languages; £150 per annum for a Librarian (Mr. Macray); £1000 for the purchase of books, and £100 *annually* for the same purpose. Dr. Trithen held the Professorship six years, and was succeeded in 1853 by Mr. Max Müller.

May 8. The recently appointed Bishop of Sodor and Man, Dr. Shirley, was borne to an early grave. At New College he was known as a steady, clever, reading man; he gained the prize for the English Essay in 1822, but did not reside after taking his first Degree. The Bampton Lectures for 1847, which he had been elected to preach, were cut short by his death, after he had delivered two of them.

The Ashmolean Society was at this date (indeed it had been for several years) in a very flourishing condition, chiefly owing to the scientific communications of Dr. Daubeny, Dr. Buckland, and Mr. Strickland.

June 23. The British Association, for the second time, held its meeting in Oxford, Sir Robert Inglis being President. Science was well represented here in all its departments. If foreign nations sent us Struve, Le Verrier, and Bunsen, we had our Buckland, Daubeny, and Manuel Johnson. The

Radcliffe Library was opened for the Evening Meetings; the Colleges were more or less hospitable. Exeter and Christ Church each gave a large '*spread;*' but the Star Hotel was the centre of action, at least in the way of refreshment, of social intercourse, and post-prandian oratory; the 'Ordinary' at the Star Hotel alternated with the Extraordinary. The Prince of Canino (*Lucien* Bonaparte, whose motto, as opposed to Napoleon, had been '*luceo*, non uro') attended the meeting as a philosopher, and named a new species of bat (which he had discovered) 'Rhedycinus,' out of compliment to Oxford, anciently called 'Rhedycina.'

On July 29, and four successive days, the University election for M.P. was in every sense HOTLY contested. Mr. Cardwell soon retired from the contest, leaving it to be fought out between Gladstone and Round. On the first day of voting, by a bad arrangement, the crush and crowding (as the voters struggled, in the Convocation House, through a sort of pen) were really dreadful. A better arrangement was made next day, and the voting went on swimmingly. At the close of the poll:—

        Inglis, 'omne tulit punctum.'
        Gladstone . . 997
        Round . . 824

An uncalled-for statement was subsequently printed, showing the great majority of First-Class men who had voted for Mr. Gladstone; for what had the *Class* to do with their *suffrage?* Was it any proof that they were better able to judge of his merits than other voters of sound mind and ripe judgment? Was it ever stated, after a City of Oxford election, that Mr. —— was supported by a majority of first-class grocers or tip-top mercers[1]?

[1] Having (at this and subsequent contested elections) voted for Gladstone, as a sort of hero-worshipper, though not able to keep pace with his

October 1. Poor Donald Maclean, formerly of Balliol and for many years Member for Oxford City, was not merely gazetted as a bankrupt, but outlawed.

Nov. 8. Died an old Oxonian, the Archbishop of York, aged 91. He had enjoyed good health to the last, and was a dignified, fine old man; his illness was of a very short duration. His death was probably in some way connected with an accident which befell him a month before. A wooden bridge in the episcopal grounds gave way as he and his chaplain were passing it, and plunged them up to their necks in the water. 'Well, Dixon,' said the Archbishop, on being extricated, 'I think we have frightened the frogs!' The chaplain prudently retired to bed: the hardy Archbishop entertained a large dinner party the same day.

His place was soon filled by the translation of Dr. Musgrave from the See of Hereford, who was succeeded by Dr. Hampden, who, in his turn, was succeeded, as Regius Professor of Divinity, by Dr. Jacobson.

Nov. 25. An extraordinary Convocation was held in the Sheldonian Theatre (which was filled at a short notice) in order to confer the Hon. Degree of D.C.L. on the Rajah of Sarawak, Mr. (afterwards Sir James) Brooke. The young men, nay, all persons present, did full justice to him in the

political changes,—I feel a comfort in learning from Sir J. T. Coleridge's Life of Keble, that he (K.) felt and acted in much the same way. 'Even when, as sometimes happened, he might not have been prepared to follow Mr. G. in what he had said or done, he still thought that, where there was no reason to doubt the honesty and singleness of his intentions, it was unjust and unwise in a private man to withdraw his support of a representative because his judgment, probably more informed and guided by a better appreciation of difficulties, differed from his own.' P.S. in 1869.—Gladstone had not then *horrified* his old supporters at Oxford by his Bill for disestablishing and disendowing the Church of Ireland.

way of loud applause, and Dr. Phillimore, on presenting him, gave in classical Latin a spirited description of Mr. Brooke's energetic and self-supported efforts.

Dec. 1. The 'odium theologicum,' which had for some time been dormant, broke out afresh against Dr. Hampden on his elevation to the Bishopric of Hereford. The Rev. Arthur Perceval particularly distinguished himself in that bad feeling, by asking even our CITY COUNCIL to petition her Majesty's re-consideration of the appointment. He received, however, a good rap on the knuckles in the reply of the Mayor, who told him 'that, in the first place, he did not think the City Council adapted to interfere in theological matters; and, in the next, that Dr. Hampden's manner of life and teaching in Oxford had gained the general respect and affection of the citizens.' This renewed attack on Dr. Hampden was well described as 'an old arrow barbed afresh; but with more venom in the shaft than vigour in the bow that aimed it.' The best answer to this attempt was the affectionate address to Dr. Hampden from his parishioners at Ewelme, and its assertion that 'the great truths of Christianity had (for the eleven years of his incumbency) formed the ground-work of his teaching.' Weigh that, and Dr. Hampden's truly Christian 'Letter to Lord John Russell' in vindication of himself, against the 'Remonstrance' of thirteen Bishops; and justice and charity will surely be found on Dr. Hampden's side. Like most of the congregation, I had considered his Bampton Lectures rather dry, and, like the rest of the University, thought no more about them for four years; but now the cry raised against them induced me to look carefully at them. After making due allowance for a philosophising tendency and phraseology (quite in keeping with his professed subject), I fully accepted his clear and beautifully expressed assertion of the doctrine of the Trinity, near the end of the last Lecture. No stronger proof could well be given of the influence of selfish, disappointed feelings than the 'Letter of Remonstrance' (against Dr. Hampden's appointment) addressed to the Queen by the then Dean of Hereford, who, on the ground of having been Chaplain to Queen Adelaide, publicly and indelicately pressed his claims to the Bishopric. The first line of his address ('*We*, your Majesty's most dutiful and loyal subject, *John Merewether*,' &c.), unsupported by any of his Chapter, was simply ridiculous. This same Dean of Hereford went so far as to threaten that, on the *congé d'élire*, he would refuse to elect Dr. Hampden; but he was coolly checked (or rather checkmated) by the following letter from the Prime Minister, Lord John Russell:—

'Woburn Abbey.

I have had the honour to receive your letter of the 21st inst., in which you intimate your intention of violating the law.

I have the honour to be, &c.,

J. RUSSELL.'

There was a smack of *premunire* in this pithy reply; no opposition was offered.

To see the name of Bishop Denison among the thirteen remonstrant Bishops astonished those who had stood by his side (in a very small minority) when the vote of 'the suspension of certain privileges' was carried in the Theatre against Dr. Hampden. In his 'Letter' of self-vindication against the charge of inconsistency, he said that he never took an active part for Dr. Hampden; but what could be more active than giving a vote at such a crisis and in such an assembly? The Bishop of Oxford, who had aided the remonstrant Bishops with his signature, subsequently bethought himself of reading Dr. Hampden's much abused

Bampton Lectures, instead of resting his judgment (as he had done) 'upon mere extracts.' He discovered that there was 'no ground for further opposition,' and handsomely expressed this tardy conviction in a letter addressed 'To the Bishop of Hereford Elect.'

A.D. 1848.

[B.A. 264. M.A. 185. Hon. D.C.L. at Commemoration, 9.]

Jan. 11. An unseemly, last effort was made to annoy Dr. Hampden by opposing his 'confirmation' at Bow Church. On the proclamation 'Oyez, oyez, oyez,' &c. inviting objectors to come forward, if there were any, a Proctor began to offer objections in the names of three obscure clergymen (cat's-paws put forward by objectors of greater note but of less courage), but (notwithstanding the invitation) he was stopped by the Vicar-General on the ground that they were sitting there under a mandate from the Crown; 'We conceive ourselves,' he said, 'bound to confirm.' After a short argument allowed for a time, another proclamation 'Oyez' was repeated, which (notwithstanding the sanctity of the place) was received with cries of 'Shame,' 'Mockery,' 'Order,' &c. from the crowded assembly. The ceremony of confirmation then took place, 'In the name of God,' &c., &c.

The battle was nevertheless followed up, and a *rule* was asked for and obtained in the Queen's Bench to show cause against the legality of Dr. Hampden's confirmation. When clergymen were so pugnacious, it was not likely the lawyers would stop the fight; indeed, some of them rushed into the contest as *something more than advocates*, Mr. Baddely, for instance, and Mr. Hope.

Feb. 1. After several days' lengthened pleadings on both

sides, the 'rule was discharged,' i.e. the application to 'show cause was *dismissed*,' the Judges themselves not agreeing!

At a meeting of the clergy held at Gloucester for the purpose of following up the Hampden prosecution, Dr. Jeune made an eloquent and manly defence of Dr. Hampden.

Dr. Cramer, too, Dean of Carlisle (who had been one of the Hebdomadal Board at the time of Dr. Hampden's quasi condemnation), came forward (at this time) to explain his share in that measure and his subsequent efforts to remove the stigma.

Above all, Archbishop Whately published a lengthened and powerful vindication of Dr. Hampden.

March 25. Dr. Hampden was consecrated Bishop of Hereford at Lambeth Palace; and so, after prodigious efforts against him, kept up to the very last, this most bitter and unprecedented struggle ended. The lively interest in the question felt by me from the first must be my excuse for having entered so fully into the history of the proceedings.

April 15. Dr. Jacobson's appointment to the Divinity Chair (vacated by Dr. Hampden) caused him to resign the Public Oratorship, to which Mr. Michell was elected in Convocation. Mr. Hansell, of Magdalen College, had retired from the contest, having, on a comparison of *promised* votes, produced 330 against Mr. Michell's 499.

In the same month Dr. Bliss succeeded Bishop Hampden in the Headship of St. Mary Hall. 'I know no one,' the old Duke, our Chancellor, was reported to have said on the occasion of appointing him, 'who understands University matters so well as Dr. Bliss;' and he might well say it and a great deal more in justification of his appointment. Indeed, Dr. Bliss was so exact and methodical in the arrangement of his papers and memoranda, so full of information, as well as ready to give it, that other persons had become rather careless of acquiring a knowledge of University matters (as their predecessors had done, more or less), being quite sure of full and prompt information from the Registrar. 'Ask Dr. Bliss,' was the answer to all enquiries, 'he knows.'

May 25. An address was voted in Convocation to her Majesty, 'expressive of loyalty and attachment' at a time of great excitement,—of revolutionary movements abroad and of 'monster' Chartist petitions at home. About this time also a memorial, very numerously signed by Graduates and former members of Oxford and Cambridge, was addressed to the Premier, Lord John Russell, asking for a sweeping University reform. ['All in good time, gentlemen,' he might have answered; 'another ten years will give you all you wish for, perhaps more.']

Meanwhile, for this spring, at least, and summer, the Church and the University enjoyed comparative peace,—scarcely disturbed by Bishop Phillpotts' love of *hot water* and the Gorham case. France might get rid of Louis Philippe and set up an experimental Republic in his place; Ireland might produce its *sympathising* disturbers of the peace; and English Chartists throw Birmingham and even London into alarm,—but Oxford unruffled could enjoy its grand concerts, its Commemoration-balls, its boat-races and its cricket-matches. The Tutors, to be sure, not satisfied with this state of things, laboured hard at the beginning of spring to give the youngsters (in a plan submitted to the Hebdomadal Board) an additional chance of illustrating the 'Art of Pluck,' by introducing an intermediate Examination[1] between the 'Little-go' and the 'Great-go.' Before they

[1] This intermediate Examination was adopted in 1852.

threw so much upon the work to be done in the Schools, did these Tutors really do their utmost to increase and improve the work done in their lecture-rooms?

June 17. The loyal address, previously voted, was presented to her Majesty by a deputation from the University, assuring her of our warm attachment and devotion 'amidst the fearful storms that were sweeping over the kingdoms of Europe.'

In the Commemoration-week the 'Radcliffe sermon' was preached by the Bishop of Hereford, Dr. Hampden, and as the best proof of the excellence of his discourse, the unusually large sum of £110 14s. 7d. was collected at the doors[1].

At this Commemoration Mr. Gladstone was presented to the Hon. Degree of D.C.L. (he was a regular M.A. before), but, in consequence of his vote for the admission of Jews to Parliament, he was most unfavourably received; not a word of Dr. Phillimore's presentation-speech was allowed to be heard. *M. Guizot* was present in the Theatre (he had followed Louis Philippe in his flight from Paris), and being recognised, he was invited by acclamation from the area to the Doctors' seats in the rising semicircle; he had declined the Oxford Chair of European Languages which was offered to him; so, at least, it was reported.

Nov. 11. My colleague, William Miller, M.A. of New College, having died, was succeeded in the office of Esquire Bedel by Mr. Harrison, B.A. of Brasenose.

In November of this year Dr. Acland, in a clever pamphlet, stirred up afresh the question of 'extending the University system of Examination' so as to include the

---

[1] In the year 1861 the collection, after a sermon by the Bishop of Cork, was only £29.

departments of Natural Science: (1) Natural Philosophy, comprehending the general laws of matter; (2) Chemistry, relating to the special properties, &c. of bodies throughout nature; (3) General Physiology, or the laws which govern life, animal and vegetable.

Dec. 1. An unusual[1] compliment was paid to Music by opening the Sheldonian Theatre for a morning concert, in order to give Oxonians an opportunity of hearing *Jenny Lind*. Assisted by a select band, she charmed the audience with her sweet notes and unaffected manner, at the reasonable price (for her) of 10s. 6d. the ticket[2]. The Theatre was, of course, very cold, but the temperature did not seem to affect the throat of the Swedish nightingale. She appeared to be much struck, and was even moved to tears by the impression made upon her at her entrance into our Theatre 'with its many black gowns.' She said, 'It was like entering a sacred building.' She left £100 of her profits to be applied in aid of the Oxford Charities[3].

A.D. 1849.

[B.A. 300. M.A. 208. One Hon. D.C.L. and one Hon. M.A. at Commemoration.]

March 22. An elaborate statute called 'The New Examination Statute,' was brought forward in Convocation. Its

---

[1] *Unusual* in those days, but since then often granted for the performance of Musical Exercises, pro gradu.

[2] This 'reasonable price' was (it was said) made a condition by the authorities on granting the use of the Theatre.

[3] This liberal act called forth the following acknowledgment:—

> 'When warbling throats produce *Bank*-notes,
> None grudge the bright half-guinea;
> The fruits we see of the *Linden* tree:
> God bless thee, vocal Jenny!'

great feature, the proposal of an intermediate Examination between Little-go and Great-go (I beg pardon, between Responsions and the Final Examination), was carried by 197 to 23 votes. But as several of the subordinate proposals were rejected, the whole statute was withdrawn to be new modelled by the Hebdomadal Board.

June 19. A very numerous and influential meeting was held in the Theatre to consider the formation of a general University Museum, with a view to promote and assist the study of Natural Science, hereafter to be a department of the University studies. Private movements and offers of subscription for such a purpose had been for some time going on, but this meeting contemplated a Public University Building and Institution, to be raised and supported by the funds of the University.

At the Commemoration, June 21, the Newdigate Prize was *not awarded*, though a great many copies of verses were said to have been sent in! In the absence of great public characters, much interest was shown on the presentation (to the Hon. Degree of M.A.) of *Captain Hayes*, who, after several years of active and distinguished service in the Indian army, had become a member of Magdalen Hall, had passed all the requisite Examinations for the Degree of B.A., but was recalled to India before he was of sufficient standing to take it. Poor, brave man! On returning to India he was among the first victims of the revolt; not, however, by assassination, but while heading his troop of cavalry against fearful odds of rebellious Sepoys.

August. Cases of cholera were reported as spreading in Oxford; great care was taken by the Board of Health to check it.

Oct. 6. The disease began to relax; there had, however, been 121 cases and 64 deaths. About the middle of

October it was publicly announced that the cholera had entirely disappeared in Oxford. Deo gratias!

Martin Tupper (who at this time inundated the public with his Rhymes) published 'A Prayer, in verse, *for* the Cholera!' When we say a 'Prayer *for* rain,' or '*for* a good harvest,' we do not mean *against* it.

> It well may pose e'en Oxford dons,
> When cons are pros and pros are cons.

October brought us the news of the death of one of the greatest ornaments and the stout champion of Oxford, Dr. Copleston, Bishop of Llandaff and Dean of St. Paul's.

In the autumn of this year, Dudley Fereday, Esq., formerly a Gentleman-Commoner of Magdalen, bequeathed £20,000 to found four Fellowships at Magdalen, or (if refused there) to some other College in Oxford. Magdalen (already large and rich enough) declined the offer, which was accepted by St. John's College, but not till 1854.

Dec. 7. The new Examination Statute was again put to the vote; its main features were approved and carried, but as four or five of the clauses were rejected, it again came out of Convocation in a mangled and damaged state. The institution of a Modern History School was affirmed, but the details were left for reconsideration. The greatest number of Non-Placets was given to the proposed plan of appointing Examiners through the medium of *a Board*, in other words taking the privilege of '*nomination*' from the Vice-Chancellor and Proctors, under whose control it had hitherto worked so well. The proposal 'that Examiners may allow *merits to compensate for defects* (so that a candidate eminent in Philosophy or History, or in Philology and Criticism, but displaying only a moderate knowledge of other matters, should be respectively admissible to the highest honours) was also decisively rejected, the votes being for it 106, against it 176.

A.D. 1850.

[B.A. 312. M.A. 196. Hon. D.C.L. at Commemoration, 5.]

Feb. 16. A public meeting was held to promote the formation of a 'Wash-house and Baths *for the Industrious Classes* of Oxford[1].' The subscription was nobly headed by Mr. Phil. Duncan with £600, and a sufficient sum was soon raised; for it was expected that the Baths, &c. (though at a very low charge) would be self-supporting. Indeed, it was soon found that gentlemen and ladies might be induced to use baths of a better kind, under the same roof and management, yet still at a moderate charge. Oxford may well cherish the memory of the two Duncan brothers. They were a blessing to Oxford, and for many years the ornaments of its society.

About this time the health of Dr. Buckland gave way, and symptoms, or rather proofs, of a *softening of the brain* showed themselves—that sad disease in any case, but most distressingly sad and mysterious in the case of so talented, active, and intelligent an individual.

Early in the spring of 1850 the conclusion of the long-protracted cause of The Bishop of Exeter versus Rev. J. Gorham, was considered by most persons at Oxford as

---

[1] Several years afterwards, a very destructive explosion of the steam seriously injured this valuable building. It was said to have been caused by ignorance, and to have confirmed the ignorant neighbours in their notion that steam was a diabolical device. Certainly the washing department was not supported.

N.B. To the disgrace of Oxford, City and University, these Baths were closed in 1868.

strange and unsatisfactory. Having been condemned in the Ecclesiastical Court, Mr. Gorham appealed to the ultimate Court of the Queen in Council, and there the Ecclesiastical sentence was reversed! One would have expected that the matter (however unsatisfactorily) would have ended there. But no! That busy, clever man, the Rev. G. Denison, published a formal Protest, denying the right of the Council to adjudicate in a matter of *doctrine*. Questions were asked in Parliament, but Lord John Russell wisely determined to take no notice of Mr. Denison's Protest. Little did Mr. Denison then think that he himself would, a few years after, be placed nearly in Mr. Gorham's position. But—' vivitur hoc pacto.'

The Bishop of Exeter, however, in a subsequent 'Letter to the Archbishop of Canterbury,' knocked down all the Gorhamite arguments; giving vent to his long-suppressed feelings of annoyance, and pouring forth his accumulated knowledge on the subject of Baptismal Regeneration. A fourth edition of the Bishop's Letter was published two days after the appearance of the first. Perhaps the most singular circumstance, in connection with this vexed question, was the Letter of Miss Sellon to Lord Campbell, declining to consider him any longer a subscriber to her 'Orphans' Home' at Devonport—on the ground of his share in the Judgment in the Gorham case. There can be no doubt that his Lordship showed more of truly Christian charity and forbearance in his reply, than the lady did in her rejoinder. The 'Sister of Mercy' showed him neither mercy nor charity, while his Lordship exercised great tenderness and forbearance. At Oxford, I think, the general impression was, that Mr. Gorham's view of 'prevenient grace' was wrong as to ninety-nine cases out of a hundred, though possibly right as to the hundredth. I could not find that the question is 'decided by the Creeds,' as Miss Sellon, the lady bishop (I beg her pardon, the Lady Superior[1]), asserts; though it seems to be determined in our Catechism.

April 23. The new Examination Statute, establishing 'Moderations' (statutably called the *First Public Examination*) and the Law and History School, after being pared down by the rejection of two or three clauses, finally passed.

In May, after an ineffectual effort to get the bishops to agree to a settlement of the Baptismal question, raised by the Gorham case, a Petition to the Queen (quite as unlikely to do any good) was got up at Oxford by certain 'Members of Convocation and Bachelors in Law,' 'that she would allow all questions touching the doctrine of the Church of England to be eventually referred to a Provincial Synod.'

Indications became very strong, in Parliament (this May), of the approach of the threatened *University Commission*, notwithstanding the vigorous opposition of the Duke of Wellington and ('quod minimè reris') Lord Brougham, who deprecated 'a rash and inconsiderate interference with the Universities!'

May 24. In Convocation a grant of £2000 was voted in aid of the endowment of Colonial Bishops.

The 'merry month of May' announced (to the no small alarm of many at Oxford) Lord John Russell's notice of the coming Royal Commission; which was followed by a powerful 'Remonstrance' on the part of the Hebdomadal Board.

May 25. The 'Cowley Enclosure' coolly, and cruelly, 'cut off forty-seven foot-paths,' within two miles of Oxford

---

[1] I believe that her Sisterhood have since gone a step higher, and speak of her as 'The Holy Mother.'

(some of them leading directly from Oxford), 'substituting for them eight new ones!' Most of the former were connected with pleasant country-walks, and were in themselves pretty, natural, and winding; the latter, of course, were dull and dusty (as being merely foot-paths by the new road side), and formal as being all in straight lines. Cowley Marsh, where at a short distance you might wander about on the turf without the formality of a foot-path, was doomed to be inclosed, for the chance of a meagre crop of oats on its soil of clay. Luckily the Vice-Chancellor, Dr. Plumptre, secured cricket-grounds for the young men, but how different (for the non-cricketers) from the uninclosed common! A great fuss has been made occasionally in Parliament and in Acts of Parliament about the 'Health of Towns,' but what can interfere more with that health than inclosures carried to the very entrance of towns, especially such a place as Oxford? This inclosure, accompanied by that of Bullingdon Common, with its nice turf for a canter, only required (what soon followed) the inclosure of Bagley Wood, to cut off not only country walks from Oxford inhabitants in general, but from its future students *in Scientia Naturali* in particular, the only remaining localities for botanical and physiological pursuits. But then—the rights of property must be respected; and if permission is asked for a botanical ramble, the answer will probably be, 'The game must not be disturbed.'

> Don't talk to us of entomology,
>   Or scientific taste for botany;
> We have not learnt your phraseology,
>   And as for science we've not got any.
> You prate of fauna and of flora,
>   With hints of ignorance you prick us;
> We warn you off, Sirs, sine morâ,
>   Back to your books and hortus siccus.

The Radcliffe charity sermon was in this June preached by the Bishop of Norwich; the collection of £55 (small indeed compared with Dr. Hampden's £110) was larger than that after the sermon of 1849 preached by Dr. Chandler, Dean of Chichester, only £33—the smallest, *at that time*, ever collected. But in this matter (as in others) there is 'a difference between a Bishop and a Dean.' The causes of the diminished collection in late years are not, however, dependent on the preacher.

June 18. On this and several successive days a very well-attended and interesting meeting was held in Oxford of the Archæological Institute. Some of the rooms in the Taylor Buildings were used for a curious display of ancient vestments, armour, &c. Professor Willis's lecture on Christ Church Cathedral was highly spoken of. Dinners and soirées formed a cheerful relief to the grave discussions of the morning meetings.

The beginning of July witnessed a most sad, and a most disgraceful event. The sad one was the death of Sir Robert Peel, by a fall from his horse. The disgraceful one was a blow with a whip on her Majesty's forehead, by a crazy but a vain fellow called Robert Pate, or *Lieutenant* Pate.

July. Radley *School* having constituted itself a *College*, the Head Master became Warden and the other Masters Fellows. Of course any collection of persons living and working together may be called a college, but no such institution, being without foundation, or endowment, can ever become a public school like Eton or Winton College.

Aug. 20. Mr. Gorham was at length inducted into his living of Brampford Speke on the fiat of the Archbishop of Canterbury, the Bishop of Exeter having refused to induct him. Though I never agreed with Mr. Gorham on the subject of Holy Baptism 'in the case of Infants,' I confess that I learnt to sympathise with him in his long persecution.

'Solemn Declarations' as to the royal power of meddling with matters of doctrine were about this time addressed to the Bishop of London by three divines,—two of whom, Archdeacon Manning and R. I. W. Wilberforce, soon after 'went over to Rome.'

In this August 'The University Commission' was issued. 'Oxford,' it said, or seemed to say, 'set thine house in order[1].'

Mr. *Allies* of Wadham was reported, in the 'Tablet' (a Roman Catholic paper) of this date, to be engaged in writing a refutation of his former work, 'The Church of England Vindicated from the Charge of Schism,' '*after which* he intends to become a Catholic,' i. e. a *Roman* Catholic; a

---

[1] Mr. Froude, in his History of England, vol. ii. pp. 414 and 416, gives a curious account of a *Commission* which visited Oxford (among many other places) in 1533. 'The visitors, having established their powers, began work with the University of Oxford. Their time was short, for Parliament was to meet early in the spring, when their report was to be submitted to it. The Heads of Houses, as may be supposed, saw little around them which was in need of reform. The daily chapels, we suppose, had gone forward as usual, and the drowsy lectures on the Schoolmen; while "towardly young men" who were venturing stealthily into the perilous heresy of Greek, were eyed askance by the authorities, and taught to tremble at their temerity. . . . Doubtless the visitors found Oxford a pleasant place and cruelly they marred the enjoyments of it. Like a sudden storm of rain, they dropt down into its quiet precincts. Heedless of rights of fellows and founders' bequests, of sleepy dignities and established indolences, they re-established long-dormant lectures in the Colleges. In a few little days (for so long only they remained) they poured new life into education. They founded fresh professorships—of Polite Latin, Philosophy, Divinity, Canon Law, Natural Sciences, above all, of the dreaded Greek, *confiscating funds* to support them.'

distinction which I, as a member of the Catholic Church of England, always endeavour to make. 'God save us from treacherous friends and false *allies!*' was the general remark.

In September appeared a very long and heavy circular (too long and too heavy to be called a *jeu-d'esprit*) affecting to be a 'Report from the Sub-Committee to the Board of Commissioners, on the State of Things in Oxford in June 1860!' It is pleasant to find those awful prognostications still unrealised. These are but a few of them:—

1. 'Since the removal of an enforced subscription to the Thirty-nine Articles at matriculation, a great influx has taken place not only of Nonconforming Christians, but also of other denominations; and though nearly all the *sect* which was formerly the Established Church have quitted the University, the number of members is but slightly diminished.

2. 'Five Baptists and four Quakers have been appointed to Fellowships in Magdalen College.

3. 'Nearly all the Professorial Chairs are occupied by distinguished clergymen in the Dissenting interest. The Sanscrit Chair is ably filled by the celebrated Brahmin Ram Roy.

4. 'A splendid Roman Catholic cathedral is rapidly progressing opposite St. Mary's;—and the Roman Catholic Bishop of Oxford has taken up his residence at his episcopal mansion in St. Giles's.'

And so on *ad infinitum*, i.e. for several pages of 'compressed typography.'

A part of the first prophecy, as to the cessation of subscription at matriculation, has been fulfilled, but the '*influx*' has been quite *gullatim*.

The fourth may ere long be partially fulfilled by the erection of a large Roman Catholic chapel (or church), though not a *cathedral*, and not *opposite St. Mary's*.

October 31. Mr. Garbett, Professor of Poetry, wrote a spirited answer to the request of the University Commissioners for information; at the conclusion, he considered 'the Commission, in an age of professed and in many points real liberalism and improvement, a despotic stretch of antiquated prerogative. It recalls the worst times and the worst precedents[1].' This reply was to have been expected from

[1] In 1648, 'The blessed Parliament' (as it was called by those who assumed to themselves the title of 'Beloved Saints') thought it was high time for the University of Oxford *to be Visited*. [Laud, who as Chancellor of Oxford succeeded that Earl of Pembroke whose bronze statue stands in the Bodleian Gallery, had been superseded by another Earl of Pembroke in 1641; he, in his turn, gave way to the Marquis of Hertford in 1643, but in 1648 was again made Chancellor by the Parliament. In that character he accompanied the Parliamentary Visitors here mentioned to 'visit the several Colleges and Halls'—and especially to enforce the Solemn League and Covenant.] The proceedings, as detailed by Ant. Wood, are highly interesting. The University authorities, headed by the Vice-Chancellor, Dr. Samuel Fell, Dean of Christ Church, behaved with great firmness—but were most of them expelled unceremoniously. This Earl of Pembroke seems to have used 'very ill language' to the Vice-Chancellor. 'At the first meeting,' says Dr. Fell, 'he said that I was a *noun-substantive* [did he not mean a *noun adjective?*] and could not stand without my Chapter; that the Devil made me Vice-Chancellor; and that it were fit I should be whipped, nay hanged.' April 12. The Chancellor, Visitors, and 'certain soldiers,' with a great rabble, went to Christ Church, and entering the Deanery (which had been previously *forced open*) the Chancellor desired Mrs. Fell to quit. [Dr. Fell himself was by this time in safe custody in London]—but she refusing that kind proposal had very ill language given her by him. She was carried into the quadrangle by the soldiers in a chair—as were also certain gentlewomen that were then in the lodgings; the children were carried out on boards. The Chancellor and Visitors then sending for the buttery book, dashed out the names of the Dean and many others; appointing other persons in their place. A Convocation was summoned

Mr. Garbett, but the Report of the Commissioners which soon after appeared, and the Evidence attached to that elaborate Blue Book, are ample proofs that Mr. Garbett and his opinions were quite in the minority in reference to the opinions of the leading men in the University. That Blue Book contained a great amount of information as to the history of the University and Colleges, from the earliest to the most recent days. The bias under which it was compiled gave of course a colouring to many of its statements; but it is for many reasons worthy of preservation and careful reference. The few copies of it obtained by the Oxford booksellers for sale were eagerly bought up.

In the autumn of 1850, the quasi-establishment of a Popish hierarchy in England (commonly protested against under the title of 'The Popish Aggression') caused great disgust by its assumption of ecclesiastical titles, 'a local habitation and a name;'—and not only disgust, but active, energetic protests and addresses to the Queen, from the University, the City, and the Clergy of the diocese.

N. B. It has subsequently become the fashion to laugh at the feeling excited by this aggressive movement; but as long as Popery is unchanged, such an assumption is sure to be followed by farther encroachment.

by the Visitors' monitory (nominated for the purpose as a Yeoman Bedel), who, not knowing Latin, caused great laughter to the Scholars, by calling out in each quadrangle (*more Bedellorum*), not 'per fidem, per fidem, per fidem,' but 'provided, provided, provided!' N.B. Before the circulation of printed Notices of Convocations, &c. the Yeoman Bedels used to summon Masters to Convocation, in the Quadrangle of each College and from the steps of the Clarendon, 'altà voce' in this form, 'Magistri ad Convocationem per fidem, per fidem, per fidem.'

CHAPTER XX.

Recollections from A.D. 1851 *to* A.D. 1856.

A.D. 1851.

[B.A. 312. M.A. 196. Hon. D.C.L. at Commemoration, 5.]

FEB. 8. The following advertisement from a private tutor (slangicè 'coach'), who called himself M.A. of Oxford, appeared in the 'Times':—

'Coaching extraordinary, by an M.A. residing in London. As the Great-go even now looms in the distance, application (to Omicron, Oxford and Cambridge Club) should be made immediately, as only two gentlemen can be admitted into the *Hansom*. N.B. Each pupil must live like a hermit and work like a horse.'

Feb. 21. Classical Oxford made a small but graceful return to classical Greece, by voting, in Convocation, books (printed at the University Press), to the value of £150, towards the formation of a library for *the University of Athens*, with the cost of the binding. Parvula pro magnis Oxonia grata rependit.

Feb. 25. Very considerable alterations were proposed and carried in Convocation, as to the Exercises for the Degree of B.C.L., substituting a bonâ fide Examination in place of the old Disputations, which had been long represented by certain threadbare '*strings*,' i. e. logical arguments on legal questions; e.g. 'Quid existimas de hac quæstione, An dominium acquiri possit sine possessione?' The disputants had their traditional Latin arguments, pro and con., served out to them by the Clerk of the Schools, with a huge folio of Justinian for references (to fill up the hour required by the Statute), till, on the Clerk's appearing with his watch held up (and mumbling something which sounded like 'tempus *præterlabitur est*'), the Professor, who had been reading a book or a newspaper all the while, stopped the disputants with the welcome 'sufficit[1].' This statement will hardly be believed, —but having myself taken a part in the solemn mockery several times, I can vouch for its unexaggerated accuracy[2].

The same farce took place in Medicine at this time, and ten years earlier in Divinity. But—'Magnus ab integro sæclorum nascitur ordo.'

---

[1] See note 2, p. 131.

[2] Cambridge was in these matters much in the same state as Oxford; as appears from Mr. Walsh's Account of that University, published in 1837. He says, 'At the present day *Acts and Opponencies* in some cases have merged into a mere idle form, in others they are compounded for by the payment of a sum of money. In the latter case, the money is deposited as a caution for the performance of the exercises; and as, of course, they are not performed, the "caution" is then forfeited to the University, and the matter is at an end. In the former case, the whole ceremony is carried on nearly in the following way: *Thomas Styles*, from the Respondent's seat, speaking in Latin: "Accuratus fuit Newton; accuratus Wood; accuratus quoque Locke." *John Noakes*, from the Opponent's seat: "Si argumenta tua falsa sint, cadunt; sed falsa sunt, ergo actum est tecum." These words are repeated until Thos. Styles has kept the requisite number of Acts, and John Noakes the requisite number of Opponencies. They then change places, and Thos. Styles refutes John Noakes with John Noakes' own syllogism;—and Da Capo ad libitum. This method of performing disputations is called "*Huddling*."'

This spring was a time of more than usual excitement. 'No peace with Rome,' 'No concealed Jesuits,' &c., were the cries in the Church; 'Change of the Ministry' and 'failures in the attempt to form another,' in the State; 'The Commissioners are coming,' in the University; 'the Sanatory Question,' in the City of Oxford. It was only a wonder that in the natural world things went on as usual; that the Examinations too were carried on with only a little more plucking than before; that the University Sermons, and Degree-days, the Sessions, and the Assizes, succeeded each other in the accustomed jog-trot way; nay, that concerts and dinner-parties were given and attended. M. Jullien advertised his Promenade Concerts, and M. Soyer gave a series of 'Lectures' on his cooking apparatus, as the self-appointed *Professor* of Gastronomy and the Ars coquinaria.

I have before had occasion to apply the common observation, that Counsels' opinions may, by a careful getting-up of questions, be obtained on both sides of any matter. At this time the Hebdomadal Board had (they believed) abundant materials in proof of the illegality of the Commission, and four distinguished lawyers, Turner, Bethel, Keating, and Kenyon, advised the University to demand, or rather 'pray,' that the Commission might be recalled and cancelled; or at least to require the legal validity of the Commission to be shown.

This year was marked by two important events, the decennial census of the population of Great Britain, and the Great Exhibition. The former did not indeed concern the University as such, though the College strictness of night-discipline afforded great facilities for the purpose. To the latter the University did not, I believe, contribute anything, the Colleges being well satisfied with looking after their own *little Exhibitions*. Of the citizens, Mr. Spiers was, I think, the only exhibitor;—his stall of papier-maché, &c. being very attractive.

April 6. Two more of our most valuable Oxford men deserted to the Roman camp,—Archdeacon Manning and Mr. Hope, Q.C.; both formerly Fellows of Merton, both highly gifted, loved and esteemed.

About this date King's College, Cambridge, at length followed the example of New College, Oxford, by giving up the privilege of graduating without undergoing the usual *Public* Examinations. The *King's* men thus acknowledged that there is no *royal road* to learning, as New College had found that, to be *semper novum*, a little *renovation* was in conformity with the spirit of Wykham's statutes.

May 21. In a full Convocation, a Petition to 'her Majesty in Council' against the 'Commission of Inquiry,' &c. was carried by 249 votes against 105; majority, 144. Mr. Neate, of Oriel, spoke against the Petition; but men came to vote and not to talk or be talked to; and permission to address the House *in the vernacular* was not then so easily granted as has since been the case. The Petition, however, was not likely to stop the current of reform that was setting in so strongly Oxonwards; for on the 17th of June Lord John Russell being asked in 'the House' whether the proceedings of the University Commission were to be suspended till the above-mentioned Petition was presented and decided upon, emphatically answered 'Certainly not.'

June 17. A statute, which proposed to increase the incomes of certain Professors, was very roughly handled.

1. £150 to be added to the annual stipend of the *Reader in Mineralogy*. Placets and Non-Placets equal; i.e. 57. It was therefore lost.
2. £150 to the income of the *Reader in Geology*, lost by one vote. Placets 60, Non-Placets 61.

3. £71 10s. to the *Reader in Chemistry*, lost. Placets 53, Non-Placets 66.
4. £170 to the *Reader in Experimental Philosophy*, carried. Placets 62, Non-Placets 57.
5. £160 to *Camden's History Reader*, lost. Placets 54, Non-Placets 61.

N. B. The above rejected propositions were soon afterward carried, excepting the Camden Readership, which, owing possibly to Dr. Cardwell's large private funds, was left, for a time, with its scanty income. In this same Convocation, the proposal ' that £30,000 (being part of £60,000 transferred from the University Press to the University Chest) be appropriated to *Museums, Lecture-rooms, and Examination Schools*,' was lost, the Placets being only 47 against 88 Non-Placets. What was meant and intended by *Museums* I do not know, but I believe my memorandum as to the *plural number* is correct. We do know, however, that ONE Museum has since been sufficient to absorb more than double the sum then withheld. As for Lecture-rooms, there can be no lack of them while so much of the Ashmolean Museum and of the Taylor Buildings is unappropriated. The increased demand for Examination Schools is a more difficult matter to decide upon. The Ashmolean Museum might be made useful in this way, without interfering with the use of a part of it by the Ashmolean, Architectural, or any other Society in their evening meetings[1].

July 2. In Commemoration-week Dr. Tait preached the 'Radcliffe Sermon,' but, like his predecessor's of 1850, it produced only £32. It is evident that this falling-off from

[1] The Ashmolean *Building* (no longer a *Museum*) has been so appropriated, but found unsuitable. The extensive purchases in the High Street in 1868 and 1869 will supply (as at least £30,000 may well supply) ample accommodation for any number of Examination Schools.

the £70, £80, or £100 of former years is not to be attributed to the preacher, but partly to the audience and partly to the nature of the service. 1st. As to the audience, or rather congregation. It is obvious to any one who has been a regular attendant at these sermons, that the persons likely to give largely no longer attend. The county gentlemen (with the exception of one or two, made Stewards for the occasion) have ceased to show themselves; and the visitors for the Commemoration-week, partly exhausted by the previous night's ball or concert, and partly engaged at late breakfasts, or getting ready for a party to Nuneham, never think of the charity sermon; or, if they do, they look upon it as a local affair, in which they have no concern, and for which they did not come up to Oxford. 2ndly. As to the service. This is still a *choral* service, for the most part badly performed by a weak choir. Now this might have been attractive formerly (especially when aided, as I remember it to have been, by the first-rate public singers, such as Miss Stevens, Bartleman, Vaughan, &c., then engaged for the concerts, but good-naturedly joining the St. Mary's choir); but now, these *stars* having disappeared, the service, as a choral performance, cannot be compared with that of the regular College and Cathedral choirs. But the greatest objection is *the time it takes*, added to a sermon usually very long. If this annual appeal for the Infirmary is to continue, it would be wise to reduce its length by dropping the Morning Service and retaining the sermon, preceded by a psalm and followed by a short but well-performed anthem. It is notorious that Undergraduates and Bachelors never appear there; indeed, the seats of the latter have been usurped by the choir, and the gallery of the former is chiefly occupied by respectable females of the middle class, who have learnt to consider this as an annual treat, cheaply purchased at the price of 6*d.* dropped into the plate. M.A.'s sometimes appear, but 'rari in gurgite vasto,' while Heads of Houses make themselves still more scarce[1]. In truth, it is not an *University* sermon or service, though Dr. Jenkyns, in 1825, first gave it the appearance of being so, by joining, as Vice-Chancellor, the Radcliffe procession from the Library to the Church.

Dec. 2. In a Convocation, of a better temper and of a more liberal spirit than that of June 17, an augmentation of £150 per annum was voted to the Readers in Mineralogy and Geology respectively, and £71 10*s.* to the Chemistry Professor.

In this Michaelmas Term *Mr. Thackeray* gave some lectures on 'The English Humourists.' They were well attended, probably better attended than he had expected, so little was he then known and appreciated at Oxford.

A.D. 1852.

[B.A. 306. M.A. 248. Hon. D.C.L. at Commemoration, 1.]

About this time died my old schoolmaster, Dr. Ellerton, who founded the annual prize for a Theological Essay. By-the-bye, why in the Annual Notice is it simply called 'The Theological Essay,' and not 'The *Ellerton* Theological Essay?' His name is indeed retained in announcing the Hebrew Scholarships, but in connection with that of Dr. Pusey and his brother, co-founders of the Scholarships.

Feb. 18. Mr. Claughton of Trinity was elected Professor of Poetry, his only opponent, Mr. Bode of Ch. Ch., having withdrawn from the contest.

---

[1] This 'Radcliffe Sermon' was discontinued in 1863—never (it is presumed) to be revived; my account of it, however, may remain as a 'Recollection' of a thing gone by.

This May witnessed the appearance of the bulky '*Blue Book*' of 800 pages, noticed before in Chapter XIX., and entitled 'Report of her Majesty's Commissioners, appointed to inquire into the State, Discipline, Studies, and Revenues of the University and Colleges of Oxford,' with an elaborate Statement of Evidence, and forty-seven '*Recommendations*,' some of them affecting the University, and others particular Colleges.

June. *Mr. Manning* (late Archdeacon), on returning from a visit to Rome (where he had been kissing the Pope's toe), informed the English public (in answer to reports of his re-conversion) 'that he had found in the (Roman) Catholic Church all that he had sought and more than, while without its pale, he had ever been able to conceive.'

In this same month the Warden and Fellows of New College, instead of replying to the many questions sent to them (in common with other Colleges) by the Commissioners, threw themselves upon their Visitor, the Bishop of Winchester, and requested him to make a thorough investigation of their proceedings, studies, &c.; which he undertook to do and did. But this *would not do;*—eventually, indeed, the College was thought to have yielded more to the demands for change than was necessary or expected.

June 15. In Convocation the donation of the Fielding Herbarium was accepted; and not only that, but £2000 was voted (from the large sum lately received from the University Press) for maintaining and adding to this collection, with £1250 for a suitable building for its reception in the Botanical Gardens.

The Commemoration week produced a well-timed novelty in the form of a rather lengthy but learned and witty *jeu-d'esprit*, entitled '*Phrontisterion*,' a quiz by anticipation of the dreaded effects of the Commission. Borrowing the idea from the 'Clouds' of Aristophanes, it introduced Socrates as 'Mr. Commissioner.' Take, as a specimen:—

> 'Professors we, from over the sea,
> From the land where Professors in plenty be;
> And we thrive and flourish, as well we may,
> In the land which produces one Kant with a K,
> And many a *Cant* with a C.
> Where Hegel taught, to his profit and fame,
> That something and nothing were one and the same,' &c.

It was attributed to Mr., now Dr. Mansel, Dean of St. Paul's, who, six years afterwards, grappled in a more serious style with German philosophers in his clever Bampton Lectures; but who (as people must expect when they mount to transcendental heights) did not find himself, on coming down to our ordinary, every-day world, exempt from polemical attacks.

In July, a contest took place for the representation of the University, between Gladstone and Dr. Marsham, which, after lasting four days, ended by Mr. Gladstone's election with a majority of 350 votes. Sir R. Inglis had 1368 votes, Gladstone 1108, Dr. Marsham 758. New political or rather theological titles and denominations were invented and adopted on this occasion; for not only the '*High and Dry*,' but the '*Low and Slow*,' were stirred up to oppose Gladstone, Alma Mater's most talented but capricious son. I have always voted for him (as I did for Sir Robert Peel, even when Oxford rejected him), and probably always shall, unless he cuts the connection, disgusted with the regular recurrence of a contested election[1]. Oxford, years ago, could quietly elect, again and again, a representative who could barely say 'Aye or No;' but then he represented the ayes and noes of his constituents!

In the last week of July an interesting meeting took place

[1] Or loses it, as he has since, by his ultra-liberal tendencies.

in Oxford of the 'Medical and Surgical Association,' very numerously attended, under the presidency of Dr. Ogle. Three eminent physicians, Sir Ch. Hastings, Dr. I. Forbes, and Dr. I. Conolly, had the Honorary Degree of D.C.L. (why was it not M.D.?) conferred on them. There was a brilliant Conversazione in the Radcliffe Library, with abundant refreshment for mind and body. It was the twentieth anniversary of the Society.

Sept. 14. Oxford lost her noble Chancellor, England her noblest son, Arthur Duke of Wellington[1]. As soon as the shock occasioned by his loss was past, Alma Mater, as in duty bound, began to look round for an 'Almus Pater' in his place. Lord Harrowby and Lord Ellesmere (good men and highly respected, but 'not quite equal to the place') were only named to be put aside. That the Bishop of Exeter should have been for a moment thought of was only a proof of (not hero-worship but) Bishop-worship in a few ultra-Tractarians. Lord Derby, once named, was at once our future Chancellor: every one retiring before him as 'the right man in the right place.' On the 12th of October he was unanimously elected Chancellor, in the usual form of elections in Convocation. The only variety was, that the Senior Proctor, Mr. Lake, in a long Latin speech, lamented the haste in which the vacancy had been filled up and the matter settled even *in Vacation-time ;* but he was most satisfactorily answered by the Vice-Chancellor

[1] It was said that he had the Oxford Blue Book on his desk when death seized him. He was trying, no doubt, to master it. I must add a better and more touching account given to a trustworthy person by the Duke's housekeeper: 'The last time I saw him alive was the night before his death He was then, I think, going to bed, and it was late. He had with him the Oxford Blue Book, with a pencil in it; and he said to Lord Charles Wellesley, who was with him, "I shall never get through it, Charles, but I must work on."'

(Dr. Plumptre), who said, 'that in all recent instances (three at least) the vacancy (and that even in Vacation) had been as rapidly filled up, and that the Statutes required it to be done 'quàm primum commode fieri poterit.' Lord Derby, besides his manifest fitness for the post of honour, by his rank, talents, high character, and reputation (not to mention his Prize[1] for Latin Verse in 1819), had also the great recommendation (to clerical electors at least) of being the Prime Minister! A slippery position indeed in these days; and so the event proved it to be, as he ceased to be Premier in the December following. In his ministerial house at the Treasury a Convocation was held on the 26th of October, for the purpose of admitting Lord Derby to his office of Chancellor. On that occasion, in his Latin reply to the address of the Public Orator, he astonished his hearers by his easy flow of classical Latinity, and especially delighted Dr. Gaisford, the Dean of Ch. Ch., Lord Derby's College.

Oct. 23. By a decree of Convocation, the ceremony of *sitting* in the Examination School '*per integrum diem*' (on which the sitter might generally say 'perdidi diem') was abolished. On the same day the Vice-Chancellor, Dr. Plumptre, who had held his office four years, resigned the seals, &c. to Dr. Cotton. The death of the late Chancellor, so near the beginning of Michaelmas Term, had made it necessary for Dr. Plumptre to hold the Vice-Chancellorship a fortnight over his fourth year—Lord Derby not having been elected till October 12.

Nov. 4. A novel delegacy! The Proctors nominated twelve members of Convocation as delegates to represent the University at the public funeral of the Duke of Welling-

[1] About the time when Lord Derby (then the Hon. E. Stanley) filled the Rostrum, Ch. Ch. carried off ten Prizes within nearly five successive years.

ton. A special place in St. Paul's was reserved for them on that occasion.

Nov. 6. An inquest having been held on the death of a young member of Jesus College, the College authorities demurred about the Coroner's fee, which had hitherto been paid by a Bursar and charged to the friends of the deceased. The matter was referred to the Hebdomadal Board, who, after due enquiry and consideration, determined that the University (through the Vice-Chancellor), in that and in all future cases, should pay the fee and incidental expenses of an inquest[1].

December 16. Lord Derby's Ministry having been left in a minority (286 versus 305) on the important question of the Budget, a resignation took place. Lord Aberdeen undertook the Government, and Mr. Gladstone (with the necessity of a re-election and the certainty of a contested one, after voting against Lord Derby's Ministry) was invited and consented to join Lord Aberdeen.

A. D. 1853.

[B.A. 356. M.A. 235. Hon. D.C.L. at the Installation, 38.]

The opening of this year was marked by the lengthened and bitter efforts by which Mr. Gladstone's re-election was opposed. No wonder that those who were adverse to him before, should be still more opposed to him now; for even his warm friends had to gulp down much that was painful, and to feel rather sore after the operation. Oxford however, as a whole, could not afford to lose, or rather could not make up its mind to part with, its distinguished but very wayward *alumnus*. After fifteen days' polling (an extension seldom claimed, but allowed by the *then* election-law) the result was,

[1] This Coroner's fee was placed by Convocation in the Table of Statutable Fees in 1869.

for Mr. Gladstone 1022 votes, for Mr. Perceval 898,—majority for Gladstone 124. The irksomeness, as well as the acrimony of this protracted battle, was most painful to witness, much more so to take a part in. It was natural that Oxford men should be vexed and angry with Mr. Gladstone, for having joined in a vote which led to the resignation of Lord Derby, their Chancellor. Loaves and fishes, deaneries and bishoprics, all knocked over! Hence the angry feelings, speeches, and letters, even of good and pious men. Mr. Gladstone was accused of joining in 'a strange combination,' an 'unnatural coalition;' but what connections and combinations could be more strange than those which were formed against him, such as that of Archdeacon G. A. Denison working in the same Committee with the Rev. Hugh Stowell! &c., &c.

Jan. 27. The sum of £500 was voted in Convocation ' in aid of the subscription for *an educational memorial* in honour of the late Duke of Wellington;' that is, for 'The Institution for Educating the Orphans of Military Men,' or some such title. Mr. Rawlinson opposed the vote, on the ground that the money would be more appropriately given, for an *academical* purpose, in connection with our late Chancellor's name,—'Ut scholares, è gymnasio isto quod extranei fundaturi sunt, apud nos nutriantur atque erudiantur.' The proposed vote, however, did not attract much attention; on a scrutiny being demanded, the Placets (for giving the £500) were 25, Non-Placets 22. Only forty-seven members of Convocation therefore were present.

In February, Dr. Newman (once of us as *Mr.* Newman, but since *doctored* by the Pope) was tried and found guilty of publishing 'a defamatory paper' in reference to the character of a Dr. Achilli, another of the Pope's Doctors, and once a Romish priest! Dr. Newman's defence was, that he believed what he had published was notoriously true; he was fined however £100 and costs. Without any idea of comparing Dr. Newman with Dr. Achilli,—the one all purity and piety, however misdirected, the other notoriously said to be the reverse,—they were so far alike, that the one was a deserter from our Church to that of Rome, the other a deserter from Rome to Protestantism in some shape or other. It must have been a painful business to Dr. Newman to find himself (no longer indeed 'a boy,' but still)—

'Infelix . . . atque impar congressus *Achilli*.'

Early in this year of unsettled ideas and coming change, a self-constituted academical body, called 'The Tutors' Association,' presented itself and the result of its deliberations before the University, on the all-important subject of academic education, and especially as to the *extension* of that education. It was of course, as an unauthorised body, an imperium in imperio; but as it was composed of the great majority of the Tutors (naturally alarmed, as well they might be, at the critical position of 'this our craft,' and at the threatened incursion into their preserves, by Professors), their report was received with the respect and consideration which its careful construction and the high character of its authors demanded. One of its chief subjects was that of 'Affiliated Halls,' with a detailed plan for their government, and a scheme for educating, feeding, and lodging students at £60 per annum; Hatfield Hall at Durham being acknowledged as their model. 'Private Halls' also were fully discussed in this Tutors' Report, as well as the 'Extension of Colleges, by means of detached buildings,' a plan which (it was thought) would give suitable employment to a large number of resident Fellows. The Tutorial Report, followed, as it soon was by the Commissioners' Report, raised an expectation, that good, large houses would be in great request, to be turned into Aulæ Privatæ. This expectation, however, has not been realised. Indeed, only two attempts at *private-halling* were made; the 'Aula Privata Magistri Butler' had a very ephemeral existence. Though instituted by a very superior man it did not succeed. Litton Hall did a little better, and actually produced two or three graduates; but Mr. Litton got preferment elsewhere in 1860, and no 'parvulus Æneas' now 'ludit in Aula[1].' 'College extension' has not succeeded much better; it would perhaps be more just to say that it has succeeded where it has been attempted, but that the attempts hitherto have been but few. Exeter College has been the boldest in this kind of speculation (for a speculation it must be), and has in this way added greatly to its numbers. Christ Church has merely turned a Canon's house into sets of rooms, Merton is about to build[2], but Magdalen, which was said to have contemplated a large detached building with one of its Fellows for Principal, and accommodation for a considerable number of students on very moderate charges, has, it is now said, relinquished the idea. The wonder was, that a wealthy and quiet society like Magdalen, which some thirty years ago sacrificed so much money in order to *remove* the old Hall because it was 'nimium vicina,' should ever again have entertained the idea of an affiliated Hall, or something very like a Hall, on any part of its extensive premises. Halls, however, of every denomination (even the old ones) appeared to be kept up with more or less difficulty at that time.

March 3. By a vote of Convocation (not however an unanimous one, there being thirty-four Non-Placets to sixty-

[1] Since the above was written, the 'Aula Privata Magistri Charsley' has been more successful.
[2] Christ Church and Merton have since set to work in earnest.

four Placets) the Vice-Chancellor was authorised to purchase four acres of 'the Parks' as a site for the proposed Museum. The wedge's edge was thus well got in; the first turf was turned[1].

March 5. How Mr. Gladstone must have 'trembled in his shoes' at hearing (if ever he did hear) that the young men's 'Union Society,' after a debate of four evenings, carried, by a majority of six votes, a censure on his recent political conduct! It would, however, certainly annoy him, as he must naturally take an interest in 'the Union' where he first tried his oratorical powers, and where his speech on the Corn-laws was said to have equalled any of the Parliamentary speeches of the time.

March 8. A judicious change was agreed upon by Convocation as to the Vinerian Scholarships,—by making them the result of a real Examination by the Law Professors and Examiners in the Schools of Jurisprudence, instead of being canvassed for and voted for in Convocation. An alteration was also made in the number and the time of holding the appointments, both as to Vinerian Fellows and Scholars.

April. Dr. Bliss having announced his wish to resign the office of Registrar (which he had filled so well and so graciously for twenty-nine years), a host of candidates soon appeared, Messrs. Cornish, Rowden, Rawlinson, Shadforth, Sedgwick, Lloyd; only three, however, came to the poll: Mr. Rowden of New College had 361 votes, Mr. Cornish of Corpus 200, and Mr. Rawlinson of Exeter 162. Mr. E. Rowden had the advantage of strong Wykhamical support;

---

[1] Subsequently the whole of the Parks and the fields on the east side of the Parks were purchased by the University, down to the Cherwell, along whose banks (or rather between the natural and the artificial streams) a delightful walk has been formed, raised above the flood-level, and well named Mesopotamia.

his being a layman (though his predecessors do not appear to have been laymen) was thought to be a recommendation, inasmuch as his time and attention would not be divided between his official duties and other absorbing claims and pursuits. He was also known to be a man of business, and has since proved himself an excellent Registrar.

May 3. A pension of £200 per annum was handsomely voted to Dr. Bliss, who still retained his place as Keeper of the Archives. Alas! that he should have enjoyed his pension and his 'otium' for so few years! He died, after being much altered and weakened by paralysis, in 1857. I used to hope that as a result of his leisure he would become to the University not merely an editor and a partial continuator of Anthony Wood, but a second Anthony Wood in a modern spirit. And he probably had some such intention; but his health soon gave way, and he amused himself, in his weakened state, with searching into and arranging the details of his own Hall and its former members.

This spring, among its other blossoms and flowers, produced a second lengthy Report from the 'Association of Tutors,' or, as they were sometimes called, 'The Commonroom Dictators.' It undertook by anticipation much of the Commissioners' work; pointed out (very fairly, certainly, and temperately) the weak points of the Hebdomadal Board, as resulting chiefly from the 'isolated position' of its members (as Heads of Houses) and its exclusive character. It suggested a new Board (with the power of initiating measures), very like what was subsequently formed under the title of 'The Hebdomadal Council,' and representing within it the Heads, the Professors, and the other members of Convocation. This Report, among several good points, strongly urged the necessity of representing the resident Masters in the new Board, *if only to keep the Professors in check*: 'for (it said) it must not be forgotten that, as a body, Professors must ever be liable to some of the same influences which tend to separate the Heads of Houses from the bulk of the residents.' There was, of course, a little admixture of Tutorial importance in this jealousy of Professorial predominance. But it is but fair to add, that if any set of men have a right to claim honour and position in return for their devoted labour, it is our excellent staff of College Tutors.

June 6. Installation week. On Monday (by previous arrangement) our Chancellor, Lord Derby, on his way to Oxford was *intercepted* (so to say) four miles from Oxford, by the Bishop of Oxford, and carried off to make a speech at the opening of the ' Training College' at Culham ; and an excellent speech it was said to have been,—especially in describing the new race of schoolmasters as contrasted with 'the man who, because he could turn his hand to nothing else, was made the parish schoolmaster, that he might not become a burden to the rate-payers.'

On Tuesday, in the Theatre, D'Israeli carried off the loudest burst and longest round of applause, excepting that which accompanied the Chancellor's 'fili mi dilectissime' on admitting his son, Lord Stanley, 'ad gradum Doctoris in Jure Civili, honoris causâ.' At the dinner, or rather *post prandium*, at Worcester College (the Vice-Chancellor's College), Lord Derby's eloquence made a great impression; he enlarged upon the Commission, and 'though he had disapproved of its being issued, he now rejoiced that the University had shown a willingness to meet enquiry and adopt improvement.'

On Wednesday, Dr. Goulburn's 'Radcliffe Sermon' produced £130!

On Thursday, the Theatre was again alive with Honorary Degrees, complimentary verses, and the musical performance of 'The Installation Ode,' written by the Professor of Poetry, and set to music by Sir H. Bishop. This was followed by 'a *portion* of the Latin Essay, and the *whole* of the English Prize Poem.' Christ Church fêted the Chancellor as a former member, and Pembroke as the Visitor of the College ' ex officio.'

August. By an Act of Parliament, of this date, it is ordered 'at any election of a Member of Parliament for either of the Universities of Oxford or Cambridge, the polling shall not continue for more than five days at the most; Sunday, Christmas Day, Good Friday, and Ascension Day being excluded.'

Sept. 14. One of Oxford's most cherished and promising sons, Mr. Strickland (Deputy-Reader in Geology), met with his death in pursuit of his favourite study. While rashly examining the strata on the railroad (near Redford, on the Manchester line) he was struck down and killed by a train coming behind him. He was a most amiable as well as a talented man. Succession, however, is the order of things in this world; accordingly his death made an opening for a still more scientific geologist, Professor Phillips, of whom as an adopted son Oxford has good reason to be proud. On the 27th of October Mr. Phillips was made M.A. by decree of Convocation.

In November, ' The Tutors' Association ' again came out very strong in lengthy recommendations and warnings as to the Professorial system. Allowing that there was plenty of room for the increased working of that system, the Report deprecated 'the introduction of violent and compulsory changes.' ' It would not be doing justice to many of the Tutors of Oxford to degrade them to mere mouthpieces, or subordinates of a superior teacher. To give such a man an ex officio authority to control the opinions and dictate the teaching of a body, some of whom may be as competent to lecture to him as he to them, would spread among our ablest instructors a sense of degradation and a feeling of disgust.' The Report, however, suggested very sensible and liberal views as to the appointment, duties, and remuneration of Professors;—suggesting, on the last head, that 'the fixed annual salary of a Professor (independent of fees from his class) should be £500,—£600 would be preferable.'

Dec. 6. Our University (how much more his College!) sustained a great loss by the death of Dr. Harrington, Principal of Brasenose; I might say also the City, for his active services as a Commissioner, &c. were highly and deservedly valued by the leading citizens.

A.D. 1854.

[B.A. 263. M.A. 189. Hon. D.C.L. at Commemoration, 10.]

The opening year loomed heavily with the approaching Crimean horrors, in the war against Russia. If it be asked, 'What had Oxford in particular to do with this, or this with Oxford?' the answer is at hand; Oxford did, in fact, very soon begin to feel its effect, first in the reduced number of Matriculations, and soon after in the departure of many of its actual members for the seat of war. When it is considered that for nearly forty years there had been no field of the kind opened to our English youths, it was no wonder that the excitement and clang of war should be responded to by young men of spirit and enterprise. And so they went, full of health and ardour and cheerful hopes, to waste that health, exhaust that ardour, and quench those hopes in the protracted miseries of a siege, and to die (as many of them did) in the trenches of Sebastopol. But though perhaps not one of these deserters from our peaceful camp would have changed the battle cry for 'cedant arma togæ,' yet 'dulcem moriens reminiscitur (Oxford)' was perhaps one of his latest feelings.

Jan. 13. The good Sir Robert Inglis (by the advice of his physicians) resigned the representation of the University, a post which for twenty-five years he had filled so honestly and so well. Sir William Heathcote was brought forward to succeed him—'haud deficit alter, Aureus!' The Latin oration of Dr. Williams, Warden of New College, on nominating Sir William Heathcote, or rather (for such it was) his eulogy on Sir Robert Inglis, 'his class-fellow at Winchester, and his friend through life,' was the finest specimen of elegant and sonorous Latinity to which the walls of the Convocation House had echoed for many a year.

The City Council at this time frequently and eagerly debated the question of assessing the Colleges to the Poor-rate; a measure which was ere long to be carried out, to the great benefit of the City, and to the great credit of the University.

Feb. 24. In Convocation a sweeping plan was proposed, which would give quite a new but not an improved constitution to the University. It was embodied in a petition to the Queen, to be allowed to alter and modify the Caroline statutes; its chief feature, however, was the creation of a second Board, consisting of eight Professors and fifteen members of Convocation, to be elected by Convocation, and endowed with an equal power of originating measures; in short, a sort of 'Lower House' as compared with the Board of Heads of Houses, the 'Upper House.' It was obviously an attempt to meet and avert a stronger measure expected to result from the Commission. All the proposals were carried, though with a considerable number of Non-Placets; but it was too late! The 'stronger measure,' with (it must be confessed) a better compacted Council, was to follow in due time.

The measure thus carried was immediately followed by a protest, signed by most of the Tutors, seven or eight Professors, and many other members of Convocation. The Tutors of course objected, because their own plan was not adopted,—which was indeed a better plan, as it proposed one combined Board upon a broader basis. One feature however, savouring pretty strongly of Tutorial self-complacency, was the formation of a Congregation, with powers of debating in English, without the power of initiating[1] any measure, but in which it was proposed to ignore the existence of all resident members of Convocation who were not engaged in the instruction, discipline, or management of the Colleges and Halls!

Resident Masters of Arts, being non-Tutors, were subsequently indebted to Mr. Gladstone or Sir William Heathcote (or both) for checking and reproving this usurping and exclusive spirit with the addition of a sensible remark, 'that the representative body thus constituted [i. e. on the Tutors' plan] would be too limited[2] and too partial to their own views.' What would be chiefly wanted (it might have been added) was sound and impartial judgment, a qualification not necessarily confined to Tutors, Deans, and Bursars of Colleges[3], that is, to those who were engaged (as above stated) 'in the instruction, the discipline, or the management of Colleges.'

March 9. The grave proceeding was repeated (as it had been ever since 1843) of nominating an Examiner in ad-

[1] A very good proposition thus far, and one that was eventually adopted.

[2] This was found to be palpably true a few years after when the Tutors, &c. were about 125, Non-official M.A. and M.D. 130.

[3] The Deans and Bursars, thus by implication united with the *Tutors*, appear to have been included in the proposed composition of the Congregation, just to preserve peace in the respective Common-rooms.

dition to the two Professors, for the Theological School. Has any one been ever known to become a 'Licentiate in Divinity' as the fruit of such Examination[1]?

The beginning of this March brought with it the death of three distinguished Oxonians,—Dr. Richards, the amiable Rector of Exeter; Dr. Denison, the conscientious but rather timid Bishop of Salisbury; and Dr. Jenkyns, the excellent Dean of Wells and Master of Balliol; the last of (comparatively) ripe years, the other two about 54 or 55.

March 17. Lord John Russell obtained the leave of the House to bring in *The Oxford University Bill*, in a very sensible and temperate speech. I need not say how anxiously every word of men (like him) in authority was weighed at that time in Oxford.

March 30. In Convocation the expenditure of £30,000 or even £40,000 was voted for the erection of the New Museum.

April the first (absit omen diei!) a Petition to the House of Commons, of Remonstrance against the Oxford University Bill, was carried (in a 'frequens Senatus' assembled in the Theatre), but only by a majority of two votes, 193 to 191! This, of course, was a futile victory, and was fairly hailed as a proof of an increasing readiness to meet the work of reform half-way, and in an honest spirit.

New College had shortly before petitioned to have the two St. Mary Winton Colleges exempted from the operation of the Bill. That this petition should be in vain did not surprise the University; but most people certainly were surprised at hearing soon after that the points in question had

---

[1] I have lately been reminded (in answer to this question) that my friend, Rev. Robert Hake, M.A., of New College, and now Minor Canon of Canterbury, actually became a Licentiate in Divinity. In his early days he had gained a Sanskrit Scholarship.

been conceded by the College. The altered position of Winchester School in relation to New College soon showed the greatness of the changes adopted.

At the end of March there appeared in the public prints an elaborate scheme, proposed by Magdalen College, 'to meet the demands of the time, and to show both the will and the means of the Society to atone for past neglect by a noble provision for the future;' in short, '*to do* what others were only *talking* of.' It was proposed, therefore, 'to prepare for the reception of a considerable number (probably sixty) of Undergraduates requiring help, in a separate building and under a Vice-gerent.'

But what has become of this grand scheme? Was it only the awakening of a giant, who soon closed his eyes again? I have hinted elsewhere (see 'Recollections in 1853') that the remembrance of old Magdalen Hall and its too close proximity might well deter the College from again hanging something like it about its neck; and I have too much respect for the rulers of that Society to doubt their wisdom in the relinquishment of such a scheme.

April 3 died the well-known and eccentric Professor John Wilson (alias 'Christopher North') at Edinburgh, where he had been for many years Professor of Moral Philosophy. He was an Oxonian, and while a Gentleman-Commoner of Magdalen College got the Prize for English Verse in 1806. He was even then a character, and a fine, manly, enthusiastic one; among other qualities, he was the life and soul of our Light Company in the O.L.V. in the field and at the feast. Strong-built and fond of out-door excitement, he thought nothing of a night walk from London to Oxford.

April 14. The second reading of the 'Oxford University Bill' was carried without a division; and when Mr. Roundell Palmer could, 'as *an Oxford man*, tender his cordial thanks to the Government for the temper with which they had treated and the attention which they had devoted to this great and important subject;' when Mr. Gladstone 'felt perfectly persuaded that the issue of the measure would redound to the great and permanent interests of the University, and increase the strength, the prosperity, and usefulness of Oxford;' it was wonderful how soon fears began to subside and hopes to arise for the future consequences of the lately 'dreaded Bill.' Of course there was still a strong party of anti-reformers, who tried to get up a list of signatures for further opposition. 'Parvis componere magna,'—the preparations going on at the same time for the Baltic armament against Russia were not half so fierce, though quite as unsuccessful.

April 20. At a meeting of the Oxford City Council, Mr. Alderman Grubb (who as Mayor would not have 'that bauble,' the City mace, carried before him when he went to Carfax Church), after stating, with great self-congratulation, that 'he had risen to his present position by trusting to his own exertions, that he had no connection with the University, and nothing for which to thank any member thereof,' moved 'That a Petition be presented to Parliament, praying that none of her Majesty's loyal subjects be denied the advantages of education in the National Universities.' His motion was carried by a majority. What result or weight it had I do not know; but, at all events, it was an unexpected compliment when, in such a quarter, the advantages of an University education were so fully allowed.

May 13. The well-known metaphor of '*The Sick Man*' (used by the Czar Nicholas in reference to the Turkish Government) was occasionally, and not always delicately, applied at this time to the moribund Hebdomadal Board; e. g. 'The Sick Man has been carefully sounded as to what time he could, with least pain and reluctance, arrange to die!'

May 23. In Convocation, the proposal to allow Colleges to annex 'Affiliated Houses' was carried; but that for the establishment of 'Independent Halls,' with special regulations for limiting expenses, was rejected by 64 votes against 23 in favour of it. Some stringent regulations for Licensed Lodging-houses (not likely, from their very stringency, to be honestly carried out) were passed nem. con.

At this same date (the Oxford University Bill having not yet reached its last stage in Parliament) nearly a hundred members of Convocation (including four Heads of Houses and seven or eight Professors) got up a Petition to the House of Commons for the passing of the Bill, at least in its principal provisions, 'deprecating a longer suspense and recognising the necessity for some changes.'

June 22. A proposal in Convocation (being nothing less than an attempt to *force* young men, as gardeners would say, into Theologians in connection with their B.A. Degree) was rejected by 113 votes to 34. It looked like a last, dreamy effort of 'The Sick Man' to show some remaining vitality. Mr. Marriott well observed, 'While I admire the courage of the Hebdomadal Board in producing such a statute at such a time, I cannot agree with them in this mode of showing it.'

Some clever Latin hexameters were circulated as 'having been picked up in a first-class carriage, on returning from the opening of the Crystal Palace on the 10th of June.' A just and elegant compliment to the Queen's well-known punctuality occurs in the introductory lines:—

> 'Ut ventum ad sedes, omnes considere jussi
> Reginam expectant, non ut te, candida Dido,
> "*Cunctantem* thalamo," sed fixo tempore certam.'

Of the rest of the lines, sixty in number, a specimen will suffice :—

> 'Et jam progreditur, patriæ justissima cura,
> Alberti conjux, hilari Victoria vultu.
> Intranti Costæ chorus assurexerat omnis,
> Lablachiusque tonans, argutaque Clara Novello.'

July 7. The Oxford University Bill having at length got into the House of Lords, Lord Derby's amendment, to give the election of the Hebdomadal Council to Convocation instead of Congregation (as proposed in the Bill), was rejected by 99 votes against 72. This assuredly was a wise determination. What a hubbub throughout the country, at every vacancy, was thus prevented! The Congregation, as newly constituted (about 256 in number and regularly resident), forms a constituency sufficiently numerous and locally acquainted with the qualifications of candidates.

Sept. 7. The dreaded cholera again showed itself in Oxford, and continued to carry off its victims through this month, though in small numbers compared with the former visitation. Happily, it disappeared as October commenced; but it was thought safer by the authorities to call up the Undergraduates a week later than usual.

Oct. 24. Our New Academical Constitution was inaugurated, i. e. the election of 'the Council,' to supersede the old Hebdomadal Board, took place; viz. six Heads of Houses, Dr. Williams of New College at the head; then six Professors, Mr. Hussey being far ahead of the others; and lastly, six members of Convocation, Mr. Mansel being slightly ahead. Mr. Marriott and Mr. Pattison being equal, a fresh trial took place on a subsequent day, when Mr. Marriott came in. Of course, the excluded *Heads* felt for a time somewhat like Samson robbed of his locks, rather sore and shorn of their dignity. One Head of a House, Dr. Cardwell, a most valuable and experienced member, was elected into the Council at the second voting, as a Professor. A fortunate thing, certainly, thus to secure his services; but as a rule the three classes should be (and were intended to be) kept distinct, as representatives of their respective bodies.

In November, Archdeacon Wilberforce, following the sad examples of Newman, Manning, and his own brother Henry (following also the course of his own recent writings), left his high position in the Church of England and joined the Church of Rome. His case was strongly put, in a paper of the time:—' This learned, amiable, and pious man finds himself, by the natural process of his own argument [about the Roman See as the source and centre of all authority], if not a heathen, at least a heretic. His baptism, his early training, his confirmation, his orders, his ministrations are all ignored and go for nothing. He must begin his religious life over again, be new baptised, confirmed,' &c.

Nov. 9. At a very full meeting of the Street Commissioners (a great many of them being of the University), a long discussion took place on a plan of getting rid of the 'sewage' by carrying it away in a covered sewer, so as to fall into the Thames below Sandford Lock! Much talk naturally followed, and much questioning of Sir W. Cubitt, but this scheme[1] on so expensive and vast a scale has not yet been shown to be practicable; and, however desirable for Oxford, what would be its effect on the Thames?

In this November nearly forty designs for the New Museum were exhibited for several days in the Radcliffe Library for general inspection and a final selection of one. The interest excited by them was immense, and the question 'Gothic or Grecian?' was everywhere discussed. The

[1] Now, in 1868, impossible, thanks to the late Act of Parliament for purifying the Thames.

designs were distinguished by mottos or devices, and almost all of them (the one adopted especially) were vouched for as not likely to exceed £30,000 in the erection.—We have lived to see (in 1861) that the sum of £80,000 has been called for, with the certainty of a still further demand.

Towards the end of 1854 appeared a work entitled 'The Literary Remains of *Henry Fynes Clinton*,' consisting of his Literary Journals, &c. He was one of the best Greek scholars connected with Oxford, as is shown by his 'Fasti Hellenici,' the produce of many years of application. But either he was ungratefully forgetful of his obligations to his Alma Mater, or she (as represented by the Christ Church Tutors of his day) had been negligent in the cultivation of his peculiar talent; for in his Journal he complains that 'during seven years of Oxford residence he never received a single syllable of instruction concerning Greek accents, or Greek metres, or the idiom of Greek sentences; in short, no information upon any point of grammar or syntax or metre.' He was matriculated in 1799, and died in 1852.

December. The Museum Committee (Dr. Wellesley, Dr. Acland, Professor Phillips, and Mr. Butler of Exeter College), after selecting six of the forty plans, reduced those six to two — one Palladian, the other Gothic, or rather Rhenish-Gothic—for the final choice of Convocation. The Rhenish-Gothic was adopted, but it will take many years before old Oxford eyes can get accustomed to a style which, while it presents many parts and points extremely beautiful, yet leaves many others naked and ugly[1],

---

[1] The effect is like that of some churches thus quizzed in Pugin's 'Contrasts:'—

> 'Some raise a front up to the church,
>   Like old Westminster Abbey;
> And then they think the Lord to cheat,
>   And build the back part shabby.'

to say nothing of the vast exposure of roof, and that broken into so many and various elevations. A considerable part of the north side and the whole of the east side should at once have been planted with poplars or other tall trees. The inside, however (and that is the main thing), is imposing; very interesting from its valuable collections, its various marbles and statues, well adapted to its purpose, and surrounded with Lecture-rooms and a Library.

Dec. 22 died the venerable President of Magdalen College, Dr. Routh, in his hundredth year. It is singular that he left no memorial of himself (in the shape of an exhibition or scholarship or prize) which might perpetuate his name in a College over which he had so long presided. His fine and extensive theological library he conveyed by deed of gift to the University of Durham, with which he had no apparent connection, but which (he probably supposed) was ill provided in that department of literature[1]. His funeral was most solemn and impressive, a large choir chanting the funeral service, with a procession round the cloisters.

A.D. 1855.

[B.A. only 237. M.A. 189. Hon. D.C.L. at Commemoration, 17.]

Feb. 18. The new Congregation held its first meeting, but only a few formal matters were gone through. The ear was certainly struck by the sound of *the vernacular* from the mouth of the Vice-Chancellor.

March 3. The first Statute of the Hebdomadal Council was promulgated according to the new form and submitted to discussion; it consisted mainly of the abolition of old clauses, to make room for the new enactments in favour

---

[1] A few years before his death one of those heavy folios fell from his hand as he was taking it down from the shelf, and striking his foot, caused him pain for some time. To the sympathy of a friend, who called soon after, he replied, 'Yes, indeed, Sir, Μέγα βιβλίον μέγα κακόν.'

of Nonconforming members, at matriculation, at examination, and at the first degree. Several amendments were proposed, but as they were not adopted by the Council, the Statute, three days afterwards, was brought a second time into Congregation, to be put to the vote, but not discussed. Dr. Marsham notwithstanding began to offer objections to the Statute, but was not allowed to proceed; he subsequently printed his views in a Letter to the Vice-Chancellor. All the clauses of the Statute were resisted, but unsuccessfully, all of them being carried by a large majority. The largest number of Non-Placets (viz. 37) was against the clause which enacted 'that Dissenters' (or, euphoniously expressed, 'persons not examined in theology') 'should take up additional books in lieu of the divinity examination.' An odd sort of composition, certainly! On the whole, the freedom of debate in English and the privilege of offering amendments for the consideration of the Council were felt and acknowledged as great improvements and effective safety-valves.

The new Council took alarm at the small number of B.A. Degrees, and invited the opinions of members of Convocation as to the cause or causes of the falling-off. The new attraction of military life and adventure (though accompanied with the horrors of Balaclava and the trenches before Sebastopol) had certainly drawn away some few, who had either not begun or had not finished their intended academic career; but one main cause might certainly be found in the severity of the Examiners and the number of *Testamurs* to be obtained before the Bachelor's gown[1] could be put on.

[1] The first Degree is attainable in a shorter time than formerly, i.e. in little more than three years, and in that time *four Testamurs* are to be gained; meanwhile, as young men must have their boating or cricketing, —nay, they should have it,—there is scarcely left sufficient time to prepare for so many Examinations.

The number of B.A. Degrees in each of the last seven years was as follows: 300, 307, 312, 306, 356, 263, 237.

March 20. A debate took place in Congregation respecting Professors, especially as to religious tests to be required of them. Dr. Ogle moved an exemption from such tests for the Professor of Anatomy. Professor Price recommended a negative instead of a positive test, e. g. 'I, (A, B) declare that I will neither directly nor indirectly teach or assert anything detrimental to the doctrine and discipline of the Church of England:'—this was seconded by Mr. Butler of Exeter College, in a very luminous speech. Dr. Pusey, in reply, concluded with what at least was very beautiful if not very convincing, 'That it would be absurd to make a distinction between theological and non-theological Professors. All the sciences moved like planets round the sun of God's truth, and if they left their course, they would be hurled back into chaos.'

In this month of March, the Council (sweeping along in its work, like new brooms) sent forth 'no end' of new Statutes and propositions,—especially about Private Halls and Professors' Stipends,—at that time modestly required not to be less than £300 a year. Dr. Rawlinson's absurd rules and limitations respecting his Anglo-Saxon Professor were, very properly, doomed to be rescinded. So also as to the Keeper of the Ashmolean Museum.

In May several Statutes of more or less importance were proposed and carried; amongst others, that no election of a Bedel, Verger, or Divinity Clerk should take place (in case of a vacancy) till some intended alterations should have been proposed. This was the first signal of the coming attack upon the old staff of the University; inasmuch however as, in case of a vacancy, an election by the existing Statute would come on (even in Long Vacation) *intra triduum*, that hasty proceeding might well be prevented from recurring.

[In June, it was ordered that no election (except for M.P.) should take place in Vacation.]

Late in May a great improvement for all parties, in paying and receiving fees for Degrees, took place; viz. that they should be paid in the Apodyterium[1] at 9.30 a.m. on Degree-days (the Degrees being conferred at 10). 'The Proctors,' it was said in the printed notice, 'will be present;' —but the extra half-hour then required was soon found irksome, and the delicate question of subscription or non-subscription to the Thirty-nine Articles (which was now first made optional for the B.A. Degree) was left to the Yeoman Bedel, before long, to be altogether discontinued!

May 19. The '*Private Hall Statute*' was carried in Convocation, nem. con., no one caring much about it. It came into the world in a chilly state and met with a cold reception; it was, in short, '*nobody's child*,' and it is no wonder that it has not thriven.

A very good and sensible Statute was passed at this time (by 24 to 11 votes, only 35 persons caring about a really important measure), which directed 'that all future Statutes should come into force *at once*' (unless some particular time were specified) without the previously required delay of thirty days,—which was tiresome to wait for and often forgotten. Also the sum of £200 was voted to be divided among the most approved of the non-accepted authors or constructors of the Museum plans. At the same time a proposal in Convocation to grant £350 for the purchase of a set of Assyrian sculptures was rejected, by 20 votes against 12.

---

[1] This term, borrowed from the ante-room attached to the baths of the Greeks, is so far appropriate as applied to the 'locus ubi vestimenta *exuuntur;*'—the vestimenta being the inferior gowns stripped off, when the *togæ superioris gradûs induuntur*. At all events it is a more classical name than that of an adjoining place, 'The Pig-market'!

May 24. A most important and sweeping Statute was promulgated 'Concerning University Fees and Dues.' It was a most elaborate and skilful production (worthy of Dr. Jeune, the Master of Pembroke and his financial talent), being (with ' Some Unofficial Explanations' which accompanied it) the result of much patient labour, research, and calculation. Among those who were especially affected by the proposed *Novæ Tabulæ* of Fees and Dues, I, as an Esquire Bedel (whose income entirely arose from such sources), was, of course, deeply concerned. I naturally felt alarmed at first; but I at once experienced the kindest consideration from the Council and, as representing them, Dr. Jeune, with whom I had frequent conferences and by whom all my statements and calculations were most equitably considered. In short, I am bound in justice to say (after six years' experience of the New Table and of the compensation granted to me for abolished *Culets*[1] and altered Fees) that I have had no reason to regret the serious alterations then made, or to complain of their results.

June 6. The above Statute, with all its great changes, was re-promulgated, in consequence of a few of the amendments of the former Congregation having been adopted by the Council.

June 2. Oxford had to lament the loss of her distinguished Greek scholar, Dr. Gaisford, whose place Alma Mater would be puzzled to fill up with any one man. The standard of classical education has, confessedly, been greatly raised in Oxford since Dr. Gaisford's early days; and consequently a great many more scholars (of a high kind of

---

[1] This term '*culet*' being now quite disused, it is necessary to add that it was a small quarterly charge put to all persons' names on the College books and forming a part of the income of the Esquire Bedels: the word, like the French word 'cueillette,' was a corruption of 'collectum.'

scholarship) have been produced; but scarcely any *one* stands out 'in alto relievo' in the department of criticism and philology which the Greek Professor's death has left vacant. Indeed we do not see scholars, detached from tutorial studies and duties, come and devote themselves to scholarlike pursuits, for the genuine love of Greek and Greek authors as Gaisford and Elmsley did[1]. Drs. *Liddell* and *Scott*, of course, take a high place as learned lexicographers, but they are too much involved in the duties of their high position (though a high position did not seem greatly to affect Dr. Gaisford) to be likely to add much to their high reputation in this line[2]. Mr. Linwood of Christ Church once gave hopes that the mantle of Elmsley had fallen upon him; but he has not as yet fulfilled that expectation. If indeed the amiable Professor Jowett would cease to meddle with doubtful theology, and devote himself entirely to the studies of a Greek Professor, he would soon either induce Convocation to raise his Professorial income to its proper standard, or shame Government into a suitable endowment of his Regius Professorship. Meanwhile, it is a comfort to feel assured, from the incidental improvement in Greek scholarship which his lectures have undoubtedly produced, that Oxford is not likely again to approach the state of things in 1540, when (we are told) Greek was so little known in the University, that if a Greek passage occurred in a lecture on a Latin author, it was usually skipped or

[1] What is here said ought to have protected me from the charge [in the 'Pall Mall Gazette' of Nov. 11, 1868] 'of *not* being aware of the scholarlike minority or under-current of studious residents in Oxford,—at the early part of this century.'

[2] It was said that Gaisford, on his visit to Germany, had some difficulty in escaping from the 'umarmung' of some of its scholars, exclaiming (in the apprehension of a 'kuss' on both cheeks) 'Ohe! jam satis, amice.'

shirked (as the phrase now is), with the observation 'Græcum est, non potest legi.' [Since then, to the comfort of all parties, the Chapter of Christ Church has handsomely endowed the Greek Chair.]

June 16. The important *Fee Statute* was finally carried in Convocation, to come into force at the beginning of the following Michaelmas Term. One or two of its clauses were faintly opposed.

In June ('*leonum* arida nutrix'), the Commemoration was greatly enlivened by the presence of our Chancellor, Lord Derby, who made a splendid speech[1] at Dr. Acland's soirée in the Radcliffe Library (in reference to the intended Museum and the extension of scientific studies) on the Tuesday evening, June 19. On the next day, Wednesday, he conducted, with great tact and gracefulness, the business of Convocation in the Theatre, conferring the Honorary Degrees, &c. In the afternoon of the same day he performed (what was indeed the great object of his visit to Oxford) the ceremony of laying the foundation-stone of the Museum. The scene altogether was most imposing. The Chancellor and the University dignitaries were elevated on a large stand or stage, in front of which (in a large enclosed area) ladies and gentlemen were assembled in great numbers, duly admitted by tickets, including a strong choir of men and boys conducted by Sir F. Ouseley. On the outside of the inclosed space stood a large, well-behaved crowd. The Chancellor's English oration, energetically spoken (not read), was worthy of the occasion and of his high reputation as an orator. The other parts of the ceremony, musical and devotional

---

[1] His Lordship in this speech (as he did in another, some time after, at a meeting of the British Association) declared himself to be, *as to Science*, quite an ignoramus.' Would we had a few more such among our Oxford nobles!

(for the Vice-Chancellor, Dr. Cotton, delivered a long prayer, every one kneeling), were well conducted. The weather too was, fortunately, most propitious.

Oct. 10. Michaelmas Term began with the new Table of Fees, for Matriculation, Degrees, &c., &c. The actual sum paid by individuals, on graduating, was not much reduced, except in the case of those who, under the old system, would have been Grand-Compounders. The B.A. pays £7 10s., nearly the same as before; the M.A. £12, about £2 less than formerly. The sum being the same in all cases, the business of paying and taking the fees was very greatly simplified and accelerated. The Table is printed in the Statute-book and hung up in the Apodyterium, so that men come knowing what they have to pay, and many with the exact amount in their hand.

During this summer, and indeed during the whole long period whilst the Museum was being built, it was very gratifying to see the good effects of the thoughtful, good feeling of the University authorities, who caused a temporary messroom and a reading-room to be constructed, close to the site of the Museum, for the use and comfort of the workmen there employed. This building was opened by the Vice-Chancellor, &c. with a dinner for the workmen; books were purchased for their leisure hours, a respectable female was established there, with a fire for cooking, and morning prayers undertaken to be kept up by the Vice-Chancellor and other clergymen.

Nov. 8. The peculiarities in the academical dress of Servitors were abolished by a liberal Statute; this good feeling had originated with Dr. Liddell, who set the good example at Christ Church[1]. The chief peculiarity was, the absence

---

[1] Christ Church indeed is the only College which still retains Servitors; Jesus and Pembroke had some within my 'Recollection;'

of the silk tassel on the cap; the other (but less observable) was the absence of little plaits or folds on the flying wings or '*leading strings*' attached to the Commoner's gown.

In the beginning of December, Dr. Macbride and Mr. Golightly brought a formal complaint before the Vice-Chancellor against Mr. Jowett, on the ground that, in his Notes upon St. Paul's Epistle to the Thessalonians, he had by implication, if not directly, assailed the doctrine of the Atonement. Mr. Jowett, on being required by the Vice-Chancellor to renew his subscription to the Thirty-nine Articles, did so without hesitation[1]. In consequence of this charge the University pulpit, during the following year, resounded with frequent vindications of this distinctive Christian doctrine in a series of sermons, by different persons, but soon after published in one volume.

A proposal at this time from the Council to appoint a 'Law Lecturer' for three years, at £300 per annum, and 'to be nominated by the Council,' was dropped, chiefly, it was said, in consequence of a Circular by Mr. Rogers, in which he asked 'why the work could not be done by one or both of the two Law Professors?'

A.D. 1856.

[B.A. 281. M.A. 250. Hon. D.C.L. at Commemoration, 12.]

This year began with a great and obvious improvement in the Cathedral Service at Christ Church, under the auspices of Dean Liddell. The prayers 'at 10 and 5' (which had been, for years immemorial, *read* by the chaplains, while the choir responded in a slovenly monotone) were now chanted

---

N. B. I see in the Oxford Calendar for 1869, that at Christ Church the term *Servitors* is changed into *Exhibitioners*.

[1] 'O yes (said he), just give me a pen.'

or intoned; not well, of course, at first, the chaplains being new to the work, but still the Service was made more like what Cathedral Service should be. It is no longer hurried through, for a congregation consisting of a single Canon and the choir, but is carefully performed before an increasing number of persons, strangers and residents, well-seated and civilly treated by the vergers[1].

The beginning of Lent Term brought with it a long (and rather sharp) printed correspondence between Professor Price and Mr. Ashpitel of B. N. C. about the total blank in the Mathematical First Class List of the preceding Michaelmas Term. Mr. Ashpitel represented the Mathematical Examiners on that occasion, and Mr. Price had been the private tutor of two or three men who (contrary to his expectation or calculation) had dropped into the second class. It is not pretended here to report the particulars of their squabble. If Examiners are fallible, the fact need not be exposed beyond their own body.

Feb. 12. In a Congregation held for altering certain clauses in old Statutes, partially obsolete, a proposal to assign the Theatre organ-loft (called in the proposed Statute '*superius pegma*') as the seat for *Doctors of Music*, at the Encænia, having been objected to by Sir F. Ouseley on behalf of his brother-doctors, was withdrawn. The question, however, as to their seat in the semicircle was still left *in dubio*,—with the tacit understanding that a Mus. Doc., if he presented himself, might sit with the other Doctors by sufferance, but not by right. I did not, and do not, believe

---

[1] What can induce Dr. Corfe to allow the extraordinary mode of chanting the Psalms at the Cathedral, i. e. not singing the verses *alternately*, or antiphonally (as is the universal Cathedral usage) but *chopping every verse in two*,—the men and boys ever beginning but never ending a sentence?!

the correctness of what was then asserted, that Dr. Phil. Hayes had ever sat there, since he always had his proper place as Professor, *at the organ*, a handsome benefaction being left to the Professor of Music by Lord Crewe for his services on the Commemoration-day. The argument that their splendid gown and hood (the most showy of all the University costumes) were obviously intended to be displayed on such a show-day, was ingenious and plausible, but it did not convince the plainer-dressed Masters in Congregation[1].

I have always, however, doubted their claim; for being inferior to the Masters (as non-members of Convocation), why should they take precedence of them and be honourably seated, while the Masters are left standing in the crowded area? I am also of opinion that the only Doctors of Music that ever (till the late unrepeated experiment) sat in the semicircle where F. H. Graaf and the famous *Joseph Haydn*; and that they sat there as having been then presented to the Degree in the Theatre, *Honoris causâ*, and not as regular Doctors of Music. See 'Recollections and *Collections*' in 1791.

Feb. 12. The Statute *De Bedellis* was promulgated in Congregation; but as I have a pretty large stock of '*Recollections*' connected therewith, it will form the subject of a separate chapter, next to this.

May 31. In the Commemoration-week the 'Radcliffe Sermon' was preached by Dr. Hook, in New College chapel (St. Mary's church being under repair); the collection was unusually large, viz. £106. A new feature was introduced

---

[1] 'The semicircle on the North part of the Sheldonian Theatre is for Doctors, Noblemen, or Inceptors in the *superior* Faculties.—A Professor or Doctor in Music, Grammar, Rhetoric, or Poetry is *but equal with a Bachelor of Arts*.' Anthony Wood, III. p. 723.

into the gaieties and hospitalities of the week, viz. a splendid *déjeûner*, under an immense spread of tents, in Worcester College Garden. It was given by the Masonic Lodge on the occasion of presenting a grand piece of plate to 'Brother Beach,' *P.P.G.W.* (whatever that means) of Oxfordshire.

June 4. Our Chancellor again visited Oxford and presided in the Theatre at the admission of twelve Honorary Degrees. The Prince Consort, the Prince of Baden, and the Prince of Prussia were present.

July 19. A Convocation was held (*in Long Vacation*) in which the Degree of D.D. *by Diploma* was conferred on the Bishop of Gloucester (Dr. Baring), afterwards, by translation, Bishop of Durham.

In November the new Music Statute was put into full play, with its staff of Professor, Choragus, and Coryphæus or Precentor. The Professor (Sir F. Ouseley) at once began a course of lectures,—a phenomenon which had not been witnessed in Oxford for many years. The Choragus (Dr. Elvey) set to work in earnest to form a weekly class for the practice of vocal music; he, and the Coryphæus (Dr. Corfe) with another class, working alternately. The classes were at first, I believe, tolerably numerous, but, as the novelty of the thing wore off, they gradually came to nothing. Dr. Elvey, I know, found it heavy work; and the 'Societates jam privatim constitutæ' of the Music Statute (i. e. the Amateur Club, the several Glee Clubs, and 'the Plain-Song Society') supplied the academics with as much music as they either cared for or could find time for. Besides this, the 12*s*. a term, paid by each member of the class, did not remunerate the instructors so well as private lessons.

Nov. 7. A remarkable funeral took place (viz. that of a young chorister of Magdalen College choir, named *Bird*) at the burying-ground of St. Cross. The boys of the school, about forty in number, followed the hearse to the cemetery, where they were met by a surpliced choir of thirty. The Burial Service was sung with great feeling and thrilling effect. N.B. The monument soon after raised to the poor boy's memory—upon a scale rather large and grand for its little occupant—provoked the following expression:—

On approaching the large tomb of a little boy.

'I saw the tomb and cried, with deep surprise,
"Surely some great one 'neath that structure lies."
I read, and found a little "*Bird*" at rest,
A bird too humble for so large a nest.'

The month of November was marked by increased energy among our young men in what they denominate 'Athletic Sports.' Not only has foot-ball been borrowed from Tom Browns at Rugby by Tom Browns at Oxford, but, in addition to foot-races, hurdle-leaping, and the like, the absurd exhibition was introduced of *men* (and *gentlemen*) jumping (or attempting to jump) 'in *sacks sewed up to the shoulders*, forty yards out and forty yards in, round a flag!' In comparison with this, which of course 'convulsed the spectators with laughter,' the wheel-barrow race and the donkey-races were quite legitimate and classical.

Nov. 11. In Congregation a sweeping but judicious Statute about the *Cycle* and duties of the Proctors, was carried by 50 votes against 39. In Convocation, Nov. 25, the majority for the Statute was 25. The new Cycle being formed on a calculation of 'Names on the Books,' not of 'Members of Convocation,' Magdalen, New College, and some others lost their frequent turns for the Procuratorial office; others, especially Exeter, gained those turns. The Halls also were admitted to the Cycle for the first time.

CHAPTER XXI.

'Nunquam omnes moriemur inulti.'—*Virgil.*

The Statute De Bedellis, A.D. 1856.

Recollections in A.D. 1857 *and* A.D. 1858.

FEB. 12. The new Hebdomadal Council, which had superseded the old Hebdomadal Board in 1854, had only been two years in existence, when they surprised the University by a Statute, De Bedellis. I say '*surprised* the University' deliberately; for when or where had the necessity or the mere idea of such a proceeding been mooted or conceived? Who was aggrieved by the continuance of appointments of older date than most of the Colleges, of an establishment only in proportion to the state and dignity of the University? For this Statute (which was considered to be simply a plan for getting a few hundreds a year to endow a Professorship or two) proposed to discontinue (as we died off) the office and title of the three Esquire Bedels and (in *name*) the three Yeoman Bedels, appointing, in the place of the six, two ' Bedels,' simply so called, and two 'Sub-Bedels'

—the former with an income of £150, the latter of £100 a year. As soon as the Statute was announced, I did my best to stir up an opposition; but being almost single-handed, no wonder I was beaten, by the great weight of the Council and the *vis inertiæ* of most resident Masters. The Statute was carried in the essentials, though clipped of some of its strange accompaniments; of this kind, was the novel idea of calling upon one of the two junior Esquire Bedels to discharge the duty of '*scriba*' or secretary to the Vice-Chancellor—that is, a new and additional office, indefinite as to time and work, and without any additional remuneration! This was, deservedly, rejected in Congregation. As a proof, by way of corollary, of the unfairness of such a proposed arrangement, the Vice-Chancellor *afterwards* had a scribe or secretary voted for him (and a very proper and almost necessary thing too), but with a proportionate salary! Another clause too was rejected, as more like the contrivance and manœuvring of a petty German prince to make a show on grand occasions, than the proceeding of an old English University; viz. after the reduction of the old staff to four, ' to clap on two *sham Bedels*, to be dressed up, on any extraordinary occasion, in the left-off costume, and carrying, *pro tempore*, the old time-honoured staves!'

Vested interests (and, I am bound to add, my own especially) were guarded and preserved; but I exerted myself against the uncalled-for change[1], not only from a natural and, I hope, pardonable *esprit de corps*, but also from a conviction (which has grown upon me ever since) that the change would unfavourably affect the dignity of the

---

[1] As I was not only pardoned but even applauded, at the time, for the spirit shown in opposing this Statute, I trust that the same indulgence will be extended to this egotistical record of it.

University and tend towards *Americanising* our Alma Mater. At Cambridge, not long before, an attempt to strike off one from the triumvirate of Esquire Bedels had been rejected in the Senate House; and I was not a little cheered by letters of sympathy and encouragement from Dr. Leapingwell, one of the Cambridge Esquire Bedels[1].

In consequence of two or three Amendments to the Statute having been adopted by the Council, it was promulgated afresh, on the 21st of February, and on the 2nd of March the Statute was first brought forward for voting. The 1st clause, viz. for 'reducing the number from six to four,' 'for dropping the titles of "Esquire" and "Yeoman" and substituting those of "Bedels" and "Sub-Bedels,"' was actually (and ought to have been finally) rejected. The majority indeed was not large—42 Non-Placets to 38 Placets. So also was the 2nd clause—requiring one of the (existing) Esquire Bedels to do the extra work of secretary to the Vice-Chancellor—Non-Placets 53, Placets 44. This latter clause was never repeated, but the former was again proposed (after being formally rejected), but not till May 19. It was indeed asserted in a circular that the question had been lost, in the former Congregation, by the accidental tardiness of several voters; but to my knowledge there were also tardy voters on the Non-Placet side. The main proposal was, however, *again submitted to Congregation*, and carried, by a slight majority. Three days afterwards the same result took place in *Convocation*, where I had hoped better things. I raised my voice even in Convocation, in a speech which I subjoin.

---

[1] Since the above was written Dr. Leapingwell died, highly respected, but has no successor; for, by a recent enactment, inconsistent Cambridge has lopped off one of their Esquire Bedels, or Bedèlls, as they write and accentuate it.

N.B. This oratiuncula, indeed the whole chapter, may be read or passed over according to inclination.

'Insignissime Vice-Cancellarie, favorem tuum et indulgentiam, ut et venerabilis Domûs Convocationis obsecro, dum hanc arripio occasionem ad liberalitatem et justitiam hujus "Magnæ Congregationis" provocandi. Hoc Statutum De Bedellis non parvi momenti esse videtur, quippe quod (elephanto simile isti famâ illustrato, propter pondus suum et magnitudinem *in duabus evecto navibus*) in duabus *Congregationibus separatim* et *frustatim* approbatum est. Modus iste ingeniosus suffragiorum ad arbitrium eligendorum et assuendorum in mentem antecessoribus nostris vix unquam venerat; nec quidem, ut opinor, in novis hisce temporibus de re ullâ aliâ conatus fiet ejusmodi. De Bedellis nihil non, ut videtur, et dici et agi possit! Et hoc, de *Collegio*, ut ita dicam, ministrorum, qui apud Oxonienses benevolentiâ, titulis honorariis et proventu liberali per quingentos, ad minimum, annos usi sunt.

Sed plura dicere cupiens, patientiâ vestrâ, Academici, non abutar. In hac totâ re non solùm ordini nostro, veteri et honesto, consulere volui, sed etiam, et maxime, dignitati et honori dilectæ Almæ Matris subservire. Annorum quinquaginta Ministerium me et amore gratoque animi affectu Oxoniæ nostræ devinxit, et mentem timore, vano fortasse sed vero, implevit, de aliis in pejus mutationibus quæ ex hujus Statuti exemplo, quasi e fonte profluere possint.

Sed futura futuris relinquamus; hodie vestrum est, Academici, hanc vexatam quæstionem suffragiis vestris dijudicare; nostrum est (ut pro collegis mecum dicam), sententiam majoris partis humiliter accipere. Ego tamen si sileam, ipsi hi parietes, ipsi nostri baculi voce φωνᾶντι συνέτοισι vos invocarent, opprobrium hujus Statuti suffragiis vestris avertere; "Magistri ad suffragandum."'

But all in vain! The majority, however, of only six votes (55 to 49) was no great triumph. One of the Esquire Bedels, Mr. Forster, has since died; Mr. Harrison will probably continue to maintain the office and its title when those who assailed both shall have resigned *their offices and titles*. The writer of these 'Reminiscences' (though old) is still (1860) able to bear his gold[1] staff without staggering under its weight. The greatest weight he feels is his debt of gratitude to Almighty God for His great mercies, and to the University for a great amount of kindness, liberality, and consideration, from first to last, and of patient indulgence and forbearance during the struggle here described.

A curious feature of this measure (the Bedels' Statute) was the fact that Dr. Pusey, as a member of the Hebdomadal Council, was the constructor and advocate of it. As its acknowledged parent, he supported his measure by means of printed circulars and speeches in Congregation. In some of these (while he displayed a tender regard for us [Esquire Bedels] as being 'overpaid and underworked'), he suffered himself to use rather strong expressions, which, on being complained of, he subsequently softened down. I trust that he will not be offended if (in justice to him and myself) I close this long-spun yarn with his very kind note and explanation :—

'MY DEAR SIR,

'I am sorry to see from some of the papers which have come out, as well as to hear from your speech in Congregation, that this question about the Esquire Bedels' office has been matter of personal pain to

---

[1] Not exactly gold (*aureus*) but silver-gilt (*auratus*)—or, as in the Statute, '*deauratus*,' an allowable word, but , as also suggesting the opposite meaning, and recent decision, of *stripping off*, rather than *laying on*, gold) not so good or classical as *inauratus*.

you. It is natural that you, as the holder of an office which has been of more importance than it can be again, should desire earnestly that it should be retained or restored. You have passed a respected life in it. But surely one may differ as to the nature of an office, or its value, without being supposed to throw any slight upon its holder. It was a pain to me to speak of the office in the presence of its holders, since I could not estimate it as they did. But I meant to avoid everything which could give offence or pain. Whatever is done, I hope you will not think anything can be meant disrespectful to yourself, who are senior to most of us, and whom we have always respected.

'With every good wish, yours faithfully,

'Feb. 29, 1856. 'E. B. PUSEY.'

In conclusion I must say, that though I have not changed my view of the measure, I am more willing than I was in 1856 to allow for 'the *different point of view*' from which others then regarded it. For many reasons I have a high respect for Dr. Pusey, though I have always thought that he had failed to improve great opportunities of keeping the balance between *too much* and *too little*, between *too high* and *too low*. If I have in any expression gone too far, I here ask his forgiveness and indulgence. As to the Bedels' Statute I accept his explanation, with all respect due to one so greatly my superior; and waiting God's good time for removing me from the duties of my office and all other earthly cares, or, it may be, the University's liberality in relieving my short remaining time by a full pension (for there would be no successor waiting for my departure), I here take leave of a subject naturally interesting to me, but, I fear, tiresome to others.

P.S. In 1866 I was allowed to retire from my office (which I had held for sixty years) on a liberal pension.

A. D. 1857.

[B.A. 269. M.A. 241. Hon. D.C.L. at Commemoration, 14.]

March 3. A new Examination Statute was promulgated by the Hebdomadal Council, in which it was proposed ' to relieve candidates from the necessity of passing in two Schools at the " Great Go," or Final Examination; to give them their choice out of five Schools instead of four; to abolish the honorary Fourth Class; to allow the sufficiency of *two Examiners'* signatures *out of three*, for the Testamur; and to dispense with the compulsory attendance on Professors' Lectures.' It was, however, received with formidable opposition on the part of the Tutors[1]; the debate, after being very lengthened, was continued by adjournment to a second day, and numerous amendments were handed in. [The confessed object (and a very good object too) of one or two of the above-mentioned proposals was, to diminish the number of failures (or 'plucks').] It was some time before the Council rallied from this rough treatment of their new Statute; and it was not till late in April that a very modified form thereof was circulated 'for consideration.' (1) The First Public Examination (commonly called ' Moderations') was to be left unaltered. (2) The final Schools to

[1] How was it (it was asked) that the M.A. members of the Council (who were sent thither to represent the opinions of the other members of Convocation) showed themselves so ignorant of, or so regardless of the wishes and opinions of the Tutors, as to sanction a Statute so sure to be opposed? Were they overlaid and outvoted by the other two thirds of the Council? Do they not sit in the Council as the Tribunes of the people did in the Roman Senate, to express the sentiments and opinions of their order? Might they not communicate with that order more formally and frequently than they do?

remain four (not five, as lately proposed);—*poetry* and *scholarship* to be restored (as before 1851) to the final Classical School. (3) The proposal to allow two instead of all three Examiners' names to the Testamur was withdrawn; (4) Enforced attendance on some one Professor's two courses to be continued. (5) A mark of distinction was proposed for those who should shine in their Divinity Examination.

May 5. Two elections took place in Convocation. For the Poetry Professorship:—Arnold 363, Bode 278.

For the Political Economy Professorship:—Neate 194, Rogers 130, Senior 128.

May 12. The new but much modified Examination Statute was again promulgated, and again roughly handled in Congregation,—several *amendments* being proposed[1].

June 11. In consequence of those amendments having been adopted by the Council, this ill-fated but well-intended Statute was promulgated a third time. The discussion, or debate, was again a long one (being adjourned to a second day), and threatening as to the result (further amendments being still poured in). These, however, were not adopted by the Council. Consequently, on June 16, when the measure (purporting to be a new Examination Statute) was put to the vote in Congregation, fourteen out of sixteen clauses were rejected by very large majorities. So ended the labours of the Hebdomadal Council[2].

[1] May 12. In Convocation, a form of Statute for the Middle Class Examination (in which the title of A.A., or Associate in Arts, was introduced) was carried by eighty-one votes to sixteen. A separate vote took place on the title, which was carried by sixty-two votes to thirty-eight. Query: Is this title of A.A. ever adopted? The two vowels do not *take*.

[2] The surviving members of the superseded *Hebdomadal Board* must have smiled at seeing its young supplanter so cavalierly treated by the new Congregation.

The Tutors, who in this question were indeed too strong for the initiative body, were influenced, I believe, by an honest conviction that the existing system was not only good, but that it had not yet had full time for its entire development. There was also, of course, a reluctance to change or modify their own mode and course of teaching, and possibly a tacit approval of *plucking*, at least, those who would not, as well as those who could not, profit by their College lectures.

June 24. At the Commemoration fourteen Honorary Degrees were conferred in the Theatre; Sir Colin Campbell, and General Williams *of Kars*, being *the great guns;* fine, interesting men, and hailed with tumultuous applause; the former so soon (July 8) to be sent to quell the insurrectionary war in India, and return Lord Clyde. On the preceding day the 'Radcliffe Sermon,' preached by the Warden of Winchester, Mr. Barter, produced only £51 12s. 6d.

At Midsummer this year (1857) I resigned the mastership of New College School, which I had held for fifty-one years, the College, always liberal, offering me a handsome pension. Not that I was done up or past my work,—but who, at seventy-one years of age, would not thankfully accept the 'jam datur otium?'

In July, Mr. Neate, M.P. for the City of Oxford, was *unseated*, in consequence of a petition charging him, or rather his agents, with bribery, in the shape of a vast number of *paid messengers*, being electors, engaged by his committee.

'Poor Mr. Neate soon lost his seat,
 Upset by his agents for bribery!
So "*the neat's-tongue was dried*,"
With many jokes beside,
 Quæ nunc esset longum perscribere.'

Oct. 27. A hard-fought contest took place in Convocation for the Clinical Professorship, vacated by the death of Dr. Ogle. An unprecedented number of voters came up for the election, *Dr. Acland*, with his large family connections and influence, being supported by 470 votes against *Dr. Jackson's* 222.

Dr. Acland had just been appointed Regius Professor of Medicine, and it was not expected by most of the Oxford residents that he would aim at the Clinical Professorship also. Dr. Acland's plea was, I believe, that he could not well illustrate his lectures as Regius Professor without access also to the sick beds in the Infirmary. Dr. Jackson, having lost his election (though supported by so large a number of votes), resigned his post as Physician to the Infirmary,— declining (as he was requested by the Governors) to reconsider his determination.

On the 6th of November Dr. Jackson was unanimously chosen to be *Consulting* Physician to the Warneford Lunatic Asylum, in the place of Dr. Ogle.

Oct. 18. The Proctors, supported by an order from the Hebdomadal Council (but descending not a little from the high tone of former days), expressed, in a circular, 'a hope that the Undergraduates would accept in the spirit in which they were offered, the following suggestions :—(1) That they refrain from appearing in public without their academic dress before the hour of 2 p.m. or after the hour of 5 p.m. (2) That they at all times refrain from *walking through* the Schools' Quadrangle without their academic dress, or *loitering* in the public streets.' Soon after, it was said that an Undergraduate being *proctorised* in the Schools' Quad, assured a Pro-Proctor that 'he thought he was all right,'— not having *walked through* the Quadrangle, but merely into it by the iron-gate, and intending *to return by the same*.

Another, on being stopped in the High Street on a charge of *loitering* there, assured a remonstrating 'Pro.' that 'so far from *loitering*, he had been "*doing the High*" for exercise, at the rate of four miles an hour!' O those *ingenious* but not always *ingenuous* youths!

Nov. 18 died, beloved and esteemed by all Oxonians, Dr. *Philip Bliss*, the most devoted and valuable *Registrar* of the University for nearly thirty years, i.e. from 1824 to 1853. I mention that office especially, though he held others, because it was in that he gained and deserved the esteem and gratitude of all who worked with him in the service of the University. By his love of order and systematic punctuality, by obtaining the large room in the Clarendon for the Registrary[1], and by his judicious arrangements there, he greatly facilitated the duties of his successors, while he certainly raised the character and importance of the office. There was a sweetness in his manner and address, which made it a pleasure to have any intercourse with Dr. Bliss. There was no coldness, no chilly reserve, no assumption of superiority, no forgetfulness that, as Registrar, he was still statutably one of the 'Ministri et servientes Universitatis.' The fact was, he was so loved and respected, that he had no fear of losing his dignity as Head of a Hall and D.C.L.

Nov. 17. Dr. Livingstone, of African celebrity, delivered a most interesting lecture in the Sheldonian Theatre,—or rather a simple but animated account of his researches and adventures in Africa. He had previously been made Hon. D.C.L., and on this occasion he appeared in the Doctors' red gown. Among other interesting, and of course more

---

[1] His predecessors had had no fixed room of office; the present Registrary was part of the *old* Clarendon *Printing Office*. About a year before his death he benefited the University by publishing the 'Reliquiæ Hearnianæ.'

important things, he declared, that having penetrated (beyond all other missionaries) into the tribe called Bazeti, he had, in an intercourse of sixteen years, so carefully studied and practised their language, that he could master it better than (from disuse) he could his own on returning to England. His details were most interesting, and his unaffected manner gained him both fixed attention and hearty applause. At Dr. Daubeny's, whose guest he was, he was the *African lion* of the evening.

Dec. 1. An uncalled-for Statute was promulgated, 'to alter the academic gown for Undergraduates.' An idea had got abroad that the Commoners disliked and professed to be ashamed of their gown; and possibly some of them had excused their increasing disuse of it to the Proctors on this plea. Indeed, there is no doubt, that as the gown *now* generally appears (shabby, from having passed down through several generations of '*men*,' stripped of one or both wings or flaps, shortened, in many instances, up to the knees, or still higher from the frequent abscission of ragged hems,—made of a worse material than formerly, and often exhibiting evidence of having been constructed by a non-academic tailor, probably mamma's or sisters' work) it too often presents an unseemly and even ungentlemanly appearance; but till of late years it certainly was not so. On the contrary, the Commoner's gown, formerly made of what was called 'Prince's stuff,' though light and airy, was not flimsy, nor flabby, nor shabby; but being worn by young men, dressed as *gentlemen* then were, it was justly considered, not an imposing certainly, but a light and graceful toga for those of our *gens togata* who had still to work for their sleeves. Certainly the Proctors of 1857 took up the idea of a change of costume so earnestly, that a Statute for the purpose was prepared by the Hebdomadal Council, and after much grave consideration, serious consultation with some influential Undergraduates (and, it is to be presumed, with some influential tailors), *a new model gown* for Scholars (whose accustomed gown was to be given up to the Commoners) was exhibited in Congregation[1]; it was shaped like their old gown, but heavily laden with velvet at the back of the neck, and a strip of velvet brought down some way in front. Altogether it had a clumsy appearance, and would make most Scholars look like 'hogs in armour!' The proposal, however, with the exhibition of the model gown, led to all sorts of suggestions, some of them very strange to Oxford ears; e. g. Mr. Neate, of Oriel, proposed that the Undergraduates should be released from the gown altogether,—a proposition for which, if carried, neither Alma Mater nor the Oxford tailors, his late constituents, would thank him. But he is one of the clever, privileged men, who are expected when they rise in Convocation (still more in Congregation, since by the recent Act of Parliament 'ici on parle Anglais,') to propose something odd, and say something amusing. Mr. Tweed, of Exeter, would not meddle with the Scholars' gown, but would give the Commoners the plain *silk* gown, worn by Students in Civil Law and Medicine [not a bad idea as to appearance, but the difference in cost would be considerable]. Mr. Lake, of Balliol, would dress Scholars and Commoners alike, i. e. in the Scholars' gown. Mr. Rogers would not alter these dresses, but (in his usual levelling mood) would make Noblemen and Gentlemen-Commoners wear the usual Commoners' gown.

One would have thought that such a reception would have stifled the statute in its cradle, in other words, that its parents

---

[1] The Clerk of the Schools, wearing this gown, was desired to walk up and down the Convocation House, to be inspected by the House.

would have withdrawn it from further public notice. But no,—in a subsequent Convocation (Dec. 10) it was put to the vote in its original shape, and rejected by fifty-nine votes to thirty-eight. Such a fuss about dress has not probably occurred since the olden days, when the new-made Masters of Arts, while keeping (as it was called) their Regency at the Act, were fined if they did not present themselves in a sort of half-boots, *ocreæ* (like the bene ocreati or ἐϋκνήμιδες Ἀχαιοί). When I was first in office there was a dispensation annually passed, after the Act Tuesday, for any further use of the 'ocreæ' and other paraphernalia, 'Supplicatio de ocreis et crepidis et socculis exuendis.'

A.D. 1858.

[B.A. 277. M.A. 234. Hon. D.C.L. at Commemoration, 7.]

In January of this year, a prize was offered by Dr. Acland and Sir Walter Trevelyan for the best essay 'On Rearing Fish in the Cherwell and Isis.' Query: Could any such 'rearing' ever succeed in streams so disturbed by boats, sewage, &c.? A former prize offered in 1856 for an essay 'On the Fauna of Christ Church Meadow'[1] and the ad-

---

[1] Since the recent masonry work and palisades round 'the Meadow,' it would be idle to look for any specimens of Fauna or Flora there :—

'Stone and iron will soon environ
All Oxford Walks, or near it ;
But be it known to iron and stone,
That men of taste can't bear it.'

This is a Parody on the old, touching lines in the starvation-days, toward the end of last century :—

'Bone and Skin, two millers thin,
Would starve us all, or near it ;
But be it known to Skin and Bone,
That Flesh and Blood can't bear it.'

joining Waters,' not having been claimed, was repeated by Dr. Acland. Query: Did anything ever come of these offers? If so, the public, which was informed of the offers, might have expected to hear of the result. Or were they too much in advance for Oxford physiologists, and therefore never acted upon?

Feb. 2. An Address, to be presented by a Delegacy, was voted to congratulate the Queen on the marriage of the Princess Royal.

Feb. 3. Authority was given to the Vice-Chancellor by Convocation to take legal measures for maintaining the privileges of the University, as to the dispute with the City, concerning the Mayor's oath 'to respect the rights and privileges of the University' on his admission to office. This proceeding, in a dignified spirit, was intended only to bring the citizens to their senses; the University, after enforcing its right, being willing to make concessions to the City. After some swaggering on one side, and forbearance on the other, the matter was amicably settled, and future Mayors relieved from a ceremony under which their predecessors, till quite recently, had never fretted, and to which (or something like it) the High Sheriff for the County does not scruple to conform[1].

---

[1] As a contrast between City and University feelings, represented by customs, on the arrival of the Judges for the Assizes, the City salutes them with a peal of the cheerful Carfax bells, the University announces the fact by the solemn tolling of St. Mary's great bell. The prisoners in the County gaol (in the days of hanging for all sorts of offences) were said to listen earnestly to these opposite sounds and, according to their respective temperaments, draw omens of acquittal or condemnation. I believe, however, that the *University knell* (as it was called) was only intended as a signal for the Heads of Houses and Proctors to meet the Vice-Chancellor at St. Mary's, to go thence in procession to wait on

Feb. 23. In Convocation, the proposal that 'No Moderator or Examiner shall examine vivâ voce a candidate of whom he has been the *private* Tutor within the space of two years,' was carried by twenty-one votes against eight. Only twenty-nine members of Convocation taking the trouble to vote on a question of no little practical consequence ! The same restriction had been previously imposed on *public* (or College) Tutors.

Feb. 25. A ceremony, most interesting to me, took place in the hall of New College; viz. the presentation of a testimonial (in the shape of an elegant silver ink-stand and a handsome silver salver) from some of my former pupils at New College School, in their own language, 'beneficiorum haud immemores.' Having recorded so many things about others, my cotemporaries, I trust I may be forgiven this allusion to my scholastic labours 'per annos plusquam quinquaginta.'

The obituary of this month of February contained the names of two persons long known and greatly respected in Oxford. The first, *Mr. Sneyd*, Warden of All Souls, was for thirty years at the head of a Society of which he was a fit and graceful representative. He had for some months been in ill-health, caused probably, or at least aggravated, by the advent of the University Commission, and the prospect of coming changes, which had 'cast their shadow before them.' Indeed, he actually resigned the Headship, to the astonishment of every one, and the great regret of his College. Still clinging, however, to Oxford, he purchased a house in St. Giles's, but before he could take

their Lordships and present them with gloves. The gloves, white kid with gold lace trimmings, are still presented, but the procession is discontinued, the Vice-Chancellor and others assembling at the Judges' Lodgings.

possession he sunk under his illness, and was laid in the 'ultima domus' of his College Chapel.

The other, *Dr. John Bull*, Canon of Ch. Ch., equally distinguished for refined manners and good taste, had also high claims to respect in Oxford, his native city, both as a sound and elegant scholar, an impressive preacher, and an admirable man of business. He had well earned the good fortune which marked his career; and if from his pluralities his revenues were considerable, his charities, private and public, were also on a large and liberal scale. Both he and his cotemporary, Mr. Sneyd, though possessing all the requisites for insuring (as far as it can be insured) a happy married life, died unmarried. Perhaps they had heard and adopted a *bon mot* of Mr. Sneyd's predecessor as Warden (Dr. Legge, also Bishop of Oxford), who, when the Prince Regent jokingly said, 'I think, my Lord, there should be a special, high tax on all bachelors,' replied, 'I quite agree with your Royal Highness,—*all luxuries should be taxed.*'

March 8. In Convocation, a statute was passed (nem. con.) which greatly improved and facilitated the mode of voting in elections in Convocation, viz. the simple presentation to the Vice-Chancellor and Proctors of a written form, previously filled up (in the Apodyterium or elsewhere), with the names of voters and the candidates voted for. The superseded plan (which will, like everything superseded, be soon forgotten) was a tedious process (attended with much crowding and pressing) of writing the respective names in succession on papers lying before the Vice-Chancellor and Proctors,—followed by an amusing rather than a solemn ceremony (at this time discontinued) of burning the voting papers in a brazier brought into the House for the occasion, before the Proctor could announce the result of the election.

On the same day, the sum of £1295 18s. was voted in payment of a London surveyor's bill for 'representing the Colleges and Halls in the valuation of rateable property in the University and City!' N.B. This valuation was only a check on the 'City' valuer, Mr. Shaw (whose bill was *only* £1432 0s. 6d.,—besides the costs for an Act of Parliament paid out of the joint rates)—not to mention Mr. Morrell's bill of £218 11s. 6d. I will only remark that these valuations were perfunctory and superficial; for instance, no one asked to enter or inspect my house (or those of my immediate neighbours); the valuer looked, *en passant*, to the frontage only, than which, in most cases, nothing is more delusive; 'fronti nulla fides.' We felt aggrieved on finding that so hasty and slight a process was made a ground for raising our house-rent and, consequently, our poor-rate, &c.

April 27. The first public examination for a Musical Degree (if that could be called public which attracted no public attention) took place in the Music School. Two persons were examined and both passed.

May 14. In Convocation there was a grand *field-day* (as the soldiers have it) for and against the Museum votes; four proposals were rejected and eleven carried.

June 15. On Tuesday in the Commemoration-week the 'Radcliffe Sermon,' though preached by a Bishop (Dr. Villiers, Bishop of Carlisle), produced only £36 4s. The sum was at least as short as the text, 'What seek ye?' As I have said elsewhere, the increasing engagements and gaieties of the week unfit visitors from attending this service; and it is too long and heavy to attract residents.

June 17. The first Examination under the Statute for the Middle Classes (or rather 'of persons not members of the University'), boys and young men, was held in Oxford (as also in eleven other places). The Vice-Chancellor (Dr. Williams) addressed the Oxford candidates in the Convocation House, and their masters were entertained in the evening in the hall of New College. Mr. Sewell of that College had devoted himself to the previous arrangements for the Examination.

Oct. 8. Dr. Williams, Warden of New College, resigned the office of Vice-Chancellor, not to resume it, as he might have done for two more years, but 'for good,' as people say; and certainly for his good, i.e. his rest and comfort. His concluding speech was a splendid specimen of good Latin and good feeling, recommended by his fine voice. It was, in short, quite a refreshing reminiscence of old times. For himself he did wisely in resigning an office which, admirably as he discharged its duties, took too much out of a man at his time of life. He had come to the office, or rather the office had come to him, much later in life than to most Vice-Chancellors. Alas! that the prudence of his retirement should so soon have been proved by his death!

Oct. 26 died the Rev. Vaughan Thomas of C.C.C., for many years an active, influential Member of Convocation; but for some cause or other, of disgust or offence, he had, several years before his death, removed his name from the University books, though constantly residing in Oxford. In his best days he was a frequent speaker in Convocation; he had been highly valued for his superintendence of some of our public institutions and charities, but rather impatient of interference with his autocracy. He was a strong partisan, and though not uncharitable to *persons*, he was unbending in his antipathies to parties and opinions different from his own. Without much claim to be considered a theologian, he had the credit (?) of leading (though but for a time) the '*persecution*' of Dr. Hampden. With all his energy he on that occasion was only put in the fore-front of the battle (a post he was always ready to occupy) by deeper and more subtle thinkers, who for a time made use of him, but soon shot ahead, far beyond him. His 'High Churchism' was not of the Tractarian kind, but rather what has been called 'High and Dry.' He was an elegant scholar and highly respected.

Oct. 27. A meeting of a most interesting nature was held in Merton College hall, when a testimonial (in the form of a complete set of Communion plate, silver-gilt) was presented to *Bishop Hobhouse* by his parishioners of St. Peter's-in-the-East. Seventeen years of devoted labours, marked by an affectionate and earnest interest in the individuals as well as families of his parish, made each and all feel his loss as something that could never be replaced.

Nov. 4. A contest took place for the Professorship of Anglo-Saxon, which had lately been put on a better footing and released from several absurd restrictions (imposed by its founder, Dr. Rawlinson), as well as made tenable for life, instead of being transmitted, at the end of a seven-years' tenure, by a Professor who has just got into his work, to another who had probably to learn his lesson. *Dr. Bosworth* (not long before incorporated as D.D. from Cambridge, and a distinguished Anglo-Saxon scholar) had 140 votes, against Mr. Metcalfe, Fellow of Lincoln, who had only 38.

CHAPTER XXII.

'Omnia fert ætas.'—*Virgil.*

Recollections from A.D. 1859 *to* A.D. 1860.

A.D. 1859.

[B.A. 300. M.A. 258. Hon. D.C.L. at Commemoration, 6.]

JAN. 14. A novel case came on in the Vice-Chancellor's Court. Mr. Parkinson, M.A., of St. Mary Hall, appealed against a fine of £5 imposed by the Proctors, for riding a race (dressed, of course, in jockey costume) in Port Meadow, in defiance of a Pro-Proctor's remonstrance on the spot. The £5 had been paid under protest, and the case excited considerable interest, as the privileges of an M.A., or even a D.D., seemed to be involved. The case was ably argued on both sides by counsel engaged for the occasion. Dr. Kenyon, the Assessor, reserved his judgment. After a considerable interval, the judgment gave back the £5 to Mr. Parkinson, on the ground that it had been imposed on a wrong Statute, but leaving the general question pretty much what it was before! Each party had to pay his own expenses.

Feb. 5. The notorious Mr. Barnum from America advertised a lecture (to be given in the Town Hall, by *permission of the Vice-Chancellor and the Mayor!*) on 'Money-making,' with illustrations of '*Humbug.*' Grave people went about, saying, 'What next? is there not humbug enough already in Oxford? As for money-making, with the exception of tailors and money-lenders, it is rather behindhand.' At the lecture Mr. Barnum was roughly treated by the Undergraduates, who called him 'Prince of Humbugs;' he coolly called them 'silly boys,' laughed at their 'geese-like sibillation,' and pocketing the large receipts, walked off with the Horatian consolation, 'Plaudo mihi ipse domi.'

Feb. 12. Mr. Gladstone, having vacated his seat by accepting the office of High Commissioner of the Ionian Islands (and that only for a couple of months), inflicted upon the University the trouble of going through the ceremony of re-electing him M.P. for Oxford. Some *feelers* had been thrown out for a candidate to oppose him, but produced no result; which also, I believe, might be said of his High Commissionership, notwithstanding his eloquent addresses to the islanders in Italian. Why not in modern or (what he is so well at home in) Homeric Greek?

March. The talked-of plan (since carried out) of removing the zoological specimens from the Ashmolean to the University Museum suggested the question, 'Why was *Elias Ashmole* never enrolled among the University Public Benefactors?' I presume the answer would be, 'Because, though he furnished the building called by his name with a certain amount of curiosities, more or less valuable, and a library, small indeed and injured by neglect and careless treatment, yet curious and unique, the University was at the expense of the building which received his collection.'

March 19. Dr. Acland's announcement that the Radcliffe Trustees had assented to his proposal to remove the books contained in the 'Radcliffe Library' to the library of the Museum, on the plea, 'that the *specimens* and the *books* illustrative of them might be studied together,' very naturally suggested the question,—'According to this, should not the books on botany be transferred rather to the Botanic Garden?' Many persons certainly were surprised that the Curators should convert the building into an University Reading Room, subsidiary to and dependent on the Bodleian. The noble structure has since been christened (somewhat arrogantly) as 'The Camera Bodleiana[1].' Query: Will the ground-floor, when fitted up for books, be called 'The Camera Obscura?' N.B. This ground-area has, at a great expense and with great ingenuity, been lighted, floored, and furnished with shelves capable of receiving the overflowings of the Bodleian for many years.

April 7. In Convocation a Statute was passed for abolishing the University Sermons 'from Christmas Day till the Latin Sermon before Lent Term, excepting those on the great festivals of the Circumcision and the Epiphany,' which were retained by the intervention of Dr. Hawkins. When the *Long Vacation* Sermons were discontinued (in 1819) I prophesied (in a written memorandum) that the discontinuance of the *Christmas* Vacation Sermons would soon follow; not expecting it would take forty years to bring it about. The sermons on what were called Court days (the Gunpowder Treason, Charles's Martyrdom, and the Restoration) were also discontinued, those days being, by authority, no longer observed. The long services and sermons might well be dropped; but a single special prayer (to keep alive the memory of man's wickedness and God's mercies) might wisely have been introduced on those days into the Church's daily service. The sermon on the Accession day is still kept up.

[1] I believe it has since been more justly called 'The Camera Radcliviana.'

June 2. The Statute '*De armis non gestandis*' was suspended by a decree of Convocation, in order to allow the formation of an University Rifle Corps.

July 1. The strong feeling occasioned at Oxford by Mr. Gladstone's imputed inconsistency (a feeling shared by many of his supporters, though they could not make up their minds to vote against 'Oxford's most talented son') showed itself in the stubborn attempt to place the Marquis of Chandos in his place. After five days' polling the numbers stood thus:—For Gladstone, 1050; for Chandos, 859; majority, 191.

It was remarked at this time as flattering to Oxford, that in Lord Palmerston's Ministry (by joining which Mr. Gladstone offended many of his constituents and tried the goodfeeling of more) there were in the Cabinet six of our First Class men (three of them Double Firsts), and out of the Cabinet there were in office four First Classmen.

July 2. In Convocation a Statute was passed (since found to work badly) by which what was called 'Compulsory Attendance' on some one Professor's lectures was abolished. And what has been the result? 'A beggarly account of empty (benches),'—'no end of Notices' of a Course, and invitations to call at such an hour at such a place; but the notices were in most cases unnoticed, the invitations voted uninviting! The idle youngsters, released from the *necessity* of attendance on a Professor's lecture, ran off from their College lecture to their boating, or cricketing, or their billiards. What would College lectures themselves be, as to attendance, if Undergraduates might attend or stay away *ad libitum?* A great cry had been raised on the commencement of the new era, under the joint auspices of Parliament, the Commission, and the Council, as to the wonders to be wrought by the Professoriate; but, notwithstanding an increased staff and better endowment, how little impression has been made, in that direction, on the minds of youthful students or on their established bias (prejudice some may call it) in 'favour of the classical literature they had learned to love, or at least to study, at school! Either, then, the Professors must wait till the incipient attention to *scientific* studies in our schools (especially our public schools) shall have borne more fruit, or they must persuade Convocation to *replace the screw* and make the young ones come, *by a gentle compulsion*, to the fountains opened for them.

At the same time a measure was carried in Congregation (and approved in Convocation in the following Michaelmas Term) which even in these days of change and reform surprised every one; so little could such a thing have been thought possible, much less desirable, a year or two before! But one '*improvement*' makes room for another, and therefore the unlooked-for proposal to abrogate the necessity of a three weeks' residence between the Degrees of B.A. and M.A. (or what was called 'keeping *the Master's Term*') excited very little opposition. There was indeed a little talk of the good use to which those three weeks might be turned, of the kindly interest with which Bachelors of Arts revisited Alma Mater, attended divinity lectures, frequented the Bodleian, and listened to sermons at St. Mary's, during those three weeks: observations which were met by counter-assertions (and for the most part true ones) as to the enforced waste of time, the interruption of higher duties elsewhere, the additional expense of hired lodgings, and the renewal of College 'battels.' Some commiseration was (and very justly) felt and expressed for the lodging-house-keepers (chiefly respectable College servants) who had always reckoned upon these Term-keepers for the payment of their rent. The arguments, however, were stronger, or at least more acceptable, in favour of the measure, which was rightly considered as a great boon to many B.A.'s who, though desirous to become Masters for various reasons, never could find time, from their pressing duties elsewhere, for such a residence. It was carried without much difficulty, and, from the increased number of Masters' Degrees for several Terms afterwards, proved to be a considerable *bonus* also to the University Chest.

Oct. 17. The Prince of Wales 'came up' to keep his first Term at Oxford, being regularly Matriculated as a member of Christ Church, though living with his 'governor,' Colonel Bruce, in a house especially taken and prepared for him, called 'Frewen Hall' (from its having been formerly lived in, perhaps built, by Dr. Frewen, M.D., of Christ Church; indeed, it seems, till the Prince took it, to have always been occupied by *the Profession*,—by Dr. Vivian, Sir Christopher Pegge, Dr. Kidd, Mr. Fisher, Mr. Wyatt). Immediately on his arrival, he was waited upon by the Vice-Chancellor and Proctors in full procession. His appearance on that occasion was that of an amiable, graceful, ingenuous youth, with more of his mother's features and expression than of his father's; not imposing certainly, but perfectly easy and unembarrassed. Considering his father's connection with Cambridge as the Chancellor, Oxford had reason to feel flattered by his commencing his academical studies with us. During the five or six Terms of his residence, the young Prince gained golden opinions by his easy, unaffected bearing, and took with him, at his departure, the loyal good wishes of all Oxford, University and City.

Oct. 18. The splendid new Chapel of Exeter College was consecrated, having been built, notwithstanding its elaborate workmanship, in an unusually short time. It is one, and the most striking, of the results of the spirit and energy which of late years have marked the progress of this Society. I have no right to criticise this production of Mr. Scott's skill and genius, but I confess, that, exquisite as it is, there is something that does not quite please my unscientific eye; and this, partly from the great exposure of roof above the beautiful stone-work (an exposure, which is a striking feature in most of our recent Oxford buildings as contrasted with our older ones), and partly from the actual contact with which (like Balliol Chapel) it is wedged into the side of the Quadrangle, at its west end. Its elevation, however, is turned to admirable purpose and effect in the interior.

Oct. 27. It was a happy thought in the speech of the Vice-Chancellor, Dr. Jeune, at the Mayor's banquet, when in allusion to the acknowledged obligations of the City to the University, he said,—'Just consider the very name of the City: if *Ox-ford* or *Oxen-ford* had not become the site of an *University*, what would it probably still have been but a resting-place for a few drovers? Instead of which it has become a city of palaces, of towers, and trees, and pleasant waters.'

I may be allowed to append to this the (to me) interesting fact that the Mayor of Oxford on this occasion was my old friend (and pupil at New College School for eight years) Thomas Randall. How well he was fitted for the important position *I* was well aware; how admirably he discharged its duties the University as well as the City loudly expressed at a subsequent dinner, given in commemoration of his Mayoralty. Discipuli palmæ sunt præmia vera magistri.

Nov. 17. The quæstio vexata of the 'Professors' fee' (which appeared to have been recently settled by a negative vote of Convocation) was again revived in Congregation, in a proposal to allow Professors to take from each pupil a fee of one guinea for each course of Lectures (attendance on these lectures being no longer compulsory). The votes, on a scrutiny, were equal, i. e. twenty-six on each side. While the Vice-Chancellor was consulting with the Doctors near him as to his giving a casting-vote, happily (or unhappily?) a tardy voter came in and decided the matter by giving a Non-Placet!—and so the Professors went away with a lengthened face, sighing—

> '*Fee*, fa, fum! we may well look glum,
> For that *tardy ninny* has cut off our guinea.
> *Fee*, fa, fum.'

Nov. 25. A large meeting of University *boating-men*, held in the Radcliffe Library (Dr. Acland in the chair), was called by the President of the Boat Club, to consider the best means of preventing boat accidents. A good deal of sensible and a little amusing talk took place, and several judicious resolutions and desirable things were proposed and agreed upon; but, as they were for the most part restrictive (to a set of youths who would kick at restriction), and recommending what could not be enforced, little if any good was likely to ensue from the meeting, except what might flow, for a time, from this stirring up of the subject. I took the opportunity of stating, as University Coroner (in correction of a report of what I had said at an Inquest) that 'only fifteen lives (*only*, that is, in comparison of a much larger reported number) had been lost in connection with boats in the last thirty years; but that of these (owing, in my opinion, though the young audience would not allow it, to the more dangerous kind of boats lately introduced) nine had been lost in the last nine years.'

November. In chronicling the striking incidents and varying shades of Oxford life, it is but fair to mention the following Notice, by the Vice-Chancellor and Proctors, as a proof of a growing neglect of manners, the natural accompaniment of a rougher bearing and a coarser *external*: 'Whereas complaints have been made that some Undergraduate members of the University are in the habit of smoking at public entertainments, and otherwise creating annoyance, they are hereby cautioned against the repetition of such ungentlemanlike conduct.'

Dec. 29. A public meeting was called by the Mayor, supported by the Vice-Chancellor, to form a plan 'for finding employment during Long Vacation for junior College-servants' (commonly called 'scouts'), amounting, it was supposed, to at least seventy-five in number. Instead of leaving them to idleness and thoughtless expenditure at the beginning of the Vacation, and debt and difficulties at the close of it, it was proposed, by opening a regular correspondence with hotel-keepers in watering places, and other frequented resorts, to obtain for them employment as waiters for three summer months, thus enabling them to save money instead of wasting it. Both the Mayor and the Vice-Chancellor spoke at length on the subject, and arrangements were made (which were carried out successfully, and intended to be permanently kept in action) for securing this employment, and thus supplying hotels with help, often difficult to be obtained during the short summer season.

A.D. 1860.

'To be garrulous and egotistical is the rightful privilege of old age.'
Guardian Paper.

[B.A. 305. M.A. 233. Hon. D.C.L. at Commemoration, 5.
At the meeting of the British Association, 2.]

Feb. 16. In Convocation, the University passed a vote of thanks to Miss Burdett Coutts, for a valuable collection of

Devonshire fossils, and also for £5000, 3 per cents., the dividends from which are to be paid to two Scholars, to be called 'The Burdett Coutts Geological Scholars.'

Feb. 23. A statute was passed, requiring those who take the M.A. Degree 'to retain their names on the College books until the "Act" after their Degree,' in order to obtain insertion in the Registry of Convocation; but will it be acted upon any more than the old regulation, which always implied that the Masters' Degree was not complete till the Act was either kept or formally dispensed with? The *Degree* is what most men care for, not the future suffrage (with the expense of keeping the name on the books); and as soon as they have been admitted thereto (say, on October 10, in one year) who is to make them keep on their names till the first week in July in the year following?

March 22 died Dr. Williams, Warden of New College, full of honours, scholastic, ecclesiastic, and academic. Throughout an active and influential life he commanded the respect and esteem of all who knew him. He may be said to have been a prosperous man, for step by step his life was marked by a series of honourable appointments, almost courting his acceptance because of his pre-eminent fitness for them. I had the gratification of starting with him at New College, in the same year (1802) and at the same age (16); we attended the same lectures, in which I often benefited by his elegant and correct rendering of Greek and Latin Classics. Throughout his subsequent career he did me many marked and essential kindnesses, both at Winchester and Oxford. His services are too recent to require any remark as to the high tone of feeling and dignity with which he discharged the duties of Vice-Chancellor for two years.

May 3. In Convocation, a statute for the regulation of licensed Lodging Houses, still more stringent than the former one, after fighting its way through successive congregations, was rejected by eighty-nine votes against sixty-three.

May 8 died (after an operation for the stone) the Sanskrit Professor, Mr. Wilson, always considered *facile princeps* in Sanskrit literature; his death left the best endowed Professorship in Oxford open to future competition,—and that was not long in coming, in the persons of Messrs. Monier Williams and Max Müller.

May 15. An unsatisfactory medical statute was partially passed (quoad gradum *Bac. Med.*) after many struggles and various alterations. It seemed very unnecessary to split into two[1] the one stringent Examination, which had been introduced in Dr. Kidd's time; so that *six testamurs*[2], from first to last, will have to be obtained before the Degree of Bachelor in Medicine can be taken! The Vice-Chancellor put his veto on one or two clauses, leaving the 'Treatise' for the Doctors' Degree as before. Query: How many young men will ever toil through all this, when a Medical Degree, equally serviceable (except in Oxford), can be obtained by *one Examination* elsewhere?

---

[1] This however is said to be better and easier for the examined, than crowding all medical subjects into one Examination.

[2] This may at first appear incredible; but beside *the two Medical* Examinations of this new statute, the Student in Medicine is required to have previously passed '*examinationes omnes* ad gradum B.A. requisitas,' *four in number*, in 1860! Before 'Dr. Kidd's Examination Statute' for the Degree of M.B. there was at least plenty of ceremony on the day of graduation. The resident Doctors in Medicine met at the College of the intended Graduate, accompanied him in a processional 'deductio à domo,' and received each of them a fee of 10s. to be charged to his account. Two of them (i.e. one besides the Regius Professor) always stopped to sign in Congregation a certificate of his fitness for a licence to practise.

June 19. The 'Radcliffe Sermon,' preached by Canon Stanley, of Christ Church, produced £62 12s. 6d., a rather larger sum than usual.

June 20. The Commemoration-day. There were six Honorary D.C.L.'s, among whom were Lord Brougham, a former Lord Chancellor, and Sir Richard Bethell, a future one. Lord Brougham was received with a strong expression of admiration for his abilities, and respect for his age. He seemed rather astonished at his own position;—having been, long before, the fierce assailant of Oxford (in the pages of the Edinburgh Review), he was now welcomed to the seat of honour with loud and lengthened acclamations. Many of the young men in the gallery probably had never heard of his anti-Oxford movements, and the elder ones willingly forgot them, for the sake of his recent good services. The noble veteran was in good health, full of energy and spirits, actually *knocking up* more than one Oxonian, considerably his juniors, in lionising Oxford during two successive days. Sir Richard Bethell, formerly a Scholar at Wadham, was duly but more calmly received, as being *at home* once more and on his own ground. The Prince of Wales was present in the Theatre, wearing the Nobleman's dress-gown.

In this Act Term, Convocation accepted an offer from the Dean and Chapter of Christ Church, to remove as a loan Dr. Lee's collection of anatomical preparations, specimens, &c. from the Anatomy School at Christ Church, to the University Museum, to be there deposited under the care of the Linacre Professor of Physiology. One of the conditions sounded rather harsh:—' That the whole or any part of the collection may be reclaimed at any time by the Trustees.' Perhaps, however, it was only an ingenious way of quieting their consciences in parting with them! Query: What will be done with the old Anatomy

School at Christ Church? Will that also be so kept up as 'to be reclaimed at any time,' and restored to its proper uses?

June 25. Oxford, for the third time, had the honour of receiving the British Association (having done so, first in 1832, and next in 1847). Especial *éclat* was given to the meeting in the Theatre, by the circumstance of the Prince Consort being present to resign the Chair (which he had filled the year before at Aberdeen) to his successor Lord Wrottesley, an Oxford and Christ Church man. The Prince's speech was manly and modest, Lord Wrottesley's long but very interesting, especially his candid review of the state of science at Oxford in his Undergraduate days, when Kidd, Daubeny, and Buckland conduced to its revival. The Chancellor, Lord Derby, who came to Oxford on the occasion out of respect to the Prince Consort, concluded the sitting by a graceful speech, proposing a vote of thanks to Lord Wrottesley for his able address, and alluding pleasantly to the days when he and Lord Wrottesley ('forty years ago') were Undergraduates together at Christ Church.

N.B. Lord Wrottesley graduated with a First Class in Mathematics, in 1819, the same year in which Lord Derby gained the prize for Latin verse.

The real business of the Association, of course, went on through the week, in the different sections in the morning, and *conversazioni* were held in the evening; the new Museum, though not finished, being thrown open with great effect for such purposes. On Sunday, Dr. Temple[1] preached

[1] Dr. Temple was not contented with preaching a sermon of a somewhat rationalistic tendency to what was, in a great measure, an ultra-Liberal audience, but, having dressed it up afresh, he presented it as an *Essay* 'On the Education of the World,' in the forefront of that unhappy volume 'Essays and Reviews.'

to a crowded congregation. On the next day, Hon. D.C.L. Degrees were conferred in the Theatre upon Lord Wrottesley, M. de la Rive, and Professor Sedgwick. Lord Rosse, who was to have shared in the honour, was prevented from attending the meeting. On Wednesday, the 10th day, the concluding meeting took place (again in the Theatre, which was well filled). The Dean of Christ Church expressed a hope that Oxford would not, at a *fourth meeting* of the Association, deserve the charge of indifference to science, which, ' with some justice,' Lord Wrottesley had, in his opening speech, laid to its charge.

Nov. 3. In the middle of the day (*Saturday*) an explosion (*not theological*) took place in St. Mary's Church, which startled and alarmed the adjacent parts of the High Street, broke almost all the windows of the church, and tore up bodily the Vice-Chancellor's seat and the adjoining ladies' sittings. The church had been for some weeks closed for laying down pipes to warm it with hot water. At first it was naturally supposed that those pipes had burst, but on a careful examination it was proved that gas was the cause. A gas-pipe had been in some way disturbed, to make room for the hot-water pipes, and partially injured; a slight escape of gas had, in consequence, been going on till the day preceding the intended re-opening of the church, when a gas-fitter, having tried some fittings close to the Vice-Chancellor's chair, carelessly dropped the match he had used; the match must have passed through a crack in the floor (which had lately been disturbed), ignited the accumulated gas, and so caused the explosion. The gas-man declared that he was thrown by it, over some seats, to a distance of several yards. Certainly a person who was tuning the organ was forced off his stool and thrown upon his back, where he lay fully persuaded that the church was falling upon him. It was indeed a providential thing that the explosion did not happen a day later, i.e. on the *Sunday*, when the University and the parish services were to have re-commenced, and a sermon by the Bishop of Oxford would have drawn together a large congregation. It was said that a Tutor at Brasenose, who was giving a lecture at the time of the accident, coolly said to his class (on an impression that the sound came from the Museum), 'There, gentlemen, Brodie has done it at last!' Had this explosion happened while the church was full, the scene (independent of the parties actually crushed by it) would have been very frightful[1].

Dec. 7. One of the sharpest contests ever known in the Convocation House took place for the Sanscrit Professorship. The value of the endowment, the length of time during which canvassing had been going on, and

---

[1] We are told that in 1541 even a false alarm produced a panic, which, while it lasted, is said to have been awful, though some of the circumstances must have made it rather ridiculous; for instance, the doors being choked up by the pressing crowd, the windows were forced open; a boy escaped by clinging to a friar's cowl, and one Doctor offered £20, another his scarlet gown, to any one who would pull him out, 'though it were by the ears!'

An alarm also took place at the City Church on a Sunday—about the middle of the seventeenth century. 'A terrible wind blew down two or three stones on the leads, during service, which occasioned a great alarm and outcry—some even shouting "murder." It happened that at the moment a *trumpet* sounded belonging to a troop of soldiers then in Oxford:—so that they in the church cried out, that the Day of Judgment was come. Some said the Anabaptists and Quakers were come to cut their throats; while the preacher, Mr. G. Philips, perceiving their error, *was ready*' (so says Sir J. Peshall—after Ant. Wood) '*to burst with laughter in the pulpit*, to see such mistaken confusion; several of the people hanging from the galleries and falling on the heads of those who were crowding to the doors.'

the high reputation of the two competitors brought up an unprecedented number of voters. An ungenerous feeling operated against Max Müller, as being by birth a foreigner.

   Mr. Monier Williams . . 843
   Mr. Max Müller 610

     Majority . 233

The year 1860 concluded with a flying visit to Oxford paid by her Majesty, Dec. 12. It seemed to have been a sudden thought, and it was very natural that the royal mother and the Prince Consort should wish to see the young Prince of Wales at his studies in Frewen Hall. It was not a visit of state; the Vice-Chancellor therefore (unattended) met the royal party at the railroad station, and accompanied it in the visit to the principal buildings and colleges, during several hours. The passing from one place to another being done in carriages (and those not open ones), the crowds in the streets caught only a passing view of the royal features; the privileged few had ample gratification of the kind within the several colleges, where her Majesty charmed every one by her gracious bearing and the hearty pleasure she evidently enjoyed in being *lionised* by the young heir to the throne, who (with his brother Alfred, the Princess Alice and her German *affiancé*) paid every attention to the Queen mother—

  (Reginæ) 'tacitum pertentant gaudia pectus.'

N.B. The young Prince, *me judice*, made one mistake; it is (at least, it was) a sort of standing rule in Oxford to wear the academic dress in lionising ladies. His silk gown and gold-tasselled cap would have looked well and graceful, without being showy or formal.

CONCLUSION.

A.D. 1860.

Having carried these 'Recollections' as far as is safe and advisable on the principle (already quoted) 'de *vivis* melius est tacere,' I here, in conclusion, request a favourable interpretation of anything which may have approached that forbidden ground, and bequeath to, I hope, a more worthy successor the task of recording events, changes and innovations which Oxford has seen since the year 1860, and will continue to see.

I have lived to see great alterations and I must say (in most respects) great improvements in all around me; in nothing more so than in the liberality of feeling and kind consideration, which have taken away much of the repulsive stiffness of former days, without unduly lowering the standard of respect and of 'honour to whom honour is due.'

I cannot take leave of these superficial 'Recollections,' which have been long floating in an old man's brain, without acknowledging the kind consideration of Convocation (following the lead of the Council, as that followed the lead of the then Vice-Chancellor, Dr. Lightfoot) in granting me a liberal pension on resigning my 'staff' after sixty years of academical service.

'Sed jam tempus equûm spumantia solvere colla.'—*Virgil.*

INDEX.

A.

Agricultural Meeting, 308.
Alexander, Archduke of Russia, 306.
Amhurst, author of 'Terræ filius,' 38.
Anti-Mendicity Society, 78.
Arnold, Dr., 152, 322.
Ashmole, Elias, 85.
Ashmolean Museum, its Curators, 84.
Association, British, 264.
Association of Tutors, 390, 393.

B.

Bampton Lectures, 235.
Bandinel, Dr., 76.
Barbers' Company, 18.
Bedels, 244, 419.
Bishop-making, 54.
Blandy's, Miss, Trial in the Divinity School, 7.
Blenheim Private Theatricals, 9.
Bliss, Dr., 362, 392, 429.
Blucher in the Theatre, 81.
Bobart, 247.
Bodleian Librarian, 170.
Bread-riots (Jan. 1800), 42.
Brougham, Lord, 450.

Bulteel, Mr., 258, 262.
Burke, Edm., a Diploma D.C.L. refused to him, 6; Hon. M.A. Degree subsequently rejected by him, 70.

C.

Capellanus Universitatis, 225.
Cemetery Question, 336.
Challenging the Honours, 58.
Chancellors of the University, 201.
Cholera, 264.
'Christopher North,' 400.
Cista magna Universitatis, 228.
Clarence, Duke of, with Lord Exmouth, 88.
Classes in the Public Examination, 61.
Clinton, Henry Fynes, 405.
Coker and the University Volunteers in 1798, 36.
Collectors, 242.
Cotton's 'bonne bouche,' 94.
Council, Hebdomadal, inaugurated, 403.
Cowley Enclosure, 370.
Cramer, Dr., 193.
Crotch, 1, 149.
Crowe, W., 229.

D.

David, St., his day, 122.
Demetriades, 88.
Derby, Earl, 386, 394, 417.
Dies Scholastica, 112.
Disputed Election of a Chancellor, 65.
Dodd's Lament, 130.
Dons and Donnas, 200.
Duncan, John and Philip, 85.

E.

Eldon's, Lord, account of his examination for a B.A. Degree, 37.
Elmsley, Peter, 115.
Encænia held in Radcliffe Library, 46.
Examinator et Examinatus in 1799, 40.
Examination Statute, New, 48.
Examination for M.A. Degree discontinued, 60.
Explosion at St. Mary's, 452.

F.

Faber, F. W., 353.
Faussett, Dr., 155.
Fire at Oriel, 45.
French Refugee Priests in Oxford, 11.
Friars' Entry, 202.

G.

Gas introduced into Oxford, 98.
Gauntlett, Dr., 98, 183.
Giles, St., his Fair, and the Gipsies, 303.
Gladstone, prophetic eulogy of, 273, 357, 385, 388, 442.
Gown, Undergraduates', 430.
Greek Professor, 411.
Guizot, M., in the Theatre, 364.

H.

Hack-Preachers superseded by Select Preachers, 54, 237.
Halls, Private, 391.
Hampden Controversy, the, 280, 325.
Haydn, Hon. Mus. Doc., 8.
Haydon the Artist, 313.
Hayes, Dr. Phil., 147.
Heads of Houses, 160.
Hertford College, 188.
Highway Robbers imitated, 5.
Hornsby, Dr., 137.

J.

Jackson, Cyril, Dean, 172.
Jenkyns, Dr., 209.
Jowett, Greek Professor, 411.
Jubilee on the fiftieth anniversary of the King's accession, 69.

K.

Keble 'College,' 188.
Kent, Duchess of, visits Oxford, 265.
Kettel, Dr., 76.
Kett, of Trinity, 16.
Knocker-stealing, 275.

L.

Landor at Trinity College, 19.
Latin Litany, 248.
Law Disputations, 377.
Lecturers at the City Church, 27.
Lind, Jenny, her Concert, 365.

INDEX.

459

Littlemore and Father Dominick, 352.
Liverpool, Lord, 239.
Livingstone in the Theatre, 429.
Lockhart, J. Ingram, 47.

M.

Macmullen v. Hampden, 333.
Martyrs' Memorial, 305.
Match against Time, 33.
Mayor's Oath discontinued, 433.
Merton College, 180.
Mo. Griff., 350.
Museum, foundation-stone laid, 412.
Mus. Doc., 415.
Music Room, 2.

N.

Newman, Dr., 291.
Nicholas, Grand Duke of Russia (afterwards Emperor), 89.
Nicoll, Dr., 156.

O.

Oldenburgh, Duchess of, 78.
Open-air Sermon, 112.
Orange, Prince of, resident in Oxford, 63, 75.
Ormerod, Mr., 93.
Osborne, Lord Conyers, Inquest on his Death, 259.
Oxford Calendar, first appearance of, 63.
Oxford Duns, 55.
'Oxford Spy,' 91.
Oxonii dux poeticus, 12.

P.

Peel resigns his Seat, 126.

Portland, Duke of, installed, 14.
Prince Consort, 451.
Prince of Wales, 454.
Proctors, 214.
Pusey, Dr., his University Sermon, 328.

Q.

Queen Adelaide at Oxford, 276.
Queen Victoria lionizes Oxford, 454.
Quercus Magdalenensis, 4.

R.

Radcliffe Sermon, 99, 381.
Randolph, Dr., 139.
Robertson, Abram, 144.
Routh, Dr., 162, 406.
Royal Visitors or Crowned Heads at Oxford, 79.

S.

Sadler, the Oxford Aëronaut, 3.
Savings-Bank, 86.
Shaw, Dr. (Shavius), 111.
Shelley expelled, 72.
Sheridan in the Oxford Theatre, 70.
Shuttleworth, Dr., made Bishop, 315, 323.
Sibthorp, Dr., 153.
'Sophs' extinguished, 123.
Southey at Oxford in 1795, 19.

T.

Tabulæ novæ, 410.
Tatham, Dr., 233.
Taylor Institution, 356.
Terræ-filius, 135.

INDEX.

Theatre, Sheldonian, unroofed, 46.
Thomas, Vaughan, 281, 437.
Tom Paine burnt in effigy on Carfax, 12.
Tournay, Dr., 195.
Tractarian Movement, 288.
Tracts for the Times, 293; No. 90, 318.
Tweedledum and Tweedledee, 24.

U.

University Commission, 370.
University Sermons and Preachers, 233.

V.

Veto of both Proctors, 345.
'Via regia,' does it mean a private road? 65.

Vice-Chancellors, 198.

W.

Wales, Prince of, 454.
Ward, Mr., and his Book, 340.
Wall-lectures in the Divinity School, 39.
Wellington, Duke of, elected Chancellor, 270; his Installation, 272.
Wetherell, Dr., 169.
White, Blanco, 118.
White, Dr., 142.
Wigs, 160.
Williams, an Undergraduate, v. Brickenden, a Proctor, 71.
Williams, Dr., 437, 448.
Winchester School 'rebellion,' 13.
Wordsworth, Hon. D.C.L., 307.

www.ingramcontent.com/pod-product-compliance
Lightning Source LLC
Chambersburg PA
CBHW022113300426
44117CB00007B/698